PREFAB
ARCHITECTURE

PREFAB ARCHITECTURE

A GUIDE TO MODULAR DESIGN AND CONSTRUCTION

RYAN E. SMITH

FOREWORD BY **JAMES TIMBERLAKE, FAIA**

WILEY

John Wiley & Sons, Inc.

Library of Congress Cataloging-in-Publication Data:

Smith, Ryan E.
  Prefab architecture : a guide to modular design and construction / Ryan E. Smith ; foreword by James Timberlake.
      p. cm.
  Includes bibliographical references and index.
  ISBN 978-0-470-27561-0 (cloth : alk. paper); ISBN 978-0-470-88046-3 (ebk); ISBN 978-0-470-88043-2 (ebk); ISBN 978-0-470-88044-9 (ebk); ISBN 978-0-470-95030-2 (ebk); ISBN 978-0-470-95055-5
  1. Buildings, Prefabricated. I. Title. II. Title: Guide for architects and construction professionals.
  NA8480.S66 2011
  721'.04497—dc22

                                                                        2010016474

Printed in the United States of America

10 9 8 7 6 5 4 3 2 1

Contents

FOREWORD

Quality Assurance, Quality Control

James Timberlake, FAIA, KieranTimberlake

Since the beginning of time, buildings have been executed in situ, on-site. From the first primitive hut through the pyramids, ancient Rome and Greece, all of our modern cities and great cultures have been served by men and women working the trenches of construction stick upon stick, brick against brick, element by element. As wealth began to afford more and more manual labor and greater craftsmanship, and time was defined as "forever," the results were profound: the greatest, largest, most opulently finished structures ever. Improving quality meant putting more labor on the problem. Increasing scope meant putting more labor on the problem. We reaped the benefits of inexpensive labor and massive amounts of time for large program scopes and the highest quality until the turn of the twentieth century.

For the last 100 years, as the economy has become more sophisticated and global, one equation has governed construction: Q (quality) $\times$ T (time) $=$ S (scope) $\times$ C (cost). No matter which variable is defined as paramount to a project—quality, time, scope, or cost—the other variables must stay in balance. Want less time with a fast track schedule? Then give up quality, spend more money, or reduce the scope. Want a lower budget? Manage costs, reduce quality, and reduce scope. Want higher quality? Increase the budget proportional to your scope and likely increase time. Project after project around the globe has been dominated by this equation.

The historical chronicles of prefabrication are well and widely published, most notably in 2008 by Barry Bergdoll in his catalogue for *Home Delivery: Fabricating the Modern Dwelling*, The Museum of Modern Art's exhibit on the historical and contemporary significance of factory-produced architecture. Prefabrication in its earliest form was less about addressing quality and time or managing scope and costs—let alone about applying an environmental ethic—than it was about a fascination with industrial commoditization, production, and replication. Focused generally on housing typologies, the scalability of offsite fabrication was more focused on meeting a theoretical need for a booming housing market than it was on the integration of systems, materials, and production with the possibility for mass-customization.

With a lack of focus on integration, early attempts at factory production collapsed without firm ground up foundations in place. As George Romney, the Housing and Urban Development Department Secretary and refugee of the automotive industry learned in the 1970s, the "top down" strategy of forcing the construction industry to adopt offsite construction while encouraging its promise was quite damaging. The lack of integration tools available to the industry, and the post-war rollercoaster economy conspired to doom the effort. People were left bankrupt, demoralized, and discouraged from ever attempting to change an industry so entrenched. Since that initial effort to change the construction industry, we have seen a steady decline in the productivity of the construction industry, leaving architects to assume the burden of change.

What has changed in the world to make prefabrication viable today?

First, other industries have changed the way they work and provide products. As Stephen Kieran and I chronicled in *Refabricating Architecture*, the automobile, shipbuilding, and aerospace industries have remade themselves completely, sometimes twice over, since 1995. Their production methods are leaner, more time and material efficient, and more worker friendly. Their output range extends from a fully mass-customized product (automobiles) to a nearly fully customized one-off product (ships). The scale of these products on average also exceeds the complexity and scale of almost anything produced in architecture. Arguably, a ship, plane, or car, all of which have to move and carry occupants and products safely, day in and day out, are more complex overall than many of the buildings the construction industry produces. Simply, the construction industry needs to deliver a product that meets the requirements of design, on budget, on time, without falling down or leaking. It often fails at this task.

Second, the critical difference is that the air, ship, and auto industries integrate—both at the source of inspiration and at the source of supply. They have a captive supply chain and during the past two decades have integrated, redefined, and then reintegrated leaner supply chains and products. Efficiency begins at inception and is consistently interpreted and reintegrated throughout the design and production cycles. The design side of these industries is also integrated—usually with captive design divisions informing and collaborating with production teams, allowing for continuous evaluation and improvement.

By contrast, the supply chain for the architecture, construction, and building product manufacturing industries is extended and fragmented. Architects often rely on uncoordinated and poorly integrated product supply references, such as the Sweets Catalog, to research, understand, and specify products. Those products are often placed into documents and projects as open choices to be further whittled down by the construction bidding and procurement process. From there, a vast array of mostly uncoordinated products is destined for an onsite construction project with the workforce relegated to coordinating, fitting, and integrating these products into a coherent whole. This process is pure chaos, even under the best and most organized conditions. Often, a vast number of trades converge on a single point of finish within a project—bathrooms and kitchens often the most cited example—where they cannot all work, let alone fit, at one time. Yet each is under great pressure to complete the work not just on time, but *ahead* of time. Add to this chaos unpredictable weather or work conditions, outside of the normative comfort zones for a normal workplace, and the stress of completing the work increases with the likelihood of diminishing the quality that most architects and clients demand.

Yet architects' tools to integrate have changed. The architecture profession has embraced three-dimensional building information modeling and production tools. We are now able to visualize and correct "busts" before they are built. We have better communication tools, some of which have been embraced by the construction industry, such as online document and project management software, enabling real-time sharing of designs, information, and results.

We are now capable of sending a fully visualized, and virtually formed, model to a production line, bypassing the document interpretation phase, with all of its back and forth checking, redrawing, and margin for additional errors and omissions, ultimately improving the quality of the final product.

Third, however slowly, the environmental ethic of the architecture profession and the construction industry has begun to change. Onsite construction has been estimated to waste up to 40% of all new products brought to site. Imagine a clean, 4 x 8 foot sheet of brand new drywall. Now imagine approximately 2 feet square of each and every sheet brought to the site ending up in a dumpster and headed to a landfill. Add to that load after load of metal stud ends, wires, components, broken glass, aluminum, concrete block, and brick and it adds up to a small building's worth of components and raw materials wasted each and every time we construct a building. The industry, the profession, and the world can no longer tolerate that sort of waste, let alone continue to absorb the economic impact of it.

Integration modeling, the backbone of offsite fabrication and manufacturing, leans the product supply chain, helps architects and constructors manage the amount of materials needed and allows for a positive repurposing of the left over materials. Further, offsite assembly offers the promise of disassembly and re-use. Rather than repurposing a whole building, we might now consider disassembly as a way forward to altogether new re-uses for building materials. The holistic integration of sustainable materials helps to produce a greener final product. Rather than haphazard applications of materials and systems in a way that purports to be sustainable—a practice I often refer to as "green bling"—offsite construction and manufacturing offers what we might call "total sustainability,"

broadly defined as being 100% compliant throughout all building materials and systems in an economic and useful manner. Offsite construction presents the opportunity for this high level of compliance through integration, document and supply controls, and material management.

In addition, despite incredible improvements in workplace safety, the construction site remains a dangerous place, fraught with potential accidents, and generally exclusive of women. The construction industry must become leaner, safer, and broaden its workforce in order to remain safe, economically competitive, and relevant. A more inclusive workplace with real safety measures, and eliminating the factor of weather by building indoors rather than outdoors for the vast majority of the project, is also a long-term sustainable measure. It ensures greater productivity, the potential for growth, and the broadening of a workforce and workplace that is unlimited.

Ryan Smith has demonstrated with numerous examples of experimentation, collaboration, and hard work by countless individuals in his book the premise that "something has to precede something else." *Prefab Architecture* is a first read—the "pre" in whichever mode of fabrication that an architect and client choose to embrace. This book provides a guide to frontloading a project, and in turn, a means of changing our economy, changing the way we think about architecture and design, and changing the affordability and the quality of what is produced. Call it "nextgen" construction logic. It is beyond theory, and beyond most of what we think we know about pods, containers, mods, and joints. This book is more than "Prefabrication 101." It is the "Joy of Cooking" writ large for the architecture and construction industries.

INTRODUCTION

Prefab Architecture is intended to reach a wide range of readers, including architects who design detached dwellings, architecture and building technology students, and researchers and practitioners interested in the application of prefabrication as a production method for building. In addition, readers of magazines such as *Dwell* will be interested in the prefab examples and possibilities.

Prefabrication—often associated with the terms "offsite," "assembly," or just simply "fabrication"—can be viewed as stuck in the trenches of nineteenth-century conventions of standardization and twentieth-century modernism. Common construction means have not changed drastically over the last 80 years. In order for architecture to come into fruition—to actually be built—it takes many years, requires heavy investment, and is fraught with confrontation, value engineering, headaches, and inevitable heartache. This is not to say that new materials and methods of production have not advanced other industries, on the contrary. John Fernandez writes, "It is widely believed that construction is the slowest of all industries of such scale in implementing proven, scientifically sound technological innovation."[1] There are many reasons for the lack of innovation in the production of architecture that will be discussed throughout this book. The reality of this lack of building construction innovation must be definitively stated as an argument for why prefabrication should be pursued.

As a beginning we need to define what "offsite fabrication" is and what it is not, to alleviate confusion on its meaning herein for the reader. Webster says that "prefabricate" means, "to fabricate the parts of at a factory so that construction consists mainly of assembling and uniting standardized parts."[2] This definition in the contemporary dictionary has an entry date of 1932, seemingly not to have changed since. Prefabricate is a transitive verb. The noun "prefabrication" is then the parts that have been produced and then are assembled onsite; but one might wonder why the "pre" in prefabrication. The only explanation is that fabrication was at one time considered something that happened on the site; hence prefabrication meant that there was a body of work that occurred before the actual onsite fabrication commenced, or in today's terms, before assembly onsite. Therefore, should prefabrication be called manufacturing? The technology of industrialization has progressed since 1932, but the word has not, leaving us to continue to say prefabrication when in fact we may mean something very different. The lack of progress in the word usage is an indication of a lack of dialogue concerning construction methods and progress in the construction industry in general.

Prefabrication, however, is a pervasive term and it would be futile to try to debunk it within this context. Suffice it to say, throughout this book, the terms "prefabrication," "offsite fabrication," and "offsite production" are used interchangeably to mean elements intended for building construction that are produced offsite to a greater degree of finish and assembled onsite. The topic of prefabrication for this book is a jumping-off point to explore many other related aspects of building culture including housing, building technology, and architectural practice today. The intention in writing this book is to relate the history of industrialized building, the theory of technology in architecture, principles of industrialized building, classifications of industrialized building, products, and how the integrated process can lead to finding a greater balance between economy, efficiency, and aesthetics.

There is a growing interest in the architecture, engineering, and construction (AEC) industry in developing approaches to building that allow for greater efficiency and precision, are environmentally conscious, make better use of a declining workforce, and provide shorter construction cycles. As an alternative to conventional building practices, there is growing reliance on assembling offsite-manufactured and fabricated components throughout the industry. The expanding middle classes cause increased demand for buildings, from the prosaic to the remarkable, and the working class offers up fewer skilled laborers to produce these buildings. As a result, the construction industry has had to rethink its processes, relying in many cases on technology transfer from the manufacturing industry. Offsite manufacture and computer numerically controlled digital fabrication toward mass customization have far more relevance to architects today than any of us might have predicted only 10 years ago.

Prefab architecture is not new, and the points in history when it was most relevant often mirrored the circumstances of today. The Crystal Palace of 1851 by Joseph Paxton is cited as one of the earliest prefabricated buildings (although there are many examples that preceded) whose production also reflected the technological advances and expanding middle classes of nineteenth-century England. This economic expansion continued throughout the latter half of the nineteenth century, and the need to house the burgeoning middle classes supported a diverse range of residential kit suppliers throughout the world. In the period during WWII, the need to build whole cities as part of the war effort again required sophisticated building production systems, although the quality of construction was often sacrificed. The skewed relationship between production quality and design quality continued in the postwar period, and its effect lingers even today in the profession's unwillingness to engage the manufacturing and fabrication industry because of the stigma placed upon prefab.

Prefabrication is not a cure-all solution that automatically promises lower costs and higher quality. While greater reliance on manufactured production has created a bland, monotonous landscape, this is also not a universal result of relying on fabrication. Rather, buildings that rely on fabrication are only as good as the demands placed on them. In that regard, by ignoring the opportunities of fabrication, architects assure that our work is increasingly irrelevant for much of the construction industry. On the other hand, a reliance on fabrication processes can offer greater precision, shorter construction periods, better value, and greater predictability. By building in a controlled environment away from the construction site, it is possible to create safer working conditions, reduce waste and promote recycling, and sustain less damage onsite. But each of these attributes reflects a sliding scale of opportunities or tradeoffs, rather than clear benefits.

At first glance, improved working conditions seem agreeable to everyone: instead of building in conditions dictated by the weather, fabricators supply controlled environments with ergonomically considered equipment. Yet in many fabrication environments, reliance on minimal skills leaves laborers with little room for skill advancement or intellectual challenge. Although prefabrication may save on material waste, it does not say anything about the environmental impact of materials used in construction other than the distance of transportation from shop to construction site (it may be noted that neither does the LEED rating system offer embodied energy accounting). As a solution to buildings that may be disassembled as easily as they were assembled and reused as industrial nutrients, prefabrication seems to be a possibility. In the entire hype surrounding prefab, these are concepts that have not been addressed satisfactorily in the construction industry.

Architects, engineers, and contractors need to develop an understanding of the history, theory, and pragmatics of prefabrication so that they may effectively develop and implement these methods into the production of architecture. As a profession, architects lack a structure for determining the reasons for deciding where and when fabrication is appropriate, and an understanding of the range of choices that are inherent in relying on fabricators. Effectively using the fabrication process in construction requires rethinking the earliest stages of the design process. This book is therefore an educational and, most especially, a professional text that offers the information necessary to make informed decisions and ask pertinent questions concerning existing commercially available prefabricated systems during design and also methods for developing new systems with manufacturers and fabricators in the future.

This book is about the role of offsite fabrication in the making of architecture, synthesizing history, theory, and technical information of offsite fabrication for ar-

chitects and construction professionals. The ultimate goal herein is to facilitate the proliferation of prefabrication into the AEC industry, finding ways to overcome barriers and push opportunities. The book is broken into four parts:

- *Part I—Context* reviews the history and theory of prefabrication technology.

  - Chapter 1 focuses on the history of industrialized technology generally, illustrating moments in that development and their impact on society and the building industry's understanding of prefabrication as a concept and practice of industrialized construction.

  - Chapter 2 illustrates the history of prefabrication from an architectural perspective, arguing that the maturation of the profession is concurrent with the developments of the Industrial Revolution and societal modernist movement making prefabrication an engrained design ethic in the culture of architecture.

  - Chapter 3 presents a theory on technology in general, and offsite fabrication specifically. Whether offsite construction occurs and the degree to which it is implemented is contingent upon three constraints including environment, organization, and technology context. The contextual concepts of collaboration, integrated practice, lean construction, building information modeling, and mass customization are presented.

- *Part II—Applications* introduces the principles and outputs that define and characterize offsite fabrication in architecture.

  - Chapter 4 discusses the principles of prefabrication including the triad of cost, schedule, and scope and their accompanying tenants of labor, quality, and risk. This chapter is intended to aid construction professionals to weigh the opportunities and challenges of prefabrication in order to make informed decisions concerning when and how to implement offsite strategies.

○ Chapter 5 is concerned with technical and constructional fundamentals that are foundational to understanding prefabrication in construction. The chapter focuses the following fundamentals: building systems, materials, methods, product, class, and grids.

○ Chapter 6 identifies and presents three elements of prefabrication, namely components, panels, and modules. Each is discussed with examples given of wood kits, precast, metal building systems, panelization, SIPs, light gauge panels, enclosure panels including glazing and cladding, and finally wood and steel modular elements.

○ Chapter 7 discusses designing for assembly that includes various concepts of its practice: designing for detailing, designing for increased manufacturing productivity, loading and unloading, transportation, and onsite assembly strategies.

○ Chapter 8 focuses on the role of offsite fabrication in reaching sustainability goals in architecture. Fundamentally, prefabrication uses less material, but can also be a method to control the material going into a building, and, therefore, increase the quality of the construction. The majority of this chapter discusses the concepts of designing for disassembly and lifecycle.

• *Part III—Case Studies* focuses on contemporary examples of offsite fabrication in architecture and construction. The case studies are distinguished by chapter topic.

○ Chapter 9 is concerned with the prefabrication fad in single, detached housing and makes an argument for using the lessons learned for mass-housing solutions. Architects working in single-family dwellings and prefabrication over the last decade are presented, including:

- Rocio Romero Prefab
- Resolution: 4 Architecture
- ecoMOD Project
- Michelle Kaufmann
- Marmol Radziner
- Jennifer Siegal
- Hybrid Architects
- Project Frog
- Anderson Anderson Architecture
- Bensonwood

○ Chapter 10 discusses commercial and interior architectural applications for prefabrication in precast, cladding, modular, curtain wall, and digital fabrication through contemporary case studies. The following architects are presented:

- KieranTimberlake
- SHoP Architects
- Steven Holl Architects
- Moshie Safdie Architects
- MJSA Architects
- Neil M. Denari Architects
- Office dA
- Diller Scofidio + Renfro

• *Part IV—Conclusion*

○ Chapter 11 concludes the book with a call for education, government, and industry to collectively work toward increasing integrated practices and prefabrication technology in the building industry.

ACKNOWLEDGMENTS

Many individuals have made this book possible and deserve a sincere thank you:

- John Wiley & Sons Senior Editor John E. Czarnecki, Assoc. AIA, and Wiley staff for their support and advice throughout the process

- University of Utah College of Architecture + Planning administration Dean Brenda Scheer and Architecture Director Prescott Muir, and staff Mayra Focht, Cathay Ericson, and Derek Bingman

- Many students over the past six years who have inspired and motivated the topics in this book from courses on offsite fabrication, CAD/CAM and materials-integrated technology, enclosures, and assembly

- A special thanks to student researchers Brian Hebdon, Jonathan Moffit, Jennifer Manckia, Chase Hearn, Adam La Fortune, Kristen Bushnell, Ryan Hajeb, Jenny Gill, Tom Lane, and Scott Yribar, who have tirelessly collected images, developed case studies, produced drawings, and engaged in critical discussions of contemporary offsite fabrication in architecture

- Thanks and love to Lindsey, my wife, and our kids for their patience and support.

A special acknowledgment goes to the individuals in the companies that opened their doors to interviews and factory visits, and provided illustrative images. Specific photo and image credits are included at the back of the book. The following individuals and companies have provided information:

Anderson Anderson Architecture, San Francisco, CA
- Mark Anderson
- Peter Anderson

Architectenburo JMW, Tilberg, The Netherlands
- Jeroen Wouters

A. Zahner Co, Kansas City, MO
- L.William Zahner

Bensonwood, Walpole, NH
- Tedd Benson

BHB Engineers, Salt Lake City, UT
- Don Barker

Blazer Industries, Inc., Aurnsville, OR
- Kendra Cox

Blu Homes, Waltham, MA
- Dennis Michaud

Burton Lumber, Salt Lake City, UT
- Debbie Israelson
- Clint Barratt

Professor Charles Eastman
Georgia Tech University
Atlanta, GA

DIRTT, Calgary, Canada
• Lance Henderson

Dwell Magazine, San Francisco, CA
• Sam Grawe

EcoMOD—University of Virginia, Charlottesville, VA
• John Quale
• Scott Smith

Eco Steel Building Systems, Park City, UT
• Joss Hudson

Professor Edward Allen
MIT/University of Oregon
Nantuckett, MA

Elliott WorkGroup, Park City, UT
• Roger Durst

Euclid Timber Frames, LC, Heber City, UT
• Kip Apostol
• Joshua Bellows

Fast Fab Erectors, Tucson, AZ
• Michael Gard

Fetzers Architectural Woodworking, West Valley City, UT
• Paul Fetzer
• Ty Jones

Front, Inc., New York, NY
• Min Ra

Professor George Elvin
Ball State University
Muncie, IN

GMAC Steel, Salt Lake City, UT
• Gary MacDonald

Guy Nordsen Associates Structural Engineers LC, New York, NY
• Guy Nordsen

Hanson Eagle Precast, Salt Lake City, UT
• James McGuire

Hybrid Architecture, Seattle, WA
• Robert Humble
• Joel Egan

Irontown Homes, Spanish Fork, UT
• Kam Valgardson
• Amanda Poulson

Kappe + DU Architects, San Rafael, CA and Berkeley, CA
• Ray Kappe

Professor Karl Wallick
University of Cincinnati
Cincinnati, OH

KC Panel, Kamas, NM
• Craig Boydell

KieranTimberlake, Philadelphia, PA
• James Timberlake
• Chris Macneal
• Richard Hodge

Kullman Buildings Corporation, Lebanon, NJ
• Tony Gardner
• Amy Marks
• Casey Damrose

Living Homes, Santa Monica, CA
• Steve Glenn

Marmol Radziner Prefab, Los Angeles, CA
- Todd Jerry
- Alicia Daugherty

Michelle Kaufmann Design (formerly), San Francisco, CA
- Michelle Kaufmann
- Paul Warner
- Verl Adams

Minean International Corporation, Vancouver, BC Canada
- Mervyn Pinto

MJSA Architects, Salt Lake City, UT
- Christiane Phillips
- Christopher Nelson

Modular Building Institute, Charlottesville, VA
- Tim Harding

MSC Constructors, South Ogden, UT
- Jason Brown

Office dA, Inc., Boston, MA
- Nader Tehrani
- Suzy Costello

Office of Mobile Design, Santa Monica, CA
- Jennifer Siegal

OSKA Architects, Seattle, WA
- Tom Kundig

Professor Patrick Rand
North Carolina State University
Raleigh, NC

Emeritus Professor Paul Teicholz
Stanford University
Berkeley, California

Professor Phillip Crowthers
Queensland University of Technology
Brisbane, Australia

POHL Inc. of America, West Valley City, UT
- Udo Clages
- Zbigniew Hojnacki (Ziggy)

Premier Building System, Fife, WA
- Tom Riles

Project Frog, San Francisco, CA
- Nikki Tankursley
- Evan Nakamura
- Ash Notaney

Resolution: 4 Architecture, New York, NY
- Joseph Tanney

Rocio Romero, LLC, St. Louis, MO
- Matthew Bradley

SHoP Architects, New York, NY
- Greg Pasquerelli
- Chris Sharples
- Georgia Wright

Steel Encounters, Salt Lake City, UT
- Derek Losee

Steven Holl Architects, New York, NY
- Julia van den Hout
- Tim Bade

Sustainaisance International, Pittsburgh, PA and Hallandale, FL
- Robert Kobet

Tempohousing, Amsterdam, The Netherlands
- Quinten de Gooijer

3Form Material Solutions, Salt Lake City, UT
- Willie Gatti
- Jeremey Porter
- Ruben Suare

Tripyramid Structures, Boston, MA
- Tim Ellison
- Basil Harb (formerly)

VCBO Architects, Salt Lake City, UT
- Nathan Levitt
- Steve Crane

PART I

CONTEXT

1 History of Industrialized Building

"Three things you can depend on in architecture. Every new generation will rediscover the virtues of prefabs. Every new generation will rediscover the idea of stacking people up high. And every new generation will rediscover the virtues of subsidized housing to make cities more affordable. Combine all three— a holy trinity of architectural and social ideals."[1]

—Hugh Pearman

Prefabrication architecture is a tale of necessity and desires. Individuals and communities have constructed shelter from the beginning as a matter of function. In order to build in remote locations, deliver buildings more quickly, or to build in mass quantity, society has used prefabrication, taking the construction activities that traditionally occur on a site to a factory where frames, modules, or panels are fabricated. Barry Bergdoll, curator of the Museum of Modern Art 2008 "Home Delivery," an exhibition that tracked developments in prefabricated housing, differentiates prefab from prefab architecture. He states that *prefab* is a "long economic history of the building industry that can be traced back to antiquity" including the methods employed to build ancient temples and timber structures. Conversely, the history of *prefab architecture* is "a core theme of modernist architectural discourse and experiment, born from the union of architecture and industry."[2] The relationship between need and desire in studying prefabrication is argued as follows: If industrial-manufacturing processes can produce other products and goods for society, then why can't the same process be harnessed to produce higher quality and more affordable architecture?

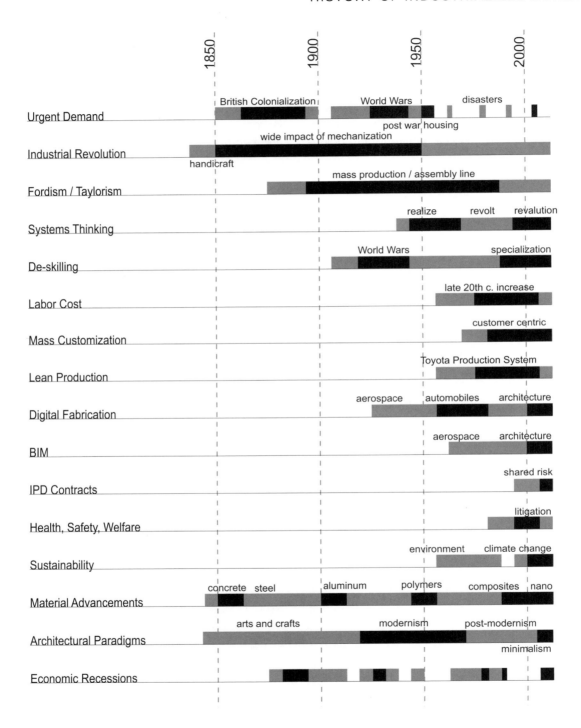

Although not to the extent of other industries, prefabrication has already been realized in many buildings; but can architecture, a discipline rooted in image, exploit the principles of offsite fabrication to make itself more relevant? Can prefabrication be a tool by which architecture can have an impact on all areas of the built environment including and most importantly housing? How might the quality of both design and production concurrently be increased? These are questions that the early and late modernists—Le Corbusier, Gropius, Mies van der Rohe, Wright—as well as design engineers—Fuller and Prouve—have asked. These are the questions architects today including KieranTimberlake, SHoP, Michelle Kaufmann, and others are asking. In order to answer these questions, we will step back and evaluate the historical linkages between industrial manufacturing processes and the production of architecture to understand the context by which we find architecture today and to uncover the lessons learned from previous attempts in prefab architecture.

This chapter reviews the developments in industrialized building that shape our understanding of prefabrication in architecture and building. Chapter 2 will evaluate the relationship between the history of the architectural profession and prefabrication, uncovering the failures and successes. It will end with a summary of lessons learned from failed prefab experiments that may be applied to reassessing the future of prefab architecture in the

twenty-first century. The techniques developed in other industries have been transferred to the construction sector to provide more appropriate production solutions to creating shelter. In addition to technology transfer, many societal and cultural factors have affected the development of prefab architecture.

1.1 British Contributions

The history of prefabrication in the West begins with Great Britain's global colonization effort. In the sixteenth and seventeenth centuries, settlements in today's India, the Middle East, Africa, Australia, New Zealand, Canada, and the United States required a rapid building initiative. Since the British were not familiar with many of the materials in abundance in these countries, components were manufactured in England and shipped by boat to the various locations worldwide. The earliest of such cases recorded was in 1624, when houses were prepared in England and sent to the fishing village of Cape Anne in what is now a city in Massachusetts.[3] The late 1700s and early 1800s was a time of Australian settlement by England. It is reported that the earliest settlement in New South Wales was home to a prefabricated hospital, storehouses, and cottages that were shipped to Sydney arriving in 1790. These simple shelters were timber framed and had timber panel roofs, floors, and walls. Speculation also suggests that infill material could have been canvas or a lighter timber frame infill system with weatherboarding. A similar system is reported to have been unloaded and erected a couple of years later in Freetown, Sierra Leone, to build a church, shops, and several other building types.[4]

◀Figure 1.1 This table illustrates the historical influences on the development of prefabrication. The value on the influence bar indicates the relative impact. White:—little to no impact; Gray—impact; Black—large impact. Note that many of the influences occur in the latter part of the 20th century with the large majority from 1960 onward.

English colonial building extended to South Africa. In 1820 the British sent a relief mission of settlers to South Africa, Eastern Cape Providence, accompanied by three-room wooden cottages. Gilbert Herbert writes that the structures were simple and shed-like, with precut timber frames, clad either with weatherboarding, trimmed and fixed on the site, or with board-and-batten siding. Door and window sashes were probably prepared as complete components.[5] These structures were not as extensively prefabricated as our contemporary understanding of offsite fabrication; however, they represent a significant reduction in labor and time compared to onsite methods that preceded. The prefabricated shelters' timber frame and complex joints were structurally and precision dependent on offsite methods.

1.1.1 Manning Portable Cottage

H. John Manning, a London carpenter and builder, designed a comfortable, easily constructed cottage for his son who was immigrating to Australia in 1830. Later known as the Manning Portable Colonial Cottage for Emigrants, the house was an expert system of prefabricated timber frame and infill components. It is described by John Loudon in the *Encyclopedia of Cottage, Farm, and Villa Architecture and Furniture* as consisting of grooved posts, floor plates, and triangulated trusses. The panels of the cottage fit between the grooved posts, standardized and interchangeable.[6] The system was designed to be mobile, easily shipped for furthering the colonial agenda of the British. Manning stated that a single person could carry each individual piece that made up the shelter. The Manning Cottage was an improvement of the earlier frame and infill systems designed by the English in that it offered an ease of erection. The

system was simply bolted together with a standard wrench, appealing to the abilities and availability of tools to the emigrants. Herbert writes, "the Manning system foreshadowed the essential concepts of prefabrication, the concepts of dimensional coordination and standardization."[7] Manning's system used the same dimensional logic with all posts, plates, and infill panels being carefully coordinated. It built upon the need for a quick erection system for emigrants but relied upon the British carpentry skills in shipbuilding.

The Portable Colonial Cottage made its way to many settlements by the British throughout the nineteenth century. Its impact on the British-settled

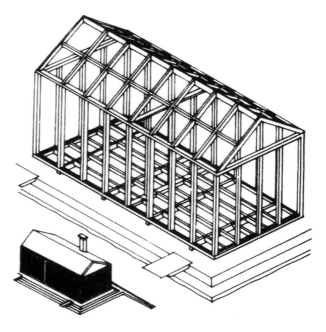

Figure 1.2 The Manning Portable Colonial Cottage for Emigrants was a timber and panel infill prefabricated system. Developed by Manning, this was a quickly deployable solution to the rapidly expanding British colonies in New Zealand and South Africa during the nineteenth century.

North America and the future U.S. construction industry is uncertain, however, it is assumed that the practices of timber architecture from Britain were the beginnings of the balloon frame in the United States. Augustine Taylor is often credited with the invention of the balloon frame in its implementation in construction of St. Mary's Church in 1833 in Fort Dearborn near Chicago. The light frame, including the platform frame and balloon frame, resulted from two primary factors: a plentiful supply of wood in the new country and a rapidly expanding industrial economy with mass-produced iron nails and lumber mills. In the span of one spring and summer, 150 houses were built. Buildings were erected so quickly that Chicago was almost entirely constructed of balloon frames before the fire of 1871. The infamy of the speed of balloon frame construction preceded the building of the entire West, mostly in light wood construction.[8]

1.1.2 Iron Prefab

Another contribution that came out of the British colonial movement was the employment of iron manufacturing for building construction. Components such as lintels, windows, columns, beams, and trusses were manufactured in a foundry and fabricated in a workshop.[9] The components were brought to the jobsite and assembled into structure and enclosure systems. Like its prefabricated timber-framed counterpart, iron construction was not as extensive as prefab today, but fathered the beginnings of the steel structural movement in the United States and elsewhere.

One of the first employments of iron construction in the United Kingdom was in bridge building. The Coalbrookdale Company Bridge in 1807 was almost entirely prefabricated and erected in pieces onsite. This was followed by a host of bridges in England that progressively streamlined the process of production and erection. Pieces were standardized, cast repeatedly, and shipped to the site to be erected by fewer laborers and unskilled laypersons garnering a saving in time and cost in comparison with the traditional construction of handcrafted wood or masonry. Some of the better-known bridges were on the Oxford Canal made at the Horseley Iron Works, at Tipton, Staffordshire. John Grantham reports that this foundry was also the first to produce an iron steamboat. The ships were constructed of heavy plates riveted together to form units. The ships could be assembled, disassembled, and reassembled. One of these manufacturer/fabricators was William Fairbairn, who in the mid-1800s built four "accommodation" boats, now known as cruise ships. This technology was transferred and Fairbairn later built a prefabricated iron plate building. In the mid-1800s English lighthouses and other building types were constructed using prefabricated iron plates and rivets.[10]

Cast iron construction, the precursor to contemporary structural steel construction, used mass-produced cast components that were envisioned as a kit-of-parts. By standardizing manufacturing, the economy of scale helped realize a savings in time and cost. The technology was primarily used as a frame and could be turned into any stylistic expression including Gothic or Baroque. In addition to the bridges, ships, lighthouses, and prosaic buildings, the single most extensive use of the material was in the standardized structure and infill enclosure of the Great Exhibition of 1851 in England, otherwise known as the Crystal Palace. The structure was largely a repetitive system of standardized components that when assembled created a massive skeleton. Joseph Paxton, the project's designer, had a background in green house design and claimed,

"All the roofing and upright sashes would be made by machinery, and fitted together and glazed with great rapidity, most of them being finished previous to being brought to the place, so that little else would be required on the spot than to fit the finished materials together."[11]

The palace was certainly not the first in cast iron architecture, nor the last, but it linked the Manning Cottage precut timber frame with the new material of the day, cast iron. The large number of factory-produced components and the details of the Palace are quite astonishing considering the era in which it was realized. In addition, the Crystal Palace is important because it represents a shift in understanding among architects, that beauty may be as simple as the functional means of production. Paxton was more interested in the engineering, fabrication, and assembly process, than in traditional aesthetic references.

1.1.3 Corrugated Iron

The early 1800s also ushered in an additional innovation in metal: corrugated iron. Although prefabrication of frames was relatively well developed in the early part of the nineteenth century, panel and spanning material were underdeveloped. The Manning Cottage and iron trusses of prefab buildings used traditional canvas or wood planking as a means of roofing. Corrugated iron provided a quickly constructed, affordable, and structurally efficient material for roofs and walls. Corrosion obviously presented problems until 1837 when many companies began to hot-dip galvanize metals in order to protect them. Richard Walker, in 1832, noted the potential for corrugated iron for portable buildings intended for export. The corrugated sheet could be nested in multiple layers during transit and were cut into 3 ft × 2 ft panels that easily could be handled by one person, and fas-

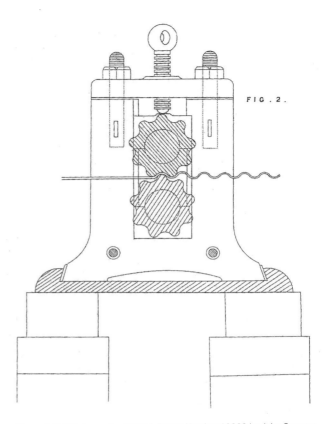

FIG. 2.

Figure 1.3 This image is of British Patent Number 10399 by John Spencer dated November 23, 1844. It is a corrugated iron rolling machine that became popular because of the wide availability of iron and hot-dip galvanizing in the 1830s.

tened into place at the jobsite. Along with Manning's Portable Cottage, Walker's marketing and exportation of corrugated iron provided one of the first widely used prefabricated timber and iron building systems in the world.[12]

Corrugated iron was employed in the Gold Rush of San Francisco in the mid-1800s. Because of the influx of people in search of new money, housing was in urgent demand. Entrepreneurs on the East Coast responded with using the latest iron technology from England and manufacturing simple shelters. Naylor from New York shipped more than 500 house kits made of corrugated iron during this time. Many of these homes were advertised in magazines and other publications so that patrons could order the shelter of their choice directly.[13] Corrugated iron in buildings did not end with the kit homes of the Gold Rush era. The use of the panel had a large impact on the proliferation of Quonset huts during World War II, and later in industrial buildings, storage facilities, and even rural churches. Considered archaic by contemporary construction standards, what is not generally understood is that corrugated iron has its roots in fulfilling a need in transportable, quickly erected architecture that was prefabricated

and shipped to be erected elsewhere. Its use in urban and rural temporary structures has continued since its inception.

1.2 Mass Production and Kit Homes in the United States

Ordering kit homes from a catalog did not cease with the Gold Rush. At the turn of the twentieth century, amidst the rapidly increasing industrial revolution and the full adoption of balloon framing, kit homes from precut timber for light frame houses became common. Among them was Aladdin Homes, formed in 1906 by W.J. and O.E. Sovereign, brothers who believed that mass-production concepts could be used to produce mass housing. The Transcontinental Railroad, connecting the East and West coasts, was completed in 1869 and facilitated the proliferation of such companies. With the rapid expansion of the United States to the West, there was an urgent need for quick, affordable, and easily constructed housing. Aladdin homes followed the precedent of mail-order, knock-down boats that buyers could purchase and assemble themselves. Clothing had also become mass-produced with patrons ordering via mail service based on standardized sizes. The brothers believed that the housing industry could benefit from the same concept that had been used in these industries. Therefore, they marketed what they called the "Readi-Cut" system in which all the lumber necessary to build a complete home was precut in a factory and delivered. This process was to remove the waste associated with onsite framing, increase speed of manufacture, improve precision, and thereby allow purchasers to only need a hammer and time for erection. Although Aladdin was the first to pioneer the precut lumber systems of production for balloon-framed homes, Sears Roebuck and Co., with their

Figure 1.4 One of the most common applications for corrugated iron has been by the U.S. (Quonset hut) and British (Nissen hut) militaries during World War II.

marketing and financial power, were able to sustain prefabricated efforts through the 1930s.[14]

Sears Roebuck's success was in large part due to its ability to offer a variety of housing options and financing. Offering model-based housing, whether from a catalog or built model home village, remains the method that many homebuilders sell today, complete with onsite financing and upgrade options. Sears took Aladdin's ideas and created a strong business model backed by national retail capital and experience in mail order shipping. In the end, both Sears and Aladdin failed and pulled both their catalogs and production from operation. This failure is in large measure due to the Great Depression and housing crisis of the early 1920s and 1930s. As a mortgage broker as well as a product developer, it is reported that Sears lost over $5.6 million in unpaid mortgages during this time.[15] Sears and Aladdin did not claim to make advances in architectural design, rather, their contribution to

prefabrication was in providing a more efficient ready-to-build system of components, a strong marketing strategy, affordability, and variety within a standardized product to the consumer. Although not explicitly working to impact the future of prefabrication in architecture, implicitly these frame systems hid their industrialized production under wood siding and roof shingles. Housing architecture in the United States during the early part of the twentieth century was marked by veneers and finishes that worked to hide the method by which production was assumed.[16]

1.3 Fordism

The advances in pre-cut light-frame systems were developments that took advantage of new processes and technologies for production. The advents of Henry Ford's Model T assembly line process provided lower cost yet higher quality automobiles. He

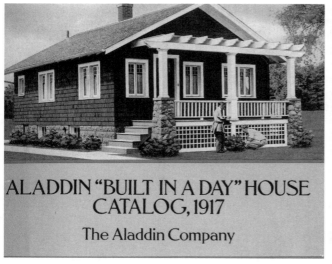

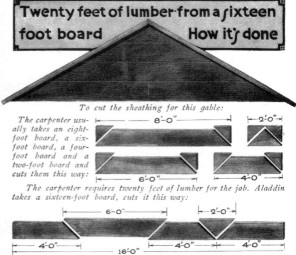

Figure 1.5 The Aladdin "Built In A Day" House, circa 1917, boasted lower cost per square foot of house in material due to its "Readi-Cut" system that maximized yield from standard lengths of lumber.

was able to provide a more precise product and also decrease labor and time per unit output. This process of standardization and assembly line production was transferred to the housing industry and, by 1910, a number of companies began to offer prefabricated houses in a variety of scales and quality.

The principles of standardization, mass production, interchangeability, and flow that pervade manufacturing can be traced to Ford. Standardization is the limitation to the variety in product produced so that machines may be able to output set lengths, widths, and assemblies. This removes the waste associated with variability options and the margin of error in end products. Mass production is a sister concept to standardization. It claims the economy of scale, that the more of something that is produced, the cheaper and higher quality it can become. Ford also invested heavily later in the production of automobiles in interchangeability. This concept refers to the ability for parts to be used on a number of different end products. A prime example of this is a 2 × 4 in the construction of houses. The houses might all be different, but all are built from this standardized, mass-produced part. Products such as threading for bolts became standardized in the Ford factory, making connections easier and faster. Flow is the assembly line concept where products are driven on a line at which laborers perform a limited number of tasks in the operation. This repetition of task reduces time.

The industrialized world understands these principles implicitly because it is in many ways the decree by which we operate as a society. These principles have become accepted as standards in and of themselves. They have been used by manufacturers of products in many industries, including the building industry. Stephen Batchelor states that the impact of Ford's

principles of production on technology development is considerable:

"but in the wider world it is seen as one of the key ideas of the twentieth century, which has fundamentally altered the texture of Western life. The arts—music, literature, theatre, painting, sculpture, architecture and design—have all been affected."[17]

There are problems with the acceptance of Fordism as a way of life. In addition to its effects on form in the arts, mass production is but one of many manufacturing strategies that can be conceived from today's technology. Therefore, as Sabel and Zeitlin argue, the production of products in the future, including prefabricated architecture, will be determined not by the technologies that have been developed by Ford and others under the mass-production paradigm, but by the social struggles of the day.[18] Just as social context was formed by the impacts of Ford's production theory, Ford's production theory is just as much a product of social desire. Consumerism is one of the social contexts in which mass production has thrived. But in recent years, the issues with the housing crisis, the constant thirst for the new, has placed the economy and its people in a terrible predicament. Although short-term desires have been met, long-term stability has not. The sustainability of this model is not everlasting in terms of both economics and environmental ethics. Mass production also presents problems with labor monotony, potentials of exploitation of the poor, and a lack of variety in the man-made landscape. More will be discussed on the perils of Fordist production and prefabrication later in the text. New paradigms are emerging that question this production method; however, suffice it to say that the impacts on the American social beliefs are long lasting.

1.4 Wartime Housing

Prefabrication in the United States was used to further the expansion westward in the late nineteenth and early twentieth centuries. Many advances in applying Fordist mass production to the development of kit houses were exploited. This time of innovation was the first major paradigm shift in the location of production of buildings from site to factory. As the great economy deflated, much of the production during the 1920s and 1930s also declined. This period was not marked by large mass-housing initiatives, marketing strategies, or even the successful business practices that marked the early twentieth-century movements. On the contrary, it displayed one-off prototypical experiment houses that tested Fordist mass production, using automobile and shipbuilding technology in building construction.

In 1932, Howard T. Fisher developed the General Houses Corporation to produce postwar housing. The product differed from the Sears and Aladdin types in that they did not aim to mimic aesthetics of the past or tradition, but were intended to reflect the manner in which they were developed, the means of prefabrication. Fisher's houses were centered on taking advantage of the Fordist mass production; his homes were to be assembled literally as an automobile. General Houses would implement building components from supply companies that were in the market place servicing other industries. Fisher's greatest technological achievement was in the development of a metal sandwich panel wall system that used similar technologies from the airplane industry developed during the war. He also had the support of industrialists General Electric, Pittsburgh Glass, and Pullman Car Co. His efforts, similar to the architects of the time, were to produce modern buildings, flat roofs, and do it in an industrial

aesthetic. Fisher was extremely optimistic about the public's taste, and his marketing strategy to sell the most innovative and contemporary housing in convenience and aesthetic is attributed to his company's near demise. Ironically, years later the company was successful in producing traditional-style houses in nine states. Fisher's innovations provided a new chapter in prefab thinking—that a house can be factory bound and offsite assembled from components provided by different companies, much like an automobile of this time was produced.[19]

General Houses gave way to a number of similar companies looking to produce modern houses for the masses. Among them are notably the American Houses developed by McLaughlin, an architect, and Young, an industrialist. Their 1933 "Motohome" also had difficulty gaining success until McLaughlin retooled and developed more traditional wood precut homes. These houses were remarkably similar to Fisher's company in that they had flat roofs and used a metal sandwich panel system for exterior walls. While General Houses and American Houses developed an innovative panel system, the Pierce Foundation prefabricated a services core that housed kitchen, bathroom, and all plumbing fixtures. The core also held heating and air conditioning services. American Houses implemented the Pierce Foundation's service core in their prototype. The service core in the American Houses showing was one of the first identifiable modular examples in prefabrication building. This prefabricated service module mirrored Buckminster Fuller's Dymaxion House pod, which will be discussed in Chapter 2.[20]

Used in military applications in airplanes and ships and in the automobile industry, steel's aesthetic appeal for designers and builders alike was alluring. Builder George Fred Keck developed both the

"House of Tomorrow" and the "Crystal House" for the Chicago World's Fair in 1933. On display were a number of examples of steel used in housing. Keck's prototypes featured steel frame and glass infill walls. The House of Tomorrow comprised a 12-sided, 3-story structure that resembled an airplane hangar more than a house. Keck used prefabricated steel elements to develop the steel superstructure, enclosure panels, and railings. It is reported that 750,000 people visited this house during the first year of exhibition but not one buyer was secured. The Crystal House built upon the steel frame concept and could be erected in an impressive three days. It too was unsuccessful in market and sold for scrap to pay off Keck's bills.[21]

1.5 Postwar Housing

The advances in the postwar era are not identified by technique, but rather are marked by business improvements. As World War II was coming to a close, returning soldiers increased market demand for housing. In 1946, the U.S. federal government passed the Veteran Emergency Housing Act (VEHA), giving a mandate to produce 850,000 prefabricated houses in less than two years. This initiative sparked numerous efforts in postwar housing design, including architects Walter Gropius and Konrad Wachsmann's "Prepackaged House" proposal, which will be discussed in Chapter 2. Although this mandate did not reach its envisioned breath of impact and completion, it gave rise to a number of prefabrication housing companies over the course of a decade. Among these companies were Lustron Corporation, Levitt Town, and Eichler Homes.

In 1948, Lustron Corportion began producing all-steel houses in airplane factories left vacant after the war. The houses were traditional in form, simple, with modest gable roofs and porches, but innovative in that they were constructed of entirely prefabricated enamel steel on the exterior and interior. Carl Strandlund, an industrialist from the prewar years, took the concept of automobile process to housing even more literal than experiments in the 1930s with metal sandwich panel technology. The method and even material in this case were literally to be fashioned after automobile manufacturing. Just as a car, the house had contained too many pieces to be feasible in construction. The components did not always make sense in their sizes in relation to manufacturing standard sizes of sheet metal and therefore created unnecessary waste. In the end, the houses were too expensive for modest income buyers. After only 2,500 homes were built, the company closed in 1950. In addition to the method of production being problematic, Lustron homes were cold, both visually and in temperature. Employing little insulation, the metal house would heat up in the summer and freeze in the winter.[22] In a recent tour of a salvaged home at the MOMA exhibit in 2008, many patrons were over-

Figure 1.6 The 1948 Lustron House was an all-enameled steel building system that used the automobile metal sandwich panel technology. This Lustron home still stands in Madison, Wisconsin.

heard remarking about the impersonal machine-like quality of the house.

William Levitt took advantage of the VEHA. Instead of producing homes in the factory, Levitt systematized the onsite process. Using principles of assembly line production and adding a separation of construction planning and execution borrowed from Taylorism, Levitt organized crews to maximize production efficiencies and material use.[23] A developer by trade, Levitt produced entire subdivisions of housing, and in 1945 he developed Levittown in Pennsylvania. The homes were unremarkable, very similar, and were the plausible foreshadowing model of cookie cutter developments in the United States.

In California, Joseph Eichler similarly developed a systematized method for onsite construction by developing entire communities of housing. However, having grown up in a Frank Lloyd Wright house and being a lover of the arts, Eichler was appalled at the lack of variety and aesthetic appeal in Levitt's product. Eichler, therefore, hired architects on the West Coast to design courtyard and exterior-interior relational plans that employed post-and-beam design and large expanses of glass. These homes were designed and built on a rigid grid, and featured standardized mechanical and plumbing systems that allowed for variety within a set system. Eichler was not only interested in style being influenced by California modernists, but was a socialist, wanting to open modern architectural design to the middle class of housing. In comparison to Lustron, Levitt, and many others already discussed, Eichler's mission was somewhat successful, building developments in Sunnyvale, Palo Alto, and San Rafael.

Eichler began in the mid-1940s and, by 1955, had become so efficient at delivering modern homes

Figure 1.7 Systematized onsite building construction was developed in the mid-twentieth century and continues today as the pervasive method of residential construction. This house in Utah is modeled after mid-century Eichler houses. There are neighborhoods throughout the western United States that are built within the principles of courtyards, large expanses of glass set within a post-and-beam structure.

that, despite the marginal increase in cost of material of an exposed post-and-beam structure, could sell a house at a comparable price with the same amenities as conventional housing. The impact of these homes on prefabrication technique is next to none; however, in studying what prefabrication promises—increased quality and reduced cost—it was influential. At the end of the day the reason these homes succeeded and continue to succeed from one owner to another is attributed not only to their aesthetic appeal and unparalleled location, but to the commitment, attention to detail, design, and quality that Joe Eichler himself was willing to offer to the process.[24]

The postwar housing program in the United Kingdom mirrored the United States. Nissen huts, the UK equivalent of the U.S. Quonset hut, provided much-needed shelter during and after the war. Models including Arcon, Uni-Seco, Tarran, and Aluminum

Temporary, or AIROH, were temporary bungalows under an organized government initiative to supply housing for the war-stricken country. The United Kingdom used innovative technologies of the time, including steel framing and asbestos cement cladding, timber framing, precast concrete, and aluminum. The homes were not overly stylized, and employed prefabricated kitchen and bathroom systems. It was at this time that many of the wartime and postwar prefabrication housing companies in the United States provided and influenced housing in the United Kingdom during their rebuilding efforts. In particular, the Tennessee Valley Authority project for the Roosevelt Dam in 1944 employed prefabricated temporary shelter for workers on the dam. This technology was used in the United Kingdom. for its recovery efforts, learning from the Americans' methods as well as receiving actual houses that were produced in the United States and were shipped across the Atlantic for rebuilding efforts. The difference in the UK programs when compared to prefab initiatives in the United States, is that the houses were intended to be temporary, focusing on speed rather than quality.[25] In addition to the TVA temporary housing program, an additional temporary housing initiative began mid-century in the United States, known as the mobile home industry.

1.6 Mobile and Manufactured Housing

In 1954, the mobile home industry expanded with the need for affordable rapidly constructed housing. Similar to the UK temporary housing programs, mobile homes were completely built as a module on a chassis in a factory and then trucked to site. Mobile homes kept their wheels, making them capable of transport, but in most cases were never moved. By 1968, mobiles accounted for a quarter of all single-family housing in the United States.[26]

Recreation vehicles such as the Airstream gained popularity in the 1920s and 1930s and during World War II. This housing type was affordable and transient, an ideal model for those struggling to find work in different regions. These trailers were used as temporary housing for migrant and emigrant workers during WWII, thus furthering its widespread use. After the war, many companies that began as recreational mobile trailer manufacturers shifted into producing permanent mobile housing. As this temporary housing type slowly became a more accepted means of permanent housing, it eventually became larger and more sophisticated in its methods of production and marketing.

A major shift in the transition from mobile to permanent housing was the move from an 8-foot-wide to a 10-foot-wide trailer, allowing for more comfortable living. This shift had not only technical adaptations, but also social implications being accepted widely. The

Figure 1.8 A late 1970s single-wide mobile house with flanking porches near Salt Lake City, Utah, built to HUD code.

10-foot-wide was no longer a trailer, but a house, intended to be transported to the site and remain. This change continued to progress as 12-foot-wide and even 14-foot-wide mobile homes were manufactured in 1969. In 1976, large mobiles called "double-wides" were introduced. Each module was pulled to site and set in place making a 28-foot-wide home. In 1976, the code changed, distinguishing permanent homes as being those designed to the standard code (i.e., IBC) and mobiles to the HUD code. Today, the HUD code homes have changed their name from mobile to manufactured housing. Sometimes confused for manufactured housing, modular homes are built to IBC code, are without a chassis, and are set onsite permanently.[27]

In the United States, architects and society generally deem the mobile home as insignificant. This is due to its lack of design variety and construction quality. Mobile dwellings have been the victims of hurricanes and tornadoes, becoming a talking point for construction professionals, many of whom would like to see manufactured housing fall forever. But the mobile home meets the basic needs of shelter, and at a cost the majority of citizens can afford. Despite society and architects' loathing of this building type, it is estimated that the manufactured home industry accounts for 4 percent of the market share for new single-family housing in the United States.[28] Per square foot it is the cheapest option available for new homeowners bar none. It has succeeded because it is *not* a part of the waste-laden architecture and construction industry methods of delivery. It has emerged autonomous and has thrived on its own terms of supply and demand for nearly a century.[29]

The manufactured home does not profess to be more than it is and its owners do not expect more of it. It

is built to a lower code. Because of this, prefabrication, the method by which manufactured housing is realized, has come under attack as a subpar method of construction for all housing. It is only recently that manufactured methods of housing production are being evaluated to create different levels or degrees of quality in mainstream housing. This can be most easily seen in the work of modular housing companies and prefab architects like Michelle Kaufmann and Joe Tanney at Resolution: 4 Architecture. The key tenants of these homes center upon the advantages that the manufactured housing industry teaches—that building in modules considerably reduces the overhead and onsite labor and can dramatically reduce initial cost. Unlike mobile homes, Kaufmann and Tanney have used modular housing to infuse a higher level of sustainability, quality control, and craft. More will be discussed concerning modular construction and other architects working in this area in Chapter 9.

1.7 Precast Concrete

The history of site-cast concrete in the Industrial Revolution is clearer than precast. Early indications that precast was used can be found in the evidence of precast fountains and sculptural pieces in early Roman and later during the nineteenth century. Precast has also been found in burial vaults in cemeteries across the United States dating back the turn of the twentieth century. Despite the advances made by the Romans, concrete was lost to the world for 13 centuries until, in 1756, British engineer John Smeaton used hydraulic lime in concrete. Later, in the 1840s, Portland cement was first used. Joseph Monier made concrete flowerpots with wire reinforcement. The greatest advance to concrete construction was taking this concept into reinforcing steel, allowing greater uses of concrete in construction. Advanced pouring techniques and the availability of raw material make concrete accessible for a myriad of functions. The first use of reinforced precast is attributed to French businessman E. Coignet, who developed a system of components similar to elements in the construction of the casino in Biarritz in 1891. Five years later, François Hennebique is attributed with the first precast *modulare,* developed for gatekeepers' lodges.[30] Although not technically precast, Thomas Edison developed a reinforced concrete housing prototype in 1908 with a technique for a single-pour house using cast iron formwork.

The development of prestressed concrete is congruent with precast developments. Prestressing at the plant allows precast elements to be stronger, lighter, and an overall better use of material. Although a San Francisco engineer patented prestressed concrete in 1886, it did not emerge as an accepted building material in the United States until a half-century later. The shortage of steel in Europe after World War II coupled with technological advancements in high-strength concrete and steel made prestressed concrete the building material of choice during European postwar reconstruction. North America's first prestressed concrete structure, the Walnut Lane Memorial Bridge in Philadelphia, Pennsylvania, however, was not completed until 1951.

In conventional reinforced concrete, the high tensile strength of steel is combined with concrete's great compressive strength to form a structural material that is strong in both compression and tension. The principle behind prestressed concrete is that compressive stresses induced by high-strength steel tendons in a concrete member before loads are applied will balance the tensile stresses imposed in the member during service. Therefore, prestressed, precast concrete was first widely used in civil engineering projects such as water culverts and bridges. Architect Louis I. Kahn and engineer August Komendant employed prestressed concrete on the Richards Medical Laboratory at the University of Pennsylvania campus, one of its first uses in architecture in 1971. Prestressed precast today is common, however, and continues to be used more often in larger commercial and industrial buildings that warrant its great strength and mass, as well as its financial investment.

Figure 1.9 Edison's 1908 single-pour concrete system was deployed as a fast and affordable housing option. Using elaborate cast iron formwork and machinery allowed for up to three-story houses to be cast in a single pour. The iron formwork proved cumbersome and difficult. It was not until Charles Ingersoll, a wealthy New Jersey manufacturer who brought the idea of making the forms out tof wood, that Edison's single-pour concept was built. Construction began in 1917 in Union, New Jersey. Fewer than 100 houses were actually realized.

1.8 Digital Production

Prefabrication, the process of building in a factory, implies a Fordist mass-production model. However, today's methods of production in automobile manufacturing have moved dramatically beyond notions of standardization, economy of scale, and flow. Today's processes of production, through the use of digital technology for both design and fabrication by means of computer aided design and computer aided manufacturing (CAD/CAM) systems, are proving to be a paradigm shift in production ideology. This enlightenment is affecting not only prefab technology development, but the social constructions by which buildings are produced, their contract structure, and the interface of players. Digital fabrication is potentially a method by which the promises of prefabrication—complementary increase in design and production quality—may be realized.

Two forces gave rise to CAD/CAM technology. First is the link to the Industrial Revolution and mass production already discussed in this chapter. The other is that of digital automation. Automation is more computer technology than manufacturing. It is the process of creating machines that are automata, or have been purposely built to mimic the process of skilled human labor, controlled by instruction given via numerical command or computer numerical control (CNC). Although today the two principles of CAD/CAM including computers and production are hardly distinguishable as separate entities in many industries, including automobile and aerospace, this separation theoretically is necessary to more effectively use these new methods to advance prefab architecture. Of all the areas of CAD/CAM technology implementation and development for the production of goods, the building industry is the slowest to evolve.

Developed in the military, the Air Force after World War II sought to expand its manufacturing system to produce repetitive and complex geometric components for planes and weapons applications.[31] But the history of CNC goes much deeper, entering into our infatuation with making the qualitative quantifiable. Lewis Mumford in *Technics and Civilization* shares the history of Benedictine monasteries in which numerical control emerged as a technique of regularization for the behavior of the monks. Mumford states that this marked a change in the human perception of time, relinquishing our physiological bodies from the rhythms of solar movements and seasons to being dictated by numerical control.[32]

Numerical control found its way into clock towers of European towns as a method to regularize trade. Bookkeeping methods advanced in tandem with trade calculation, and soon after, the notions of perspective drawing, cartography, and planetary science expanded. This all has come into fruition by virtue of the implementation of mathematics to understand spatial and social ends. This infatuation has not receded; in fact, the Industrial Revolution opened the door to modern-day computation through a 1 0 1 0 sequencing. Numerical sequences became important to America in the materials, patents, and communications systems related to the telegraph and railroad era.[33] By the turn of the nineteenth century, these standards became known as the "American System of Management and Manufacture."[34]

One of the first developments in automation can be traced to Joseph Marie Jacquard, who developed a

Figure 1.10 Jacquard, in 1801, developed a numerical control system for automating weaving patterns in a loom allowing textile design and manufacture. This was accomplished by using punch cards as the numerical input similar to numerical sequencing drives in contemporary computing.

manufacturing until computers became widely available. Early systems developed by Herman Hollerith in the mechanical tabulator based on punch cards were not that different from the Jacquard punch card system until advances were made to coded tapes, and ultimately into the hard drive of machines by uploading information. It was not until the 1950s that computers were used for manufacturing production, opening up possibilities for digitally controlled machinery.[35]

Up until the 1990s, numerical control was limited to only those who could afford the technology. Today, small manufacturers and fabricators use CNC machinery for their day-to-day operations. The advances that led to this proliferation can be attributed to the following:

- Development of smaller, more powerful computers that were affordable and able to process data at much greater speeds and to realize a return on their investment,

- Software that made the process of design to fabrication more accessible, and

- A general knowledge of how geometry could relate to production via numerical control.[36]

New machines during the 1990s were also developed to accommodate a variety of scales at different price tags. The decade brought a host of software applications from mechanical engineering such as CATIA, and other parametric platforms that allowed individuals to rationalize the design process of highly irregular nonplatonic geometry. Many product and mechanical engineering applications linked data concerning materials and methods of production with the human interface so that design decisions and their impact on production logistics

machine that read punch cards in order to control the weaving pattern in a loom in 1801. The Jacquard Loom is an excellent example of the theory of programmable machines. Punch card technology stayed relatively rudimentary in its effects on building and

could be integrated. This same idea is now being implemented into architecture and construction practice by way of building information modeling, or BIM. On the surface, digital design and manufacturing has the potential to offer innovative solutions, increase quality, and stabilize cost. The promise of prefabrication that was touted by Ford and others may be realized in this new paradigm as society and the building professions continue to shape its future direction.

chapter 2 History of Industrialized Architecture

This chapter proposes that the history of the architectural profession and the Industrial Revolution are parallel in their development, thus shaping the ideals of American architectural manifestos, architectural history in the United States, and contemporary values of the profession at large. The chapter will review the evolution of the architectural profession as it emerged in the twentieth century in the United States and the lessons learned from failures in prefabs during this time. The lessons can be applied to future successes in the twenty-first century.

2.1 Beginnings of a Profession

Architecture is a discipline that stems from a craft industry. A master builder during the Renaissance was an architect, engineer, and contractor. Brunelleschi, for example, served as master builder to oversee the design and construction of the Duomo in Florence in 1436. This model of practice continued until the Enlightenment Period, an era in which traditional thought was questioned. Often referred to as the Age of Reason, science began to take a role in everyday life in the eighteenth century. The Enlightenment

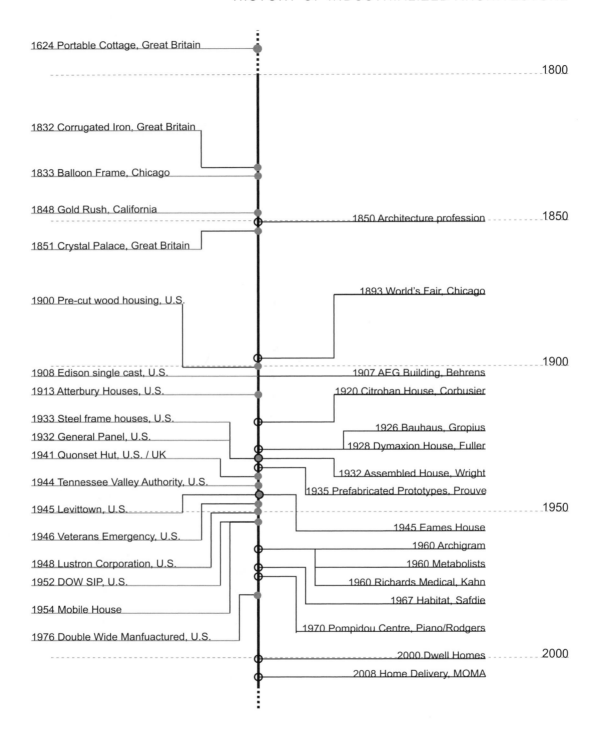

1624 Portable Cottage, Great Britain

1800

1832 Corrugated Iron, Great Britain

1833 Balloon Frame, Chicago

1848 Gold Rush, California

1850 Architecture profession   1850

1851 Crystal Palace, Great Britain

1893 World's Fair, Chicago

1900 Pre-cut wood housing, U.S.

1900

1908 Edison single cast, U.S.   1907 AEG Building, Behrens
1913 Atterbury Houses, U.S.   1920 Citrohan House, Corbusier
1933 Steel frame houses, U.S.
1932 General Panel, U.S.   1926 Bauhaus, Gropius
1941 Quonset Hut, U.S. / UK   1928 Dymaxion House, Fuller
1944 Tennessee Valley Authority, U.S. 1932 Assembled House, Wright
                                      1935 Prefabricated Prototypes, Prouve
1945 Levittown, U.S.   1950
                                      1945 Eames House
1946 Veterans Emergency, U.S.   1960 Archigram
1948 Lustron Corporation, U.S.   1960 Metabolists
1952 DOW SIP, U.S.   1960 Richards Medical, Kahn
                                      1967 Habitat, Safdie
1954 Mobile House
                                      1970 Pompidou Centre, Piano/Rodgers
1976 Double Wide Manfuactured, U.S.
                                      2000 Dwell Homes   2000
                                      2008 Home Delivery, MOMA

extended to every walk of life, from philosophy to mathematics, from politics to architecture and engineering. These movements manifest themselves in architectural education by the establishment of systematic teaching methods and models for the education of masses in the building sciences. The École Polytechnique in the late 1700s and the subsequent École Centrale des Arts et Manufactures in the early 1800s established the "modern architect." Jean-Nicolas-Louis Durand educated many generations of professionals and teachers of architecture for more than 30 years. Within his philosophy of architecture was a deep understanding of the architect in industrial production. Consequently, education placed an equal emphasis on technique and composition.[1]

Other counties in Europe, as well as the United States, adopted this model of education in the early nineteenth century. In the early 1800s, there were three primary methods of becoming an architect: being trained at the École des Beaux Arts; being schooled in an engineering-oriented academy, also in France; or apprenticing in the office of a master architect, who had either studied or trained under the same education system set up in the 1700s by the French. Most architects of the time had a combination of the three training options in some fashion. However, the United States had an additional option to training—a culture of the self-taught professionalism that stemmed from the young American pioneering spirit. These self-taught technical pioneers were a bit skeptical of formal education and therefore, a shop culture or apprenticeship was always favored in tandem with university learning. In addition, in-

Figure 2.2 This 1893 image from *Teknisk Ukeblad,* a technical journal in Norway, illustrates the "gentleman architect" disassociated with the act of technical construction, producing artistic representations of buildings on linen sheets.

◀ Figure 2.1 This timeline illustrates the historical events in prefabrication technology. The left column of the timeline includes the nonarchitectural events discussed in Chapter 1 while the right column lists selected architectural events covered in Chapter 2.

dustrial development, unlike in France, occurred at a fast pace in the U.S. Many of the first schools of architecture were developed in institutions where scientific research was rapidly progressing and readily accepted, including Harvard, MIT, and Penn.[2]

Science was highly favored and viewed by society at large as positive to the future of progress. In order to compete in the building market, an area that was readily overtaken by craftsmen and do-it-yourselfers, architects had to distinguish themselves as useful tradespeople. The first organization of architects stated that their purpose was to promote "architectural science." This allowed architecture to be carefully situated as a benefit to society through the measure of science of building. In retrospect, this might have done architecture more of a disservice in the U.S. market than was anticipated, as today architects are still trying to define their profession and role in society and within the construction culture. More importantly, however, "science" implied that there existed a systematic method of delivering a technical education by which one could become an architect. This was also the case for engineers, mechanics, and others associated with building industry trades. Although the system for becoming an architect was not scientific in our current understanding of applied sciences, it created a sense of professionalism that doctors and other scientists in society had at the time.[3]

Architects identified themselves as traditional and self-proclaimed leaders of the building process. In a similar timeframe, contractors were generally singular individuals or small-scale companies that managed small projects, working on everything from the larger general contracting and managing of sub-trades to the actual laying of bricks and mortar. In 1850, as architecture was emerging as a profession, contractors began to take on larger projects managing all aspects of building construction. During this time, the architect's control and supervision of construction and advisory role to the client was called into question. Speculative office buildings and other development projects gave contractors much more power than architects over the final outcome of building projects. As advances in building materials and methods increased and trades became ever more specialized, the architect eventually became less significant in the building industry, being seen as less of a resource to the client when compared with the builder. Architects' contractual control over

means and methods of construction has continued to wane since. This legal disinterest in building construction separates the architectural design process from prefabrication principles, disconnecting decisions of design from decisions of production, causing buildings to be overbudget, often not meeting the client's basic needs.[4] Many of the root problems associated with architects' lack of interest and understanding of the entirety of culture and market of the building industry can be traced to this critical shift in responsibility.

It was not until the end of the Civil War in the mid-1800s, with great advances in transportation of trains and ships, that manufacturing and service systems of buildings emerged. This was the Industrial Revolution, a time of changes in technical systems and belief systems, as a desire for "better, faster, cheaper" became an engendered societal value. During this time, U.S. blue-collar and white-collar workers were of equal value in the building industry. For example, Cyrus McCormick, a producer of harvesting machinery, was paid and respected comparable to Le Baron Jenney, a French-educated architect who later became the founder of the Chicago School. This marriage of shop culture and academic learning made a unique combination in the United States that fueled its developments in technology innovation. The developments of manufacturing methods and science in civil construction projects such as railways paved the way for the developments of steel tower construction. The methods of assembly line manufacturing and fabrication gave way to new theories and approaches to prefabrication technology in architectural production.[5]

The World's Fair in Chicago in 1893 embodies the conflicting roots of architectural theory in the United States that incorporate both Beaux Arts tradition pronounced by Jeffersonian architecture of the Virginia State Capital and the industrial aesthetic brought by advances in iron technology from England and France via Benjamin Henry Latrobe. While the White City that was built on the outskirts of Chicago adorned all of the traditions of the Beaux Arts, downtown was full of a new architecture, steel-framed stone and glass-clad structures that spoke of the new age of industrialism. The 1800s were a time of great advances in manufactured and prefabricated components in buildings. Cast iron and subsequently steel structures and curtain wall formations became part of the architectural vocabulary. This technology was based on standardization. Mass-produced parts were developed as systems for buildings to be constructed. Ornament became less and less important in favor of utility. However, this was not only a matter of economics, rather it was coupled with a desire to express the industrial nature of building production. Brick and stone were abandoned in favor of parts produced in factories near and far.

Richard Hunt, designer of the Tribune Tower, was instrumental in the World's Fair. He brought neo-renaissance to America in 1855, organized his studio according to Parisian examples, and was one of

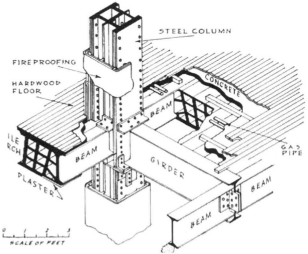

◀ Figure 2.3 The Reliance Building was designed by Atwood in the Daniel Burnham's architectural firm and engineered by E.C. Shankland. The basement and ground floor were constructed in 1890 and were designed by John Root. The remaining floors by Burnham's office were completed in 1895. This building is an all-steel frame that deviated from classical conventions and employed large expanses of glass, making it the first skyscraper.

▼ Figure 2.4 This is a detail of steel frame construction employed in early skyscrapers such as the Reliance Building.

the founding members of the American Institute of Architects. Hunt's protégé, William Ware, founded the first architecture school in the United States, at MIT, which was built on the principles of the École des Beaux Arts. Although Hunt's influence on American architecture was concerned with neo-traditional tenants, society seemed to be interested in a different direction, looking at the possibilities of industrial technology to revamp the production of building. While half of architecture was holding onto an ideal of traditionalism, the Chicago School was a different story.

The skyscraper technology was a result of post–Civil War developments in standardization, technical perfection, and a systematic kit-of-parts technology. William Le Baron Jenney, the father of the Chicago School, educated architects such as William Hilabird and Martin Roche, and influenced Daniel Burnham, John Root, Louis Sullivan, and later Frank Lloyd Wright. His inventions and innovations were taken up by Mies van der Rohe and are the modern building methods used today in cities of steel and glass. Wright refused to be educated by or to join the Beaux Arts movement. Sullivan, his mentor, condemned the White City exhibit in Chicago in 1893, believing that it was both nostalgic and regressive. Sullivan developed his own aesthetic based on a joining of ornament and utility; the very approach Wright mastered and that eventually became representative of American architecture—a bringing together of both innovation and tradition. The Chicago School was in two concurrent worlds, one a studio culture of arts tradition and the other a desire for technological innovation.[6]

The balance between innovation and tradition is a continual pursuit. Some might point to modernism of the early and mid-twentieth century as a balance of both classicism of architectural theory in composition and industrial utility in standardization. However, even in the movements that followed, architectural examples of production developments and nonarchitectural examples were continually diverse. Prefabrication, however, as an aesthetic gained its largest ground during the period of the modern revolution, beginning with the works of Behrens and his followers Walter Gropius, Mies van der Rohe, and Le Corbusier; and later with the American, Frank Lloyd Wright. Architectural history is one of modernist dictums, a search for new and innovative approaches to design and production, which is inextricably linked to prefabrication.

Peter Behrens trained himself as an architect, seeing architecture as the profession to offer social change. Behrens was appointed industrial designer for the German Electric Company in 1907, and designed lamps, appliances, as well as various factory buildings. The AEG Factory, designed by Behrens in Berlin in 1908, raised the awareness of industry as beauty. Behrens designed the factory like the machinery that was housed within it—its aesthetic was a direct re-

Figure 2.5   Peter Behrens designed the AEG Factory in Berlin in 1908. Behrens was mentor to future modern architects Le Corbusier, Mies van der Rohe, and Walter Gropius.

flection of its use. Although Behrens was influential in moving architecture into the realm of utility as design, arguably the most significant achievement that can be attributed to Behrens is his mentoring of three future key players in the advancement of modern architecture and prefabrication, namely Germans Walter Gropius and Mies van der Rohe, and Swiss-Frenchman Charles-Édouard Jeanneret-Gris, otherwise known as Le Corbusier.[7]

2.2 Gropius and Wachsmann

Walter Gropius was concerned about two ideals in architecture: industrialization and social equality. Using the industrial aesthetic of Behrens, his mentor, Gropius created an architecture that expressed absolute function. In 1919, he established the Bauhaus. Initially, the school was meant to be a marriage of all the design arts with a broad pedagogy. However, as additional teachers were brought on, Gropius and Adolf Meyer in 1926 designed a new building for the school, and industrial production began to take center stage in the school's mission. Gropius emphasized that the new curriculum would adhere to the following:

"The nature of an object is determined by what it does. Before a container, a chair or a house can function properly its nature must first be studied, for it must perfectly serve its purpose; in other words, it must fulfill its function practically, must be cheap, durable and 'beautiful'."[8]

He later expressed that in addition to education, one of the primary goals of the Bauhaus was to create designed objects for the masses. Gropius left Germany in 1934 and arrived in the United States in 1937. Due to his infamy from the Bauhaus, and participation in the Weissenhof Estate in Stuttgart, he was offered a job as the director of the architecture program at Harvard University. His interest in prefabrication was obvious from the days at the Bauhaus, harnessing the technology of offsite fabrication to reduce the cost of housing. In 1910, in collaboration with Behren's office, he proposed a mass-produced shelter for the German Electric Company. In the early 1930s, Gropius developed a copper-clad panel system before the idea was crushed, due to the war in Europe. Finally, in another collaboration, Gropius and Konrad Wachsmann produced perhaps his most well-known contribution to prefab architecture thinking; the mass-produced "Packaged House," designed for the U.S. market as a wartime housing proposal.[9]

Gilbert Herbert's *Dream of the Factory-Made House* tells the story of the design and manufacture of the project that consumed these two partners for a period of over five years. Gropius was an architect, who thought much like an engineer. Wachsmann was a self-taught architect, trained as a carpenter who maintained an undying interest in prefabrication throughout his life. His career was one marked by obsession with technology, an embrace of mechanized production, a master of detail and connection, and a lover of systems logic.[10] This team, consisting of public influential Gropius and technician Wachsmann, seemed to be the perfect combination to produce a much-needed product for the housing industry during and after the war. In 1942, the team designed a panelized system using a patented four-way connector developed by Wachsmann. All the components of the houses were produced in a factory and would be assembled onsite. They teamed with the General Panel Corporation to produce the house. It was not until 1947 that the factory production line was set up and prepared to manufacture houses. Unfortunately, by this time the government had pulled funding and the project lost its opportunity.[11]

The intricacies of why and how the system failed will be discussed later in this chapter. Gropius and Wachsmann were seen as architectural heros, trying to provide housing for the masses by using factory production technology. They were designers, but also acted as engineers, industrial designers, and manufacturers. Granted, they were not the only group producing factory homes; in fact, nearly 200,000 homes were produced by these means during and after the war. But Gropius was a father of modernism, a Dean at one of the most prestigious schools of architecture, and had great influence in the architecture culture. Their influence on the understanding of the role of architecture in society was causing a stir among practicing architects of the day. The team's message was that architects could take a project from conception to production, perhaps in the fashion of Brunelleschi, the master builder of centuries earlier. Complete creative authorship and cost effectiveness seemed a possibility, at least on paper. The message Gropius and Wachsmann sent is that if they could succeed with prefabrication in the least of the architectural typologies—housing—then maybe architecture could have more of an influence on the lives of Americans everyday.

2.3 Mies van der Rohe

Mies van der Rohe was also interested in industrialized building as a means of design. From Behrens it's obvious that Mies learned an attention to detail and craft. His thirst for precision and quality in design and construction seemed unquenchable. Mies

designed to use the factory; many of the parts were standardized; however, in the assembly process, the components were customized. The requirement for hand assembly in order to give the appearance of simplicity and refinement made any cost savings from the factory process negligible. Mies is quoted as having said,

"I see in industrialization the central problem of building in our time. If we succeed in carrying out this industrialization, the social economic, technical and also artistic problems will be readily solved."[12]

Unlike Gropius and Wachsmann's goal to provide housing for the masses, Mies did not have such aspirations and his designs were anything but affordable. Mies's greatest gifts to architectural history and the future were his passion for the steel and glass tower. Mies mastered the aesthetic of the slender steel structure. This became a mark of not only a refinement of the Chicago School, but created an entirely new typology for modern America across the world. Architects used this system of glass, steel, and aluminum during Mies's life and today in most skyscrapers that line the skyline of the world's major cities.[13]

"The first fact—a fact of technology—is that the building frame made of straight steel or concrete members is going to continue in use because it is efficient, economical, and easy to put together. In short, the rectangular cage as refined by Mies, however limiting it may appear to those interested in more sculptural expression, is sure to govern the shapes of most of our buildings for a great many years to come."[14]

Mies's contributions to prefabrication are not in the development of a new technology for production,

Figure 2.6 Mies van der Rohe's Seagram Building in New York City employs functional detailing manifest as aesthetic ornament.

panelized systems, or modules, but rather to the mainstreaming of the modern aesthetic in the societal acceptance of the steel and glass tower. He also influenced an entire generation of architects enamored with creating such artifices. The aesthetic sensibilities of Mies's pavilions in Barcelona and the Farnsworth House in Illinois are, in many respects, the embodiment of the minimalism that has found resurgence in late twentieth- and early twenty-first-century residential architecture. Today many prefab houses marketed by architects and others are modern in their implementation of simple materials, clean lines, and high level of transparency. Consciously or otherwise, Mies's influence on the understanding and expres-

sion of architecture, especially in prefabrication, will have an impact long into the future.

2.4 Le Corbusier

Before working for Behrens, Le Corbusier was trained as an artist/craftsman and apprenticed for Auguste Perret, the early master of reinforced concrete. It was from these experiences that Le Corbusier gained an appreciation for new materials and methods of architectural production. In 1923, far into the Industrial Revolution, and long after his training, Le Corbusier wrote *Towards a*

New Architecture. This personal manifesto argues that the beauty of modern architecture is discovered in its utility. He applauded the perfection of the automobile, airplanes, and ships that were, he felt, examples of beauty and function. He considered these technological feats to be the "Greek Temples" of the modern era, and once the ideals of modernism were identified by society, architecture would eventually follow. His statement "the house is a machine for living" was to be taken literally, because for Le Corbusier, it was either "architecture or revolution." He saw architecture, and mass-produced architecture in particular, as the answer to social ills. As part of this effort to create a machine for living, Le Corbusier designed and built a prototype called the Citrohan House. The word "Citrohan" was used as a pun, referring to the French automobile at the time, *Citroën*.

It is unclear that Le Corbusier ever intended for his houses to be built in a factory, or prefabricated,

Figure 2.7 Le Corbusier's ideas for a "machine for living" included the 1920–1930 Citrohan House. This house was inspired by the manufacturing methods employed in early standardized automobile production.

rather that the methods of mass production and assembly line labor would be employed onsite, in a more traditional manner. He believed that the architect could set up a system of construction that was based on rationalization through standardization. The Citrohan House linked the beginnings of Le Corbusier's five points of architecture including the domino or concrete frame with exterior and interior infill walls to allow openings to occur where needed for view and light. Factory-made windows and doors as well as prefabricated brisole covered the facades of his buildings. The houses were designed on rigid grids, but not necessarily in standard material dimensions. Le Corbusier's conceptual and practical linkages of design to production were somewhat lacking. Although similar designs were built, Le Corbusier never realized these mass-produced and prefabricated ideals at the scale and magnitude discussed in his writings.

Although none of Le Corbusier's buildings were built using prefabricated methods, his ideas about using the manufacturing industry were widely known by architects of the era. Le Corbusier saw beauty in the standardization of everyday objects. He viewed the purist object, as his architecture manifest, as the embodiment of utility and refinement. These ideals have provided much of the basis for contemporary low-cost, mass housing experiments in prefab architecture. Arguably the most influential architect for modernism in the twentieth century, Le Corbusier's influence on the role of prefabrication and mass production in housing is far reaching. Prefabricated architecture today continues to suffer from the infatuation with the small, modern purist box. Just as Le Corbusier's plans did not grow legs, so many of the prefab experiments in architecture today may meet basic needs, but do not satisfy societal desires to enhance the home dwelling. This can be seen in the pithy of housing projects Le Corbusier completed that are now overtaken and manipulated beyond recognition by the inhabitants. In many cases the house blocks have failed and been torn down.

2.5 Frank Lloyd Wright

Frank Lloyd Wright was independent and believed in an open (politically and physically), nonprejudiced, and adventurous America.[15] It has been written that he was well aware of the work of the modern masters in Europe, as they were aware of his work in the United States. Like Gropius, Wachsmann, Mies, and Le Corbusier, Wright believed in new, innovative architecture. He was trained by Sullivan to embrace the new but reference the traditional. Wright has become the most celebrated American architect because of his contributions to advances in spatial understanding and material prowess.

In 1932, Wright spoke about what he called the "assembled house." These houses were to be made up of standard units that became the spatial building blocks which would define the various rooms. The modules conceptually were a kit-of-parts and could be added to and taken from. Wright knew of the advances in prefabricated kitchens and baths having read and seen Buckminster Fuller's Dymaxion and the Pierce Foundation's service core. He spoke of insulated metal panel infill walls and customization options for clients.[16] Wright was extremely skeptical of prefabrication because he felt it lacked tactile qualities, and it called into question authorship of the designer. However, he was advanced in his thinking of how prefabricated buildings could

extend to become living organisms.[17] Despite his skepticism with offsite fabrication in building, Wright moved beyond theoretical rhetoric, and as early as 1916 had designed a precut lumber system for single-family houses based on the balloon framing system. It is recorded that many other experiments in steel and wood by Wright were tried during the 1920s and 1930s but all failed to gain commercial success. His methods never varied much from the standards of onsite construction and his demand for quality in hand-crafted detail made his houses expensive and inaccessible for the larger population.

The greatest success by Wright in realizing affordability was in the Usonian homes of the late 1930s and early 1940s. The Jacobs Home in Madison, Wisconsin, is an example. This house did not use any of the prefabrication methods Wright initially spoke of in 1932, but it aimed at affordability and was designed based on a logic of rational construction. The core of the home was built of masonry and housed the fireplace and kitchen/bath services. The core also offered the house lateral stability, being constructed from reinforced masonry. Infill walls made of plywood and planking were used for the exterior enclosure. The house was small, but highly detailed. A regular grid and standardized materials had great potential for prefabrication. However, at the end of the day, Wright was unable to achieve the level of handcraft he desired through prefabrication and to negotiate his desires for aesthetics with what he understood was affordable production. Wright never wanted his houses to be "mass produced" in the true sense; his architecture was client- and site-driven first, and technology-driven second.

2.6 Architectural Engineers

Although Buckminster Fuller and Jean Prouve were not formally trained as architects, their influence on prefabrication architecture is highly regarded. Fuller and Prouve's contributions are just as significant, if not more so, than the masters already discussed. In addition, their works were in some ways more successful, being accepted and widely known in nonarchitectural circles. This success can be attributed to the technical excellence of the designers and the final product outputs.

Buckminster Fuller, an engineer by training, practiced during the time of Gropius, Mies, and Le Corbusier. His rise to favor among architects has much to do with his ability to rationalize complex geometry common in structural algorithmic geodesic, tensegrity, and finally his stealthy mass-produced housing designs. In 1928, Fuller patented the Dymaxion house, which contained, among other things, an airplane-looking mast and cable structural system. Later in 1936, he designed a prefabricated bathroom unit for the house and in 1940 he produced a deployable unit for the army. By the time 1944 came around, Fuller was well known for his innovative designs in prefabricated mass-produced housing, which gave way to the making of the Wichita House. With the war ending in the mid-1940s, the airplane industry was having difficulty. Fuller was approached to convert airplane factories into housing production facilities. This fulfilled the need to keep employees working during the postwar employment slump.

The Wichita House was a technical marvel, fabricated as an airplane in aluminum, fastened with rivets. Fuller even used principles of airplane design, encouraging airflow around and through the house. All the services were grouped at the center of the house and the rest of the living spaces were subdivided into wedged-shaped rooms like the dividing of a circular pie. The real innovation in the evolution of the Fuller proposals was in weight. The Wichita House was only 6,000 lbs and when shipped could fit onto a single truck. Fuller claimed that it could be erected in a single day. Although the Wichita House was successful in that it provided factories with postwar work, Fuller pulled the plug on the production claiming that it was not ready for large runs. The company was sold shortly thereafter.[18]

Jean Prouve was also not an architect, but practiced designing and fabricating furniture. A Frenchman, he trained with architectural engineers including Robert Mallet-Stevens and Tony Garnier. In 1935, Prouve designed a small mass-produced shelter and built a prototype as a vacation house for a client. Although he never spelled out his design philosophy, it is clear that he believed in taking advantage of the most advanced methods of manufacturing and fabrication available to create new dynamic buildings.[19] He stated,

---

"Studies carried out independently of the practice should be avoided, or even forbidden. All that is extraneous seldom conforms to requirements and leads to loss of time. The constructor will have comment to make on the spot. The designer must also be able to discover his mistakes quickly and recognize them in advance; there must therefore be a constant dialogue between the designer and the constructor who must work as a team."[20]

Prouve's shop fabricated military huts for the French and later produced postwar housing. These designs were lightweight, easily erected prefabricated

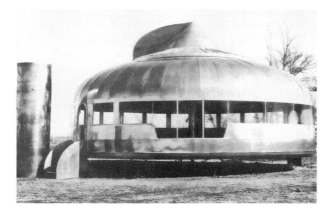

▲ Figure 2.8 Using the infrastructure of manufacturing factories during the war, Buckminster Fuller set out to develop an affordable housing solution in the Dymaxion house, which uses aluminum structure and skin and a tensile structure that hangs from a central mast. This model was built in Wichita, giving it the name of the Wichita House.

▶ Figure 2.9 Buckminster Fuller developed this prefabricated bathroom pod for the Dymaxion house series.

shelters used as a temporary housing solution. From the beginning, Prouve's designs used a cold-formed steel frame and wood roof and floor infill panels. In addition, in 1949, Prouve prefabricated 25 experimental houses that were erected in a suburb near Paris. Known as the Meudon Houses, they still exist today, but have been remodeled beyond recognition.[21]

Prouve worked to minimize waste and maximize benefit. He was able to achieve the most space for the lightest volume possible. He designed for craning of modules, frames that provided structure for infill panels, and systems fabricated offsite in a

▲ Figure 2.10 This service station, designed by Jean Prouve, has been restored and is currently on display on the Vitra Campus in Wel am Rhein.

factory. The aesthetics of his architecture and furniture followed the pattern of fabrication of molding, forming, bending, bolting, and welding—the manipulations of manufacture. The number of prefab projects was also much higher than any of his architectural predecessors. Nobody quite knows why, but Prouve was ousted from his own shop and ironically spent the remainder of his design career consulting without a direct connection to fabrication. However, many of the principles of design and production in architecture today can be traced to Prouve's design-build factory in the early twentieth century.

2.7 Late-Twentieth-Century Prefab

"In the second half of the twentieth century, however, the relationship between architecture and the mass-produced house changed. Architects…seemed to lose the will to change the world by direct intervention and instead put their faith in influence and example." [22]

The Case Study House Program of 1945 was initiated to produce California-style prototype houses that had a strong connection to landscape. The projects were meant to be affordable single-family homes, well designed, and easily constructed. Over 20 years, 36 homes were built, but most designers never collaborated with fabricators and most were unique site-built pieces of architecture, relished and venerated even today. Homes were designed by architects including Richard Neutra, Craig Ellwood, Raphael Soriano, and Pierre Koenig. Many of the homes were prefabricated components of steel frames and infill panels. The embodiment of prefabrication in the Case Study

series can be most explicitly seen in the Charles and Ray Eames House. [23]

Charles and Ray Eames were a husband and wife industrial design team. Like Prouve, the Eameses saw architecture and furniture much the same. Interested in architecture and influential in modern design of the mid-century, they envisioned their home to be built entirely from off-the-shelf components. Every element of the house was to be ordered and supplied from an industrial manufacturer. The steel frame was also made of standardized parts. Charles Eames said that the primary objective for the house was to create the cheapest space possible, with the highest level of industrialization. The house was not repeated, but represented maximizing the available industry at the time. The house could theoretically be duplicated if an instruction list and drawings were handed over. This systemized design and building process was not "affordable" nor was it particularly efficient. The Eameses eventually went on to abandon architecture in favor of their forte, industrial design, but their principles of prefabrication followed them into those arenas for the rest of their careers. [24]

The second major late-twentieth-century exploitation of prefabrication was in the high-tech movement. These architects include Brits Archigram, Michael Hopkins, Richard Rodgers, and Norman Foster. In the 1960s, Archigram consisting of Peter Cook, Warren Chalk, Ron Herron, Dennis Crompton, Michael Webb, and David Greene, among others, was essentially a paper architecture firm, creating manifestos of the future through propaganda and marketing imagery. Archigram's creations were highly industrialized wonders consisting of "walking cities," "instant cities," and "plug-in cities." Archigram did not actually develop any technical specifications for these ideas nor were any prototypes constructed; however, the partners provoked discussion and theory about the future of architecture and urbanism. Other architects did develop the group's ideas into full design proposals and construction but most experiments were singular enterprises, expensive and highly customized. Among these experiments in prefabrication include a house designed by Rodgers in 1968, called the Zip-up House, built from superinsulated aluminum sandwich panel walls with rounded corners and glazed ends. It was a tubular design in which modules could be added to make entire subdivisions. In 1975, Hopkins and his wife, Paty, built a home similar to the Eameses', constructed from standardized off-the-shelf steel components and even sporting primary colors found in the Eameses' work. Richard Horden, protégé of Foster, in 1983 designed the Yacht House in which ship technology was employed in the construction of a system consisting of light frame and panel infill. The high-tech movement and prefabrication was an era of architectural ideas. As far as recorded history of these trials, no fruitful collaborations with industrial manufacturers and fabricators were made and the systems were so customized that they were not affordable beyond a single prototype.

At the World Expo in 1967, Fuller built a large geodesic that was a three-quarter sphere, 61 meters high. As with previous experiment, Fuller's ideas of the geodesic never held with the mainstream. At the age of 24, Moshie Safdie, at the same World Expo, designed his first built project. One hundred fifty-eight houses were constructed from 354 modular units. There were 18 types of modules in reinforced precast concrete manufactured offsite. The modules were

stacked one on the other and voids between them formed outdoor gardens and decks. The modules were too heavy to be easily installed or relocated, had too many variations, and required specific tools and forms for the pours. In addition to offsite difficulties, onsite work required large cranes and intensive labor to attach the modules together. This plug-and-play concept did not save any money and, in fact, was far overbudget. Safdie left his dream of prefabrication in mass housing, calling his experiment a failure, and at that time claimed that prefabrication in architecture was impossible.[25]

Paul Rudolph stated that Safdie's material choices were the problem due to difficulty of fabrication and erection of the modules. Rudolph realized a modular housing project in a development called Oriental Masonic Gardens in New Haven, Connecticut in 1971. The technology was certainly not innovative, but the project used the mobile home typology in a multifamily development that was a reinterpretation of vernacular building. Architects of the era had signed off on mobile housing as not worthy of inspection, and here Rudolph was interested in grappling with a low-cost, high-design solution. The project suffered from great monotony with the barrel roofs of the mobile home, and dimensions repeated in mass, creating more of a ghetto than a vibrant neighborhood fabric.

The 1960s also brought the Japanese Metabolists. Like Safdie and Rudoloph, these projects used modular systems but differed in that the modules plugged into a structural and service core. The most famous of projects is the late 60's Nakagin Capsule Tower by Kurokawa. Kurokawa believed that the modules could be extracted as easily as they were plugged when tenants moved or module interiors needed to be updated. The project was originally

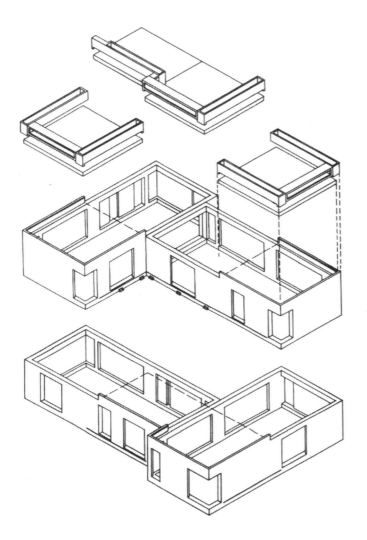

Figure 2.11 Moshie Safdie designed this housing complex called "Habitat" for the 1967 World Expo in Montreal. At age 24, Safdie developed a complex of 158 dwellings from 354 precast modular units.

designed as a hotel for late night laborers not able to commute back home after work. The capsules were completely fabricated offsite with modern conveniences. Ironically, the building is now outdated, has never been changed or extracted from the core, and is in disrepair. The investment in the steel structural and service core was so expensive that the initial cost of the project was much more than a building of its size in traditional onsite con-

struction. Should this concept of interchangeable modules become more widely accepted, the ability to remove elements is where lifecycle cost savings may be gained.

Prefabrication architecture in the late twentieth century, outside of small single-family houses and affordable multifamily housing, included projects on a much larger scale, custom, and for the public.

Figure 2.12 One of many prefab housing projects during the 1960s and 1970s, Paul Rudolph realized this modular housing development in New Haven in 1971. This adaptation of mobile housing units organizes the modules in juxtaposition to one another to create a sense of community.

Louis I. Kahn, an American architect living, working, and teaching in Philadelphia during the 1950s, 1960s, and 1970s, was a modernist, but wanted architecture to return to its roots in monumentalization, having much more of an impact on public sensorial perception of the built environment. His aesthetic was not that of industry, but of monumentality, solidity, and craft. Kahn also taught at Penn. Students and faculty revered him and his influence on materials in architecture is still felt today. Kahn's interest in prefabrication was not in the technology per se, but in revealing a material or a system and its method of construction for aesthetic and design ethics. Kahn's view on architecture can be summed up in his question "what does a brick want to be?" This question continues to challenge the greatest of designers and pushes architects to reveal the nature of materials and their method of employment in construction. In 1956, Kahn contacted August Komendant, a German engineer, to help him design a precast, prestressed, and post-tensioned concrete structure for the Richards Medical Laboratory at the University of Pennsylvania. Until that time precast, pretressed concrete had only been used for civil engineering projects involving long-span applications such as bridges and highways and in special construction. The adaptation of prestressed concrete for Kahn's architecture, let alone any building, was a major technology transfer for the construction industry. With Komendant, Kahn was able to design and build an intricate system of precast columns, and vierendeel girders, and beams that expressed the logic of the structure and embodied the overall parti. The prestressed units were combined through post-tensioning. This process made the members much more slender and elegant than site-cast counterparts. The fabrication of the components was accomplished by Atlantic Prestressing Company at a bid of $75,000

Figure 2.13 Kahn and engineer Komendant designed Richards Medical, a precast, prestressed concrete building, for the University of Pennsylvania built in the late 1960s. This is one of the first uses of prestressed concrete in building construction.

lower than the competition. It was estimated that traditional in situ cast concrete would have cost an additional $200,000 in the early 1960s. The final cost by Atlantic was $82,000 over their estimate, an acceptable margin by the client. In addition, the erection went remarkably well. The project was famously successful in meeting schedule. Kahn's success had much to do with his willingness to engage an expert in the precast design industry and work to come to a creative solution for the prefabricated structure.[26]

The late modernists used an exaggeration and reductive attitude in the design to expose the very inner workings of a building as an aesthetic. This had been done tentatively, but in the late 1960s, the Beaubourg Centres de Pompidou, designed by Italian architect Renzo Piano and the British architect Richard Rodgers, brought high-tech monumental expressionism to an unprecedented level. The construction from 1971–1977 marked a time in Paris with cranes constantly moving parts here and there from the back of trucks into place onsite. To accomplish this, the most technologically and pre-

fab-advanced building up until this time required the collaboration of the best in engineering. Piano and Rodgers worked with Ove Arup, who employed Ted Happold—and became Buro Happold Engineers—and Peter Rice, who would go on to work with Piano and other architects on complex technical projects.[27]

The most innovative element in the building was the superstructure. Completely exposed to the viewer as an exo-skeleton, it was made up of elegantly designed columns, girders, beams, and cross-bracing with a detail of a gerberette that acted to counterbalance the loading of the building and live loading of the occupants. This detail proved to be the most expressive and difficult to manufacture offsite. The gerberette weighed 17 tons each and was a testament to the capacity of fabrication to produce large-scale steel structural components. The story of the prefabricated components at Beaubourg is the story of Pompidou in general—that all components and pieces are subservient to the larger architectural ideal that must be maintained in the face of opposition by means of budget, schedule, technical requirements, or otherwise. Beaubourg was not an expression of utility in prefabrication, but in prefabrication on steroids, hyped to become something much more than it was intended—not a tool of construction and production but the very image of architecture itself. To this end, prefabrication had its place going into the 1990s and beyond.[28]

Piano and Rodgers' design redefined the role of prefabrication in the creation of architecture and building. The modernists of the generation before including Gropius, Mies van der Rohe, and Le Corbusier dreamed of offsite technologies as a way to realize a new aesthetic and affordable housing—

a solution for a need. The modernists of the late twentieth century seem to be less concerned with prefabrication as a means of providing social solutions as a method of production that could realize unprecedented scale, quality, and form—an answer for desire. Innovation trumps social equity in the late twentieth century and on into the early twenty-

Figure 2.14 Designed by Piano and Rodgers and engineered by Ove Arup's Peter Rice and Ted Happold in 1968, this building was entirely assembled from prefabricated components from 1971 to 1977 when it was completed.

first, and none truer than in recent buildings including the highly digitally designed, fabricated, and constructed Disney Concert Hall in Los Angeles. Spanning over a decade in the making and millions of dollars over budget, the concert hall is an edifice of beauty and the antithesis of efficiency. Under its stainless skin lies a story of struggle, financial challenges, geometry errors, sophisticated CAD/CAM production techniques, and lawsuits. For those who worked on the project or funded the enterprise, it is a building that they love and hate. Its innovation for architecture is its capacity to push the digital delivery of prefabrication to its limits.[29]

2.8 Lessons Learned

Prefabrication is evolutionary, not revolutionary. Similar to how advances are made in the medical field, solutions to problems are discovered through practice and through failure. Each failure leads to an understanding of what does not work, getting closer to what does. The advances in offsite fabrication for building have followed a rough road of disappointment and some successes. Each example offers insight into how prefabrication should or should not be harnessed to deliver architecture. Each is unique in its context, but similar themes throughout suggest ways in which architects and construction professionals may take advantage of prefabrication, while leaving its ills behind.

The details in Chapter 1 of nonarchitectural examples of housing including Sears Homes, Lustron Corporation, advances in precast concrete, and the most prolific prefab type, the mobile home, in most cases have nothing to do with architecture. So why are architects so concerned with prefab? Collin

Davies explains why this relationship between architecture and prefabrication is important:

"(prefabrication) challenges architecture's most deep-seated prejudices. It calls into question the concept of authorship, which is central to architecture's view of itself as an art form; it insists on a knowledge of production methods, marketing and distribution as well as construction; it disallows architecture's normal obsession with the needs of the individual clients and the specific qualities of particular places; and its lightweight, portable technologies mock architecture's monumental pretension. But if architecture could adapt itself to these conditions and succeed in (prefabrication), then it might recover some of the influence it has lost in the last 30 years and begin to make a real difference to the quality of the built environment."

The failures of prefabrication are not only among architects. Developers and businesspeople over the course of its history have also failed. These lessons are just as important, if not more, to determining how to harness prefabrication's promises in architecture and construction. The failures suggest the following:

2.8.1 Proprietary Systems Do Not Work for Mass Housing

Mark and Peter Anderson write,

"One of the lessons that can be learned from the many previous attempts at prefabricated housing production is that uniquely proprietary systems of single-source components are too costly to develop and have almost always ended in economic failure, even when excellent in design, detailing, and production concept."

A summary of proprietary systems and failures for mass housing include, in order of history:

1928, 1944: Fuller Dymaxion and Wichita House: circular geometry and custom aluminum skin with patented bathroom and kitchen service pod

1932, 1933: Fisher General Houses Corporation and McLaughlin American Houses: airplane-like, metal-stressed skin exterior panels

1932: Wright Usonian "assembled house": custom masonry service core and exterior wood assembled panels

1933: Keck House of Tomorrow and Crystal House: steel kit-of-parts; components to be assembled

1942: Gropius and Wachsmann's Prepacked House: four-way connector, frame, and exterior and interior infill panels

1948: Lustron Corporation Houses: enameled steel exterior and interior, custom built in steel fixtures and cabinets

1967: Safdie Habitat: variety of precast housing units linking together in unique configuration

1968: Metabolists Capsule: structure and service core with precast plug-in modules

All of these architects, companies, and their proprietary systems were competent and technically ready for market. The issue with these systems is that they do not lend themselves to manipulation and maintenance over time. For example, Fuller's proposals were technically advanced but would have required a continual stock of supply in order to maintain the building systems during their lifecycle. Especially in the case of service pods, systems are updated frequently enough that the near entirety of the home is outdated after its first decade or two of life. Often built to a lower quality than commercial construction, residential housing is one of the most durable (long lasting) of any of the building types. This is due to the ability of owners to manipulate their space affordably and through fairly rudimentary methods.

The other cases all have similar issues, that affordable housing does not warrant entirely new systems of development. Not only do systems that become outdated need replacing, but also aesthetic preferences change over time. Proprietary systems tend to also be proprietary in their aesthetic agendas, imposing specific ideas, styles, and materials that are difficult to change and adapt to individual living patterns. Proposals that are conceptual have accommodated change including Safdie and the Metabolist projects, but as their histories confirm, are rarely, if ever, changed because of the sheer cost of demounting a module in order to update the technology or replace the module altogether. In addition, plug-and-play proprietary systems rely on heavy infrastructure, all of which cannot be manipulated without deep, invasive, and expensive intervention, difficult to justify in the lifecycle costs of the building.

The Andersons continue,

"We have come to believe that the most effective path to achieving the benefit of prefabrication come from an incremental transition from site-based craft and assembly to offsite componentization of building elements, accompanied by a deeper analysis and understanding of social and economic forces outside of design and mechanics."

A list of successful nonproprietary systems and their descriptions in order of history follows.

Nineteenth century: Manning Cottage: standardized timber and infill system highly transportable

1832: Corrugated iron: rolled sheet metal into ribbed corrugation, stackable, light, and versatile, still widely used today

1833: Balloon frame: milled and cut standard lengths of light timber for walls, floors, and roof structure

1851: Crystal Palace: cast iron standardized connections and member lengths, interchangeable, one-off, but at an affordable scale with financial support to pull it off

1906–1940: Aladdin Homes and Sears Homes: precut balloon frame systems, mail order offering a variety of products put together with nails and hammer

Although custom for the building proper, the Crystal Palace of 1851 relied on standardized, interchangeable pieces that dramatically reduced both its erection time and labor force required to fabricate. The palace could also be reconfigured due to the flexibility of the system.

In comparison to the previous list of failed housing experiments, the list above offers an insightful counterpoint to explain the phenomena of defining proprietary systems for architecture. These examples point to one technology in particular that was created over a century ago in the United States: the balloon frame. In 2003, approximately 75 percent of all new housing in the United States used this method. About 28 percent of this segment used stick-framing concepts, but brought the operation into the factory using panelization, or the systematizing of 2X construction on flat beds, similar to the familiar prefabricated trusses,

Figure 2.15 Taylor is credited with the development of the balloon frame in Chicago in 1833. Light wood framed walls provided an ideal solution to the rapidly expanding West during the 1800s in the United States.

or structural insulated panels. The remaining housing stock is built as manufactured housing or some other material such as block, concrete, and so forth. Prefabricated stick-frame panels and modules are the primary methods used to deliver factory-based housing today. These technologies, including panelization in its various forms, modularization, or other sandwich-panel applications, which will be discussed in detail in Chapter 6, use the concepts of the stick frame, but simply bring the operations of building indoors. The flexibility, speed, and ease of assembly have made this fundamental unit of construction a market staple.

2.8.2 Prefabrication Is About Design and Development of a Technology

Prefabrication involves not only the design of a beautiful product, with detailed connections, interlacing materials that come together in either standardized or unique ways, but also has to be designed from a production standpoint. Architects are not generally proficient at product and production design and are not

trained to be industrialists. Our forte is form and design; generally speaking, the process by which something is made is secondary to our passion of creating uniqueness. Two primary examples of looking past production methods and focusing too much on design for design's sake are Le Corbusier's Citrohan House and Wright's Usonian Assembled House.

The Citrohan House was to be built as an automobile. This is what Le Corbusier stated in his writings, but as previously discussed, it is unclear whether he actually intended for the methods of production to be implemented in its construction. What is clear, however, is that Le Corbusier was enamored with the industrialization of society and saw architecture as needing to reflect this aesthetically. His study of automobiles and other modern advances illustrate this fascination, but his buildings, mostly in site-cast concrete, seemed to be more concerned with form and material than with any kind of design for production runs, factory to site connections, or mass production. Thankfully this is so, because Le Corbusier has given architecture a wealth of knowledge concerning what to do and especially what not to do in public housing, that may not have been available had he continued on the mass-produced Citrohan. The lesson from Le Corbusier is that architecture for architecture's sake cannot fulfill the needs of a society to have affordable, quality housing because production design must be part of the process.

Colin Davies states,

"The distinction between construction design and spatial design is an important one. Architecture commonly assumes responsibly for both and treats them as if they were equal value. The house building industry knows otherwise. A building technology, whether developed over centuries or invented in a factory, is a precious thing in which much practical ingenuity has been invested. It takes real experts to develop a building technology, preferably with hands-on knowledge of materials involved and tools used to shape them. New technologies designed in isolation on the drawing board are very unlikely to be successful. Technologies have to be developed, not designed, and you need a factory to develop them in." [30]

Wright similarly struggled with what he viewed was an implicit contradiction in building, that design and construction could not be mediated. He did not always believe this and spoke and practiced to try and deliver an affordable mass-produced house using a system of variation and standardized core and infill systems in the Usonian. The most successful example of this, the Jacobs House, was still over budget and Wright continued to make changes onsite throughout construction. His passion for connection with owners, and collaboration in the schematic design process, always overplayed any search for a system of mass production. This points to two primary obstacles for architects working in prefabrication: site specificity and authorship.

First is the notion of site-specific design. Kenneth Frampton sums up architecture's understanding of site specificity,

"It is fairly obvious that so called high-tech architects who have reinterpreted the craft of building in terms of modern productive methods have in effect been engaged in creating buildings which are largely determined by production methods…Against this, we may set the place-form or the foundational, topographic element that in one way or another is cast into the ground as a heavyweight site component that offers a form of quite literal resistance to the productional superstructure poised on top of it." [31]

Place-form refers to the site as a sculpted solid, designed as a subtraction, like a bas-relief. The site is a place that is formed to be a receptacle for the installation of the product-form, or the fabricated layering of lightness most often in steel or timber frame and layers of varying transparency and translucency. For architects of today and generations before, site plays a critical role in authenticity. But is site a requirement for architecture? Wright certainly thought so, as does Frampton. Mark and Peter Anderson wrote a book titled *Prefab Prototypes: Site Specific Design for Off-Site Construction.* [32] The title and the discussion that follows in the introduction to the monograph points to the inherent conception that architecture equals site. What is often missed, however, is that in order for architecture to have more of an impact on the everyday lives of people, it must also equal production. The Andersons' concern, like that of so many architects, is that prefab leads to a lack of individuality and authorship in the design process.

Davies concludes,

"Architecture's sensitivity to nuances of "place" is admirable in its way but is has become a fetish…The idea that the form of a building should emerge naturally from the unique combination of factors generated by a particular client and a particular site is appealing but unrealistic. Most houses are standard products adaptable to almost any site. There is nothing wrong with this. It has always been so. Vernacular architecture, the only kind that everybody loves, is an architecture of standard construction details applied to standard building types." [33]

Architects are also concerned that prefabrication threatens authorship, leaving credit dispersed among many as opposed to being attributed to the singular architect. This concern was manifest in a recent lecture by a renowned designer explaining their concept of a new theatre to be built in New York City. Advanced materials, methods, and prefab systems had been devised to realize the architecture. Noticeably absent from the presentation were the names of the collaborators, including the engineers, fabricators, and contractors who made the project a reality. One of the greatest fallacies in the culture of architecture is that buildings are attributed to one author. Architects must move beyond this obstacle of heroism if we are to create truly great solutions to the problems of the present day. Prefabrication can only thrive in a culture of collaboration.

This conundrum is not necessarily the fault of the current generation of designers. Previous generations, many discussed in this chapter, have shaped the way in which we understand our profession. The reality is that architecture and building is a creative endeavor, but creativity is developed out of adaptations and re-interpretation of standards, patterns, and languages in both design and production history. Architects are interested in production, but in many cases superficially, only if it adds to support a conceptual notion of our design ideology. But if architecture is going to be truly interested in prefab making design and production more closely related, architects must embrace shared authorship.

2.8.3 Prefabrication Has More to Do with a Business Plan Than a Product

Failures in prefab business planning can be seen in both works of architects and developers. From 1948 to 1950, the Lustron Corporation built prefabricated porcelain-enameled steel houses. The rise and fall of this company is told in detail by Thomas Fetters in *The Lustron Home*.[34] It is not that Lustron's product was low quality or dysfunctional. The home was ideal for the time in which it was built, using technologies from the airplane industry during the war. Its enameled steel structure, able to be cleaned with a garden hose, and amenities of built-in kitchen appliances made its appeal wide. It is reported that over 60,000 people toured the Lustron show home in New York City in 1948 and advertisements in *Life* magazine generated over 150,000 inquiries.[35] By the time Lustron was forced to foreclose in 1950 it had constructed 2,680 homes over its two-year life. Consisting of 234 dealers in 35 states across the United States and having shipped to the far reaches of Venezuela, Alaska, and other military locations, Lustron is considered a success by many standards. But Lustron's primary problem that led to its ultimate demise was poor financial planning on the part of its administrators.

Lustron was in debt well before production and relied on the RFC (Reconstruction Finance Corporation) that pulled funding in late 1949. In its short life, Lustron could not muster enough market demand to continue operating independent of outside funding. The reasons for RFC's pullout were primarily political. Fetters indicates that a series of bad publicity articles linked RFC's investment to Lustron as an irresponsible use of public funds. Congressional hearings ensued to make the RFC responsible for its spending practices. In addition, this was a time of postwar concern over overtly government-backed housing initiatives that might have been construed by the public as being associated with communistic or socialistic operations. Although enough funding had been loaned to update machines in the factory, production processes had been streamlined, and the designs retooled to offer more options within a standard type, Lustron's name had been tainted and the public, what small handful had been interested, were no longer interested.[36]

The architectural example of overlooking the business support for prefabrication can be seen in Gropius and Wachsmann's prepacked housing proposal. The plans, details, and perspectives of this system, as well as the many prototype experiments of connections, illustrate a thoroughly developed system of assembly. It was precise and carefully considered. Wachsmann went to great lengths to ensure that the technique would not fail, designing the construction system including supply chain, fabrication, assembly line production, shipping, and installation. In 1942, Gropius and Wachsmann were prepared to produce 10,000 homes per year and a prototype was even run in the factory. It is not entirely clear, but apparently Wachsmann felt compelled to refine the details and methods of production continuously. Herbert writes that despite the enthusiasm, expertise and reputation of both of the men, government and private investment backing, and collaboration with industry partners, the project was not ready and missed the opportunity to succeed in 1942.[37] Wartime demand declined and, despite its technical prowess, the housing proposal failed.

It was in 1946 that the VEHA was established to encourage manufacturers to replace factories used to produce goods for the war. The VEHA wanted factories to produce housing for the millions of dwellings needed to shelter returning veterans and growing families. Putting in more efficient equipment and refinement of the system further by Wachsmann caused the factory to be prepared just too late as the federal funding was cancelled. The story of its failure, however, was not in the lack of funding as in the case of the Lustron Corporation series of unfor-

tunate reliance on the RFC and politics that caused its downfall; rather it was the infatuation with the production proper that blinded the men to the realities of the need for marketing. The genius of the construction system, developed over years if not decades by Wachsmann's experience in previous prototypes during his war service, was not enough to gain the interest of consumers. The reality is that homebuyers were not interested in the method of production or in the ingenuity of the fabrication and assembly system no matter how sophisticated it appeared; rather patrons were interested in everyday practical features of the completed dwelling: durability, conveniences, and probably the most valued, resale potential.

Therefore, prefabrication, whether in housing or with other building types, must adhere to the principles of both technique and business marketing. Prefabrication, as with any technology or product, is vulnerable to the failings in business, finances, and political context in which the prefabrication system is deployed. In these examples, prefabrication can exist by meeting these principles without architecture, but architecture certainly cannot exist without meeting these basic tenants of prefab.

2.8.4 Situation Should Warrant Prefabrication

One of the major lessons from the failures in prefabrication trials of the past is that offsite construction should not be used in every situation and each project should be specifically evaluated for the potential to use prefab methods. Each project has a client, location, and labor context in which it must operate.[38] These parameters have a large impact on whether or not prefabrication will be used, regardless of how much the architect or other construction professionals want it to be used or how sophisticated and attractive the system might be in appearance and function. In many of the examples of prefabrication by architects, we have learned that the decision to use offsite production was not with consideration to client, location, and labor context, but rather a design idea that was envisioned to push a technical aesthetic agenda forward. Certainly with the early modern masters this was the case as well as in many postwar experiments. However, in some cases, one-off specific projects that use prefabrication for the novelty without consideration for the context in which it emerges can be deemed irresponsible and even unethical. These principles will be discussed in more depth in Chapter 3.

2.8.5 Must Come from an Integrated Process

Many failures in prefabrication occur because of a lack of integrated process early in the planning stages of a project. The timing of thinking about prefabrication in a design process should be early on in a building venture. Alastair Gibb states that an overall strategy for offsite fabrication is required because the benefits of prefabrication are not in the individual elemental cost, but are realized in possible secondary effects of saved time on site, reduced financial paperwork, RFPs, change orders, and so forth.[39] By working toward selecting prefabrication as the method of implementation early on, it encourages the client, design team, contractor team, and key fabricators to work collaboratively to realize an affordable appropriate technology for a given context.

Joel Turkel of Turkel Design states:

"The future of prefab is an increasingly non-architectural problem. Traditionally, architects have tried to design things to be prefabricated using either existing or new means, as opposed to designing functional and integrated delivery methods…Real development for the industry will come from young (professionals) who are able to… think in terms of complete front-to-back business models. They are aware of the needs and limits of manufacturing processes but also are versed in new technologies, entrepreneurial methods, how capital works, strategic partnerships, and the important of marketing and branding. This group will not design buildings but rather solutions for distributed delivery methods…leading the way toward rationalized industry wide changes to benefit us all, rather than just promoting an individual vision or aesthetic."[40]

---

chapter 3 Environment, Organization, and Technology

Project teams may employ offsite construction to realize building project goals for efficiencies and innovation. Although owners, designers, and contractors may want to develop and use prefabrication, they are in many respects at the mercy of the context in which it is employed. In their book, *The Process of Technological Innovation*, Tormatzky and Fleischer outline three criteria that have proven necessary for technology to thrive within other industries. These are environment, organization, and technology.[1]

• *Environment* refers to the market, industry, infrastructural, and cultural context.

• *Organization* refers to linkages, communication, and responsibility given to members of a collaborative.

• *Technology* indicates the availability and characteristics of the technology itself.

Sometimes, prefabrication is defined as a *technology*, being only material and digital output. However, in order for it to thrive, it must answer the demands of all three contextual parameters. Prefab encompasses a process-oriented approach responding to the en-

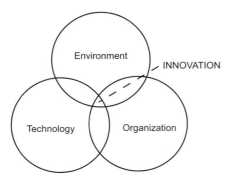

Figure 3.1 Three criteria that have proven necessary for innovation to thrive within collaborative contexts include environment, organization, and technology.

vironmental context, organizational structure, and digital and material capacity of manufacturing. These principles in large measure determine whether or not prefabrication will occur at all or the extent to which it may be realized. These three principles will be discussed in this chapter in order: environmental context, organizational context, and technological context.

3.1 Environmental Context

Technology is not deterministic, but rather it is affectively determined. This misconceived idea of technology having a life of its own, on a mission to shape society, is especially prevalent in architectural culture. Technology is often blamed by society for the negative aspects of the environment. The television, for example, is blamed for the disintegration of the family; automobiles for the segregation of cities; and cheap oil for the bland landscape of monotonous glass skyscrapers in cities. These technologies are not to blame, but the people behind their deployment. However, the purpose in discussing technology is not to determine which are "bad" or "good," since this is subjective, but to highlight that technol-

ogy emerges from social and cultural needs and desires. This will help architects and builders interested in developing and using new technologies, including prefabrication, to do so critically, and with an awareness of the potential opportunities and challenges. The environmental contexts in which prefabrication can be categorized include *team, type,* and *location.*

3.1.1 Team

A project team is made up of a number of players, each with a different vested interest. This is why they are often referred to as stakeholders. Clients are building owners or developers, who may be individuals, groups, or a representative of the owner. They are the impetus behind a building project, providing the funding and financing of the project. In large measure, the client determines the procurement or delivery method employed, as well as the ultimate size, shape, and finish of the facility. The client, therefore, determines the construction method used, whether prefabricated or not, and the extent to which prefabrication is employed with the help of architects and engineers on the design team. Design team members take the goals and program of the client and work to develop a design and delivery strategy that will meet the project budget, scope, and schedule. Design teams can have a large impact on whether or not prefabrication is employed, depending on the collaborative working relationship and trust given to the team by the client. Contractors may also be the determining factor, especially if the construction method in a traditional design-bid-build contract is not decided on from the beginning. Although prefabrication has less of a chance of success in this model, and can be detrimental being decided upon so late in the process—during the bidding and construction phases—contractors may use pieces of a project that are prefabricated in order to increase productivity.

There are a few characteristics to determine whether a project team will be more or less likely to employ prefabrication. These determinants include:

- Experience: A team that has used offsite fabrication on other projects or has had exposure to prefabrication previous to the building project will be more likely to use it again. Most clients, and many designers and contractors, view offsite fabrication as alternative, meaning that the project has more initial risk than with traditional delivery methods. There is no data to substantiate this, and is actually quite the opposite; however, the perception remains. Design team members and contractors who have experience in using prefabrication have the confidence and skill set to deliver it again. These skills may be quite a bit different than onsite construction, where the act of coordination of shipping, setting, and stitching demands integration of process.

- Control: A client who wants to maintain control of project costs, schedule, and quality of output may choose offsite production. This is not to definitively say that prefabrication is always less costly, but that a client will experience a higher degree of predictability, understanding the schedule and quality that will be achieved at a specific price point. This reduces the exposure of design and contractor team members as well. Onsite construction leaves too many unknowns unresolved before breaking ground. A client and design team that do not want to make decisions regarding construction early on in the development process will have difficulty with the level of resolution needed to deliver prefabricated architecture.

- Repetition: A client and contractor who build together often may find offsite fabrication beneficial because the systems that are developed may be deployed in other projects. This is especially true for project teams that work together on a series of building ventures. This is certainly the case with clients such as Travelodge Hotel in the United Kingdom that have developed an International Standard Building Unit (ISBU) fabrication system that is proven and continues to improve on cost and schedule in each iteration. The added benefit is that project team members also continue their relationship with the fabricator, who may or may not be the contractor, but becomes a key player in delivering the facilities. Apple uses this model on their stores, and the subcontractors become key stakeholders in delivering increasingly innovative projects sequentially.

- Manufacturing: Project team members who have experience with product development, manufacturing, and fabrication in other industries may be acquainted with the opportunities that are presented by these technologies for building construction. It should be noted that clients without this experience are often nervous about how little work is occurring onsite and then want the project to be completed more quickly when offsite constructed elements begin appearing. This is especially true with smaller-scale residential and commercial prefabrication.

- Financing: A client who has the capital to invest in prefabrication at the beginning of the project has a higher chance of seeing offsite fabrication succeed. Initial investment in offsite production may be higher depending on the level and degree of prefabrication. Contractors who have the capacity to bond a project—to pay out early in the process and remain throughout the delivery, as opposed to larger draws later in construction—will have an easier time investing in prefabrication. Projects that look to lease options for panels and modules are an added benefit with prefabrication. Additional financing options presented by prefab will be discussed in Chapter 4.

3.1.2 Type

The project type can determine the degree to which prefabrication is employed. It is often thought that highly proprietary, unique projects that have little repetition should not employ offsite fabrication. The reality is that customized products for buildings require less repetition, but still require control that can only be delivered by offsite methods. Whether trying to increase the productivity of standard building types, or on a unique specialized project, offsite fabrication can be harnessed to increase the quality of the building elements and increase the predictability of the end result. A few general guidelines can be stated, however, regarding the type of project that is more or less prefabricated:

- Duration: Projects that are under extreme schedule constraints can benefit from reduced project duration offered by prefab. Examples of short schedules include corporations that are trying to open by a certain date, school and dormitory facilities that must open for a new semester, and embassies that must be built for U.S. operations in a foreign country. There are hardly any building types today that do not demand a short schedule for construction, but for some, it is the driving issue on the table from the start of project conception. Looking to prefabrication for these types of projects at the same time schedule is being identified will aid the project team in making more appropriate decisions regarding the prefab methods to employ to meet project schedule goals.

- Repetition: Building projects that have a great deal of repetition can benefit from prefabrication. Kullman Buildings Corp. uses lean production methods on modular buildings to produce high-tech health-care facilities, communications structures, and highly finished bathrooms and kitchen service pods. These units are repetitive, being constructed in mass quantity for clients such as the federal government, communications companies, hotels, and student dormitories. Precast projects likewise use casting beds to deliver repetitious elements for projects such as prisons, warehouses, stadiums, and parking structures. Repetition may be used to deliver one building or it may be capitalized in a number of building projects similar to one another. For complex geometrical designs, geometry may need to be rationalized for more efficient fabrication. The Salt Lake City Library reduced the need from thousands of casting beds to seven by the design team rationalizing its precast cladding panels for repetitive casts.

- Unique: Architectural projects that employ unique forms, unique sustainability requirements, or unique programmatic solutions demand a higher degree of control of the end product. In these situations, offsite production can make these projects a possibility. Frank Ghery's curved surfaces are all developed as a set of panels by A. Zahner Architectural Metals. These surfaces would be nearly impossible fabricated onsite. Dimensionally accurate, geometrically complex projects use prefabrication to remove tolerance and quality control offsite. These types of projects are not necessarily faster; quite the opposite. Offsite fabrication is given the research and development prototype funding required for delivering the system. These specialized projects are concerned with quality and innovation.

- Procurement: The delivery method selected by the client can have a large impact on the determination and extent of prefabrication. Although offsite production can be used in any contract structure, design-bid-build contracts are more difficult as they suggest means and methods of construction to be determined by the contractor during and after bidding. Often construction managers are used in this type of contract, making decisions regarding construction methods without input from the client. This can be mitigated by selecting design-build, or integrated contacts that allow for early prefabrication decision making with the contractor and key fabricators and subcontractors present at the design and planning phases.

3.1.3 Location

The real estate industry's chant, "location, location, location," is no more appropriate than in the building industry. Perhaps there is no greater determinant for the extent to which prefabrication is employed than with the site and labor context of the location of the project. The following are characteristics of location that determine the extent and type of offsite fabrication:

- Geography: Sites that are accessible, where land is affordable and construction seasons are year round, prefabrication makes less sense. However, remote sites where onsite methods would be difficult to reach and would necessitate labor crews commuting each day would benefit from fabricating elements offsite and erecting them quickly onsite. In addition, sites with large topographic elevation changes or sites with limited access would demand that cranes place larger panels and modules onsite. Dense urban centers that have expensive land and limited access require that buildings be built faster. This often is why urban sites use fast-track methods. Prefabrication may be employed to increase speed of construction. In addition, dense urban sites may require construction vehicles to have limited access to the building site; therefore, offsite fabrication that can be erected in less time will require fewer logistical constraints for street blockage during staging.

- Manufacturing: Sites that are located away from industrialized cities and manufacturing capacities will have less of a chance of prefabrication than those that are close. This is less of a concern as prefabricators—especially modular builders—are becoming more common throughout the United States. In addition, unique projects may have the budgets to invest in specialized manufacturers to deliver a system from Los Angeles to New York City, for example. Specialized manufacturers ship throughout the world. However, for budget-restricted projects, if manufacturers cannot be found in the local region, the cost of transportation may be greater than the savings as a result of prefabrication. In general, if there are few manufacturing facilities, onsite methods are more accessible from a logistics and cost perspective.

- Material: Just as with manufacturing accessibility, material availability can determine the extent to which prefabrication is used. Offsite fabrication is dependent on material type. This will often determine how the material is harvested, processed, manufactured, and installed. Some areas of the United States are steel frame areas, while some are concrete, for example. This distinction is becoming less of an issue, however, as the cost of one system may still be significantly less if the infrastructure and labor force of a specific system is available in a particular region. Teams should identify the material available during early stages of a building project to determine what prefabrication capacities might be possible.

- Labor: The cost of labor is a major factor in the overall cost of a building project. If labor is expensive, as it is in Europe and Japan, prefab methods that reduce the number of workers and the time spent in labor benefit the project more significantly than in locations where labor is inexpensive and available. In addition, locations that do not have a labor force due to the remoteness of the site can benefit from prefabrication as previously discussed. On specialized projects, the lack of skilled labor to accomplish the building may require offsite fabrication far away from the region, but the manufacturing labor must be within an affordable distance to justify the transportation expense.

• Regulation: Although prefabrication at a myriad of types and scales is becoming increasingly common, building officials and regulatory agencies cannot keep up with the advances being made.

Municipalities that are unaccustomed to reviewing, approving, and inspecting offsite fabricated elements for construction may not be willing to approve permitting submittals quickly and may require special engineering or third-party verifiers to determine the validity of the system for health, safety, and welfare reasons. Projects that are fabricated in one state and are shipped to another often require third-party inspectors—hired by the manufacturing company—to report to the local authority that has inspection jurisdiction for site work, setting, and stitching.

BEIJING NATIONAL AQUATICS CENTER

An example of environmental context determining production can be found at the Water Cube: The Beijing National Aquatics Center, which became a familiar site on the news and Internet broadcasting during the 2008 summer Olympics. The building is a fantastic display of structural steel laced together in an intricate diagrid. Arup, the engineer, suggested prefabrication as the method of delivery to limit expensive onsite welding. Prefabrication would save time and ease the construction coordination. This was rejected, however, by the Chinese, who used the large and available labor force for onsite welding. Approximately 12,000 spherical nodes and 22,000 tube and box sections were individually fixed onsite. The labor force consisted of 3,000 workers including more than 100 welders. Arup's usual process of information development in a finite element analysis and steel detailing software and then transfer to CNC machinery for cutting was discarded in favor of taking advantage of the available labor force. Although digital tools were used to coordinate the complex three-dimensional (3D) geometry, expediency, and efficiency in construction, in many ways it was not needed in the project. To this end, social context determined the technical resolution.[2]

Figure 3.2 The Water Cube, built for the 2008 Olympics in Beijing, was built using a large local labor force of 3,000 workers including more than 100 welders. The design and construction team evaluated offsite construction, but the client chose onsite construction in order to sustain many Chinese construction laborers.

3.2 Organization

The team, type, and location of a project have a large impact on the extent of prefabrication that is employed. However, just as important a factor is the collaborative context of the team in which the project is realized. In any building project, team members must make early determinations of the capacity of the project to use offsite production. This requires a collaborative and integrative process of delivery.

The construction industry is, in general, inefficient and fraught with errors and litigation. Traditional contracts rigidly delineate responsibilities with much elaboration on the consequences of failure. These contracts reinforce risk-abating behavior, causing project teams to not engage in integrated practice models, much to the disadvantage of all stakeholders. Owners are losing money on projects, architects are not seeing the quality of design increase, and contractors are bearing a great deal of financial burden and risk in the process. In addition to the

financial litigation, there is too little investment in technology, training, and education for prefabrication. This includes innovation in the form of collaborative delivery approaches fostered by more flexible and responsive contracts.

3.2.1 Design-Build

The extent of integration depends necessarily on the legal context in which players come together. As opposed to design-bid-build (DBB), design-build (DB) projects "reduce the overall project duration."[3] Procurement methods such as DB allow for early decision making regarding prefabrication systems that can lead to improved coordination and constructability, and finally reduced construction time. In addition, Konchar and Sanvido, in a 1998 study, found benefits of DB in terms of cost and quality, an added benefit with prefabrication.[4] Design-build also allows for the delivery process to potentially create a smoother flow of information between design and construction organizations. Instead of a handover method, where

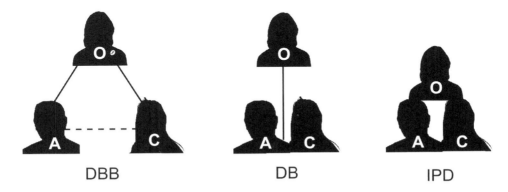

Figure 3.3 Project delivery methods used in construction suggest a more integrated model, moving from design-bid-build to design-build and the development of integrated project delivery contracts. These efforts are aimed at breaking down the poor communication that leads to finger pointing and litigation common in the U.S. construction culture. Prefab is an integral principle in the emerging area of integration.

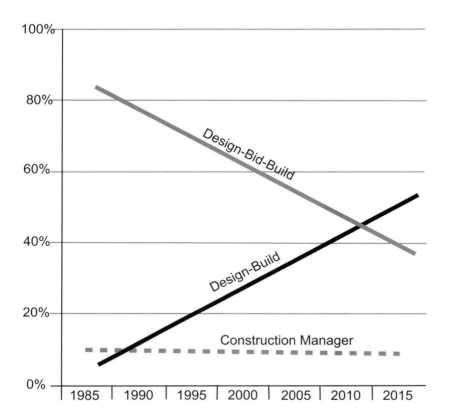

Figure 3.4 Design-build contracts, including integrated project delivery in the United States, have consistently increased in project delivery since their inception in the 1980s from a few percent of total construction projects to just over 40 percent in 2010. On the other hand, traditional design-bid-build contracts have steadily declined in use. Construction manager delivery has stayed relatively the same. This points to the desire and reality that owners and project team members are moving to more integrated delivery models, making prefab more realizable today and in the future.

one group of individuals designs a facility and then throws the job over the fence so to speak for another team to catch and run, DB methods can collaboratively identify prefabrication as the construction method and execute it as such. DB contracts allow project players to "focus less on specific deliverables between organizations and more on overall deliverables to the owner."[5]

One way in which to deliver more quality and cost benefit is through increasing the integrated process. A study at the University of Texas documents that owners are moving away from the traditional selection of providers based on low bid to preferred providers.

The study notes that projects with collaborative relationships are more successful from both the owner's and contractor's perspectives.[6] One of the key elements in integrated processes is the selection and participation of all project personnel as early in the project as possible. This can only benefit the successful deployment of prefabrication. The selection-based model in which owners bring contractors to the table early in the design process, especially key subcontractors such as precasters, or steel construction erectors or fabricators, allows for decisions to be made regarding difficult portions of projects during the design phase, thus reducing costly changes later during construction.

Although design-build is well tested today, it has its problems in that it is usually architect led or contractor led. DB entities can be incorporated AEC firms that deliver the entire package, but usually they reflect joint ventures that go after a project short term, only for the duration of the project being considered. These partnerships can start off with a degree of uncertainty, without an understanding of who does what and when. Conversely, continued partnerships that join for multiple projects can yield better results the second or third time around. The concern is that if the process is architect led, design will overwhelm values of production, and in a contractor-led model, construction will be the only consideration, finding ways to possibly reduce design features in favor of cost or schedule reductions.

3.2.2 Performance Contracts

Outside of traditional DB and DBB contracts, performance-based contracts are an emerging method of project delivery. These contracts are usually fixed-fee, results-driven contracts that allow service providers to work using their own best practices. Instead of prescriptive approaches, the emphasis is defined by the owner's goals and project players are rewarded based on their performance of meeting those goals. Beginning in 2007, the General Services Administration of the federal government is now using this method extensively. This type of contract may be important as prefabrication goals are established in the owner's list of values for a project to reduce cost and increase productivity while not relinquishing quality. Performance-based contracts can be implemented with shared incentive plans where all members integrate on most phases of the building delivery. Without a clear partitioning of the organizational contributions, if one wins, all win, but

likewise, if one fails, risk is shared across the collaborative. Prefabrication, just as performance-based contracting, is dependent on trust and risk sharing in order to succeed.

3.2.3 Integrated Project Delivery

In 2007 and 2008, two industry organizations published contracts that took the desirable elements of both design build's speed and information sharing, and performance contracts which emphasize outcomes via shared risk and incentives. In 2008, the American Institute of Architects (AIA) published two separate integrated project delivery (IPD) families: the so-called transitional AIA A295, built on a construction management at risk model, and the single purpose entity (SPE) family, developed as the contract embodiment of the principles espoused in *Integrated Project Delivery: A Guide*, published by the AIA in 2007.[7] ConsensusDOCS emerged before the IPD families with its Standard Form of Tri-Party Agreement for Collaborative Project Delivery, more commonly referred to as ConsensusDOCS 300, published in 2007.[8] The clear difference between ConsensusDOCs, IPD contracts, and the traditional DBB delivery is the concept of "relational contracting."[9] This can be explained as contracts where parties create an organization and agree to risk share with collaborative and collective decision making.

Fostering collective decision making will allow project teams to communicate more freely with information than has been possible before. This will allow for construction information to be shared across discipline lines. For example, traditional contracts do not allow for architects to share their digital information directly with contractors or subcontractors. In prefabrication, this does not benefit an integrated delivery of products because fabricators must develop their own shop drawings and get submittal approval. The future of practice facilitated by IPD contracts should allow for free information sharing so that the design information can transition into shop information. Examples of this can be seen in KieranTimberlake and Tedd Benson's Loblolly House that employed no shop drawings in the delivery process. This project will be discussed in Chapter 10.

The major difference between the AIA IPD contracts and the ConsensusDOCS can be summarized as follows:

"The primary philosophical difference between the two sets of documents is that the ConsensusDOCS agreements provide for an immensely diminished role for the Architect in project execution. The Architect has very few formal responsibilities in the Owner-Contractor legal relationship under the ConsensusDOCS. Thus, under the ConsensusDOCS, the Architect is conceived more as the Owner's consultant rather than the integral project administrator and facilitator as established by the AIA agreements." [10]

This should be of concern to architects trying to develop projects that work toward prefabrication but are limited in their capacity to offer meaningful information to the construction of the facility. The AIA A295 family of contracts allow for an easier transition between traditional delivery and full integration of project players. It uses a similar structure of architect and contractor working collaboratively to provide preconstruction services including cost estimating and constructability reviews, but it creates a collaborative working environment by integrating the duties of each player with the activities of the others.

The SPE family, also developed by the AIA, bears no resemblance of traditional contracts. The AIA has been quoted as saying that it developed this model from product design and production deliveries such as the automotive industry that holds a DB to produce a product through a combination of its own forces and independent contractors. Effectively, the project players under SPE become a limited liability company. Although all are under one entity, project players, such as the architect, may receive reimbursement for the costs they incur and may earn profit through performance. Providing incentives during the construction process provides motivation for architects, engineers, contractors, and fabricators to work collaboratively so all benefit. If one earns a profit, all earn a profit. Likewise, the team agrees to indemnify one another in the event of litigation, causing all disputes to be resolved outside of the courtroom. [11]

Few projects have been run under any of these contracts. As case studies become more prevalent, the pros and cons of each contract will become more transparent. In a recent AIA Utah meeting, Craig Coburn, a lawyer in Salt Lake City, discussed the potential pitfalls of this delivery method, but agreed that he sees great benefits for all project stakeholders. In the interim, IPD provides more work for lawyers as an entire industry relearns its relationships to one another and breaks down the prejudices of the disciplines. Autodesk, in an effort to push their software system Revit Architecture, have engaged in IPD contracts for tenant improvement projects for offices and retail centers in major cities in the United States.

AUTODESK GALLERY, SAN FRANCISCO

At the Autodesk Gallery in San Francisco, Anderson Anderson Architecture and McCall Design Group partnered with client Autodesk, architect HOK, and contractor DPR Construction Inc. in an IPD approach to deliver a media-intensive, 16,000 S.F. exhibit space for digital design and fabrication. The project was entirely developed and executed through Autodesk's Revit software. The space consists of exhibition hall, digital design studios, education spaces, and integrated digital fabrication systems within the architecture. The design process and concept work together to emphasize four integrated points reinforcing the owner's intended message: parametric modeling in support of integrated practice, sustainability, and design innovation. With these goals in mind—and the intention to draw upon the unique site and to distinguish a multi-industry software maker's creative project from more static exhibitions of physical products—the architects introduced the intention to design a space of "creative immersion in an ever-refreshing, media-saturated, special-for-me experience blossom floating within San Francisco clouds."

As part of a larger, integrated office, conference, and gallery complex of 35,000 S.F., the overall project was managed under an equal IPD partnership of two architecture firms (Anderson Anderson Architecture and HOK, designer of the adjacent office spaces); the builder (DPR Construction); and the owner (Autodesk). This new IPD contract method aligns the interests of all parties and equally adds incentive cost savings, project speed, quality, and design innovation. Together, the project team has delivered a LEED Platinum sustainable project, the highest rating for green construction. The project was delivered in an extremely tight design and construction timeframe, meeting target budget and time schedules, with substantial additional programs added to the project during the course of construction, thanks to under-budget savings and the nimble and collaborative contract structure. With its design partner, McCall Design Group, Anderson Anderson Architecture subcontracted and managed a diverse team of engineers, consultants, and technology design collaborators. The project achieved a top, 100 percent quality and innovation rating in the IPD contract incentive evaluation provided by an independent peer review.[12]

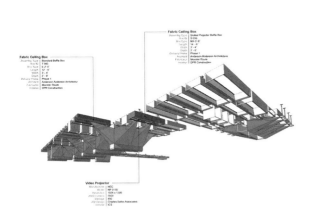

Figure 3.5 In an IPD delivery, Anderson Anderson Architecture developed a parametric model for similar but unique ceiling boxes that project and accept images and define areas of user engagement with the retail space. This project used an IPD approach for a 16,000 S.F. exhibit space that received a LEED Platinum rating.

Figure 3.6 The "MacLeamy Curve" illustrates the concept of making design decisions earlier in the project when the opportunity to influence positive outcomes is maximized and the cost of changes minimized, especially as regard to the designer and design consultant roles. Decisions of prefabrication must be made in a collaborative manner early in a project so as to control the cost and realize its benefits.

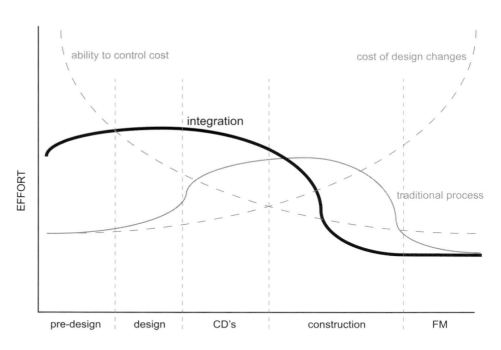

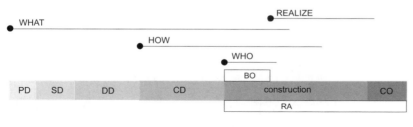

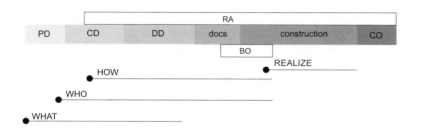

Figure 3.7 The project flow from predesign to closeout in an integrated delivery is different from the traditional method in that it does not use the conventions of SD, DD, and CD which tend to create workflow barriers. These phases of a traditional design process do not encourage collaboration. IPD suggests the identification of project goals early, so that decisions regarding production methods are considered from the beginning. The "what," "who," and "how" are integral to the design process and involve not only owner and architect, but also contractor and key subcontractors such as prefabricators who will have a major stake in the project delivery. In an integrated delivery, documents are simply an extension of early decisions regarding the "how"—shortening the overall time of design delivery. In a prefabrication project, they may take the form of bridging documents, allowing the fabricator to develop elements of the package for construction. Early participation of regulatory agencies, subcontractors, and fabricators allows shortening of the agency review and buyout phases. Because the project is coordinated to a high degree before the construction phase begins, offsite fabrication and onsite assembly are more efficient and provide a shorter construction period.

3.2.4 Integrated Practice

Working in an integrated delivery for prefabrication has many benefits. Michael Mulhern, Vice President of TriPyramid Structures, a subcontracting component manufacturer, has indicated that on a building project during design, fabrication, and erection, the discussion of what is the right material or system involves not only technical considerations but also financial and aesthetic. Each member of the design team offers a voice that demands a great deal of trust from the other key players on a design and build project.[13] Relying on manufacturers may be difficult for architects concerned with a lack of control; however, many models are turning toward reliance of architects on manufacturers to provide design services because of the subcontractor's expertise with a specific material or system that is being implemented, increasing the quality and innovation on building projects. Mark Dodgson, in *The Management of Technological Innovation,* suggests that this kind of collaboration demands a horizontal structure rather than a traditional vertical organization; where collaborators on a building project are trusted and given enough freedom in the process in order to ensure a successful and innovative end.[14]

Some examples of design-oriented manufacturers include the aforementioned TriPyramid Structures, who regularly employ architects as project managers working collaboratively with their clients on projects such as the Apple stores. Designed with Bohlin Cywinski

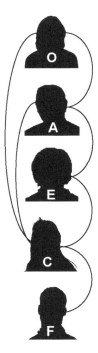

Figure 3.8 Traditional delivery limits the flow of information from owner to architect and contractor, architect to engineer and contractor, and contractor to fabricator. This removes the communication between the design team and the prefabrication team. Integration suggests a horizontal organization, allowing information exchange across stakeholders.

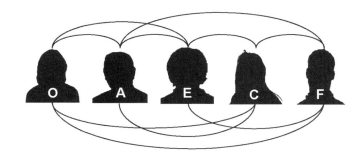

Figure 3.9 The Apple flagship stores that now dot the globe have been an experiment in technology development via an intense collaboration with client Steve Jobs, architectural firm Bohlin Cywinski Jackson, engineers Dewhurst Macfarlane/TriPyramid Structures, and material scientist and manufacturer Depp and Sealy Glass. This image shows details of the Apple "Cube" on Fifth Avenue in Manhattan.

Jackson Architects, the innovative client Steve Jobs; James O'Callaghan, a structural engineer; and subcontractors Depp and Sealy Glass, this team has accomplished progressively innovative glass staircases in numerous Apple stores internationally. A. Zahner Architectural Metals also employs architects as project managers and often collaborates with highly visible architectural firms. Most recently, A. Zahner's collaboration with Herzog and de Meuron on the San Francisco De Young Museum is an example of an innovative development of material and digital process. 3Form, Inc., an emerging eco-resin architectural panel manufacturer, is collaborating with Zaha Hadid, FOGA, and Diller, Scofidio + Renfro. In connection with the Diller, Scofidio + Renfro on the Alice Tully Hall at the Lincoln Center for Performing Arts in New York City, the team has designed and produced an innovative material: translucent wood (impregnated wood veneer sandwiched in between resin panels) and compound curved panels using the digital design and manufacturing methods of CAD/CAM. The Alice Tully Hall will be discussed in more depth in Chapter 10.

Using an in-house material science, architecture and engineering group 3Form works with architects in order to develop new interior/exterior translucent panel materials for specific design applications. 3Form works through geometry rationalization, digital modeling, and CNC tooling form-heated resin to manufacture custom panel shapes and sizes for interior installation applications. By focusing on a high level of collaboration, 3Form has set a precedent for working with and through architects to achieve an increased level of innovation. 3Form's method follows Stefan Thomke's explanation of a characteristic practice of innovative manufacturers in *Experimentation Matters,* where the iterative design to production process is front-loaded, placing material and digital innovation at the beginning of a project to avoid late-stage developments that are problematic because they hinder innovation in favor of the "quick fix." They rely on experimenting frequently through the use of new and traditional modes of technology to unlock performance goals. Finally, 3Form organizes for rapid experimentation and manages projects as experiments. This combi-

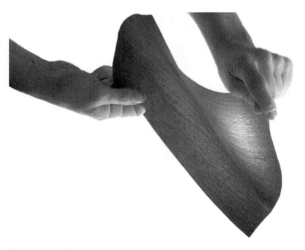

Figure 3.10 Translucent wood tests by 3Form in preparation for the development of backlit panels at the Alice Tully Hall in the Lincoln Center for Performing Arts, New York City.

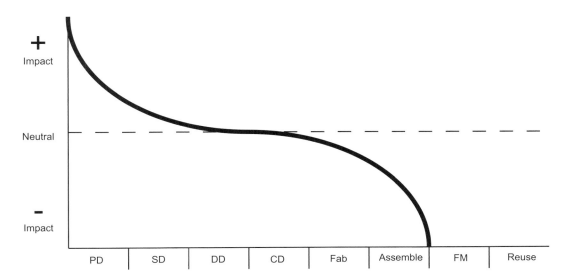

Figure 3.11 This chart shows the impact, both positive and negative, in a traditional delivery model in making decisions regarding prefabrication. The later in the project lifecycle prefabrication is implemented, the less likely its benefits will be realized. Integration demands an early decision-making process for methods of construction. Bringing prefabrication to the table during project conception will help to realize its benefits.

nation allows the company to fail early and often in order to avoid risk and costly changes onsite.[15]

Prefabrication is about process. Without an integrated delivery, prefabrication has less of a chance of succeeding. Either a large budget must drive innovation in prefabrication, or an economy of scale that justifies its investment in proprietary systems. However, within an integrated model, decisions regarding prefabrication can be made up-front so that failures are early and appropriate solutions can be found that meet the economic, environmental, and social requirements of any building project. A.F. Gibb states that in order to realize the maximum benefits of prefabrication, a project-wide strategy must be developed at an early stage in the process.[16] Integrated practice is a project-wide strategy that depends on the delivery method (contract structure) defined from the very beginning and conceptually brings all players

to the table in order to innovate. Although there are many definitions of this emerging practice in architecture and construction, integration can be defined not by its current practice or contract structure, but by its potential to realize a realigning of the players and process in a building project.

In conclusion, Mark Dodgson states in *Technological Collaboration in Industry* regarding organization of teams for innovation:

"There is no one correct solution or answer for every alliance; each one must be designed and managed in its own unique fashion to fit its own circumstances… The innovation process is iterative, and its management should be integrated throughout its various stages. Strategic management cohesion is necessary through the process."[17]

3.2.5 Lean Construction

Integrated practice is concerned with integration at all levels of project delivery; however, it focuses on flattening design to production. Lean construction, a sister concept, is likewise a project-wide strategy, but is primarily concerned with integration at the levels of production and assembly. Both are key principles in realizing prefab architecture whether in design or in production.

In the 1930s, Toyota struggled while making trucks and poor-quality vehicles. Kiichiro studied Ford's process on a trip to Michigan and read Henry Ford's book *Today and Tomorrow.*[18] Kiichiro liked what he saw of mass production and the American System of Manufacturers, but also noted many ways in which this process could be improved. Namely, waste was apparent at many intervals. The Toyota Production System (TPS) was not developed over-

Figure 3.12 A typical construction site is laden with material waste, representative of the waste of time and resources associated with onsite methods. The use of prefabrication in an integrated delivery allows for a leaning of the construction process in time and material.

night. In 1950, after World War II, Eiji Toyoda, cousin to Kiichiro, visited the Ford plants again and returned with a mission to extend Toyota's impact globally, taking on the super manufacturers of the day. Toyoda felt that using traditional methods would not accomplish this; they needed to take the best from Fordist mass production and adapt it to achieve high quality, low cost, and flexible outputs. He determined that the best way to accomplish this was to remove waste from production.[19]

Mass production is laden with waste. For one, the system of production in the United States has changed very little from the turn of the twentieth century. The process uses many different kinds of machines, each doing one operation. The products are all stored and moved to a different location in which they are assembled. This has led to much waiting time for products so that assemblies could be completed in swaths. Toyota noted disorganization and lack of flow in the process that they could capitalize on. Using the model of supermarkets, Toyota implemented a pull system by which manufacturing occurred in a continuous flow, which removes unwanted waste from the production stream. Its focus gradually has evolved to include not only production efficiencies but flexibility in the system to allow for ideas of mass customization and customer-centered enterprise that pervades business today. Today, the principles of TPS are known more widely as "lean production." Much has been written about lean production, including Womack and Jones's book *Lean Thinking,* that adapts the principles of Toyota to more conventional business practices.[20]

Lean principles are broad and beyond the scope of this book on prefabrication in architecture, but a few basic concepts establish the grounding for this theory. Prefabrication, evaluated from the perspective of lean principles, requires a concerted effort for architects to not only innovate in the areas of formal manipulation and image production, but also in the area of the social and organizational structures that define the design and production process. Finding a balance between process (people/organization) and product (object/technology) is both the challenge and opportunity of prefabrication in architecture. The first step in the lean process is to determine what the customer wants from the process itself. This defines the values of the project.

In addition to vehicles, Toyota produces prefabricated houses. The company has applied lean concepts of manufacture to building production. Although prefabricating housing since the 1970s, Toyota announced in 2004 that it established a new branch to begin full-scale production of factory-built homes. That year, Toyota Home built 4,700 homes. Each year since Toyota has increased its production and has a goal of 7,000 units a year by 2010.[21] Toyota Home saw the housing industry as no exception to the principles of lean thinking. The company has taken 5 of its 14 principles used in auto manufacturing and applied them to the prefabricated housing market. The houses are built in modules prepared to 85 percent completion before shipping to the site. They include doors, windows, plumbing, and electrical as well as finishes.[22] The basic tenets include:

- Just-In-Time

- Jidoka

- Heijunka

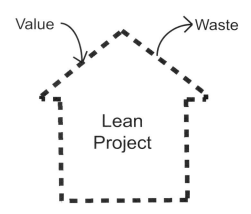

Figure 3.13 Lean construction includes removing waste—time and material—and creating value, or anything that is of benefit to the owner. Prefab is a key component identified by lean construction advocates.

- Standard Work

- Kaizen

Just-In-Time organizes each portion of the process so that it arrives just as it is needed to complete the final product. Raw material inventory is built into assemblies, usually at the scale in which it can easily be moved and inventoried. Collections of finished assemblies are then pieced together to form the larger building components such as walls, roofs, and floors. The basic structure, or "skeleton," of the modules is erected with all the hardware installed in preparation for future wall, roof, or floor "infill" portions. Each of these modules is assembled and prepared by automated machines and teams.

Toyota's lean manufacturing approach has made itself unique by diligently finding ways to reduce waste and increase efficiency. Taiichi Onco described seven waste or "muda" that required immediate elimination and constant refinement in its production of housing.[23]

1. Overproduction: Each Toyota Home house is built to order.

2. Transportation: Continue the product on its way.

3. Motion: Workspaces need to be clean and organized with the flow of assembly.

4. Waiting: Obstacles of waiting for processes to be completed due to linear organization.

5. Processing: Tasks that have no value to the customer include cleaning, paperwork, etc.

6. Inventory: Stock only what the customer needs.

7. Defects: Imperfections or missing parts can double the time for a simple task.

Jidoka is to use automation only when the human task has been perfected and deemed to have no handcraft value. By studying the perfected technique that has been removed of all its waste, the automation can take over without having to go through the costly research and development stages to eliminate waste. Toyota also believes that the machine should never replace the worker, but work along with them to manufacture a more precise quality product. Jidoka is used to increase the precision and quality of the prefabrication. According to a survey performed by the Japan Prefabricated Construction Suppliers and Manufacturers Association, 23 percent of Japanese homeowners would strongly consider purchasing a prefabricated home. The primary reason for their interest was due to the perceived high level of quality.[24]

Heijunka is the system by which Toyota Home keeps inventory low and in constant supply. Toyota accomplishes this by manufacturing directly to customer order. Standard work allows for Toyota Home to keep a well-stocked supply of raw materials. The future owner of a home will go the Toyota Home Park, where they may browse the many options and select specific attributes. The Toyota Home website allows patrons to virtually apply a variety of claddings, colors, and exterior/interior ornament in a customizable environment to suit their needs and tastes. All of these options are based on the same raw materials kept in stock, so when the order is issued they can be pulled off the shelves and sent through the process of assembly to component to module to whole house erection onsite.

Standard work: Not all of the elements that are compiled to make the Toyota Home modules and finally the completed structure are customized. From the decades of producing automobiles, Toyota understands the principles of using standard components and systems and how they make the drive toward efficiency much simpler. Each year a handful of car models are produced, many of which are modifications of the previous years' production. A basic model with minor modifications over several years allows Toyota to understand the core structure of the automobile, and thereby produce the part with greater effectiveness and reduced cost. Therefore, the modules for building are standardized with customization built into the configuration and relationships between modules.

In addition to the modules, miscellaneous materials for the homes installed onsite are manufactured in the factory, in order to ensure the same level of tolerances across all of its fields. Approximately 80 percent of the Toyota Home plant is computer controlled to allow for only the slightest variation between parts. Technology unique to Toyota is shared between the motor and housing branch. For example, the smart key system used on the Prius hybrid car is also used on the home, so the front door recognizes when the owner is near and unlocks and locks the door when he/she is coming or going. The same scratch-resistant technology for the automobiles is used on the interior and exterior walls of the home. Engine mount isolators that are used to create a smoother, quieter ride are used between steel and floor decking to minimize noise transfer from floor to floor, a common problem with most residential construction.[25]

Standard work allows the manufacturer and consumer to be extremely confident that the product they produce and receive will be of the utmost practiced quality. Toyota's confidence is expressed in offering a guarantee of up to 60 years on the life of the prefabricated house.

Kaizen is the human element of lean manufacturing. The production line technicians are asked to begin each day as if it were the worst day, developing a critical awareness to recognize and solve problems. Kaizen asks employees to find solutions as a team, focusing on a series of small tested solutions rather than a macro-level fix-all solution. Toyota Home employs the entire staff of design and production including architects, engineers, manufacturers, machinists, and computer scientists. The diverse fields act as a team to produce a quality product efficiently. If a problem arises anywhere in the process, it is easy to bring in representatives from each of the disciplines. Those who design and those who fabricate work on the same level and collaborate with their unique tasks to find a worthwhile solution. The lack of hierarchy and emphasis on communication and problem solving allows the prefabrication process to move quickly and efficiently.

Horman and Kenley report that across a variety of circumstances and contexts, 49.6 percent of construction operative time is devoted to wasteful activities.[26] Eastman and colleagues state,

---

"Conceptually, during the lifecycle of a construction project, a project team is responsible for transforming labor and material into a building. In other words, design and construction can be viewed as a series of activities, where some add value and others do not. There are numerous time-consuming, non-value-adding actives in the design process, such as correction of errors and rework, the physical handling and organization of documents, and transportation, inspection, and movement during the construction process."[27]

Again, value in lean practices is measured in removing waste and providing a quality/on-time product for the owner/client. The Construction Industry Institute reports the wide differences between manufacturing and construction industries documenting that waste constitutes 57 percent of business practice while in manufacturing, waste is 26 percent. Value adding activities are 10 percent in construction and 62 percent in manufacturing. The key is to identify waste in construction and determine a method for removing it and replacing it with value adding possibilities.

The Construction Users Round Table (CURT) is an organization that is made up of some of the largest companies that build on a frequent basis. It recently published "Key Agent's of Change," a chronicle that indicated that lean needs to become the new culture in the industry and that this requires a shift in everyone's thinking. In these efforts, CURT has redefined lean construction as lean project delivery, to emphasize that the principles of lean are not just about construction or even its precedent in manufacturing, but about the entirety of the building industry including architects and engineers. It is a paradigm shift to integrate the design and construction delivery process to encourage new methods of contracts, innovations in design and supply chain management, and especially to encourage advances in the development of offsite fabrication for onsite assembly.[28]

3.3 Technology Context

The word *technology* is derived from the Greek word *techne*, implying skill, artifact, or the contemporary word *technique*. The second part of the word, *logos*, means the study of something. Technology, therefore, can be defined as "systematic knowledge transformed into, or made manifest by tools." Those tools are in turn, applied to human needs.[29] Rather than viewing prefabrication technology as being deterministic (concerned with the tool), it is determined by the human process (study of tool making).

At the 2006 AIA National Convention, Pritzer Prize–winner Thom Mayne stated fervently, "If you want to survive, you're going to change; if you don't, you're going to perish."[30] Mayne was talking about the advances in digital tools that are providing opportunities for increased communication and fabrication capabilities. Mayne was discussing the potentials of building information modeling (BIM) and automation (CNC manufacturing). In stating this, Mayne perpetuated what is perhaps architects' most blatant irresponsibility: Despite the fact that technology dominates our buildings, our practices, and our lives, architects know relatively little about it. No technology will save us from work, but it can be an added value that makes the principles of integration more obtainable. Both CNC manufacturing and BIM will be reviewed below as contemporary movements that allow for greater levels of process collaboration and product customization. Prefabrication is increased by the use of these tools within integrated deliveries.

3.3.1 Automation

David Nye states in *Technology Matters*,

"Since technologies are not deterministic, it follows that people can use them for many ends. For much of the nineteenth and twentieth century, sociologists and historians assumed that the machine age could only lead to a crushing homogeneity. But in practice, people have often used technologies to create differences."

Consumers prefer variety and even the manufacturer Henry Ford eventually had to give in to the public's demand for a range of models and options of the Model T. Although no longer identifiable due to the appropriation of inhabitants over the years, the identical post–WWII houses that were originally built confirm this. A worry concerning prefab's monotonous effect on our environment is only a fear if we are not confident in our abilities as architects and builders to use technology toward social and cultural ends. If we do not provide variation, clients and building users will eventually demand it.

Consequently, prefabrication has received a bad reputation in the United States. This stems from the history of manufacturing for mass production by virtue of assembly line production. Standardization became the enemy, creating banal uniformity in lifestyle and landscape. Before Fordist standardization, Fredrick

Taylor, in the late 1800s, separated labor into skilled and unskilled workers. This theory was an effort to manage mass production. Each task was given to a specific person who performed the task repeatedly. This placed a great social divide between an upper class and lower—management versus day laborers. The assembly line production system under Taylor's theory produced an unhappy work force, unproductive and unsustainable in the long term.[31]

The lack of variability in the workflow as well as the lack of environment diversity has led to an emergence of customization of products, demanded by consumers. Continuing with the discussion of the automobile industry we can look to the Toyota Production Systems as a method of using the principles in Ford and Taylor but building upon them with principles that offer variability, customization, and job diversity. With regard to a theory of prefabrication, Toyota aided industry in moving from a standardized method of production to a customization. Not that each customer could special-order a car, which is evermore becoming the model today with the Scion and other Toyota models, but that the same tools and methods that were used to develop and produce one kind of automobile could be programmed through automation to work to produce another as well, with small increase in cost per unit.

"In modern times we've focused on new manufacturing methods, shifting from mass to lean production, and are now at the next wave of manufacturing innovations: mass customization."[32]

Although manufacturing has moved progressively from standardization to customization, the concepts of mass production are the modes of production still used and understood in design and construction to-day. Dana Buntrock in *Japanese Architecture as a Collaborative Process* indicates:

"Project teams need to look above Fordist mass production mentality of set lengths, widths and material specifications; they need to look beyond economy of means (larger quantities lead to greater economy), beyond the assumption that unskilled laborers to produce affordable building components, and beyond the idea that assembly line production to facilitate speedy and efficient production methods. Today's post-Fordist technology suggests not the standardization of building components but customization, utilizing digital information to automate machines, such as CNC, to produce infinitely diverse outputs."[33]

The technological development since 1770 has gone through waves of early mechanization, steam power and railways, electrical, Fordist mass production, and now information and communication technology.[34] This information technology revolution that has affected so many other industries is only now being harnessed for its ability to flatten the design to delivery of building, and provide visions for new materials and methods of production for architecture. There is a trend toward increased automation in construction via computer-automated design (CAD) and computer-automated manufacturing (CAM) software and computer numerically controlled (CNC) machines in the factory. This process allows for design information in 2D or 3D to be used to manufacture and fabricate through automated machines.

Stephen Kieran and James Timberlake prefer *personalization* to *mass customization*.[35] This seems a much more apt description of what is meant by mass customization, where customers personalize predetermined configurations. The basis for the theory is to increase variety and customization with-

STANDARDIZATION TO CUSTOMIZATION

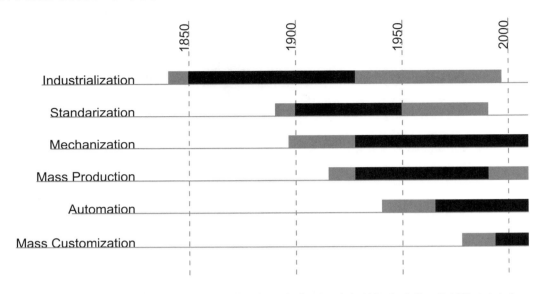

Figure 3.14 This is a listing of the developments in manufacturing technology from industrialization in the mid-1800s to today's mass customization by virtue of CAD/CAM technologies. These concepts are not exclusive, but represent when concepts developed and how we understand industrialized building today. Below are definitions:

Industrialization: As related to the industrial revolution of 1848, this marked a change in an economic and societal thinking by virtue of advanced machinery that is still pervasive today.

Standardization: A result of the industrialized society, products became standardized. This was most prevalent in developing standards related to military production.

Mechanization: This is an effort to move standardization to greater economies of scale, but introducing additional mechanized processes that were developed during the war years, but furthered by virtue of more advanced mechanical machinery, thus reducing human labor.

Mass production: Thriving on the economies of scale, this concept is to produce as much of the same thing in order to bring down the cost of a single item. It has grown concurrently with consumer demand.

Automation: The development of digitally informed manufacturing machinery via computer numerical control and CAD/CAM software.

Mass customization: This concept brings together mass production and automation to deliver an economy of scope. Mass customization works to maximize the benefits of mechanization and automation production methods, reducing labor costs, but works to preserve the benefits of variability and customization in the output.

out increasing costs. More than this goal, however, the concept has become consistent with meeting the individual needs of customers without sacrificing efficiency, effectiveness, and affordability.[36] As

mass production is a system that has inherent limitations, mass customization works to alleviate the apparent contradictions in our current understanding of production.

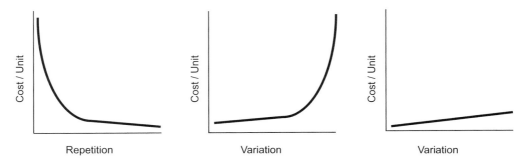

Figure 3.15 *Left:* Fordist mass production relies on the economies of scale: as repetition increases cost per unit decreases. Middle: Likewise, as variation increases, the cost per unit exponentially grows. *Right:* Mass customization suggests that variability is possible within an acceptable margin of cost increase.

3.3.2 Building Information Modeling

Increased productivity in construction has occurred through two primary digital technologies:

- Digital automation for product design and manipulation including CNC and CAD/CAM software

- Digital integration in the sharing of information via 3D information models or building information modeling (BIM)[37]

According to Goodrum and colleagues, productivity as a result of digital tools increased to 30 to 45 percent in average timesaving per installed quantity of product when employing high versus low levels of automation and integration. The integration of digital tools (i.e., BIM) has a more significant impact on project performance when compared to automation tools (i.e., CNC). In increasing labor productivity and the overall cost versus scope of a project, integrated contractual and information exchange, flattening the process of delivery is more critical than the novelty of the automation factory tools that are being deployed to, in many cases, simply create more interesting form.

This study points to a distinction between BIM and CAD/CAM software. The differentiation is primarily between component and entity-based programs that are being referred to as BIM herein, and design development environments such as CAD/CAM software that run CNC tools. BIM allows for information to be associated with 3D objects and are purpose-built to develop building design with presets such as doors, windows, and wall types. CAD/CAM software does not have embedded content, but rather relies on the designer or modeler to develop all of the information that is linked directly to CNC output. BIM platforms may also run CNC machines, but currently are limited to primarily 2D operations. Information can be exchanged from BIM platforms to CAD/CAM for digital fabrication output. Sometimes, BIM is a catch-all word to describe immersive digital modeling environments, encompassing CAD/CAM software.

Commercially available BIM software applications include:

- Autodesk Revit

- Graphisoft ArchiCAD

- Bentley Architecture

Common CAD/CAM software applications include:

- CATIA

- Pro/ENGINEER

- Solidworks[38]

While BIM has existed in some form for at least 20 years, it has emerged as a major topic in the AEC industry in the past decade, due to a confluence of factors, including the growing dissatisfaction among project owners with the cost of delays and change orders typical in construction projects. The Construction Users' Roundtable (CURT) issued a white paper in 2002 documenting the financial costs of poor coordination in construction documents and faulty communications among the members of a project team.[39] The paper called for dramatically increased collaboration among the participants in construction projects, which BIM can facilitate if augmented. This movement received considerable impetus when the General Services Administration mandated that all Final Concept Approvals (rough schematic design) include a BIM spatial model starting in fiscal year 2007.[40] Another major factor in the recent emergence of BIM is that the technology itself has significantly matured. This has in turn led to several developments: pioneering projects by architects like Frank Gehry using BIM to create buildings that would otherwise be prohibitively complex, demand by architects for BIM tools responding to initiatives like GSA's, and the efforts of software developers to make BIM tools more useful.

Enhanced continuity is at the heart of the rationale for adopting BIM in the AEC industry. Used in one sector alone, it can enhance that part of the process: Architects can increase their productivity, contractors can shorten construction times and reduce waste, and owners can manage their properties more easily. The traditional system in the AEC industry operates on the basis of separate pools of information cautiously shared among owners, designers, and constructors. Everyone is aware of the inefficiencies this system creates and clamors for greater collaboration within project teams. A crucial component of a more collaborative system is a means of effectively accumulating and incorporating an enormous amount and variety of information over the course of a project. BIM allows for increased information sharing.

Architects also stand to gain a great deal from a more collaborative environment. Architects essentially create, gather, and organize information in their work. The value of their work (and their role in the overall construction process) depends on the extent to which the other participants in the building process rely upon that information. Under the current process, the information contained in a set of drawings and specifications falls far short of what is required to actually build a building. Contractors, fabricators, vendors, and others must add an enormous amount of information to that which they receive from the designers in order to actually construct a building. The two largest categories are constructability information and details contained in shop drawings and other submittals. If the information added by constructors were available during the design phase, architects would be in a position to incorporate it in their designs rather than scrambling to respond to it as they do now.

Parametric modeling is the ability to change aspects of the BIM for simulation and have them updated in real time. Parameters in a BIM may be changed and the BIM automatically reconfigures the entire project to reflect the changed parameter(s). In addition, purpose-built third-party software developers have written compatible software applications for use with the core and addendum platforms. These modelers are developed for specific purposes to be performed during the design, development, and construction of a building project. Some purpose-built modelers provide functionalities in schedule and cost modeling, free-form modeling that offers NURBS-based geometry rationalization ability, and third-party modeling programs that offer the ability to perform various green, programming, code review, and other analyses on a developed BIM model.

Arguably, the largest benefit of BIM is in productivity gains. The traditional distribution effort for architects, for example, according to the AIA B151, is 15 percent for schematic design, 30 percent for design development, and 55 percent for construction documents. This distribution is proportional to the amount of effort required for the design team's services. When using BIM technology, a reduction in time required to produce detailed construction documents is realized. If this time savings can be shifted to the front of the process in predesign and schematic design to allow for project players in an integrated fashion to make decisions regarding function, form, productivity, and prefabrication and construction methods, this will not only save time in design delivery, but also in the delivery of construction. Linking the BIM model to manufacturing allows this process to be even more streamlined. This shift in operations, however, will require project players to front load the design process as previously discussed and therefore, shift their traditional billing cycles in a project. With the many projects that do not extend beyond development, this billing method will enable all parties involved to come closer to realizing the project in the end.

Some architecture and engineering firms have begun to put BIM to use to improve project delivery. Ghafari Associates in Dearborn, Michigan, has designed several projects for General Motors that feature a virtual model of the project so complete that contractors rely on it to fabricate every piece of the building offsite. In a 442,000 SF engine plant addition in Flint, Michigan, construction was finished five weeks ahead of an aggressive schedule and there were no change orders due to site conflicts.[41] Despite the fact that such projects are driven by purely technical considerations and have comparatively simple requirements, they prove that BIM can have a significant impact on project delivery and that the goal of a complete BIM model can be achieved and put to use in the real world.

The future of prefabrication relies on BIM. Linking time to the three-dimensional information, simulation of construction process can anticipate what challenges will arise during construction on a day-by-day schedule. Two-dimensional paper documents do not allow for this kind of analysis. BIM tools have the potential to interface with automation equipment, such as CAD/CAM shop methods. Because the model represents accurately the objects' properties for fabrication, CNC facilitates tooling to precise dimensions. BIM has great potential to allow multiple manufacturers and fabricators to produce objects in their shop simultaneously and then deliver and assemble onsite seamlessly because of the dimensional accuracy of the model and fabrication equipment. Boeing has used this model of delivery receiving sections of the plane from various suppliers that are then assembled in their factory.[42] This has obvious benefits to reduce cost and construction time as workflows can overlap.

In order to harness BIM for manufacture and pre-fabrication, construction-level information must be included in the model. This has recently occurred in two ways:

- The building model is a detailed design expressing the intent of the designer and the client. The contracts are expected to develop their own independent construction model and documents including shop drawings and submittals from subcontractors.

- The building model is a detailed design that will be further detailed for the use of all aspects of construction, planning, and fabrication. In this method, the design model is a starting point for elaboration of the construction team.

The first method is very similar to how traditional construction delivery occurs in a DBB contract structure. This is seen by architects to be an alleviation of risk and liability during the construction process. The AIA B151 states that drawings delivered by design teams for construction are intent only. The transfer of liability then after bidding is to the contractor. This has required contractors and their subcontractors, including prefabricators, to develop all submissions from scratch. Marrying the design intent from the design team with the drawings necessary for fabrication results in many rounds of submissions, communication, and, more often than not, mistakes on the jobsite assembly. This process is based solely on design intent according to Eastman and colleagues and is "inherently inefficient and irresponsible to clients." The author encourages designers to provide BIM model information to fabricators and detailers and allow them to elaborate the design information as needed to both maintain the design intent and refine the design for fabrication.[43]

BIM models allow for quantity takeoffs. The elements are included in the design model, facilitating the quantities, specifications, and properties that can be used to procure materials from the various prefabricators. As Eastman and his colleagues state, to date, object definitions for many manufactured products have not yet been developed to make this capacity a reality; however, in a few industries such as structural steel and precast, these results have been beneficial.[44] BIM can provide an accurate idea of the design and material resources required for each portion of a given work. This improves the planning and scheduling of subcontractors and helps to ensure a just-in-time arrival of people, equipment, and materials. This potentially reduces cost and allows for better coordination on the jobsite. Prefabrication can play a critical role in facilitating this if coordination and accommodation is made with regard to materials and products during the early stages of an integrated process.

Many firms are working to move toward BIM. In a recent survey by the AIA titled "The Business of Architecture," more than 34 percent of firms have acquired BIM software.[45] In another study by McGraw-Hill Construction of architects, engineers, contractors, and owners, just under half of all participants reported using BIM or purpose-built modelers. In this study, 6 out of 10 architects reported using BIM.[46] In talking with firms in the Salt Lake City region, many have adopted BIM but see great challenges in the time and cost associated with adoption into every portion of the firms' daily practice operations. Virtually all see a major gap between digital modeling in BIM for productivity and linking to consultants, owners, and construction scheduling. For these firms, many say they are waiting for the right project that will allow the space to use BIM, or they are waiting to be pressured from the owner to do so.

The ultimate implementation of BIM would be an open-source platform where building projects are digitally conceived, programmed, designed, visualized, subjected to various simulations, reviewed for code compliance, and constructed directly from the digital model which then would serve the owner in operating the facility. The BIM model (or models) would be a series of interconnected data structures and be directly accessed by all project participants. The realization of this goal would change how projects are created at every stage, yielding new models of design and construction practice. This goal, while theoretically feasible, faces many serious obstacles in reality. No one expects it to be achieved in the near future, although advancements are being made every year. The majority of architecture firms are using BIM to develop 2D drawings in a more automated manner, but the linkage to specifications, product information, and prefab is still lacking. The responsibility for this advancement is not limited by the technology; rather, as discussed in this chapter, it is determined by the environmental and organizational context in which technology is deployed.

PART II
APPLICATION

chapter 4 Principles

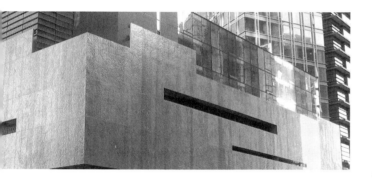

United States construction expenditure in 2008 was estimated at $1.3 trillion. This is double the next closest country, Japan, who spent $600 billion. With construction being a large portion of the U.S. gross national product, the lack of investment in productivity and innovation via process and product technology including prefabrication is staggering. This is not a new problem. In 1996, the Construction Industry Institute wrote:

"The U.S. construction industry, contributing over $847 billion annually to the U.S. Gross National Product is experiencing competitive pressures which have squeezed margins to historic lows. The construction industry now ranks as the second worst performing industry in terms of return on investment—only the airline industry rates poorer. Intense competition has forced companies to seek any avenue to preserve profits, and when such is threatened, to aggressively seek to recover losses through litigation. This business climate has led to adversarial relations which greatly hinder the construction process."[1]

Therefore, it is no wonder that in 2008, the National Institute of Standards and Technology (NIST) re-

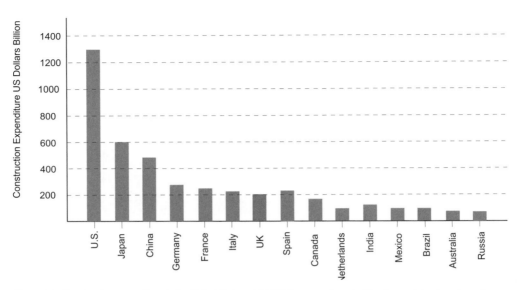

Figure 4.1 Construction expenditure in the United States at $1.3 trillion more than doubles the next developed country, Japan. However, countries such as Japan and the United Kingdom invest more per capita in technology advancement for construction than the United States by way of material and digital developments including prefabrication.

quested that the National Research Council (NRC) appoint an ad hoc committee of experts to provide advice for advancing the competitiveness and productivity of the U.S. construction industry in the next 20 years.[2] The committee's specific task was to plan and conduct a workshop to identify and prioritize technologies, processes, and deployment activities that have the greatest potential to advance significantly the productivity and competitiveness of the capital facilities sector of the U.S. construction industry in the next 20 years. The committee developed five recommendations:

1. Widespread deployment and use of interoperable technology applications, also called building information modeling (BIM);

2. Improved jobsite efficiency through more effective interfacing of people, processes, materials, equipment, and information (lean construction and integrated practice);

3. Greater use of prefabrication, preassembly, modularization, and offsite fabrication techniques and processes;

4. Innovative, widespread use of demonstration installations; and

5. Effective performance measurement to drive efficiency and support innovation.

All five activities identified by the committee are interrelated. The effectiveness to which each can be implemented will enable the others to make headway. The third recommendation is prefabrication, preassembly, modularization, and offsite fabrication techniques and processes. The reasoning for this recommendation is that many other countries, with the United Kingdom and Japan at the lead, have implemented prefab systems and experienced benefits in both residential and commercial sectors of the industry. These benefits include labor, schedule, cost, quality, and safety. Given the developments in the construction industry, as players become more integrated than ever before by virtue of employing BIM and integrated processes, prefabrication will have more traction and greater impact on productivity.

Paul Teicholz, at the Center for Integrated Facility Engineering (CIFE) at Stanford University in 2007, calculated the productivity within the U.S. field construction industry relative to all non-farm industries from 1964 through 2004. Teicholz developed this data by dividing contract dollars from the Department of Commerce by field worker hours of labor for those contracts from data at the Bureau of Labor and Statistics. The contracts include

soft (design costs) and hard (construction costs including: materials, delivery, and labor). During this 40-year period, U.S. productivity outside of construction has doubled while labor productivity within the construction industry is estimated to be 10 percent less than what it was in 1964. Labor historically represents 40 to 60 percent of construction's estimated cots. Owners are therefore actually paying 5 percent more in 2004 than they would have paid for the same building in 1964. This would seem to make sense because buildings are much more complex from a systems and performance perspective today than they ever have been, however, manufactured products and prefabricated elements are more affordable and accessible than ever. In other industries, automated

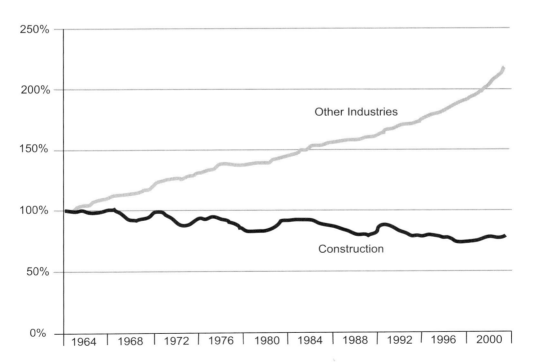

Figure 4.2 The percentage of U.S. industrial productivity from 1964 to 2004. During this 40-year period, productivity outside of construction doubled while labor productivity within the construction industry is estimated to be 10 percent less than what it was in 1964.

Figure 4.3 The triad of construction is *Cost,* including labor and material; *Scope*, the breadth and extent of the project; and *Schedule,* or duration of the project. These principles determine the quality and risk associated with each building project.

practices have produced lower labor cost with increased quality, but this statistically is not the case with construction.

Teicholz states,

"Contractors have made greater use of offsite components which take advantage of factory conditions and specialized equipment. Clearly this has allowed for higher quality and lower cost production of components, as compared to onsite work. Although the cost of these components is included in our construction cost data, the labor is not. This tends to make onsite construction productivity appear better than it actually is."[3]

4.1 Principles

A building project, regardless of its production method, is an ambitious undertaking. The sheer number of individuals, teams, materials, products, systems, communication, and finances that are implicit in the finished building is difficult to fathom. The process of a building coming into being can be likened to an orchestra, where all the players and their instruments of practice are important to the success of the intended finished product. The lifecycle of a facility refers to its conception, design, construction, and postconstruction facilities management. During each phase of the lifecycle of a building, different players take on a different role, are more important or less, depending on the time in the performance. Each building undertaking has a number of key principles that it must answer to. Although not all of the issues may be critical for a given project, generally, a building must respond to the following principles of construction and their effect on productivity:

• Cost: capital and operational investment

• Labor: skilled and unskilled human workforce

• Time: schedule or duration of the project

• Scope: extent or breadth of the project

• Quality: design and construction excellence

• Risk: exposure to potential financial loss

The owner team's priorities regarding the project will determine how much emphasis is placed on cost, schedule, and scope. Buildings are expensive and owner teams are rarely unrestricted in their ability to fund them. In addition, most projects are on a limited schedule to allow for occupation by a certain date. Related to cost, schedule, and scope are the principles of quality and risk. An owner's demand for choices of performance in systems, aesthetics, durability of finishes, and other elements of a project are directly related to decisions of a balance between the elements of cost/schedule/scope and quality. For the given program, the design team usually establishes the relationships between quality, schedule, and budget where a change in one affects all. For example, an owner team may opt to select a lower quality of material in favor of saving on cost or to allow the project to be completed on time. In this balance of goals, risk is an important component.

Key risk considerations for the owner team are whether the project can be accomplished with a desired quality within the allotted schedule and budget. The design team is concerned with whether the project can be accomplished with an overall acceptable quality, while meeting the owner's program (scope) and contracted fees (budget). The contractor team is concerned with meeting the project contract (scope) within the time and allotted cost.[4]

Offsite fabrication is the practice of assembling components of a structure in a factory and transporting complete assemblies or subassemblies to the construction site where the building is to be located. Offsite production in architecture has the potential to bring a balance between cost, schedule, and scope closer within reach by virtue of fabricating larger elements of buildings. The principles of cost, schedule, and scope will be discussed herein and how prefabrication specifically may be leveraged to achieve this balance of construction principles.

4.1.1 Cost

All building projects occur only by means of capital and the decisions designers and construction professionals make determine the ultimate cost of the building project. Cost is a necessary principle of consideration in any building project, but especially in projects that implement prefabrication as additional integrated team management and project planning is required.

Prefabrication has been touted as being more cost efficient than other onsite methods of construction. This is because cost consists of three aspects for which prefabrication conceptually has solutions: *material, labor,* and *time*. In theory, if any one of these is reduced, cost is also reduced. But prefabrication does not implicitly mean a reduction in overall project budgets. In fact, a myriad of contemporary examples use prefabrication not for its benefits in efficiency of cost but in precision and increase in quality of product to realize greater predictability. For projects in which cost is of concern, as in the majority of both public and private works, prefabrication must be employed intentionally and with a high degree of planning.

A primary method to reduce cost is to reduce the amount of material implemented in a building project. In an onsite construction, materials are purchased and procured to site where they are staged for installation. Often, the materials are over-ordered to ensure that a quantity appropriate for the task is acquired. In a factory, the concept of material purchase is not for a single project, but perhaps for many projects; this is known as "Just-in-Time." The materials are present no sooner or later than needed, reducing the amount of overall material used. Multiple projects are being fabricated in any given time, thus sharing material resources and concurrent supply chain management. In addition, material and products are not stored onsite, but similar to material prepared for components or modules fabricated in the factory, the subassemblies are delivered for installation onsite only when they are needed. Staging and maneuvering a site can consume a large portion of a contractor's time and therefore increase the overall costs of the project. With prefab, material is delivered when it is needed, in a manner that requires less onsite installation material, and results in reduced time and overhead.

Although prefabrication may save considerably with regard to delivery and staging of material, factory-produced components for buildings may initially be more expensive. Setup of a factory environment for the production of goods is a considerable investment. On small projects, unless a prefabricator is established to produce the specified products for the building project, investing in a new process in most cases is cost prohibitive. Many times factories can be adapted to produce similar objects for a specific purpose. Even with the advent of CNC equipment, fabrication setup takes time and, therefore, money. The quantity of the project must warrant the investment in the infrastructure when cost is a primary consideration or the products being specified are general enough in nature to be within the fabricator's capacity of delivery.

Other costs that may be incurred with prefabrication include increased transportation costs and craning/setting for larger pieces and components. Although prefabrication requires larger trucks for transport to site, many of which are expensive and require much labor coordination, transportation for onsite construction does not usually take into consideration the daily trips by personally owned vehicles to pick up forgotten or overlooked materials in order to finish a job. Many times these transportation costs are simply folded into the larger bid for a subcontractor in an onsite delivery. Prefabrication may also require larger cranes, increasing the cost for construction. Conversely, the number of lifts a crane will have to make with a prefabricated building is fewer in theory than with onsite construction.

Additional costs may include factory overhead, making bids higher than their onsite counterparts. On most construction projects, whether using prefabrication or not, the general contractor provides much of the setup costs associated with onsite power, portable toilets, first-aid, and, in some cases, job trailers. Therefore, not taking into consideration the fabricator's overhead versus an onsite subcontractor, the cost of prefabrication can be deceptively high. This is usually made up, however, in the values of schedule savings and quality increase. Many prefabricators, like Amy Marks at Kullman Building Systems, believe that offsite fabrication should come with a premium. Rarely are products able to be produced better, faster, and cheaper. Although on occasion, offsite comes in at a lower cost than onsite methods, this is not usually the case from a material standpoint.

Prefabrication also brings to the forefront the negotiations between capital costs and lifecycle costs. Capital costs, sometimes referred to as initial costs, are categorized into fixed and variable. Fixed costs consist of site acquisition, permits, and impact fees. Variable costs include soft costs such as preconstruction design fees and hard costs related to physical construction. Capital costs can drive the selection of whether a project is built onsite or offsite. Although a building may be built with a low initial cost, the payback may not be as beneficial over the long term. Higher initial investment in construction is difficult to justify to owners in the capitalist society of the United States, where speculative building suggests a quick low-cost investment for a high return. Real estate is therefore looked on as a commodity to be bought, sold, and traded. This is no truer than in market rate housing and speculative commercial building. Prefabrication should be viewed as a lifecycle investment, perhaps costing more initially, but providing better value in the long term.

Related to capital and lifecycle costs is the concept of proprietary systems. A proprietary prefabrication system that is closed may be very sophisticated and technically competent in and of itself, but may not serve the lifecycle of a facility well. All buildings must be maintained. In addition, systems such as enclosure and services in buildings are changed out relatively frequently. With a prefabricated proprietary system, once a system needs to be fixed or updated, remodel construction is difficult, especially when the fabrication company has gone out of business and replacement parts cannot be located. Many car buyers have experienced similar problems with their vehicles. In most cases, it becomes cost effective to eventually abandon an outdated model and simply buy a new car. In a building, the entire system may be changed out or worse the building demolished to make way for a more standardized system that does not require specialists to fix.

Soft costs related to design of prefabrication may be higher in unique one-off constructions. Structural engineers, mechanical engineers, and fabricators are often part of the design process from the beginning in prefab, increasing the upfront costs. Their involvement must not outweigh the ability for the system to recoup these expenditures. In a design-assist contract, key subcontractors are brought on to design prefab systems during early stages with design teams. This requires upfront soft cost capital. Prefabrication requires that manufacturers be paid with deposits to secure the work and begin the fabrication process. This means that larger loan draws for prefabricated portions of a construction budget may be required at earlier stages of building. Integrated contracts require design teams and contractors to shift efforts to earlier in project schedules, potentially shifting billing cycles to earlier phases in overall project duration.

HIDDEN COSTS IN PREFAB

Although prefabrication manufacturers for construction will claim that prefabrication is cheaper because of the time and labor savings, which can be substantial, the hidden costs in prefabrication may include:[5]

- **Overhead:** Manufacturing facilities employ full-time staff and have facility costs such as equipment purchase and maintenance, renting space, and monthly utilities;

- **Profit:** Offsite fabricators, as a business enterprise, must make a profit and therefore to cover these overhead expenses may charge as much or more than a general contractor for the same scope and any savings due to efficiencies in time and labor may not be passed on to the customer;

- **Transport:** Transportation due to prefabrication is higher per unit volume because of the chunking of the panels, modules, and components that are often shipped with more air than tightly packaged, onsite-erected materials and products;

- **Setting:** Although weight is usually not as much of a concern, craning a prefabricated element can be awkward and require skilled laborers or dedicated crews to set the elements;

- **Design fees:** As prefabrication requires more coordination with construction and fabrication teams, architects and engineers may charge higher rates for the investment of time.

4.1.2 Schedule

Arguably the greatest benefit to productivity of offsite fabrication is a reduction in onsite construction duration.[6] The savings in time on prefabricated building projects come in the ability to simultaneously construct in the factory while site work is being completed. Rarely are precast foundations used, therefore site work and foundation can be constructed onsite concurrently with prefabrication work of structure, enclosure, services, and interiors being produced in a factory. Whereas traditional onsite construction is a linear process by which subcontractors wait until the preceding trade has completed their work, in a factory, teams may work concurrently allowing entire sections of a building to be constructed by more than one trade. In addition, multiple fabricators can be manufacturing subassemblies that are brought together and assembled onsite.

Time savings may also come by way of employing lean production techniques. Reductions in schedule may not initially come to fruition in one-off or highly customized production runs, but can occur through an increase in repetition. In order to have concurrent factory and site work occurring, delivery may need to become front-loaded, meaning that the majority of planning occurs before construction through an integrated process. Decisions regarding prefabrication are made early so that schedule savings may be realized from the start of construction.

Prefabrication offers more predictability in finish dates. This is due to the ability to procure materials and processes more quickly and the fact that prefab occurs in a controlled environment where weather does not have an effect on the labor force. Interest on financing is compounded at a higher rate and therefore more costly on longer construction dura-

tions. Public buildings may have more leeway on schedule, but for daily income-generating companies, the ability to open according to schedule determines whether they are able to go into business at all. A business opening at a certain time of year, needing to open for a retail season; schools that need to open for students in a new semester; and hospitals that must open beds for populations that may be underrepresented with health care, are all buildings that are restricted by schedule. For example, in the author's experience, while working for an international A/E firm designing microchip plants in East Asia, each day that was over schedule in construction was a loss in hundreds of thousands of dollars in revenue for the technology company. In addition, for operating existing buildings, the less retrofit and remodel disruption the better.

Adrian Robinson at Buro Happold Engineers shares his experience with schedule reductions when using prefabricated steel modules on a hotel project in the United Kingdom. The Travelodge Hotel engineered by Buro Happold broke ground the same time as a hotel of similar size across the street, near Heathrow Airport. The Travelodge Hotel was entirely dried in while the hotel across the street had not finished steel framing. Amy Marks at Kullman, fabricator for a few of KieranTimberlake projects, states that on average they are seeing a 50 percent time savings reported from their contractors for offsite methods over onsite in the steel and concrete commercial building sector. This is especially true in her opinion in projects that employ larger modules and panels in greater quantities. The economies of scale for cost are not as much a factor as the economies of schedule in prefabrication for larger commercial buildings. In residential construction, Michelle Kaufmann reports that in her experience with prefabrication, comparing the first Glidehouse she built onsite using the stick

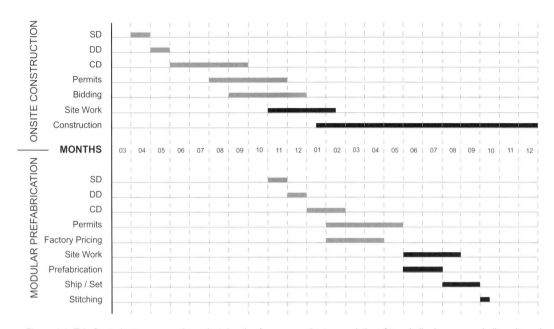

Figure 4.4 This Gantt chart compares the project duration from conception to completion of two similar houses, one built onsite and the other offsite. Prefabrication saves over 50 percent in total project duration as a result of modularizing the units. The greatest savings in schedule can be seen in the concurrency of onsite and offsite work in the prefab project as well as overall construction time. Michelle Kaufmann designed both houses.

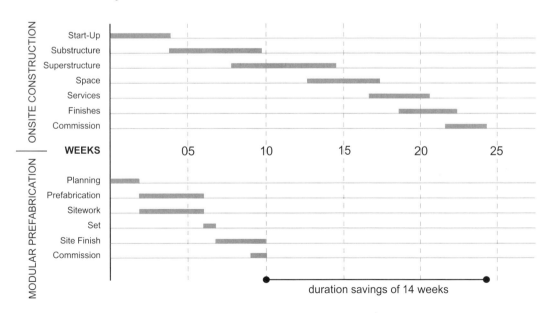

Figure 4.5 Comparing a small construction project using the methods of onsite versus offsite demonstrates a savings of 50 to 70 percent in project duration by Kullman Building Systems.

framed method to the second Glidehouse, prefabricated as a module offsite, the duration of the project was nearly half for the modular prefab. This can be attributed to the concurrency of the onsite and offsite construction activities as well as the direct construction of the house proper not including the foundation or utilities.

Weather can also affect the duration of construction on a job site. In a site-cast concrete multi-family housing project in Utah, the cold weather of the winter delayed the project three months due to unexpected snowstorms and below average temperatures that required crews to install warming blankets during curing. This labor-intensive process cost the project leasing revenues for the months that were over schedule. In a recent housing project, Irontown Homes, a modular builder in Spanish Fork, Utah, was able to fabricate building modules one month ahead of schedule. Seeing that the duration of the project could be beat, the project team decided to ship the modules and set during the middle of winter. Onsite, a blizzard ensued, taking the setting schedule an additional day than was originally planned, whereas building an onsite house in the same weather conditions would not have been feasible. As Tedd Benson of Bensonwood Homes says, "In the factory, the sun always shines."[7]

4.1.3 Labor

Safety of workers is increased by virtue of the conditioned, dry interior environment of the factory. Onsite construction not only requires workers to potentially be exposed to harsh conditions of weather and precarious positions near roads, hazardous protrusions, and the like, but also requires workers to travel long distances, even across state lines, in some cases, in order to complete a project. Projects outside of metropolises require onsite construction workers to stay in temporary accommodations and travel home on the weekends. Prefabrication offers an opportunity for shorter commutes. This reduces cost and risk of workers traveling to and from the jobsite on highways when they are fatigued after working long hours. Systematizing the construction process in a factory presents opportunities for workers to establish a regular schedule, not having to do early mornings in hot regions, for example, in order to beat the late afternoon sun. In many cases, this does not allow for a full day's work, while a factory environment provides full eight-hour days, or in fast-track projects, back-to-back alternating of shifts, thus further reducing total construction duration.

Factory work is regulated with respect to levels of noise, dust, air quality, material waste, and recycling.[8] The International Labor Organization estimates that there are at least 60,000 fatal accidents on construction sites across the globe annually. This equates to one accident every 10 minutes and 17 percent of all fatal workplace accidents.[9] In the United States, fatal and nonfatal injuries due to construction double that of the manufacturing industry.[10] In fact, the only category in which manufacturing has a higher number of injuries is in equipment injury, but only by a total of 10 individuals. By moving to prefabrication, the construction industry and its workers can experience a much safer environment by a factor of 2. Lingard and Francis found that employees in site-based roles reported higher levels of conflict at home and exhaustion than employees who worked in regional or head offices. This should be no surprise to anyone connected to the construction industry, and it must be acknowledged that long weekends and long hours contribute to poor emotional health. This study also points to the higher rate of turnover of employees in construction than that of the military, technology, and management sectors.[11] Prefabrication certainly cannot cure the evils of construction, but by bringing the work into the factory, prefabrication has the opportunity to invest in programs that control employee satisfaction in the workplace.

Nutt-Powell comments that prefabrication allows for manufacturers to employ unskilled workers. In onsite construction, skilled work is required because of the range of tasks necessary. A knowledge of how individual pieces of a project are coming together as a whole requires skills beyond many entry-level positions in the construction trades. If a worker makes a mistake onsite, it is detrimental to the progress of the project. The reality of most construction sites is that unskilled workers are commonly unsupervised. In the factory, unskilled work is more easily managed. The laws of supply and demand dictate that some laborers earn more than others. Therefore, lay construction workers naturally select jobs that are higher paying, and not necessarily what they are most qualified or skilled to perform. Conversely in prefabrication, factory workers can be paid the same for different tasks, rewarding wages based on performance. This encourages laborers to gravitate toward jobs that they enjoy. Nutt-Powell argues that this potentially increases skill levels in construction tasks.[12]

Society places value upon certain kinds of work and rewards individuals accordingly. Although the factory worker we have been discussing in this chapter may have an opportunity to become quite skilled in a particular task, the work is still considered unskilled, meaning that the market does not compensate it well. In addition, these jobs are monotonous, leaving those who perform them in the same task over and over without variation or a challenge. In order for prefabrication to be ethically accepted among the building industry, it must shed the stigma of human rights infringements with which it is associated. With computer technology and an increase in the complexity of factory production techniques in the later part of the twentieth and early-twenty-first century, as well as the employment of single-piece workflow and lean project techniques, it is likely that the prefabrication architecture laborer is much more skilled than any mass-production laborer in previous generations, moving to more intellectual, computer, or even management tasks.

The macroeconomic context in which a construction project finds itself has much impact on the feasibility of using offsite production methods. In residential construction, when work is plentiful and the economy is strong, prefabrication is able to compete with onsite methods, as a surplus of work shifts operations offsite. In times of economic depression, builders will opt for methods that pay unskilled onsite workers, despite the resultant longer durations. This is truer in the western state markets like Salt Lake City. For example, panelization of frame walls gained much strength during the 1990s and early 2000s; however, according to Burton Lumber, a prefabricator of panels and trusses, the recent recession has virtually removed their panelized market share. In discussing the issue with their customers, builders, and architects, Burton Lumber found onsite-framed construction to be cheaper because bids are coming in a record low from immigrant day laborers. Once the economy rebounds, however, the company would like to be more poised than ever to handle offsite production methods in greater variety and capacity. This is a challenge prefab will always have to compete with, until the market share becomes the majority, making it more expensive in general to build onsite.

Conversely, Kullman Building Corp. has seen an increase in market share of steel and concrete construction for commercial buildings since the economic downturn. Architects and contractors are trying to find new ways to build and questioning the traditions that are associated with the recent real estate recession. As more architects move to using BIM in their design and delivery process, Kullman is able to keep costs, schedule, and predictability closer in tact. On higher capital investment projects in the commercial sector, owners and contractors want to know with the greatest accuracy cost and schedule. Going to greater degrees of prefabrication in the factory and finishing elements to above 90 percent allows for little onsite uncertainty to creep in.

PREFAB IMPACTS ON LABOR PRODUCTIVITY

Productivity is a measure of efficiency in labor. With offsite fabrication, technical changes including machinery in the factory, evolutions in material science, and finally digital revolutions in BIM and CNC have positively impacted the productivity of labor in construction. Goodrum and colleagues published a study in which these improvements and productiveness were evaluated as a result of the functions of prefabrication. Advances in machinery, physical tools for manufacturing, and prefabrication technology, or in short, **equipment technology, have impacted labor productivity through the following means:**

• Amplified human energy to increase output

• Increased levels of control, precision, accuracy, and quality

• Added variability to production manipulation

• Increased information processing via CNC tools

• Improved ergonomics for reduced fatigue and increased safety

Material advances have increased productivity through:

• Reduction in the mass of materials

• Increase in strength of materials

• Curing and cooling time for materials

• Installation flexibility in different weather conditions

• Offsite customization of materials

Based on 100 construction-related tasks, the researchers found that labor productivity for the same activity increased by 30 percent where lighter materials were used. In addition, labor productivity also improved when construction activities were performed using materials that were easier to install or were prefabricated. Productivity cannot be a factor of material and production technology alone; however, the report shows a significant increase in productivity in projects that incorporate not only material advances in prefabrication but equipment and information technologies as well.[13]

4.1.4 Scope

The scope of a project refers to its breath, size, complexity, and the involvement of individuals and teams required to complete the undertaking. This extends not only to those involved in the physical construction, but also to the entire design and delivery team. Increases in scope are to be expected in both design and construction due to increases in coordination, integration, and requirements of early prefabrication decision making before construction occurs. Integration occurs necessarily at both the physical and organizational levels in prefabrication.[14]

Integration requires that design teams are united in their efforts and that contractors be involved in the building planning process during design. If prefabrication is going to be used effectively, it not only needs to be appropriate for the context, but the contractor will need to have an understanding of and give information to the design team regarding general concepts of construction early on. Therefore, establishing a design intent, manifest by the construction documents by which the building will be built, and also a construction intent—a concept for manufacture, delivery, and installation—that is integrated with the

design of the project is necessary. Therefore, there is not only an integration of teams in decision making, but potentially also an integration of products or outputs of prefabrication that suggest a more integrated building system.

To control the scope of the project, supply chain management must be instituted. Supply chain management (SCM) is the management of a network of interconnected businesses involved in the ultimate provision of product and service packages required by end customers. SCM spans all movement and storage of raw materials, work-in-process inventory, and finished goods from point of origin to point of consumption.[15] The term *supply chain management* was first coined by a U.S. industry consultant in the early 1980s, however, this concept emerged from the industrial revolution forward through Ford and Taylor in the assembly line production system. Today, SCM has entered into an era of integration. This is highlighted with the development of Electronic Data Interchange (EDI) systems in the 1960s and developed through the 1990s by the introduction of Enterprise Resource Planning (ERP) systems. Integration in SCM has continued to develop into the twenty-first century with the expansion of Internet-based collaborative systems. Increasing value adding and cost reducing strategies through integration characterize this era of supply chain evolution.[16] Prefabrication over onsite methods allows contractors to oversee the integration of supply chain management more effectively through the use of digital tools to increase quality and reduce cost as well as control the greenness of materials being implemented.

With scope of a prefab project, productivity increases, however, not at the expense of a need for increased communications before, and during, con-

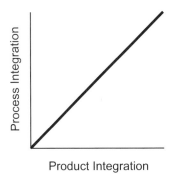

Figure 4.6 Prefabrication suggests the flattening of both the integration of process and products of construction.

struction. Mistakes onsite in scope and schedule can cost weeks and possibly even months of delays. A mishap in the factory can be retooled by realigning and rescheduling. This environment is much more controlled but also flexible. The reduction of change orders is experienced when bringing work into the factory. However, when changes are necessary because not all problems or challenges are identifiable during the design phase, a labor force in a factory is more adaptable and often does not have to include a different subcontractor as plans change. The cost of changes can often be absorbed within the operations of the factory because they are made up through other efficiencies. The inflexibility of the jobsite leads to exposure of vulnerabilities of the project team to financial distress and possibly a change in scope of the project altogether.

On the other hand, small, quick adaptations in the field can often be made faster than with factory-produced elements. For example, if a module has been shipped to site 95 percent complete and there is a change that needs to be made based on onsite foundation as-built, this cannot be mitigated easily in the field; rather, the module must be trucked back and readjusted. With onsite methods, these types of fixes are flexible. Therefore, if the product is still in the factory before shipping, there is a great deal of flexibility, but once shipped, it is entirely the opposite.

4.1.5 Quality

Quality is twofold: quality of production, which is the primary focus of this chapter, and quality of design, often associated with the work of the architect. In order for prefabrication to succeed in architecture, both must be considered of equal value. These principles are seemingly opposites. As soon as production

quality increases, architecture becomes more standardized, bland, and unvaried, while a highly customized design inevitably suggests a lack of production efficiency. But, prefabrication is not synonymous with standardization, and therefore is only as good from a design perspective as the demands placed upon it. It requires the creative abilities of architects, engineers, fabricators, and contractors to envision a method to increase both the quality of design and production to the mutual benefit of both. This is the challenge of prefab architecture.

There are insurances in designing for quality including regulatory or code standards, product warranties, and design and fabrication tolerances. Codes vary from municipality to municipality. Prefabricators trying to offer their products to a larger market share are faced with the reality of meeting the most stringent regulation for the market regions they are trying to serve. This variation is not as great since the creations of the IBC, however, within the IBC regional variations for structures including wind and seismic loading as well as environmental variations such as increase envelope performance often require adjustments to offsite-produced elements. In order to mitigate this discrepancy, many states have implemented their own third-party inspection system so that prefabricators may have their products evaluated by a company certified by the municipally and hired by the manufacturer. This can allow for more variation in the product and for cases when a jurisdiction requires something out of the ordinary, the prefabricator does not have to change their entire line of product for just one situation. Third-party verifiers are therefore responsible for everything that happens in the factory and the local inspector verifies everything that happens onsite, including foundation and prefab-element install utility, and site utility hookups to the prefabricated elements.

Onsite construction is still a handicraft culture. Whereas other industries use automation and precise methods of production, construction relies on skilled laborers in order to produce its goods. Using prefabrication can increase the precision of the products and therefore allow for greater control over the end product. As such, warranties on products are potentially more extensive from the factory. The offsite manufacturer can guarantee window wall units, panels, and modules for quality and workmanship as well as replacement of parts from the factory. This is due to the ability to guarantee the product because fewer hands have touched the installation. If the prefabrication is manufactured and installed by the same company, an increased level of warranty may be instituted as well.

Along with increased precision is the ability for manufactured components to have less dimensional tolerance. In a factory, tolerances are automatically easier to control. These tolerances not only extend to how close a component is to its intended size, but how it relates to other components or site-built components, foundations, and so forth. This is not only because machines automate the process of production, but also laborers repeat tasks so that they are consistent across iterations. Owners expect a reliable product at the end of construction. Prefab limits their risk and eliminates unknowns in a highly multivariable problem of construction. Offsite methods allow for a product that is not only higher in precision, but is more likely to be on time and on budget. The outcome is more predictable from end to end. This may be through standardized components that have previously been tested as successful, or in a one-off project that may be tested through multiple prototypes in the factory before producing in large quantity or producing a final one-of-a-kind component. Much of this can be done while site work is being prepared. It is not that onsite

construction cannot be high quality; rather, high quality is achievable at a lower cost with offsite fabrication than otherwise.

4.1.6 Risk

During the process of trying to achieve both design and production quality, risk to each party is inevitable. Systems already developed implemented into a building project are relatively accepted, tested, and proven. Owners who are risk adverse shy away from prefabrication of systems that are not available in the marketplace because they do not want to assume the liability of added cost or schedule from any untried methods. Other owners may see the risk as an opportunity to do something that will place them as an innovative company or organization. Architects and engineers, likewise, risk much when taking on a customized prefabrication project. Fabricators may be the most willing to take on such projects because they understand the parameters that are required to accomplish the tasks and stand to benefit financially from the endeavor. On projects that use prefabrication to realize a unique project or leverage offsite for its capability to control cost and schedule, all parties assume risk until prefabrication has been tested to outperform onsite methods.

Any variation from the standard in construction presents potential financial vulnerability for owner, designers, and contractors alike. However, the reality is that many prefabricated products are well proven and the unwillingness has more to do with not wanting the hassle or feeling ambivalent of the end result—the opposite of quality in design and production—than it does with issues of risk. In residential construction, prefabrication methods continue to have a negative image, associating it with temporary or HUD code portable construction. As such, lending institutions may be more reluctant to provide funding. In the custom residential market that looks for financing through a traditional construction/perm loan, prefabrication may present problems. If a lending institution is unfamiliar with prefabrication, project players may want to research different institutions that may be more accustomed to lending for mobile home or manufactured home construction. Some prefabricators will finance projects themselves, offering the capacity to cover costs during construction with initial down payments.

Construction/perm loans are a combination of financing to build the building which then rolls over into a permanent mortgage. Prefabrication offers potential opportunities for variable loan and leasing options. These types of financing provide a precedent of what construction financing may look like in the future. Short-term interest-only lines of credit allow the contractor to make "draws" on the funds as necessary in order to deliver the project. In traditional construction, the "draws" are set up on a schedule associated with the scope of the project. Banks are more hesitant to give large single draws and therefore when a portion of the project requires such construction, companies may have trouble with making cash liquid for subcontractor payments. In prefabrication, the factory traditionally will require more dispersed draws. An example by Irontown homes is 25 percent to start ordering materials/shop drawings, and to reserve a place in the fabrication queue. Another 25 percent is required to begin onsite construction; another 25 percent at mid-fabrication; and the final 25 percent at the end of factory construction, just before shipment. The specifics for the remaining draw schedule for site-built and button-up construction are determined as a project moves closer to construction. Unlike onsite construction, prefabricated elements could potentially not be tied to the land upon which

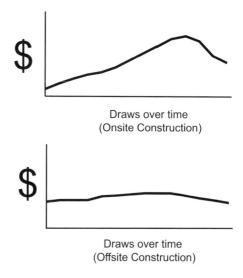

Draws over time
(Onsite Construction)

Draws over time
(Offsite Construction)

Figure 4.7 For traditional construction loans that make draws throughout a project, offsite construction allows for a more consistent draw schedule throughout the construction process compared with onsite construction that has difficulty anticipating the large draws that are necessary and often difficult to make cash liquid in a short amount of time.

they inhabit, making their investment higher than other building construction that derives its value primarily from land investment. Prefab architecture can potentially be relocated in the event that a business changes locations or a homeowner changes cities.

Extended producer responsibility (EPR) is a concept of having producers of components for prefabricated architecture remain responsible for their materials and products in the secondary market. EPR includes stewardship for the durability performance during the intended life of the building.[17] EPR can become a source of financial revenue for users as well, to buy, trade, and exchange building elements in the marketplace. As Jon Broome states, "involving people in the housing process is a necessary pre-condition for a sustainable housing."[18] EPR suggests a leasing option for prefab elements. By paying a monthly rate, the leaser sets the terms with an agent, which is usually the value of depreciation of the product while being leased. This has been used widely in portable modular construction, but has not been employed in many other areas of construction. Prefabrication offers the opportunity for the market to use this concept in tandem with extended producer responsibility to have prefab users not actually own the panels or modules, but employ them for a time under a lease agreement. The provider would maintain the system and then update it for a new leaser once the term has expired.

Similar to car leasing, this model may in the future be used for solar panels, or other plug-and-play systems on buildings may be leased for a time with the residual being captured by the client. Similarly, permanent structures may lease portions of their building systems or units returning the elements to the leasing agency, dealer, provider, or the general contractor, depending on the arrangement. A tax exempt municipal lease is currently used as a useful financing alternative available to state and local government agencies including public school districts and some charter schools, that allow payments on a predetermined rate for a specific number of payment periods with a nominal buyout fee due at the end of the lease term. After the buyout of the modular building in question, purchasers receive a title of ownership. Lease to own options can be paid out annually, quarterly, or monthly as terms are negotiated per project. Currently, banks are not familiar with this model to finance building projects. This is a significant hurdle that will have to be overcome in order for alternative financing for prefabrication to become possible.

PREFAB LEASING OPTION

DIRTT, an interior modular panel system, has an alternative lease option. The real base behind the lease option is cashflow distribution over time and moving the costs of DIRTT to the expense column in an operational budget instead of the capital cost in a tenant improvement or new construction project. The secondary market would be the primary beneficiary of lease option of prefabricated system moving walls to new ownership or lease that pay significantly less than for new. This is not unlike refurbished computers one can purchase from Apple at a significant discount. DIRTT would then move from Class A office space at initial purchase to less-designed spaces as life progresses such as Class B, C, and into more warehouse, back-office applications. This model is just starting and its success has yet to be documented.

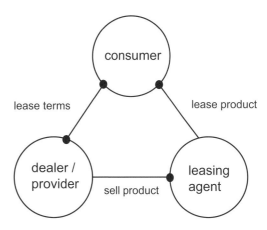

Figure 4.8 Extended producer responsibility may be a solution to construction financing in the future. Prefabrication is amenable to this model because elements may be leased to consumers, much the way an automobile is leased, where the user pays for the depreciation value of the product during the leasing period. This may also help to foster the sustainable practice of recycle and reuse of building components throughout the industry.

Linked to quality and risk is the concept of research and development. Onsite construction projects rarely have the capacity for research and development. Due to the design-bid-build process, contractors are trying to find the least common denominator to accomplishing a project. This means finding loopholes in the contract documents, discovering where costs may be cut from the beginning of construction, or simply giving a false bid so that the job is secured and then worrying about how to deliver later on down the road. Many contractors of onsite work admit that providing an educated guess to a portion of the bid is what they must do because each project presents unique uncharted territory of labor, material, and schedule. Prefabrication architecture allows the offsite fabricator to be an integral part of the bidding process or work with teams early in a deign-assist delivery to determine costing and bring the design within a constructible and affordable balance. Unique or specialized portions of buildings that require prefabrication may be seen as more risky to the owner and contractor, but trying to pull these specialized systems onsite presents much more of an added risk. Even in low-risk projects, trying to obtain higher quality through more predictable means in the factory is a lower-risk enterprise.

4.2 Tradeoffs

Much of the discussion of the principles of prefabrication, including cost, schedule, labor, scope, quality, and risk, can be presented in terms of tradeoffs. Prefabrication is not a catch-all solution, but must be implemented with regard to a specific place and time in a building project. Figure 4.9 is an onsite and offsite production comparison with regard to the principles just reviewed above. This is meant to be a help to architects and builders in determining the advantages and disadvantages to consider when planning or

moving to implement prefabrication in a project already in progress.

Looking closely at this comprehensive list of prefabrication parameters, general categories may be abstracted. First, productivity is the common denominator in any discussion concerning offsite in comparison to onsite methods. This is a result of increased coordination between project players including architects, engineers, owners, contractors, and subcontractors. Traditional onsite delivery of buildings in the United States is anything but logical or efficient. Unlike other production industries, construction is fragmented. This fragmentation produces waste in the delivery of buildings from design and engineering to supply chain and procurement. This is, in large measure, due to the separate contractual structure of the industry putting architects and contractors, design, and production on opposite sides of the table. Integrated processes allow for delivery to be flattened and productivity to be increased. Prefabrication and integration are collateral principles.

4.3 Conclusion

A study by Hook relates a building system developed in Sweden called the timber volume element (TVE) that uses 90 percent produced-offsite fabricated elements. The system reduces construction errors found in onsite construction and has been documented to reduce waste. Despite the added benefits of increased efficiencies and quality with decrease in cost of TVE for housing, the system has not gained confidence in Sweden.

▶ Figure 4.9 The principles of construction, including cost, schedule, scope, quality, and risk, are presented with a comparison of offsite versus onsite methods. This table is meant to be a help to architects and builders in determining the advantages and disadvantages when planning a new project or moving to implement prefabrication in a project already in progress.

Principles	Offsite	Onsite
Cost		
Financing	interest reduced on shortened schedule, even draws, and leasing options, alternative methods might be seen as risky for lenders	traditional construction loan / mortgage financing, lending freezes make construction actuation difficult
Administration	administrator overhead reductions	bureaucratic layers for decision making
Insurances	lower contingency costs	higher contingency costs
Transportation	two stage delivery shop and site	raw material delivery only
Change orders	extra cost and delay	accommodated changes
Overhead	larger shop overhead—people, equipment, space, utilities	overhead is absorbed into construction budget
Schedule	duration reductions recapture investment earlier	schedule overruns are common increasing overall budget
Material	less scaffolding, formwork, and shuttering	increased scaffolding, formwork and shuttering
Craning	costly heavy duty cranes for setting	no cranes for small projects, large stationary crane for larger
Initial cost	higher investment in product	lower initial cost for normative projects
Lifecycle cost	greater ROI over long term	greater maintenance requirement
Profit	subcontractor overhead costs project more, savings from scope, material may not be passed onto customer	overhead fees are more transparent to owner
Design fees	higher due to coordination requirement	standard fees
Lean	reduce time waste increase value	waste laden process
Productivity	full 8 hours of work, sophisticated machines, digital tools available	productivity increases difficult
Economy	when strong plenty of residential work, but less commercial, when weak, less residential and more commercial	residential and commercial ebb and flow with markets
Schedule		
Duration	finish date met 50% reductions	schedule overruns are common
Scope coordination	extra coordination needed between site and plan	more time for coordination and opportunity to adjust dimensions
Schedule reliability	longer lead time, reduced erection time, reliable duration	shorter lead time, longer construction and less reliable
Permitting	streamlined in familiar jurisdictions opposite in unfamiliar	dependent on jurisdiction
Weather	sun always shines	delays due to weather are common
Work flow	concurrent scheduling	linear process
Subcontractors	fewer conflicts better sequencing	simultaneous trade crowding difficult
Supply chain management	coordinated and streamlined	uncoordinated and wasteful

(continued)

Principles	Offsite	Onsite
Labor		
Local labor	less local labor needed	local labor needed
Working conditions	improved working conditions and more stable job market	variable working conditions and more sporadic job market
Skill level	craft and technical skills needed	craft and problem skills are elevated
Subcontractors	fewer conflicts better sequencing	
Unskilled labor	supervision of labor, quality control process	unsupervised labor leads to portions of project being reconstructed
Labor comfort	ergonomics increased	physically difficult
Safety	reduced exposure to accident	accident prone job site
Health	better life style and mental health	more opportunity for variety in work
Skilled labor	less chance for skill development	more chances for skill development
Commute	factory near house—full 8 hour days and no out of town travel	out of town projects require commute times
Productivity	full 8 hours of work, sophisticated machines, digital tools available	less productive use of labor force
Union	declining due to immigrant population making less room for offsite	accommodates variety of labor types
Scope		
Supply Chain Management	long term supply chains for materials established	supplies restricted to project-based purchases
Coordination	extra coordination needed between site and plan	More time for coordination and opportunity to adjust dimensions
Flexibility	changes often cannot easily be made in field	Limited adjustment can be made easily in the field
Impact of changes	less accommodation	more accommodation
Maintenance	reduced maintenance and operations	higher maintenance and operations
Transportation	two stage delivery shop and site	raw material delivery only
Flexibility	changes not made in field	adjustments made in field
Design	requires higher level of detailing for assembly, only 50% with bridging documents	design intention communicated only
Production	predictable output, mockup and prototype required	difficult to anticipate, depends on skill level of construction crew
Regulatory	3rd party verifiers	local agency to inspect
Predictably	increase expected outcome	less predictable delivery
Staging	less material on site, but must be coordinated well	staging is logistically difficult
Accessibility	specialized companies, takes research and work	smaller construction companies

Principles	Offsite	Onsite
Quality		
Reliability	more reliable quality can be achieved in shorter amount of time	less reliable (depending on the site conditions and skill level of labor)
Coordination	integrated effort between factory and site	flexible coordination and adjustments
Design	integrated design and construction process	separation of design and construction
Production	predictable output, mockup and prototype required	difficult to anticipate, depends on skill level of construction crew
Regulatory	3rd party verifiers with industry knowledge	local jurisdiction with varied experience
Predictably	increase expected outcome	unpredictable quality
Innovation	R&D capacity and control	no research and development time or resources
Design flexibility	more restricted	more freedom
Equipment	easier access	equipment to and from site
Environment	lower waste, air and water pollution, dust and noise, and overall energy costs	difficult to manage waste and energy in construction
Handling	potential for damage during handling	smaller elements easier to handle
Joining	fewer joints, but difficult to detail	more joints, more potential for failure
Tolerances	great capacity, not forgiveness in module on site	forgiveness with details constructed on site
Fit	fewer points for water and air infiltration	more locations for infiltration
Quality of materials	quality control in SCM sourcing	contingent upon source
Warranty	opportunity for comprehensive warranty of products from one supplier	dedicated to each system supplier
Risk		
Cost	overall higher cost potential, more predictable	standard bidding process brings waste, cost is unpredictable
Handling	transit damage potential, cumbersome large scale unit install	multiple trips, smaller pieces for easier per install handling
Public perception	negative	NA
Innovative	greater innovation possible	more difficult to achieve innovation complexity
Safety to labor force	safe indoor labor conditions	statistically more dangerous
Tolerances	discrepancy between onsite and offsite elements present problems, element tighter tolerances	tolerances can be accommodated easily in onsite installation
Fit	if not fit, changing size of element is costly	onsite accommodation to fitting issues resolved without added cost
Quality	when increased, risk goes down	higher exposure to risk due to material and joint failure

Hook hypothesizes that the loss of acceptance of the TVE can be attributed to an incomplete prefabrication strategy that needs a value creation formulated in the traditional construction context. Simply, if the end user does not see value in the prefabricated system, or has an unfavorable perspective on the technology, it will have difficulty succeeding in capitalistic markets. Hook suggests that demonstration projects, technical descriptions, and quantifiable measures be illustrated to owners with their cost benefit so that wise decisions can be made.[18]

The TVE program illustrates the pervasive misunderstanding by the public of prefabrication in construction. This example is in Sweden, where a culture of prefabrication has been present for many more years than in the United States. Offsite methods may take longer to be accepted by the client and public than were first anticipated in North America. Although the public may not be accepting, more importantly, construction professionals must understand, accept, and implement offsite construction for increased productivity. In a recent study by Blismas in 2007, construction professionals in Australia were surveyed to determine the lack of market penetration of prefabrication. The results indicate the following barriers to industry adoption of offsite methods:[19]

• Lack of knowledge by clients and industry professionals including architects, engineers, and contractors

• Lack of information on proven precedents that show an added value for the cost

• Outmoded design and construction culture that promotes separation of disciplines

• Lack of availability of process and program (contracts)

In addition, the United States has specific barriers to prefabrication that are unique to our construction context. Despite the obvious need for offsite production for increasing construction productivity in the United States, traditional onsite methods continue to persist. Eastman and colleagues speculate that the reason why prefabrication has not taken hold in the United States is related to issues of labor in construction including:[20]

• Construction companies in general are small, consisting of fewer than five people in 65 percent of firms. This makes investing in technology difficult and changing operations toward using methods that rely on offsite manufacturers a challenge. To change delivery methods would seem to be easier since layers of bureaucracy are not present, but smaller firms are a result of smaller building projects that do not have the budget to invest in new methods of prefabrication and automation.

• Labor has proportionally decreased productivity as inflation wages and benefit packages have stagnated, union participation has declined, and the use of immigrant workers has increased, discouraging the need for labor-saving innovations such as are found in offsite fabrication.

Therefore, if offsite production is to replace onsite methods, proponents of prefabrication must be more vigilant. The principles outlined in this chapter, including cost, schedule, labor, scope, quality, and risk, must be researched in theory and practice so that constituents in the construction industry may have the knowledge, information, contract structure, and capital to implement these technologies and processes sooner than later.

chapter 5 Fundamentals

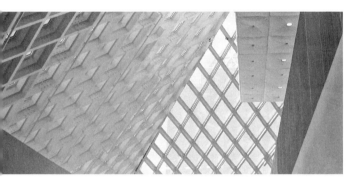

This chapter will discuss the fundamental technical and constructional principles related to prefab architecture. These fundamentals include the following categories:

- System: Structure, Skin, Services, Space

- Material: Wood, Steel/Aluminum, Concrete, Polymer/ Composite

- Method: Manufacturing and Fabrication

- Product: Made to Stock, Assembled to Order, Made to Order, Engineered to Order

- Class: Open versus Closed

- Grid: Axial and Modular

5.1 Systems

Building systems are generally thought of in five different categories: *site, structure, skin, services, and space and stuff.*[1] Prefabrication can be used to deliver everything but the site. Most "stuff," including furnishings and fixtures, are so easily changed and their lifespan varies from year to year that it will not

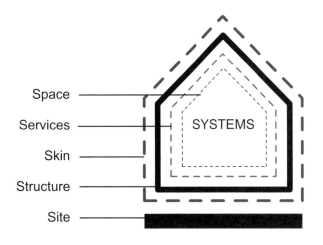

Space

Services

Skin

Structure

Site

SYSTEMS

Figure 5.1 The major building systems that have emerged in construction are identified graphically from most durable to least: site, structure, skin, services, and space.

be considered as a prefabricated system. Therefore, for the purposes of organizing the information herein, the focus will be on offsite fabricated structure and enclosure systems with a brief discussion of interior space and service systems of buildings in relation to architecture.

5.1.1 Structures

Structures are load-bearing and lateral-resisting systems that transfer dead loads induced by gravity on the mass of the building and live loads induced by habitation, wind, rain/snow, and dynamic loading of thermal and movement stresses to the ground. Structures include foundations, frames, load-bearing walls, floors, and roofs. Buildings are made up of two general types of structures to resist vertical and horizontal loading:

• Mass structures can be solid load-bearing to transfer load not through distinct elements, but through surfaces and solids. Mass structures are built of stacked wood, laminated wood, concrete, or

stressed skin panels in metal or wood. Mass structures are less common.

• Frame structures act as skeletal systems in post and beam, space frame, and diagrid. These are primarily made of wood, steel/aluminum, and/or reinforced concrete—materials that are strong enough to resist both tension and compression stresses and support multistory buildings. Frames are the most common structural system due to their flexibility for non-load-bearing infill and ease of erection.

Frame systems are composed of vertical columns or posts and horizontal spanning elements such as beams or girders. Frames are inherently gravity load-bearing, but rake under later loads due to wind, seismic, or other dynamic loads such as disproportionate live loading. Therefore, frames require some type of lateral load-resisting system. Three major types of lateral systems exist: *brace frames, shear wall,* and *rigid frame.*

• Brace frame: The junction of column to beam can be laterally braced with diagonal members of steel. There are various types of braces. In the United States, the most common are "X" bracing and chevron bracing. In seismic regions, sophisticated systems of braces have been introduced including eccentrically braced and unbonded braces. Brace frames provide a stiff structure and are more cost effective than a rigid frame or shear wall in many instances because they can be bolted together quickly onsite. The braces may be welded and bolted directly to the beam and column connection or use a gusset plate that transfers load between the elements. Brace frames, however, leave unsightly and spatial obstructions in bays at gusset plate connections that limit flexibility in future change or in routing utility services through the building.

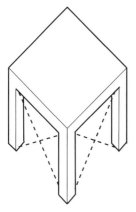 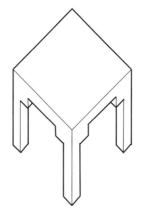 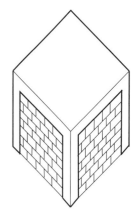

Figure 5.2 The three lateral load-resisting systems include left: brace frame; middle: rigid frame; and right: shear wall.

- Shear wall: Shear walls provide lateral resistance to horizontal loading. Shear walls infill bays between columns and beams. Traditional onsite construction may use site-cast concrete or reinforced block as a shear wall. Prefabrication would suggest that the shear panels be fabricated offsite and placed into structural bays. Panels can be fixed to the steel sections by welding or bolting connections along the edges. Steel connection plates are embedded into precast panel corners and anchored with steel shear studs. This connection is filled with mortar to ensure that the panel is secured to the corner of the column and beam.

- Rigid frame: Most frame structures are separated from enclosure. Save in the case of exterior shear walls that act as exterior enclosure infill, frames must be enclosed in order to provide exterior protection from elements, thermal differences, and interior space separation/fire separation. Frame load-bearing structures can be framed in a variety of relationships with infill such as inline (integrated), online (aligned), or offset (separated). Frames require infill so the treatment of thermal insulation becomes critical. Exposing frames to the exterior

and interior presents problems with thermal bridging. Best practice would suggest putting the frame on the interior with insulation on the exterior, or to place the frame on the exterior of the enclosure; however, this is difficult not to create thermal bridges with floor-spanning elements that must attach to the vertical frame structure and thus create a bridge for energy transfer.

- Cores: Buildings can contain a core that provides a center area of services such as stairs and elevators. Since these vertical shafts need to be fireproofed, site-cast concrete is usually used to act as shear core as well. Steel frame structures can be attached to these cores in three ways: (1) steel embeds are placed into the concrete core with a flange that engages the structural steel beams to be bolted; (2) the steel connection plate is set flush in the concrete wall and is welded to the beam onsite; or (3) the core is cast with a recess to accept the steel beam on a steel embed–bearing plate. In all of these cases, care must be taken to minimize onsite welding as much as possible. In this case, using precast cores instead of site-cast cores and providing embeds, faceplates, or recesses in the precast walls that can accept the steel structure may increase the speed of construction and quality of precision.[2]

• Space frames: A space frame is a 3D truss formation that consists of lightweight interlocking members that create a latticework. Space frames are used for long-span roofs and can be formed to make hollow columns or girder elements. Their strength-to-weight ratio is high, making this an ideal solution for few points of support and prefabricated structures that have a high degree of repetition. Space frames derive their strength from the inherently rigid triangulation. They are rigid but also ductile, with movement and bending occurring across each of the individual elements or struts. Space frames are attributed to Alexander Graham Bell at the turn of the twentieth century, but Buckminster Fuller made them popular in architecture.

Space frames have become less common in the latter part of the twentieth century due to their cost, but still present an opportunity for prefabrication when implemented in higher profile buildings where structure is left exposed.

• Diagrid: Short for "diagonal grid," this is a structure that uses triangulation as well. Members are placed on the diagonal, as opposed to horizontal and vertical standard frame structures. The diagrid is then able to act as a vertical gravity load-bearing structure and a lateral load-resisting structure simultaneously. As such, this requires less material, upward of 25 percent, than would be required in a conventional structural system that uses post and beam and a separate lateral resisting system. Diagrids can often be found in nature such as in plant formations and bone structures. In this context, they are referred to as "lamella structures" in which members are con-

◀ Figure 5.3 Cores offer lateral resistance to buildings and may also contain vertical services such as stairs, elevators, and mechanical shafts.

▼ Figure 5.4 Space frames have existed since the turn of the twentieth century, but did not take hold in architecture until Buckminster Fuller made them popular. Architecture students at the University of Utah constructed this space frame in the 1960s on the Salt Lake City campus.

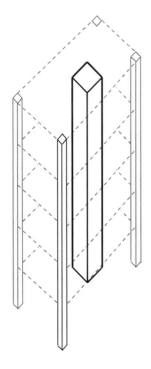

nected along a pattern of intersecting diagonal lines to form a mesh surface. Contemporary architecture has many recent examples of diagrid structures, for example, in the Hearst Tower, designed by Norman Foster; the Seattle Library, designed by Rem Koolhaas; and the Tokyo Prada store, designed by Herzog and de Meuron. Diagrid frames may be prefabricated in large grid panels and connected onsite as a superstructure.

5.1.2 Skins

Building skins or enclosures mediate between interior and exterior environments. The protection from exterior extreme temperatures and elements is the primary function of an enclosure system. Architecturally, enclosure systems provide the primary aesthetic communication of a built work. Structures and services are becoming ever more specialized, but building enclosures are still the responsibility of the architect. Therefore, how a community receives the building and how the building performs environmentally is a result of enclosure design. Envelopes constitute both exterior wall and roof systems.

Exterior skins as both the separating and linking element between interior and exterior environments must perform a variety of tasks, including:

- Function: Pragmatic purpose of the building skin, comfort, shelter, view

- Construction: Elements of the building skin and how they are assembled

- Form: Aesthetics of the building skin, cultural and contextual response

- Environment: Performance of the building skin in lifecycle

Figure 5.5 A diagrid structure uses 25 percent less frame material than with a traditional orthogonal grid. This grid is used in the Seattle Public Library, designed by OMA Rem Koolhaas.

Each of the four aspects must be fully considered to create architecture that responds to the needs of its inhabitants and the societies for which it is built. Architects and construction professionals are under increasing pressure to deliver on both construction and ecology of building skins. How a building skin is developed as a series of elements that can be fabricated and quickly assembled has a large impact on overall project budget. This sequence must be well integrated into the entirety of the other criteria. Likewise, the long-term performance in both initial and operational energy as well as durability and maintenance should be considered with respect to the other three criteria in order to justify the investment of the building skin.

Arguably, the building skin is the most dominant system among structure, services, and space.[3] This is true not only in terms of design aesthetics, but in the functions it must perform and the impact it has on ultimate energy performance throughout its lifecycle.

The building skin in many respects determines the weight and ultimate sizing of structure, as well as the performance of services and interior systems of the building. From a performance perspective, skin must ventilate; protect from radiation, conduction, convection, and daylight; insulate and potentially integrate energy systems. Other functional criteria include flame spread and structural loading. All of these functional criteria have an impact on the aesthetic criteria. In addition, functional, aesthetic, and ecological considerations determine the constructional criteria that will be employed and the degree to which prefabrication is used in a given building.

Construction and design are inseparably linked as structure and enclosure design determine the visual appearance of the building. Load-bearing components, such as beams, supports, and walls, and the spacing of them define the rhythm, division, and proportion of the building skin.[4] Classifying building skins according to construction or assembly can be based on the following criteria:

- Load transfer (bearing and non-load-bearing): Bearing skins include traditional structures such as stacked masonry, timber, or contemporary cast concrete barriers. Non-load-bearing structures are the most common today and separate building structure from the exterior enclosure skin. These are composed of wood, glass, metal, ceramic, or stone claddings. From the perspective of function, construction, aesthetics, and energy, the separation of skin and structure is a natural evolution of contemporary desire for flexibility within the lifecycle of a facility.

- Shell arrangement (single-skin or multilayered): Solid wall construction can act as a single skin, relying on one material or layer to perform both structure

and enclosure. Today, however, with increased expectation on building skins to perform a variety of functions, layers are assembled each having defined functions to serve. Air gaps may be provided for water condensation as well as placing insulation and vapor barriers in strategic relationship with one another in order to control dew points and condensation in the building skin system. Even the most rudimentary wall in residential construction is incredibly sophisticated in the functions it must perform.

- Transmission (transparent, translucent, opaque): Across the board of load transfer and shell arrangement, a variety of levels of transparency, translucency, and opacity are possible. Contemporary glass facade systems offer the capacity to open up expanses of exterior wall for view; however, this also introduces concern of radiation transmission. With contemporary materials and arrangements of shells, enclosures are able to perform much better than just 10 years ago while maintaining desired transparency.

- Structure–enclosure–space relationship: The integration of these three elements has an impact on one another. Spatially, building skins can be placed in front of, behind, or in line with the structural systems of a building. The placement of the building skin, in larger measure, determines the aesthetic communication as well as the energy performance by way of creating or mitigating thermal breaks. This also affects interior spatial arrangements, as structure interior can obstruct space definition and arrangement, but also present opportunities for expression when designed in an integrated fashion.

Prefabricated facades consisting of panels of wood, glass, metal, stone, or precast/GFRC cladding are produced in factories and installed onsite. These systems are multilayered, multimaterial, with each layer

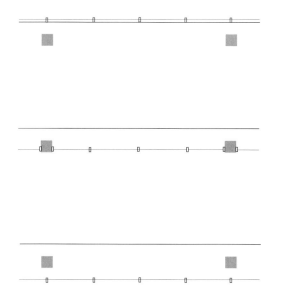

performing specific functions of protection from water, air infiltration, visibility, thermal transmission, and so forth. These layers are assembled in the factory and erected onsite to the superstructure; or an armature is attached to the superstructure and cladding elements in glass, metal, concrete, or stone are placed on the frame in the field. Commonly used non-load-bearing enclosure systems are glass curtain wall, metal facade, precast cladding, and masonry (including stone and brick). Less common but becoming popular are wood and polymer (plastic) facades.

◀ Figure 5.6 The relationship of frame structure and enclosure determines the expression of the building as well as the thermal performance. Enclosures may be outside of the vertical structure, in line with it, or inside of the structure.

Figure 5.7 These large, glazed prefab units are being fabricated in China for the Highline 23 project in New York City, designed by Neal Denari Architects. Front, Inc. developed the glazing system.

5.1.3 Services

The services of a building include the heating, ventilation and air conditioning, plumbing, electrical, and any conveying equipment such as elevators and escalators. The air handlers, condenser units, air-to-air exchangers, and heat pumps are by default prefabricated mechanized units. Mechanical ducting for airflow has been automated in design to fabrication for many years. Prefabrication of services as it relates to architecture refers to a higher level of unitization. Services may be produced as modules that can be located in buildings. Bathrooms, kitchens, communication rooms, utility rooms, and service walls are outfitted in the factory and then placed efficiently inside building structures. Conceptually leaving so-

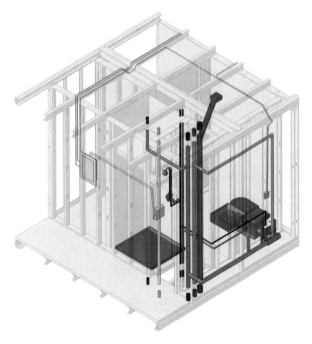

Figure 5.8 This bathroom service pod is fabricated with plumbing, fixtures, and finishes and shipped to be installed as an interior module within a building structure.

phisticated equipment and higher-level finishes inside of the units to factory work before placing them onsite controls the quality and warranty. For example, restrooms and kitchens for utilitarian functions that have a high degree of repetition are ideal for service prefab. This includes service kitchens for restaurants; and kitchen and bathroom units for housing, dormitory, and hotel construction. More on these types of service units will be discussed in Chapter 6.

5.1.4 Space

Materials used to define interior spaces are by definition not exposed to inclement weather. Therefore, polymers, finish wood panels, and newer materials not appropriate for exterior applications can be exploited on the interior. Interior systems provide the primary human dimension of architecture by which its inhabitants experience space. Architects therefore, have specified interior spaces in most cases to be the more expensive per unit volume portion of buildings. An exhaustive look at space-making elements of buildings is beyond the scope of this book. Materials for interiors can be subdivided into panels, tiles, coatings, and coverings.[5]

All of these systems may be easily applied in a factory environment, shipped, and erected onsite. This is rarely done, however. Interior space is the most temporary of all building systems, but it is also the most expensive over the lifecycle of a facility, considering the rate at which change occurs. Interiors can be changed every time a new tenant or owner moves in. To accommodate this need, manufacturers are beginning to develop prefabricated interior systems that allow for easy assembly and disassembly. A company called DIRTT (Do It Right This Time) has developed a prefabricated interior temporary partition and floor system. The wall system is an open-source product that can accept many different types of materials from 3-Form resin panels to wood paneling to glass tiles as well as different electrical configurations.

5.2 Materials

Prefabrication can be accomplished in virtually any material. Although most elements today are some type of composite made from one or more materials, the primary material in a compilation determines the flow of the material through its lifecycle from who harvests the material, manufactures, fabricates, and finally installs it. The building industry trades are set up to handle certain types of materials throughout this lifecycle due to tooling, manipulation, and install expertise. For example, in the last decade, structural insulated panels have fallen under the purview of framers, albeit not successfully in many cases, because they traditionally are used as exterior structure and enclosure walls for housing. For our purposes, materials will be organized by wood, steel/aluminum, concrete, polymer, and composite. The primary material can also determine in what system, element, and building type it is used.

Today there are more choices of materials than ever before. With the advent of nano materials and composites, the traditions of concrete, wood, and steel may seem historic. However, these materials are still high performers for their cost and the reality is that alternative structural materials outside of these three seems highly unlikely in the near or long-term future of building. In prefabrication, alternative materials are having greater impact, as their potential to make way for innovative solutions is greater. This is because

they can be carefully controlled and manipulated with a specialized labor force that understands these new materials and may be able to implement them with specific skill sets. Materials have properties and performance characteristics related to the parameters of how they are used in buildings and what job they perform. Outside of aesthetics, materials must perform a range of functions from structure, attachment, infiltration, and thermal resistance.

For example, materials for structures are generally steel and concrete because they are readily affordable and available. Labor crews have been established to handle these materials and their associated systems. Tools, machines, and factories are well established to develop and manipulate steel and concrete. Design standards exist for both steel and concrete structures regardless if they are developed on- or offsite. Glass, polymer, and aluminum are found in enclosure systems that are non-load-bearing because they are lightweight and offer light transmission, but are less suitable for structures. In smaller buildings, wood can be used for structure and enclosure as well. Glass is manufactured as large sheets and polymer in recent years has been used as panel, shell, and pneumatic pillows on enclosures. Facade construction has implemented precious metals including copper, bronze, and durable alloys such as stainless and titanium.

John Fernandez in *Material Architecture* classifies materials by families according to their extrinsic and intrinsic properties.[6] Families include metals, polymers, ceramics, natural materials, and composites. A family, such as ceramics, has consistent material properties across its material types including brick, concrete, stone, glass, and the like. These materials are brittle, made from the earth, and are dense and hard. Metals, polymers, ceramics, and natural materials are intuitively understood because we experience their tactile qualities every day. However, composites that constitute a combination of one or more of the material families are more difficult to understand. This is also the fastest growing area of material discovery and use.

Intrinsic properties include mechanical, physical, thermal, and optical qualities. These are inherent properties to the material in its physical form. Extrinsic properties include economic, environmental, societal, and cultural implications suggested by the material. Architects and engineers selecting materials for design must consider the full range of implications of a material. This includes how the material will perform in a given function and the process of manufacture and fabrication. Many extrinsic properties of a material have implications for things that are usually considered outside of the purview of architects, such as poverty alleviation, embodied energy consumption, and toxicity.[7]

5.2.1 Wood

Wood is a natural material made from water and cellulose bound together with lignin. The cellulose cylindrical tubes grow vertically and as such have a grain pattern that is the means by which nutrients are distributed from the roots to the leaves or needles. Grain also determines the strength characteristics of the tree, being stronger loaded parallel to the grain as opposed to perpendicular. Trees can be hewn and used as logs for construction, but wood is typically turned into lumber, milled or cut to specific shapes to be used as building elements.

Wood can be categorized into two classifications. Deciduous trees are broad, leafy trees that when harvested and milled become hardwood. Coniferous trees are spindly needle trees that grow tall and slender and when made into lumber are called softwoods. Generally, softwoods are physically soft and hardwoods hard; however, this is not always the case, as with balsa wood, which is a hardwood but has one of the lowest densities of any wood in existence. Hardwoods traditionally are used for finishes, flooring, millwork, and window frames. Softwoods, historically more accessible, faster growing, and more affordable are used for light wood framing, but certain species are also used for applications in lieu of hardwoods.

Wood is a friendly material, easy to manipulate with hand or mechanized machinery, has low toxicity, is biodegradable, easy to recycle and reuse, and, if kept dry, has a high serviceability. Wood has been prefabricated in some senses since it was first harvested, taking logs for stacking, shaping them into framing timbers. Because of its ease of manipulation and relative affordability and renewability, wood has also become the material of obsolescence, being used for low-quality residential construction. Over the course of history, wood has become increasingly engineered to make more structurally astute or higher performing products.

Early log construction in Europe, the United States, and Asia used the plentiful timber resources to stack, place as columns, quarter, half, and create edge-sawn members. Since this time, with the advent of the mill and machinery, logs can be cut into a myriad of different shapes and sizes, and peeled with a rotary blade to create veneers used to develop plywood, and laminated structural members or engineered lumber. Pressed wood panels that uses glues and epoxies, although often toxic to human health, have allowed scrap and waste wood too small for other applications to be reconstituted into structural elements such as panels, posts, and spanning members.

Although not common in the United States, wood in Europe and Scandinavia can be seen in products such as entire laminated wood panel walls that are structural and used for enclosure such as edge-gluded, cross-laminated, board system, ribbed, stressed skin box section, and channel-section walls and floor panels. Other common structural members used in the United States are the familiar 2X floor and roof trusses, wood I-joists, glue-laminated beams, laminated veneer lumber, and many different panel materials such as plywood, oriented strand board, and composite panels for sheathing floors, roofs, walls, and fabricating millwork. Wood is also heavily used for building skins as planks and boards for siding, flooring, decking, and other less structurally intense applications.

In all of these applications, wood today is used primarily in components, individual pieces of lumber placed together onsite to make walls, then sheathed to provide lateral and gravity load strength. Wood is

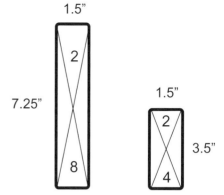

▲ Figure 5.9 This illustrates the difference between nominal and actual dimensions of lumber. Left: Lumber that is 6 in. or less has an actual dimension that is ½ in. less than the nominal dimension. This 2 × 4 is actually 1-1/2 in. × 3-1/2 in. Right: Dimensional lumber that is 8 in. or greater has an actual dimension of ¾ in. less than the nominal dimension. This 2 × 8 is actually 1-1/2 in. × 7-1/4 in. Standard lengths of dimensional lumber are in 2-in. increments from 6 to 14 in. standard with some members available up to 24 or 36 in. in length.

▼ Figure 5.10 Engineered lumber includes elements that are manufactured for increased strength with reduced use of wood material. Common elements used today include from left to right: glue-laminated beams fabricated from 2X lumber, stacked horizontally and glued under pressure; laminated veneer lumber and paralam beams produced from laminated strands or veneers; wood I-joists that contain an OSB web and ripped lumber top and bottom chords; plywood laminated from an odd number of wood veneers; and prefabricated wood roof and floor trusses.

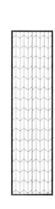

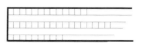
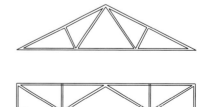

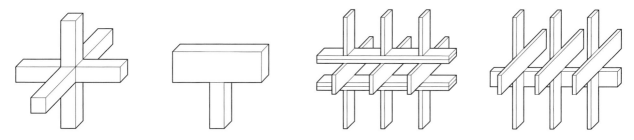

Figure 5.11 Wood framing methods from left to right: Continuous post-and-beam rail connection; post-and-continuous beam construction; platform framing builds one floor at a time, the second floor wall framing bears on the platform floor framing; and balloon framing employs continuous vertical studs from which floors are "hung."

slowly but surely being used to develop prefabricated elements as well. Not only are engineered glulams, veneered beams, and strand columns becoming more common, but wood is being used in the shop to produce entire exterior wall panels, some of which include additional layers such as waterproofing, vapor barrier, insulation, siding, gypsum board, including integrated baseboards. In addition to prefabricated panels, wood is being used to create entire modules, the primary material of the manufactured home industry and growing residential and commercial modular industry.

Traditional types of construction onsite in wood are labor intensive and unnecessarily complicated. In addition, a quarter of all material used in light wood frame construction is waste.[8] Prefabrication in larger timbers, panels, and modules allows the efficiencies of construction while increasing the quality of the manufacturing process, saving resources and simplifying the recycling of waste. Wood is an extremely porous material. Prefabrication in a factory allows wood to stay dry and at a constant temperature during fabrication. The greatest advantage of prefabricating in wood is the precision of the cutting and fitting in the factory. Usually put together with nails or screws, factory-produced wood components, mod-

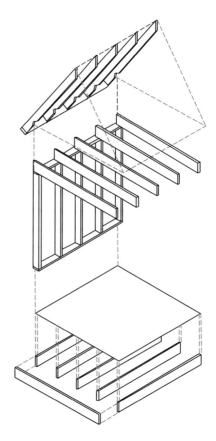

Figure 5.12 An exploded isometric drawing of a platform-framed, single-story house with rafter-framed roof. This illustrates the common elements of light frame construction including framing members and panel sheathing.

ules, or panels can be shipped to the site and put together quickly with extremely tight tolerances. With its capacity to be renewed, manipulated, laminated, and recycled/reused, wood is an obvious choice for prefabrication and will arguably continue to lead the residential and small commercial markets in the United States in the foreseeable future.

5.2.2 Steel/Aluminum

Metals can be described as ductile, hard, conductive, precise, and strong. Metals are used for a variety of applications in architecture from structural applications of mild steel to enclosure frames in aluminum and exterior cladding in precious metals of copper and titanium. Metals can be classified as either ferrous or nonferrous. Ferrous metals contain much iron, which leads to their defining characteristic of corrosion or rusting when exposed, brazed, or washed. Ferrous metals are more widely used in construction, especially in structural applications, because iron is accessible and available anywhere, making these metals more affordable to process and fabricate. Ferrous metals are versatile: They are strong, ductile, and durable. Finally, ferrous metals can be treated with coatings such as galvanizing and manipulated easily with tools to create a variety of architectural products.[9] Nonferrous metals are less accessible than ferrous metals, but are naturally corrosion resistant. These metals are not used in structural applications generally, but employed for cladding, roofing, enclosures, and other weather-exposed applications.

• Common ferrous metals include:

  ○ Cast and wrought iron

  ○ Mild steel

  ○ Stainless steel

  ○ Carbon

• Common nonferrous metals include:

  ○ Aluminum

  ○ Copper

  ○ Zinc

  ○ Titanium

Metals used in architecture are not pure, meaning that they are a combination of more or less noble metals. The process of combining metals is called alloying. The metal is improved to increase its strength, corrosion resistance, or aesthetic properties. Alloying is either treating the surface of the metal with a chemical, called surface alloying, or combining the bodies of the metals to change the fundamental composition of the metals, called bulk alloying. Surface alloying processes include plating, cladding, hot dip galvanizing, and other coating methods to improve the corrosion resistance, surface hardness, or aesthetic properties. Bulk alloying is used primarily to change the strength characteristics of the metal.

Mild steel, a nonferrous alloy, is primarily used as a structural material. The difficulty of welding steel connections onsite naturally requires fabrication in a factory. Mild steel, the most common material used on contemporary steel frame construction, requires plating in order to protect it in exposed weather conditions. During erection, surface alloying can be breached, leading to corrosion susceptibility of the steel. Therefore, in steel construction, the more work performed in a factory the better, from a cost and quality perspective. Steel is an expensive material when compared with wood and concrete, but its strength-to-weight serviceability is superior. Able to be erected quickly, steel is a prevalent choice in

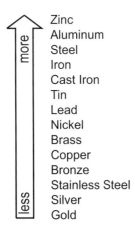

more

less

Zinc
Aluminum
Steel
Iron
Cast Iron
Tin
Lead
Nickel
Brass
Copper
Bronze
Stainless Steel
Silver
Gold

Figure 5.13 The galvanic series determines the nobility of metals, the differences in the conducting potential of metals. Electrons may be transferred from the surface of one metal to the other. The less noble metal will corrode as a result of the reaction. The further apart two metals are from one another on the list, the more likely corrosion is to occur in the less noble metal. This figure illustrates which metals are more likely to corrode due to galvanic action because they are less noble.

prefabrication. Because of its strength and speed of erection, steel is the most economical and efficient material for structuring long-span, high-rise, and unique geometric designs.

Steel, is an elastic material and has excellent tensile and compressive properties. Steel has a yield point;

when this is exceeded, the material behaves in a plastic manner, continuing to deform under stress. Steel is also dimensionally accurate, suited for precise frames, panels, and framing elements within a panel or modular construction. Structural steel is assembled with bolts or welds for attachment. Bolted connections allow for steel structures to be disassembled later. A simple uniform connection technique in prefabricated structures is important for ease and speed of assembly. Welding as much as possible should be dedicated to the factory.

Standard steel sections are forged, heated, and formed. This process leaves their final shape with a radius from interior and exterior corners. This must be taken into consideration when detailing and fabricating as the thickness of the material changes over its section. Aluminum, on the other hand, is precise in its manufacture due to extrusion and cutting. It also has much more variety in its shapes and sectional profiles. In a recent project in which steel angle was used to sandwich glass on a prefabricated bus shelter project, the author had to change the sectional profile not because of structural issues but because a radius corner of the tube steel did not provide enough bite on the tempered 3/8 in. glazing unit.

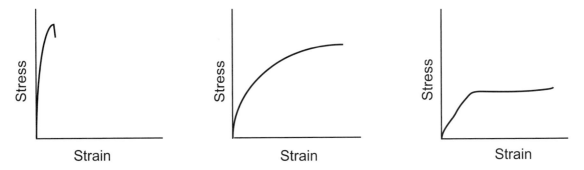

Figure 5.14 Stress and strain curves illustrate Young's modulus for a given material. Stress is a measurement of strength. Strain is a measurement of deformation. Stress/strain curves are used to describe the physical properties of materials in comparison to one another. Left: concrete; Middle: steel; Right: polymer.

Aluminum is a nonferrous alloy made of the third most abundant element of the earth's crust. Aluminum is ductile and well known for its corrosion resistance. The metal is not easy to extract, however, and its mining causes permanent disturbances to landscapes. Fortunately, aluminum is highly recyclable, meaning that it can be recycled repeatedly with little embodied energy and it loses little material properties that it had in its previous life. The following aluminum series are used for construction applications:

• Series 4000 Ornamental

• Series 5000 High strength

• Series 6000 Architectural

• Series 7000 Aircraft

• Series 8000 Aeronautical[10]

Generally, aluminum is not used as a structural material, however, in prefabrication it is having greater impact. Aluminum is light and durable, therefore it is used for prefabricated panels and modules, and is able to be assembled, shipped, and erected quickly. Aluminum has historically been used in the automobile, aircraft, and aeronautical industries as a structural frame material. KieranTimberlake have used industrial application Bosch structural aluminum sections on the Loblolly House and Cellophane House structural frames because of its speed, accuracy of erection, and capacity to be disassembled. These projects use no welding and are bolted with simple tools. Aluminum is extruded so shapes can be any profile that a die can form. However, just as with steel, there are standard shapes that are accepted by the industry for detailing.

Metal alloys are also used for lightweight cladding applications. The high strength-to-weight properties allow metals to be an ideal cladding material. Sheet

Figure 5.15 This is a list of common steel sections used in construction today. They include from left to right and top to bottom: Angle L-shaped section; double angle; Tee T-shaped section; cee C-shaped section, sometimes called a channel; wide-flange W section (column); W section beam; Tube HSS-shaped section; zee Z-shaped section; and a pipe SHS-shaped section.

Figure 5.16 A list of common aluminum sections from left to right and top to bottom: Pipe, tube, bar, hat, I-section, Z, H, T, L, C. Aluminum is extruded, making the manufacturing process more accessible than steel. Aluminum, therefore, can be extruded into any shape desired.

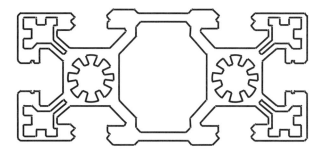

Figure 5.17 Bosch aluminum sections have been developed for industrial applications. The slots allow for fast, durable, and nonpermanent attachments, making this an ideal material and sectional profile system for prefab architecture.

metal can be manipulated and formed into a variety of shapes and geometries, making contemporary forms in architecture possible through automated machinery. A discussion of sheet metal fabrication is beyond the scope of this book. More information on the topic can be read in *Architectural Metal Surfaces,* authored by L. William Zahner.[11]

Light-gauge steel is comparable to light wood frame construction in its applications and sizes. Light-gauge steel can be used in place of 2X nominal lumber or in tandem with light wood framing. Although light gauge and wood framing are the same size, light-gauge steel has a higher strength-to-weight ratio. The sections are manufactured with a zinc coating to ASTM A563 standard. For studs and rafters, members are formed into C-shaped sections. For top and bottom wall plates, and for joist headers, channel sections are used. The strength and stiffness of the member is derived from the cold-formed shape of the steel. C-shaped members have holes placed in them every 2 ft on center to allow for wiring and plumbing runs without having to drill holes in the studs.[12]

Light-gauge steel members are attached to one another with self-drilling, self-tapping screws. Screws

Figure 5.18 Perforated, dimpled copper wall cladding panel system to be fabricated by A. Zahner Architectural Metals for the De Young Museum in San Francisco, designed by Herzog and de Mueron.

Figure 5.19 Common cold-formed light-gauge metal section used in construction. From left to right: Channel used for top and bottom plates, C-sections used for vertical studs, Z-sections for bridging and blocking, C-section stiffened, H-section or hat channel, and double C-section.

are also zinc-coated for protection from corrosion. Welding can also be employed on prefabricated elements that use light-gauge steel due to the added strength and rigidity. Cold-formed light-gauge steel is extremely versatile material and can be used outside of conventions of standard partition framing walls. Minean International has produced exterior structural panelized walls. This has allowed for low-rise housing structures to be built rapidly, without the use of heavy steel framing or concrete in multifamily projects in Portland, Oregon. This will be illustrated in Chapter 6.

5.2.3 Concrete

Unlike wood and metals, concrete is heterogeneous, mixed from Portland cement, sand, aggregate, and water in a process of hydration, which cures, or hardens, the concrete. Based on the quantities of these base materials and admixtures for performance, the properties of concrete are determined. In general, as a ceramic, concrete is a brittle material, relying on fiber and steel reinforcing for its tensile strength. The material is incredibly versatile to any formwork, affordable, but requires an inordinate amount of labor to produce architecture. From frames to panels and module, concrete can fulfill a myriad of structure and enclosure functions. Being relatively nonporous, concrete is durable and long lasting. In the factory or onsite, concrete is formed through casting of the mix in a wet state into formwork. With bar reinforcing and microreinforcing, concrete must be controlled to ensure that proper adhesion and location of reinforcing to the concrete is made. In order to increase the quality of concrete construction, performing these functions offsite ensures a consistency across numerous pours that is difficult to achieve onsite. Repetition and quality-control processes accomplish this, with a key element being formwork. Formwork materials may include wood, steel, composite polymer, or polymer liners.

Concrete capacity and variety has increased steadily since its inception in the 1800s. Admixtures have altered the performance of concrete from accelerating and retarding curing time to increasing tensile capacity and durability. There exist two types of additives to concrete to change its properties:

• Particle inclusion: Concrete is mixed with other particulate to produce a desired effect of the cementitous matrix base. Two common additives are aerated autoclaved and fly ash inclusion. Aerated autoclaved concrete expands the concrete when curing, creating a lightweight product. Fly ash inclusion is where ash, a byproduct of coal burning, is introduced to make the concrete more workable, less permeable, and more ecological because it reduces the quantity of Portland cement necessary. Portland cement embodies much energy in its processing.

• Composite: This introduces reinforcing to the concrete matrix to change the properties of the material. This may be large reinforcing, such as steel or fiberglass reinforcing rods; or microreinforcing, such as steel or glass fiber whiskers introduced in the mix. This method has increased the strength of concrete dramatically. Bentur reports that in 1850, concrete had a compressive strength of less than 5 MPa, less than 20 MPa in 1900, and less than 30 MPa in 1950. Today, with advanced concrete additives and reinforcing mechanisms, concrete is reaching strengths of 100, 200, and there are even reports of 800 MPa.[13] Some of these advanced technologies include higher performance or ductile concrete that is easy to place, compact without segregation, provides high early strength, and is stable and durable long term. Ductile concrete has a compressive strength of 200 MPa and a tensile strength of 40 MPa.[14]

Admixtures to concrete and reinforcing clearly add to the overall cost of precast, but these recent developments suggest that structures and enclosures have a long way to go in precast construction methods. These composites are ideal for applications in cladding materials, structural material, and many other uses in which prefabricated elements can be produced in a factory in a controlled fashion. The future will only tell the expanse of concrete-based composites in offsite construction. More on precast construction will be discussed in Chapter 6.

5.2.4 Polymers

Polymers are a contemporary material found in nearly every industry sector. There are two types of polymers in existence. Natural polymers are made in a benign state from rapidly renewable resources such as rubber trees and soy plastic. Synthetic polymers are produced from oil under the earth's crust from crude oil. Per unit volume, polymer resin is consumed more than steel today, and is growing at a rate of 10 percent annually.[15] Polymers make sense in construction because they perform functions difficult for other materials to perform such as waterproofing, vapor barriers, sealants, adhesives, flexible fabrics, and as a base in composite matrices.

In synthetic polymers, three major categories exist:

- Thermoplastics: Sometimes just referred to as plastic, these polymers are characterized by being able to be rapidly recyclable, have a high degree of plasticity, and can be reformed by adding heat during processing. Thermoplastics can harden during curing, and be recycled and hardened again, although this process affects the alignment of the molecules reducing the quality of the material. Common thermoplastics include polycarbonate, polyester, polyethylene, polypropylene, polystyrene, polyvinyl chloride, and EFTE.

- Thermoset: This polymer becomes permanently hardened when heated or cured. The curing process of thermosets causes a chemical reaction that creates permanent connections between the material's molecular chains. Due to their molecular bond, thermosets have superior durability and will not change shape due to extreme thermal and chemical conditions once set, thus often outperforming other building materials. Generally, thermosets are not recyclable. Common thermoset polymers include formaldehyde, polyurethane, phenolic resins, and epoxy resins.

- Elastomer: Although there exist many natural rubbers, synthetic rubbers are more common in construction. As with thermoplastics, elastomers are recyclable. These polymers can be found throughout buildings due to their superior elastic range. Silicone and neoprene used for gasketing on window frames, sealants on exterior barrier walls, and adhesive for glazing are common applications. EPDM, an elastomer, is one of the most common roofing materials because of its plasticity and durability.

Prefabrication can employ all of these polymer types within the factory environment to develop elements of components, panels, and modules. Polymers used in applications of barriers, sealants, and adhesives require a great deal of care in installation. Many times enclosures fail not because of faulty material, but due to faulty installation methods. Controlled factory conditions in which quality control can be monitored ensure that polymers are installed properly. In addition, most polymers are toxic to human health, making the handling and disposal of such more controlled in a factory environment. Other than barriers, sealants, and adhesives, polymers for textiles and foils are used to develop flexible tensile fabric structures. These inevitably must be fabricated as a sophisticated system in the factory. A popular system today is EFTE foils.

Material advancements are allowing building skins to become ever more transparent and structural. EFTE foils can span great distances for relatively little material to produce long-span membranes. In addition to long-span capacity, EFTE pillows and other polymers are increasing in their thermal resistance. Users are also demanding more of their building skins including thermal performance and breath-ability. Multilayered performative skins that are thermally active ventilat-

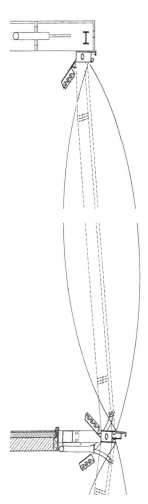

Figure 5.20 EFTE polymer foils are being employed for exterior enclosures. This section is of a pillow foil that when injected with air becomes an effective translucent thermal barrier for an enclosure.

5.2.5 Composites

Composites are the combination of two or more materials to modify the properties of both. Most often, there is a base or matrix material that provides the primary material properties. Another material is introduced to alter the performance, aesthetic, or capacity of the matrix material. The most common types of composites are concrete matrix composites in the way of glass fiber and carbon fiber reinforced concretes (GFRC and CFRC) previously discussed; metal matrix composites, including base metal alloying in which fibers of different metals are introduced to a matrix metal such as stainless wires in aluminum; and polymer matrices (GFRP and CFRP) are also becoming more common. The most prevalent composite polymer matrices are thermoset resins. The process of manufacturing elements in composites determines the strength and purpose of the composite. This is related to the arrangement of the reinforcing to the matrix or orientation of reinforcing to the base. These orientations may include one direction, cross-laminated, random whisker pattern, and others. Polymer-based composites use pultrusion, or the process of fibers being drawn through a resin bath and then "pulled" through a die that shapes the saturated fiber.[16]

ing, heating, cooling, and radiating, present many opportunities for design and thermal comfort, but also offer opportunities to generate energy. Integrated PV, wind, and yet-discovered renewable energy sources will all allow building skins to perform greater functions in ecology and energy generation. As these technologies continue to develop, prefabrication will have to be implemented in order to control the quality of these systems. At the level of lower budget projects, prefabrication also has the capacity to increase quality so that standard wall systems are better built with layers interacting in the manner designed.

 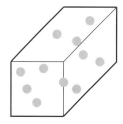

Figure 5.21 Composite is composed of a base matrix and the introduction of a secondary material. Composites are classified by: L—reinforcing describes fibers that are strategically oriented to increase the strength of the matrix, and R—particle inclusion by which the matrix is changed at its base throught he manipulation of the mix.

5.3 Method

The manufacturing process has been an interest of contemporary architects as a source of inspiration for possible geometry designed, materials developed, and finishes achieved. Manufacturing methods vary according to material and desired manipulation, however, there are generalized methods by which materials are tooled to achieve a desired output. Manufacturing here is used to describe machines, labor, and tools to create products for market. This is a broad definition that includes fabrication or the process of taking goods to develop prefabricated elements. Manufacturing can be categorized into four general areas that often overlap and, in some cases, are not entirely clearly delineated.

5.3.1 Machining

This is the process of removing material through a mechanical operation. Machining tools include saws, drills, mills, routers, and lathes. Saws cut straight lines using circular blades. Blades have teeth that are precisely defined to achieve a separation of material in one axis. This can be used in woodworking, metal manipulation, and even cutting stone. In order to achieve angled cuts and curves, additional axes of direction may be introduced, but sawing is still generally used for long straight operations of material removal. There are three methods of CNC machining:

• Water-jet cutting uses high water pressure to deliver abrasives that cut through material. This technology is extremely precise, delivering etching and cutting in the x-y axis, respectively, while simultaneously being able to cool the material. Metals, for example, can be easily cut without thermal stresses being induced and pieces can be cut without being held down by clamps.

• Plasma cutting is similar to water jet and is used on metals and ceramics. Plasma uses concentrated heat to cut at precisions of thousandths of an inch. Although it is quick and accurate, the heat can deform thin sheet metal. However, it is ideal for cutting thick plate steel up to 3 in. that will be finished later.

• Laser cutters also work in the x-y axis, removing material through a light amplification by stimulated emission of a radiation (laser) beam of light.

In comparing the three CNC processes, plasma cutting is the most affordable but has issues with heat. Laser cutting is more flexible and more precise than plasma, but still has issues with heat-induced deformation. Water-jet cutting machines are just as flexible, but do not cause discoloration or deformation from heat. However, water-jet cutting is slower and requires greater maintenance.

Drills are one-axis machines that mechanically cut by a rotating bit being pressed in a vertical direction. CNC-controlled drills locate material for the drill to automatically make holes and tap threads for connections in more than three directions. Punching is used in sheet metal and is capable of making simple holes in any pattern at a maximum diameter or size of the thickness of the material being punched. Milling and routing machines use a head that holds bits that cut in a circular fashion. The bits have multiple abrasive edges to remove material. Milling and routing is the most flexible of operations of machining. Today, CNC mills are available in six axes, able to rotate in the x, y, and z and many other directions in order to achieve curvature in wood, metal, stone, foam, or virtually any other material. This has become the tool of choice for most CAD/CAM outsourcing companies that perform complex geometric manufacturing.

Figure 5.22 Machining metal, wood, and polymer sheet can be two-dimensionally cut with a laser cutter. This laser cutter is a smaller version of what is found in many manufacturing shops.

Figure 5.23 A telltale sign of wood laser cut sheet material are black edges that have been burned by the radiation of the laser.

Lathes turn the base material around one axis while a tool engages the material to remove and create circular defined elements, tapered pieces, and cut threads on a length of dowel material. Grinding and sanding remove material by abrasives. This can be manually controlled to finish an element that has been CNC tooled or is controlled by CNC to achieve a precise dimensional and aesthetic finish.

5.3.2 Molding

This is the process of deforming, casting, and pressing. Punching may be included in this group as well. The processes of molding are defined by the type of stresses that are induced into the workpiece while in its cold state. The deformation of the piece as material moves from its elastic to plastic state causes a permanent deformation and desired shape. The deforming operation is used for sheet, wire, and tubes, which include operations of cold forming through compression or tension, shear forming, and bending. Bulk forming includes operations of drawing, rolling, forging, and extruding. Although primarily used

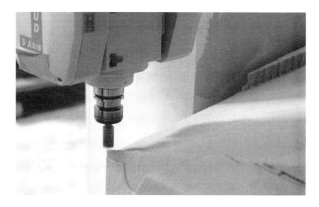

Figure 5.24 A six-axis milling machine is able to cut nearly any material. This mill is 3D precision cutting foam at 3-Form in preparation for a vacuum-forming process with resin polymers.

in cold forming, heat-applied methods also exist for polymer and soft metals materials such as aluminum that are extruded or pultruted.

Pressworking is the process of shaping sheets of metal in a die. This involves either shearing or cutting to make the shape of the piece that will then be formed through bending. Presswork is an alternative to CNC cutting tools, but can be used for repetitive processes that do not require customization of the aforementioned. Blanking is the process of shearing the sheet metal to create a shape. The piece may be trimmed or shaved to get a fine edge. The pieces are then bent by means of folding, twisting, or manipulating through crate shapes. Different bending operations exist where again a die is used to bend sheet or plate metal. Stamping is a power punch that forces a flat blank into a die cavity. This can be used to create shapes such as auto pans. Cold stamping and hot stamping are both used for thinner or thicker sheet metal. Stretch forming is similar to bending, but changes the thickness of the material through force of a hydraulic ram while applying heat to create unique custom panels.

Bulk forming includes drawing, forging, and extruding. Bulk forming relies on a great deal of heat and force to create form. CNC processes are not used as much for bulk forming, but the operations are still widely used today. Drawing pulls rods and tubes through a series of dies to reduce the material's size or change the sectional shape. This can be done in cold or hot form. Similarly, extrusion is the same process but the material is pushed rather than pulled. This is an ideal operation for long and straight elements of curtain walls in aluminum. Forging is hammering to create parts while heat is added. It is not as precise as other methods but it is still used in traditional craft-based metal works.

Casting uses a material in fluid state poured into a negative (mold) to achieve a desired 3D object. Casting processes use expendable molds, which are destroyed after having been used once. Molds tend to be constructed in wood or plaster. Reusable molds allow for many casts. Die casting uses steel or other hard materials that can be reused for multiple casts. The casting dies are created through CNC milling ma-

chines for precision. Casting creates a rough shape that in most cases must be finished by machining. Sand casting processes use expendable molds as well, but require more simplified forms. This has been employed in industrial applications; however, it is also used in larger architectural applications when other casting methods are not accessible. Die casting is a common method of forming parts by forcing hot metals under pressure into reusable molds. Vacuum casting removes air pockets that are sometimes contained in the fluid during the casting process.

Injection molding is used primarily with thermoplastic polymers. It is a form of die casting that can result in a variety of objects. Two die plates sandwich polymer material to create a shape. The interior space, or the impression, defines the formal shape and final finish. Most common polymer objects we use today are injection molded. Another common method of molding polymers is thermoforming or vacuum forming. This is primarily used for thin sheets of thermoplastic or heated thermosets and polymer composites. The sheet is pulled close to a mold within a vacuum bag or suctioned mold to create the desired shape.

Figure 5.25 This small suction-molding machine was developed to produce skateboards from carbon-fiber polymer composite (CFPC). Air pressure pulls the die plates together to form the board.

Figure 5.26 The fabrication process at 3-Form using heated thermoplastic couched in a sandwich die to be bagged and vacuum formed. These complex dies were created on a six-axis CNC mill.

Molds are made of foam, ceramic, wood, or wax, depending on the temperature and type of polymer. Blow molding or compression molding is a process used for thermosets in which objects are blown into dies to fill a volume or cavity.

5.3.3 Fabrication

This is the process of taking the previous operations of manufacturing, including machining and molding, to create fabricated elements for buildings. Fabrication is the largest of the categories often including some of the steps of molding and machining. Fabrication is the final process before a product is released for use. The key feature that defines fabrication from the other processes of manufacturing is the concept of fastening. "Joining," or bringing two or more manufactured pieces together, can be done through a myriad of methods. The general categories of fastening include mechanical, weld, and adhesive.

- Mechanical fastening uses metal-based bolts, screws, rivets, nails, and staples. Mechanical fasteners cause pieces to be affixed to one another

through the force imposed by the fastener. Just as important as the fastener is the preparation of the pieces to be fastened. The size of holes to be drilled or punched and the tolerance of the joining are important considerations in evaluating the joining method. Joining with mechanical fasteners can also be a source of architectural expression, illustrating the method of attachment. Mechanical fastening can increase the capacity of an offsite-fabricated building to be disassembled and reassembled later. A detailed explanation of fasteners is beyond the scope of this book and exists in many other sources.

- Welding is the process of joining parts without mechanical fasteners. This is done on metals through the process of heating the parent metals and allowing filler to join the pieces together permanently. Brazing and soldering are similar to welding but are used at lower temperatures and for metals such as lead, tin, and silver. Welding is used for structural and higher loaded conditions in which pieces need to be affixed. Various processes exist for welding including gas welding, the oldest and most traditional, and arc welding, which is most common today using both MIG and TIG welding procedures. The types of welds that can be used include spot welding for lapped pieces; tack welding and structural welds of fillet; and penetration welding. Welding should be saved for factory operations. Welding machines or robots that perform a variety of spot and arc operations speed up this process in the shop.

- Adhesives are glues that join materials together in a bonding action. They are generally used in lighter load application, but many advanced high-performing adhesives are available today for greater structural capacity. In joining pieces, adhesives work best over larger surface areas, thus lapped joints and adjacent pieces are joined with a lap at the butt to ensure adhesion. Butt joints with adhesives should be avoided. Adhesives are more common in glass, ceramics, woods, and polymers. In many cases, they do not allow for easy disassembly or recycling.

5.4 Product

Building fabrication may be standardized or custom. However, these terms do not capture the complexity of the manufacturing and fabrication industry. Fabrication techniques vary with each project. The chief concerns in prefabrication for the fabricator are costs, lead times, and flexibility surrounding custom products. Four terms have emerged in the manufacturing industry to describe the levels of prefabrication completion and associated effort that will be

expended in manufacturing. These terms and definitions aid in helping project teams understand the scope of the project that is being discussed and developed. These include Made-to-Stock, Assembled-to-Stock, Made-to-Order, and Engineered-to-Order.

- Made-to-Stock (MTS): MTS products are best handled through inventory replenishment strategies. In order to keep inventory replenished, manufacturers have used standardizing, or reducing complexity and increasing repetition. Supplier-managed inventory has proven successful for some companies and projects, where suppliers take on the job of determining requirements, and maintaining and distributing materials. Examples of MTS products include warehoused building goods such as lumber, wood, steel, and aluminum sections, ceiling tiles, and panel material such as gypsum board or plywood.

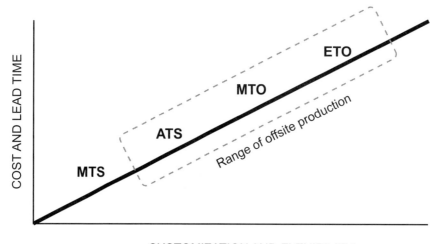

Figure 5.27 The terms Made-to-Stock, Assembled-to-Stock, Made-to-Order, and Engineered-to-Order are used in manufacturing to define the extent to which a product is customized. This is generally considered proportional to the cost and lead time necessary for production. Prefab architectural elements are considered ATS, MTO, and ETO. Sometimes MTS, (off-the-shelf) and MTO (flexible) are used exclusively to describe standardized versus prefab customized products.

• Assembled-to-Stock (ATS): ATS products have set designs and established standards. Many of the attributes of MTS are found in ATS, but customization is introduced. The principles of assembly line production and mass customization are often associated with ATS, where customers request variation within a set system of form and relationship of elements to one another. Outside of the building industry, computer companies and shoe companies are now offering customizable options for their standardized products. Examples of ATS fabrication in architecture include International Standard Building Units and Mobile Homes.

• Made-to-Order (MTO): MTO products are pulled forward through their supply process to arrive onsite just in time. These products are not sitting on shelves in MTS or have a set geometry as in ATS, but have determined the design and engineering options within a product. MTO are not made until the last responsible moment but do require more lead time than ATS products due to their increased variability from product to product sold. Examples include custom windows, doors, and other elements that have a myriad of options and are made custom for a project within a product line. Many modernist prefab systems on the market today represent MTO.

• Engineered-to-Order (ETO): ETO might also be called designed-to-order. These products represent the most complex and demanding products available. This is, by far, the largest category of building creativity and development in architecture. It also represents the greatest challenge for manufacturers and fabricators trying to determine how to deliver entirely custom products at competitive pricing. ETO products generally have the greatest lead times and the highest price points. Examples of ETO products for building include precast elements, facades, and other per-specification construction.

Architects specify MTS, ATS, MTO, and ETO elements for buildings. Looking at design through the lens of these manufacturing principles, prefabrication can be a tool by which the design team can control cost. If a product truly does not need to be custom, perhaps a more simplified method of delivery is possible. ETO producers operate shops that manufacture components, panels, and modules which are designed and engineered before production. Some prefabricators maintain large inhouse engineering departments as a holistic delivery of their services, while others outsource engineering and detailing. In addition, some use installers to place their ETO products in buildings. MTS, ATS, MTO, and ETO are not entirely exclusive. ETO uses MTS, ATS, and MTO in order to manufacture their products. In addition, a prefabricator that is primarily dealing with MTO can offer, on a limited basis, ETO products as well. Many prefabricators have their bread and butter and find a market niche in one specialty product.

Some products have become so specialized that design service providers have emerged to fill the market need. They include engineers of ETO products. They are the outsourced companies that produce steel detailing, specialized curtain wall consultation, tilt-up providers, modular dealers, and so forth. Another method in which ETO products are procured is in the form of specialist coordinators. These subcontractors do not actually design or manufacture prefabrication components, but provide a service of bringing together design, supply, and fabrication. More and more subcontractors are moving to this model, offering their services, but with no ability to manufacture. Ecosteel, a metal building system provider, performs engineering, design, and detailing services to coordinate the delivery and construction administration for their building systems. Due to this specialization, smaller manufacturing and construction firms (the majority in the United States can be described as such) can perform the production in a factory and the installation work onsite.

The typical information flow for ATS, MTO, and ETO in building construction has three major parts:

• Project acquisition: preliminary design and tendering

• Detailed design: engineering and coordination

• Fabrication: delivery and installation

The problems with this existing method is that it is labor-intensive, adding to the effort spent developing and maintaining documents as well as being fraught with errors that are not discovered until products are assembled onsite. These errors are extremely costly and can lead to further litigation down the road. Using integrated process leverages BIM technology and contracts for shared risk in order to allow project teams to streamline the delivery process. This will allow prefabrication of ATS, MTO, and ETO products to be more cost effective and accessible.

Finally, although the terms MTS, ATS, MTO, and ETO are used to describe the various levels of manufacture with their respective levels of cost, lead time, and flexibility, often MTS and MTO are used to distinguish between standardized and customized products.

5.5 Class

Prefabricated products may be closed or open. In closed classes, a single fabricator produces all the elements. The fabricator can develop entire buildings or partial elements, which must be coordinated with products fabricated by other producers. Automobile products, for example, are based on a closed class concept. Compared with the slight variations and interchangeability of automobile manufacturing, the difficultly with buildings is the uniqueness of each iteration. Closed class buildings are proprietary and the range of design options can be too limiting given a specific location context of the site.

Open classes offer the possibility of using products from different manufacturers that are not allotted to a single building purpose. This nonproprietary approach allows elements to be combined as required. This strategy should not be confused with the traditional method of selecting from a catalog of elements. The question is how to increasingly make something that is open but also specific. In many cases elements that are "open" are combined to make elements that are "closed." An example is in a steel load-bearing frame that is closed being combined with an infill fit-out that is open.[17]

The assumption may be that the more prefabricated the element is, the more closed it becomes. This is not always the case, in fact, many modular systems are designed to be able to be manipulated, added to, and maintained during their lifecycle. In addition, modular systems may have chases, open floor cavities, and access panels designed within the system to allow for easy change-out of systems and upgrades. The difference in designing open versus closed systems is to accommodate inevitable additions, upgrades, and maintenance throughout the life of the project with the end goal to have the building be reconfigured for reuse, relocated for reuse, or disassembled for reuse of components.

5.6 Grids

Grids are a geometric system of organization allowing building components and prefabricated elements to have standard dimensions. These are generally based on square and rectangular organizations thus creating straight components, flat panels, and box-like modules, although not necessarily. Structural systems are often placed on an axial grid, while panels and modules are developed on a modular grid.

• Axial grids use a central axis of a building element that is in line with the reference grid. In steel construction, W-sections are placed on grid lines, irrespective of the dimensions of the structural section. Although this is effective from a design perspective, it can present problems in coordinating how other materials and elements combine with the frame. If each column, beam, or structural element is a different dimension, a 2D and 3D grid loses its capacity to have standardized panel or infill elements associated with the frame in a standardized connection. Specialized connections will have to be accommodated at each joining of primary structural system on an axial grid with other enclosure and interior systems.[18]

• Modular grids are based on the actual location and dimension of the building elements. This takes into account the three-dimensional reality of the elements, including their height, width, and thickness. Modular grids are therefore primarily used in panel and modular systems. Modular grids in the United States are based on 2-ft increments. This is because the most basic MTS products are manufactured in 2-ft dimensions including 4 ft × 8 ft sheets of plywood, 2-ft increment lengths of studs, and so on.

Various building systems may use different grids. For example, an axial grid may represent the location and relationship between load-bearing frame elements, while an internal fit-out grid determines the location of

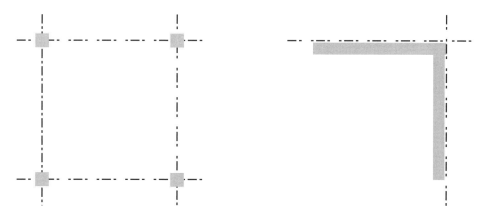

Figure 5.28 There are two different types of organizational grids in building construction: Left: *Axial* grids organize building frames at the center of structural members while Right: *Modular* grids organize buildings on face of the structure, enclosure, or any other defining building element.

all space-enclosing or defining elements. A services grid may be used for highly sophisticated service systems such as dropped ceilings or raised floors that allow plenum spaces for utility runs. Any building systems—structure, enclosure, services, space, and even finishes and furniture—may have their own grid logic. This requires scrupulous dimensional coordination between the different building systems and the elements that support them.[19]

The relationship between structural elements and fit-out elements present a standard negotiation on any project, but becomes an especially potent topic with regard to prefabricated architecture. The main structure is usually a frame with non-load-bearing in-fill enclosure panels, room modules, or interior non-load-bearing partitions. This creates the capacity to replace the infill systems at any given time, if detailed properly. Also, the location of structural frame and in-fill determines the layout of interior spaces to some degree. Integrating structural frames (embedding) within other systems is an option, aligning one face with the other system, or separating the systems entirely. In prefabrication this must be coordinated seamlessly, especially when one system is site-built and another is fabricated offsite.[20]

chapter 6   Elements

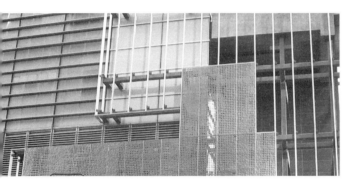

Elements of prefabrication refer to the form or configuration of the output. *Components, panels,* and *modules* are general categories in which buildings are fabricated or manufactured offsite and assembled. These categories are not industry standard names, as no hard, fast rules exist to categorize prefabrication. The definition of components, panels, and modules can be confusing. For example, panels for building interiors are sometimes referred to as modular wall systems. This is not to be confused with modular building, which uses entire finished modules that are set onsite. Categorization of components, panels, and modules is simply an organizational method to describe a prefabricated element that is more or less finished before arriving onsite.

In general, it is desirable from an efficiency standpoint to move to manufacturing larger components, panels, and modules to a greater degree of finish so that on-site erection is faster. However, in some cases, such as larger structural frames, the chunking of elements is not desirable, nor feasible, until on the jobsite. Rarely are components, panels, or modules discrete systems; rather they are a combination of elements that may be employed to accomplish the functions

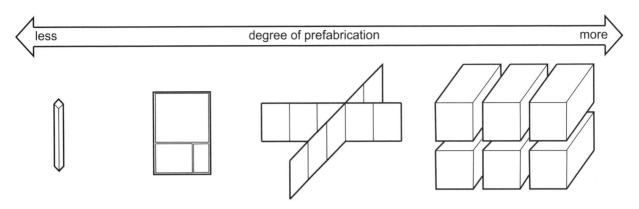

Figure 6.1 Prefabrication can be classified by the extent to which elements are completed prior to assembly onsite. *From left to right: materials, components, panels, and modules.* Generally, the benefits of prefabrication can be realized as projects move to increasingly greater degrees of prefabrication.

and aesthetic goals of the project. Panel construction has levels of finish at 60 percent while most modular systems are finished to 85 percent. Fully finished modules have a level of prefabrication up to 95 percent, leaving the remaining 5 percent for onsite foundation work and utility hookups.[1] Jennifer Siegal, architect from southern California, uses a model in which the fabricator takes the project from manufacture through installation, but also includes everything within a 5-ft radius of the house. Therefore, it could be said that outside of onsite landscaping and utilities from the street to the immediate location of the building, the facility is 98 to 100 percent handled by an offsite fabrication company in a turn-key contract.

6.1 Components

Componentized prefabrication allows for the greatest degree of customization and flexibility within the design and execution phases. Components, however, become numerous on a construction site and are difficult to account for, therefore in a prefabrication method, the responsibility becomes one of the design and production team to ensure that the system

is well defined from the beginning. This may require a method for design communication that begins to present "typical" conditions. Using a BIM environment, especially with componentized elements for structure, enclosure, and so forth, allows for an accounting of the elements and their relationship to one another. Componentized systems also require that more joints, connection, and thus more chances for misalignments, water and air infiltration, and quality can be reduced. Componentized systems include wood kits, metal building systems, and precast concrete construction.

6.1.1 Wood Kits

Wood or timber frames are quickly and efficiently fabricated and assembled. Frames today can be manufactured with custom joints, many of which now include metal fasteners. Heavy timber frames are less common in the United States, but can be seen readily in Scandinavia, especially in Finland, where the culture of wood framing has a deep tradition and is used for standard construction as well as specialized building types. In the United States, however, timber frame companies primarily serve the market of lodges and exposed timber construction public buildings. These types of structures can be found throughout the East Coast, Pacific Northwest, and Mountain West as reclaimed timber, beetle-infested timber, and new-growth wood is harvested for buildings that communicate a particular design aesthetic. Timber systems often are combined with infill panels to provide lateral resistance and enclosure to the exterior. Timber framers may or may not produce these infill panels, depending on the specifications and qualifications of the manufacturer.

Euclid Timber Framing is a custom timber manufacturer and erector near Park City, Utah, on the back of the Wasatch Mountain Range. Euclid has built its business on heavy timer luxury homes and lodges that surround the ski resorts in northern Utah. Euclid uses specialized equipment from Germany to CNC tool timbers. Kip Apostol, the president of Euclid, is also the U.S. dealer of Hundegger, a CNC wood tooling saw. He is a seller, distributor of units as well as parts, installer, and servicer of machines throughout the United States. Developed nearly 30 years ago in Germany, Hundegger machines are considered the "Rolls Royce of CNC timber tools," owning 90 percent of the market share worldwide for timber tooling.

Every day wood kit companies are making the transition to the CNC machines as they offer versatility, precision, and speed. Originally built for dimensional lumber, the K2 Hundegger machine can tool any piece that is 24.5 in. × 48 in. × any length. This includes components that are dimensioned and logs. With this equipment, a new industry is emerging in the United States dealing in precut timbers. Half a dozen outsourcing companies in the United States precut using Hundegger equipment for other timber frame suppliers, cutting specialized joinery timbers for post and beam high-end lodges and houses, as well as pole barns.

The PBA machine by Hundegger, developed nearly 10 years ago, was built to service laminated structural and enclosure panels used widely in Europe. A patented MHM system—standing for massive holz mauer, or translation: solid wood wall—is a laminated timber panel that uses the orientation of planks joined with aluminum fasteners to form a structural solid wall. MHM systems can be used alone or in combination with frames. Hundegger equipment is able to prepare panels through the tasks of cutting, pressing, and nailing panels. The soft aluminum nails allow panels to be machined by the PBA in the factory. The PBA machine will also tool the panel for custom joinery between panels or frame to panel. Panels up to 16 ft × 14 ft may be tooled, but this is often too large for handling. Usually, the PBA is used to tool two 8-ft × 14-ft panels for loading and unloading safely. Wood used for the panels can be low grade, as the solidarity of lamination adds strength. Therefore, wood sources may include new-growth soft wood, recycled timber, beetle kill, or burned wood from forest fires.

Hundegger CNC machines are entirely digitally operated. The machines are run on software that can accept all major CAD programs. A setup requires 15 minutes, and machining constitutes 10 seconds of cut time on average. The machines have the capacity to preplane, cut, assemble, and postplane. An inkjet printing function allows for bar codes, layout lines, and/or sequencing to be printed in an inconspicuous place and can be sanded off after installation. The tool may also engrave this information if the timbers or panels are finished before installation onsite.

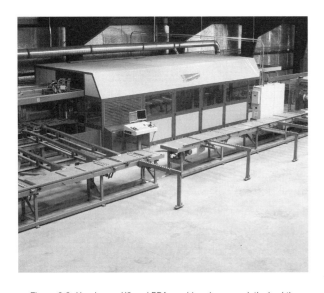

▲ Figure 6.2 Hundegger K2 and PBA machines have revolutionized the CNC wood fabrication industry. These machines are being used in Europe to produce large, solid wall systems.

MHM walls also have a thermal performance benefit. Joshua Bellows at Euclid has been performing research in preparation for the company producing an MHM system for the United States. He states that MHM panels have an 80 percent thermal performance increase over standard construction in Germany. The PHPP, or Passive House Planning Package, developed in 2007, is rapidly becoming a performance engineering rating system for buildings that deliver efficiencies to reach net zero energy. Projects for DOE Solar Decathlon and a few buildings in the United States have now been designed to this standard and are seeing positive results. This strategy is simply to superinsulate the walls to R-60 with spray-in foam insulation at 12 to 14 in. This amount of insulation is costly. The MHM system conversely uses no insulation in its layering but continues to perform well in research studies. A recent

house in Germany was awarded the highest rating by the Passive House Standard.[2]

Although CNC machines have increased the capacity of timber prefabricators to produce frames and panels, skilled craftspeople of timber framing continue to play an important role. In order for the MHM panel system to succeed in the United States, an industry that understands the technology and its capacities will have to emerge. Currently there are no MHM systems that have been fabricated or installed in the United States, but research is showing that this is one of the fastest growing components in the building industry.[3] Kip Apostol at Euclid currently maintains Hundegger PBA machines for only 12 manufacturers in the United States. Although these companies have the capacity to tool MHM components, the equipment is being used for structural insulated panel machining.[4] In Germany and areas of Europe, this technology has become commonplace. Andrea Deplazes argues that timber construction in Germany has emerged in the past 20 years from the tradition of onsite-framed lumber to a tradition of MHM panels for walls, roofs, and floors. "The 'basic element' of modern timber construction is therefore, the slab, and no longer the linear wood member. The slab consists of three or more layers of sawn timber, for example, laminations or strips obtained from a relatively low-quality wood."[5]

Wood is an extremely versatile and environmentally responsible material. It is one of few renewable structural materials. Under wise and prudent forestry practices, wood can service buildings for many years. Wood and timber prefabrication methods will continue to evolve based on the ingenuity of the designers, manufacturers, fabricators, and

Figure 6.3 MHM, or solid wood wall, is a component and panel prefab system that has been developed in Europe. Using Hundegger, CNC machinery panels are laminated and tooled quickly based on digital information. The panels are used for walls, floors, and roof applications. There is great potential for this technology growth in the U.S. residential and commercial market.

builders. Experts in manufacturing and fabrication are continually emerging in the discipline, but rarely in the design fields. Deplazes states, "It is therefore not the timber specialists, timber technologists,

biologists or performance specialists who are being put to the test here, but instead, first and foremost, the architects."[6] One thing is clear, that panel construction in SIPs or in MHM is more expensive than standard light framing, but with it comes quality and structural/thermal performance that cannot compare to stick framed onsite methods. More on SIP construction, which has become prevalent in the United States, is discussed in the panel section later in this chapter.

6.1.2 Metal Building Systems

Metal building systems are steel framed and clad with metal corrugated sheets that have been formed from cold form presses. These steel frames are inherently rigid, either as moment frames or braced frames, and are extremely light. Metal building systems have been used as far back as 1908 for small industrial buildings, but it was not until the late 1940s that the metal building industry began to make significant inroads into the nonresidential low-rise market. The metal building industry has roots in decades of precedents including the early Gold Rush housing, English shed buildings, and most especially, the Quonset Huts during the war era. During this time, cold forming of sheet metal panels were generally galvanized, attached to a 4:12 slope roof and completely utilitarian in function and aesthetic. The 1960s welcomed prepainted panels in many colors.

Until recently, architects have frowned upon metal building systems because since the 1950s and 1960s, metal buildings have been sold and erected through an authorized builder, not to a customer. The authorized builder in most cases is a specialized general contractor. This specialization allows the metal building to increase in quality while maintaining cost, but it also leads to a lack of variation in the product. Authorized dealers became so prolific in the 1950s that metal building system companies met in Chicago and organized the Metal Building Manufacturers Association. In 1968, the Metal Building Dealers Association was organized. In 1983, the MBDA changed its name to the Systems Builders Association.[7] Hybrid Architects in Seattle and Anderson Anderson Architects in San Francisco have used metal building system ideas of efficiencies and freedom of the structural frame and infill to infuse with architectural solutions.

One of the major benefits of metal building systems is the research that has been developed to size and detail the steel, its manufacturing, digital-to-fabrication process, shipping, and install. These standards make the design process much more streamlined. Architects working metal building systems should consult suppliers to develop the system according to their desires. Deviations from the standard system may present cost increases, and offsite/onsite coordination is needed in order to maximize the efficiencies without sacrificing quality of aesthetic and construction. Benefits of metal building systems include a deep cavity between structure and exterior and interior surfaces measuring upward of 12 to 14 in., depending on depth of columns and girders. This allows for large amounts of thermal insulation to be placed in the envelope cavity. In addition, large portals and spans are achievable with the steel frame so that surfaces may be opened where desired for windows and doors. The fenestration systems are detailed in the shop and fabricated and erected onsite as a kit. It is estimated that over 50 percent of all single-story, nonresiden-

tial construction are metal buildings today. Within the metal building market, what might be considered warehousing or industrial buildings only constitute slightly more than 34 percent. The use of metal building systems for banks, schools, churches, and housing is continually growing.[8]

There are two major components of metal building systems:

1. Structure, including superstructure frame, infill light-gauge steel in cavity and

2. Exterior enclosure wall panels

The primary structure of a metal building system is a frame. The types of framing are categorized as follows:

- Single-span rigid frame: No interior columns, spans from 120 ft standard to 200 ft nonstandard, tapered members or not.

- Tapered beams: Moderate clear spans, straight columns and tapered girders to maximize depth at mid-span. Top flange is sloped and bottom flange is horizontal. Column to girder is a rigid moment connection.

- Continuous beam: Post and beam, interior columns, girder sizes reduced, more economical, interior columns straight, and exterior tapered. Girders are also tapered.

- Single-span truss: Same as tapered and continuous beam, but roof is supported by trusses rather than girders.

- Lean-to: Relies on adjacent structures for lateral loads. Canopies or simple additions to existing or new metal building systems are included.

Wall panels or cladding for metal buildings are classified as field or factory systems. Girts are cold-formed "C" or "Z" sections that attach to steel columns and girders/beams of the primary frame.

The girts may attach to the flange or web. They do not perform structural functions, except to support wind loading of pressure and suction on exterior cladding. Girts are field-assembled but can

ECO STEEL

Eco Steel, formerly Northern Steel International, is not a manufacturer, but a dealer who provides metal building system contracts for foundation design, structural design, delivery, and erection, including windows and doors and installation of exterior walls and roof. The goal of this system is to dry-in the enclosure as soon as possible so subcontractors can finish out the interior. The system is more robust than wood construction with wind and seismic ratings, as well as high R-value walls and roofs that have no thermal gaps. The insulated panel construction is offered in thicknesses from 2 to 6 in. with insulation values in PUR from 16.26 to 48.78. Panel widths come in 24 to 42 in. and the insulation material is foamed in place, isocyanurate, with a nominal density of 2.4 lbs/cu ft. Panels are attached to girts with fasteners; however, the joining of the panels conceals the fastener. The finish on panels may be painted metal, corrugated, ribbed vertically, stucco, and quartz sand finishes on the exterior. This panel may be exposed on the interior as a smooth metal surface or it may be finished out with traditional gypsum wallboard.

Eco Steel has excelled at taking a standardized metal building system and customizing it to architects' design specifications. The company uses BIM modeling for architectural and structural configuration, sizing, and detailing in order to communicate with the manufacturers of the steel. This allows for construction to be simulated before it occurs on the jobsite, reducing risk and error. Eco Steel takes BIM models from architects, or develops their own from 2D drawings. All of the customized steel is prepared, predrilled, and trucked to the site for erection. As a result of this process, Eco Steel has an average 30- to 45-day

Figure 6.4 Eco Steel works with architects to develop innovative solutions to employing metal building system technology. For this two-story house: Left: Steel frame is erected onsite while Middle: custom production of polyurethane-injected composite metal panels and Right: installation of metal panels for exterior wall and roof enclosure.

continued

lead time from contract and receipt of final design drawings to production and delivery. Eco Steel provides the engineering in collaboration with the architect, including sizing and detailing for fabrication.

On average, the company's buildings are coming in at 20 to 30 percent cheaper than cobbled together buildings with many different systems. Architect Steven Wagner, in collaboration with Joss Hudson at Eco Steel, designed Forj Lofts, a multifamily complex in Rohoboth Beach, Delaware. Partnering with Eco Steel allowed the architect to design a metal building system efficiently. The process eliminated subcontractors from the construction site and cut out many of the subs associated with standard multifamily housing. Cost was controlled because the manufacturer provided fixed costs, initially offering transparency to the process. Eco Steel works on projects that prefer speed, predictably, and consistency of quality throughout the delivery in favor of low-bid procurement methods.[10]

Figure 6.5 Forj Lofts in Delaware is a two-story multifamily housing project that Eco Steel developed in collaboration with architect Steven Wagner. The project came in 20 to 30 percent cheaper than traditional methods due to schedule and material reductions.

be factory-assembled as well. Girt systems have an outer skin of cold-formed sheet metal that is corrugated for rigidity and, in some cases, an interior sheet metal panel as well. The liner panel is used for finishing the interior in architectural applications and to encase insulation. Factory systems are foam-injected, rigid enclosure panels that are affixed to frames or girts. Advantages to field and factory assembly of metal building wall panel systems include:

• Field: cold-formed sheet metal skin and layers added for insulation and interiors

○ Rapid erection of panels

○ Competition of many manufacturers who produce these systems

○ Replacement is simple

○ Opening created easily

○ Light-weight erection, no cranes or heavy equipment

○ Large foundations and heavy spandrels are not required

○ Acoustic surface can be added to interior easily.

• Factory: interior liner panels, exterior metal panels, and insulation

○ Light weight

○ Hard surface interior liner

○ Side lap fasteners are normally concealed for clean aesthetic

○ Documented panel characteristics, testing

○ Reputable manufacturers[9]

6.1.3 Precast

Precast construction is the casting of concrete components offsite in a plant and shipping to site for assembly. Precast Concrete Institute is the trade organization that certifies precast operations under stringent quality control of plants throughout the United States. There exist two primary distinctions in precast: architectural precast and structural precast. Architectural precast refers to any element, whether structural or not, that has a finish that is more than a standard gray. This usually means that precast will be seen, leaving it exposed at building occupancy. Finishes that are available with architectural precast include brick facing tiles on nonstructural cladding panels, and textures such as aggregate face, acid wash, and sand blast. A more recent development is bar relief, created with foam that is milled elsewhere and used as casting faces for panels. This uses rubberized form liners for release leaving a defined smooth and custom surface.

Wood forms with rubberized form liners can last 50 to 100 pours and are more affordable to manufacture than steel forms. Steel can last thousands of pours, are better quality, but must be manufactured by a steel fab shop and can therefore be quite expensive. Fiberglass formwork lies in the middle of durability and cost of wood and steel. Architects should specify the type of formwork depending on the number of pours to justify the initial setup cost. In order to produce special surface and detailed components, concrete material innovations including admixtures for water reduction of high volume pours have been developed. For quick curing, precast concrete elements are made with Type III Portland cement and a high early additive. In addition, the precast process may include adding heat to accelerate the hardening of the concrete and adding moisture for full hydration of the Portland cement and water. Precasting plants are able to produce fully cured elements from laying of prestressing or reinforcing strands to removal of finished elements from the beds in a 24-hour cycle. These developments have allowed precast to meet the needs of speed, cost, superior strength, and aesthetic variation in construction.

When using concrete construction, the selection of precast over site-cast has obvious benefits. Precast is carried out at ground level where beds may be dispersed and casting occurs concurrently. Mixing and placing concrete in a plant is highly mechanized and carried out in sheltered conditions when necessary. Concrete used in precast is generally stronger at 5,000 psi when compared with onsite concrete at 2,500 to 3,500 psi. Reinforcing steel is also stronger in precast than site-cast at 270,000 psi prestressing.

The large majority of precast today is prestressed. In this operation, strands of steel, or tendons, are stretched with a hydraulic jack prior to concrete being poured. Embeds and weld plates are placed during curing in addition to welded wire fabric and other reinforcing as necessary. Ten to twelve hours after pouring, the concrete has reached a compressive strength of 2,500 to 4,000 psi, and has appropriately bonded to the steel reinforcing. The next day the elements are released with the strands cut between the bulkhead, placing force on the concrete and not the reinforcing cage. This can cause the element to camber if designed as such. The components are loaded or stockpiled in preparation for shipment.

Less common, post-tensioning is the process of combining precast elements into larger assemblies onsite. This is done usually in long-span beams, girders, and tall shear wall applications. Post-tensioning uses tendon cavities placed in sections before casting in the factory so elements will meet onsite end to end. After assembly, the tendons are inserted into the aligned cavities horizontally or vertically, and tensioned with a hydraulic jack. Grout may be required to protect steel at joint conditions from corrosion. Methods for joining precast are in continual development. Joining is performed by the precast elements having weld plates with anchors cast at the plant. When the elements join onsite, they are attached with welding or bolting. The major frame of a precast system uses metal connections that are left exposed but when joined onsite are drypacked to ensure fire and corrosion protection. Bearing pads are inserted between concrete members at bearing points to mitigate grinding due to high stress, temperature movements, or loading. Bearing pads are polymer or elastomer based depending on the application and anticipated stress.

Besides joining precast components together, other components such as wall panels, facings, interior partitions, hangers, and the like must also be attached to the precast elements. Attachment methods are organized into three categories:

• Embed: An anchor bolt or anchor with weld plate is cast in the factory within the precast element. Embeds are the preferred method from both a quality of structure and aesthetic perspective. However, this requires strong coordination between the different systems of the building. In the factory, templates are used to place embeds while concrete is wet. In a fast-track project, coordination may not be possible at this level. Also, protrusions of embed plates and bolts may hinder shipping and damage connections before arriving to site. In this event, the other two methods are used.

- Epoxy set: This method uses a drilling and cleaning of the hole and then placing a bolt or hanger that is then set with anchoring cement, lead grout, or a thermoset polymer such as epoxy.

- Expansion anchor: This method also requires pre-drilling. An expansion anchor is placed into the cavity. The bolt, screw, or hanger is then placed within the anchor and when engaged expands to put pressure on the concrete and restrict its movement.

The erection of precast is similar to that of steel. Precasters claim that it is faster than structural steel framing because the deck is integral to the system. It is, of course, faster than onsite cast-in-place concrete because formwork is not site-customized and curing wait time is not necessary. James McGuire at Hanson Eagle Precast, a Heidelberg company in West Valley City, Utah, states that on a stadium project, precast saved the client an entire year in construction time.[11] The building was in a dense urban setting creating limited access by trucks. Precast allowed the Utah Jazz basketball team to begin a season early in their new downtown facility. Erection of precast can also take place under adverse weather conditions because curing is complete. Since concrete must not be cast in extreme temperatures or rain, site-cast concrete is at the mercy of the specific construction season.

Although precast is lightweight in comparison to site-cast, it is still heavier than wood and steel construction, making transportation from factory to site more difficult. Large sections of precast can be formed up to 12 to 14 ft in width, or the maximum legal dimension of a semitrailer. This also limits the possibilities for larger sections than the width of a deck of a double tee and makes offsite fabricated modules in precast difficult. The precast industry in the eastern United States is well established, therefore the precaster often will not also be the installer. In the West, this is quite the opposite. On difficult projects, deep coordination is necessary to establish a method for install before manufacture. For Hanson Eagle, they install 90 percent of all of their products. They prefer this method as it allows increased control of the product.

Precast can be shaped to form virtually any three-dimensional shape. Straight casting beds can present problems between how a component is designed and how it is formed, as the concrete shrinks making joining elements difficult onsite. Surface finishes and treatments cannot simply be applied to faces of parts but often have their own distinctive geometry, which may require subtraction of volume from the concrete itself. Stone cladding, brick patterns, and thermal insulation layers are common examples of considerations that may affect more than appearance, but also the assembly of precast. Larger elements in which different concrete types are necessary across a given sectional element for cost and performance must be considered. Structural analysis software exists for precast to check the elements' resistance to forces during the stripping, lifting, storage, transportation, and erection. These forces during this process differ from the designed forces included for building habitation.[12]

 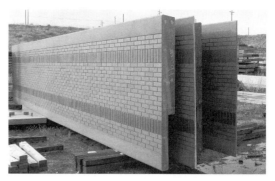

Figure 6.7 From left to right and top to bottom: Brick facing tiles being placed in bed before casting; brick facing precast cladding panel at the plant prior to shipping; professional basketball arena in downtown Salt Lake City built entirely out of precast elements saved over a year in construction time; column and floor plate precast system being erected onsite, prison modules installed onsite; and aashto beam transported on a tractor and articulated semitrailers.

PRECAST ELEMENTS AND SPECIFICATIONS[13]

- Solid flat slab
  - Width: varies; Depth/Span: $\frac{1}{40}$ of its span, ranging from 3.5 to 8 in.
- Hollow core slab
  - Width: 2, 4, and 8 ft; Depth/Span: 8 in./25 ft, 10 in./32 ft, and 12 in./40 ft
- Double tee
  - Width: 8 ft, 10 ft; Depth/Span: $\frac{1}{28}$ of span—depths include 12, 14, 16, 18, 20, 24, and 32 in.
- Single tee
  - Width: 8 ft, 10 ft; Depth/Span: 36 in./85 ft, 48 in./105 ft
- Beam and girders
  - Width: $\frac{1}{2}$ of depth. Depth/Span: $\frac{1}{15}$ of span for light loads and $\frac{1}{12}$ of span for heavy loads for rectangular, inverted tee, and L-shaped beams. Projecting ledgers on inverted-tee and L-shaped beams are usually 6 in. wide and 12 in. deep.
- Column: usually square but can be piers and rectangular
  - 10 in. column supports about 2,000 S.F. of area

    12 in. 2,600 S.F.

    16 in. 4,000 S.F.

    24 in. 8,000 S.F.
- Spandrels, cladding, walls, modules
  - Size is dependent on transportation regulations

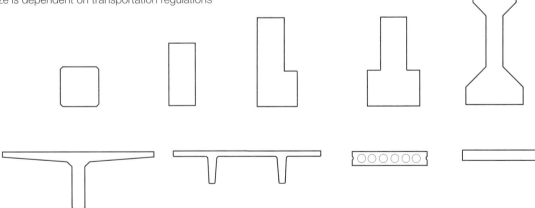

Figure 6.6 Although precast can be formed into virtually any shape specified, common profiles exist in the industry. The following are cataloged from Hanson Eagle Precast. Top Left to Right: Square Column, Rectangular Beam, L-Shaped Beam, Inverted Tee Beam, and Aashto Beam Single Tee. Bottom Left to Right: Single Tee, Double Tee, Hollow Core Slab, Flat Plate Slab.

6.2 Panels

Panels are planer elements used to build structural walls, floors, and roofs, load-bearing or non-load-bearing enclosures, and interior partitions. This section of the chapter will look at light panel wall systems common to the U.S. market including wood panelization, Structural Insulated Panels (SIPs), and light-gauge metal frame panels; non-load-bearing exterior glazing units and cladding panels; and tilt-up concrete construction.

6.2.1 Light Panel Systems

According to *Automated Builder*, a magazine that monitors the construction industry's use of prefabrication in housing, 56 percent of all residential construction in the United States is manufactured, modular, and panelized in technology. Panelized systems constitute the largest sector of the three, accounting for 43 percent of all prefabricated homes.[14] Panel systems for housing have been developed because of the flat nature of many building products such as metal and wood sheet material, interior finishing panels, and the ease of using the panel cavity for distribution of services such as plumbing and electrical lines. Although these potentials are present, they also present weaknesses in panel construction.

Michael J. Crosbie, professor at the University of Hartford, performed a study under a HUD grant in which panel systems were compared for their capacity to integrate utilities.[15] The study breaks panel systems for housing into four general categories of wood panels, SIPs, concrete panels, and metal panels. The study selected 15 systems for the test and evaluated them against 10 integration techniques that were individually scored. From this study, the researchers conclude that decisive factors in panel choice include:

- Panelized systems that offer factory integrated wiring and cable utilities and a finished product have the advantage of reducing installation time and complexity onsite while preserving the insulation value of the wall, which results in better energy performance. Preengineered panel systems with good utility integration do not require field changes.

- Panel systems that are designed to make utilities accessible after construction without damaging the panel or covering over the utility chases offer a significant advantage for future utility upgrades.

- Panel systems should integrate electrical wiring and preferably cable. It is not critical that the system include the integration of water piping because plumbing should not be installed in exterior walls. Pipes typically run through partition walls inside the house, and vertically through chases specified for their use.

- Panel systems that do not embed utilities in the panel's insulation core offer the best insulation integrity and are easy for utility upgrades after construction.

- Panel systems that have no visible interface are preferable, although integration techniques using decorative building components such as baseboards are a good choice.

- Panel manufacturers should ensure that integration systems are protected during the panel's transportation to the site.

6.2.2 Panelization

Panelization describes framing of light wood or light-gauge-metal-framed walls produced in a factory.

This process speeds up the delivery of walls to a site where framing crews install quickly when compared with onsite framing. The ideal behind panelizing, what would usually be a site-framing process, is to lower cost and increase speed. Ever more builders are becoming contractors, or paper pushers, who want every portion of a framed building to be delivered in one package. Sitting on a construction loan accrues interest. The faster contractors and developers can finish a house or small commercial building, even if the offsite construction methods are a bit more expensive, the return will be greater by finishing than investing in a less expensive method of delivery onsite. The response by prefabricated truss companies has been to deliver prefabricated light frame wall panel systems to fill this need.

Lumber panelizers have emerged throughout the western United States to serve the fast-growing markets of Phoenix, Las Vegas, areas of California, and the intermountain Denver, Salt Lake City, and Boise areas during the early 2000s. In recent years, as the economy has recessed, onsite framers have become affordable due to a lack of demand. Their bids have become so low that it is difficult for panelizers to compete. Burton Lumber in Salt Lake City has recently closed down their panelizing operations but finds that truss fabrication continues to maintain popularity. Burton states that the market was not infiltrated enough with panelization and immigrant labor has caused onsite-framing methods to be more affordable in the recent recession. Truss fabrication, however, has taken over more than 50 percent of the market years ago and therefore is more affordable to deliver than stick framed roofs. In addition, roofs tend to be more complex in geometry and factory production makes more sense for precision, accuracy, and quality.

Offsite panelization for light wood frame construction still makes good sense from a quality versus cost perspective, however. Larger projects that demand panels be erected quickly and in mass are continuing to see a market demand. Burton Lumber believes that just as prefabricated trusses emerged in the 1960s and did not take market share until the mid- to late 1970s, absorption of the cost of panelization will be seen during the second decade in this century, nearly 15 years after early adopters began using it in 2000. That being said, it is important to note that portions of the United States take to certain offsite methods better than others. Although California has been building with certain aspects of prefabrication, it continues to use onsite stick framing of roofs in many regions, much of this due to affordable immigrant labor.[16]

6.2.3 Structural Insulated Panels

Another common panelized wood system for residential and light commercial applications is Structural Insulated Panels. SIPs are a sandwich panel used as structure and enclosure and strictly infill enclosure for larger steel or concrete frame structures. SIPs are manufactured from varying thicknesses of two layers of oriented strand board (OSB) sandwiching an EPS (expanded polystyrene) or PUR (polyurethane) core. In addition to OSB, fiber cement, metal, gypsum board, and other materials are beginning to be introduced as sheathing for one side or the other in SIPs. Comparatively, SIPs have been tested and found to be stronger, more fire resistive, and a better insulator than conventional framing and insulation cavity wall systems in construction.

Architects, engineers, and design professionals have been designing and building stressed skin sandwich panels for nearly a century. Frank Lloyd Wright used a sandwich panel of sorts in the Usonian houses. The concept of a structural insulated panel began in 1935 at the Forest Products Laboratory (FPL) in Madison, Wisconsin. FPL engineers speculated that plywood and hardboard sheathing could bear a portion of the structural load in wall applications. Their prototypes were constructed using framing members within the panel, combined with structural sheathing and insulation. The panels were used to build test homes that were monitored for over 30 years, then disassembled and reexamined. During this time, FPL engineers continued to experiment with new designs and materials in an effort to attain several goals: improve energy efficiency, combat dwindling resources, and provide low-cost housing. In 1952, Dow produced the first commercially available SIP. It was not until the 1960s, when rigid foam insulation became readily available, that SIPs became affordable and accesible, but still they had difficulty gaining ground. In 1990, the SIPA (Structural Insulated Panel Association) was formed as a trade organization. Today, SIPs are a common building material, but continue to struggle breaking into some residential markets where cheap labor encourages onsite stick framing.

Undoubtedly the largest benefit to the SIP market was the advancement of CNC technology. Today SIPs are laid out digitally in the computer to maximize panel widths and heights. CAD/CAM allows panels to be precision cut, delivered, and erected. Most SIP manufacturers are also dealers, some even offer more robust contractor services of full SIP house kits with windows, doors, siding, interior finishes, and millwork. SIPs are prefabricated in the factory to specific sizes and cut openings so that onsite erection is fast and effective. Because SIPs are manufactured from sheets of OSB, standard dimensional widths are 4 ft actual. Lengths can vary but are based on 2-ft increments of 8, 10, and 12 ft with custom length increments up to 25 ft. Thicknesses of SIP panels are either 4.5 or 6.5 in. actual dimension from OSB face to OSB face for walls, and in EPS roof structures can be up to 12.25 in. in thickness dimension to accommodate larger spans and increased code requirement for roof R-values. This accounts for the thickness of the OSB and the standard cavity that the foam contains that is routed out for 2 × 4 or 2 × 6 to be couched between OSB sheets as a spline between panels. Splines using OSB inserts may also be used to connect one panel to the next. The final option for panel connection is a cam lock that provides an excellent tight connection and can be removed easily without nails. Cam locks are less common in SIPs today due to cost. Panels may be used as walls, floors, or roofs. Most manufacturers have span tables for rules of thumb in designing SIP buildings. A hired engineer or the manufacturer's engineer will have to provide final design on the SIP structure.

To accommodate electrical wiring, SIPs are manufactured with vertical and horizontal cylindrical chases. Manufacturers locate these according to the building layout and code requirements for outlet spacing. Other penetrations into or through the SIP wall and floor/roof may need to be made. In all of these conditions, once equipment or lines are run, expandable foam filler is necessary to ensure a tight envelope. Plumbing should be minimized on exterior wall locations in general, but for SIPs, exterior wall plumbing is nearly impossible.

Although 70 percent of the market share in SIPs is attributed to residential and light commercial. SIPs are also used for coolers, due to their superior insulation properties. SIPs lose 3 percent in efficiency while frame walls lose up to 25 percent, depending on quality of construction. Less lumber in the wall leads to minimal thermal bridging. Although SIPs are available with either a PUR foam core or EPS core, PUR foam is a far better insulator and has higher performing fire, flame, and smoke ratings. Unlike some blowing agents, a number of which are scheduled for phase-out by the Environmental Protection Agency (EPA), PUR foam is not a volatile organic compound and, hence, does not contribute to ozone depletion. SIPs made with PUR foam are also stronger than panels made with EPS and can withstand higher compression (axial), transverse (flexural), and raking (lateral) loads. While EPS is simply glued onto the outer skin material; injected polyurethane foam adheres to every surface (skin materials, top plates, cam locks, electrical boxes, etc.) to create a strong and durable bond between the foam and mating surface. Compared to other types of PUR, HFC-245fa polyurethane foam offers the best insulation and protection against moisture transport due to its density, cell structure, and good adhesion to the OSB skins.

The following are specifications of SIP panels compared to standard batt-insulated stick frame walls:

- 2 × 4 wall R-12

- 4.5 in. EPS R-17

- 4.5 in.PUR R-25

- 2 x 6 wall R-19

- 6.5 in. EPS R-21

- 6.5 in. PUR R-40

Some of the concerns with SIPs include high flexure. Therefore, care should be taken to ensure roof and floors are sized for deflection in addition to strength.

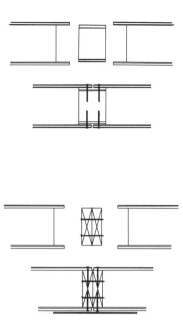

Figure 6.8 Typical 6-1/2 in. SIP details in plan: Top: SIP panel-to-panel spline joint is best for mitigating a thermal bridge; Middle: SIP panel-to-panel 2 × 6 spline joint is stronger, however, creates a thermal bridge; Bottom: corner joint.

Often a crane is necessary to set panels, adding to the cost of a smaller residential project considerably. Onsite, SIPs need to be kept flat, off the ground, and dry. SIPs should not be stored for a period over six days and during that time they must be at least 6 in. off the ground and covered with a breathable, waterproof tarp. A recent jobsite in Utah experienced damaged panels that were left uncovered during a snowstorm. Extreme heat can also cause damage. Lastly, due to their tight construction, air infiltration is a minimum with SIP buildings. Therefore, SIP systems require some sort of mechanical ventilation to bring fresh air into the structure and exhaust the moisture-laden or stale air to the outside. Often they can be combined with filter systems or other fresh air devices. According to PATH, the natural ventilation rate of SIP buildings should not be less than required by the local code or 0.35 ACH, when no local code exists.[17]

As with any new prefabrication technology, often design and building professionals are not equipped with knowledge to implement the technology. SIPs, a relatively simple technology, have had difficulty making an impact in Utah, for example. The closest manufacturers exist in Idaho and Montana. The Wasatch Front is a Seismic D Zone requiring special engineering for SIP-panel anchoring and hold-down locations. This difficulty alone has caused many ar-

Figure 6.9 SIP construction images of a 13-unit development in Park City, Utah, from left to right and top to bottom: SIP panels on a flat-bed trailer ready to be hoisted into location; SIP roof panel sections cut out onsite to make way for skylights; SIP roof panel in place; hoisting armature still attached.

chitects, engineers, builders, and especially owners to not adopt these panels over conventional framing methods. The author and a research team at the University of Utah are documenting the construction process of a 13-unit development that is built entirely out of SIP walls and roofs. The project was not originally designed for a SIP grid of 4 ft, nor does it take into consideration the structural capacity of SIPs, embedding walls with posts and double 2X members in order to provide adequate structure. Coordination between the SIP manufacturer and the architect was poor, adding to schedule delays and the difficulty with the installation of the SIPs. In addition, the framing subcontractor had not built with SIPs before, causing the first two houses to take nearly two weeks for panel erection. The rest of the units only took a few days each to be set up. The quantity of the project warranted the investment of the time required for the first couple of units. However, this case study represents the reluctance of many in the design and construction industry to move to offsite fabrication as the initial investment may not necessarily see a benefit and, in fact, may be a financial risk.[18]

6.2.4 Steel Panelization

Light-gauge-steel framed walls are usually employed as infill for commercial structures or materials to build interior partition walls. Being manufactured as panels in a factory allows metal panel systems to be quickly erected onsite, saving time and money. Minaean International Corp., based in Vancouver, Canada, has developed a light-gauge steel construction technology that has been used to erect buildings that are from four to eight stories within three months. In connection with a Hambro steel joist floor decking system, Minean's product, known as the "Artisan Quik Build," boasts high efficiency, and low manufacturing

costs for the developer. The prime niche for Artisan remains in buildings ranging from four to eight stories wherein the system achieves the highest amount of cost effectiveness combined with a stout structure providing sustainability, high sound and fire ratings, comparatively low construction duration, and minimal waste onsite.

The initial thrust of the company was to produce an offsite system for developing countries. This part of the company is still active; however, in 2000 they began developing a system of light-gauge wall panels for North American markets as an alternative to steel and concrete superstructure buildings. The 2004–2007 construction boom advanced the system, which uses prefabricated steel walls manufactured in a factory from rolled steel, put together on a hydraulic compression table and shipped to site. Although the panels are not finished on the exterior or interior, the simple act of prefabricating the walls saves weeks in a construction schedule.

Mervyn Pinto, CEO of Minean, says that his company considers this offsite system superior to other site-built framing methods.[19] In a four-story, 40,000 S.F. (10,000 S.F. per floor) building, prefabricated steel frame walls and floors took a total of seven working days per floor. This includes two days for fabrication and transport, and one day for system install per floor. The rest of the time was in pouring a concrete deck and curing. Clearly the system wins out from a schedule perspective over onsite methods. From a cost standpoint, prefabricating light-gauge steel frame panels is competitive with site framing at the four-to-eight-story residential and commercial range. On a recent three-story building in Portland, Pinto states the panels bid out at $2.00/S.F. higher than a traditional onsite system. But with the benefits of timesaving, no warping,

Figure 6.10 Shaver Green in Portland, Oregon, using a light-gauge steel panelized process. Top: Left: panels being fabricated in the factory; Middle: panels stacked horizontally on a flat-bed trailer ready for transport; Right: panels being hoisted from trailer bed to location for installation. Bottom: Left: assembly completed and sheathing being placed on the structure; Right: finished building.

shrinkage, and many of the issues of finishing expedited due to the precision and speed of assembly, the system presents added benefits over onsite construction.

Minean recently completed a building in Portland called Shaver Green, an affordable housing project that received a LEED Gold rating. The speed of construction at Shaver Green was 15 working days per floor. This six-story building was completed in six short months. Each of the floors was completely manufactured offsite with Minean's steel framed walls and Hambro's composite open-web prefabricated floor system. Pinto states that the project, a five-townhouse, 80-apartment unit community center, bid and was built at $1,975,925 by Yorke and Curtis General Contractors. The steel panelized system gave the bid a $20 to $25/S.F. advantage over concrete or steel superstructure frame building. The City of Portland has continued working with this system in other residential projects, as it sees the cost and timesaving benefits.[20]

6.2.5 Curtain Walls

Glass facades, sometimes referred to as curtain walls, are exterior non-load-bearing transparent or translucent enclosures. Usually deployed in larger or

KAMA WALL

Kama Wall similarly uses metal stud framed walls panelized in a factory, but has developed an innovative high-performance enclosure system. Kama uses heavier gauge cold-formed "C" channel steel studs placed into larger top and bottom "C" channels. The studs are rotated from their standard position in stud framing and staggered on the interior and exterior of the top and bottom channel. In between is placed polystyrene rigid foam insulation. The system allows for the strength of a load-bearing wall, but with the insulation values seen in SIP construction. The system is more costly than wood frame or SIP, but is also more durable and usable in Type II construction. This application is ideal not only for multistory residential and light commercial but also as an infill wall system for spandrel wall locations in high-rise office buildings and condos where large expanses of wall are needed that are thermally peformative and affordable.[21]

Figure 6.11 Kama Wall System is a staggered light-gauge frame with rigid foam core. Top: residence constructed from Kama Wall; Bottom: commercial building using Kama Wall for infill enclosure.

taller commercial buildings, these systems primarily are fabricated of glass and aluminum classified as:

- Stick systems:

  ◦ Built in-situ from aluminum profiles that are attached to the building frame

  ◦ Consist of vertical mullions and horizontal transoms in extruded sections

  ◦ Highly susceptible to thermal expansion and contraction so joints must be detailed to allow for free movement without compromising thermal performance and water tightness

  ◦ Erection sequences planned to accommodate tolerances

  ◦ Prefabricated insulated glazing units and aluminum sticks, labor-intensive onsite

- Unit systems:

  ◦ Separate prefabricated pieces or units fabricated with glazing and aluminum in the factory

  ◦ Attached directly to building frame

  ◦ Must accommodate dimensional tolerance for building structure

- Point supported systems:

  ◦ Hole drilled into pane of glass where fixing elements for load transfer are inserted

  ◦ Fixing elements are manufactured in stainless or titanium

  ◦ Joints between glass panes are sealed

  ◦ All is manufactured in a factory and assembled onsite

  ◦ Tolerances must be tight and critical connections for thermal and water tightness are at sill, head,

and jamb conditions where frames are usually placed

- Multilayered glass facade:

  ◦ Glass facades that consist of two layers of glass, one in front of the other

  ◦ Higher thermal and sound performance but costly

  ◦ Able to distribute mechanical in this space in winter

  ◦ Double-skin principle used to allow for natural ventilation stack venting in summer

- Composite systems

  ◦ Unit and mullion systems with column cover, spandrels, and infill panels

  ◦ Detailed shop and fabrication drawings required

  ◦ Accommodate changes in dimension across a surface

  ◦ Often detailed as rainscreen system

  ◦ Coordination with other enclosure systems of building

Unit systems are the most prefabricated of any of the curtain wall types. Prefabricating unit system enclosures have many advantages in speed and quality of the unit; however, they have difficulty adapting to existing building structures. These fully prefabricated elements must be positioned and mounted onsite. The greatest weakness in unit systems is the potential for monotony and difficulty of closing joints. In order to provide proper thermal insulation and weatherproofing, joints must be carefully detailed so that they are attached to perform load transfer but also to not make a thermal bridge or possibility for water and wind infiltration. Since the units are fabricated and then transported to site, the elements must be structural in and of themselves. The dimensional tolerance of the unit might be more precise than the structural frame in steel or concrete in a larger, taller building, therefore differential tolerances between the unit and the onsite frame can reveal gaps. For onsite-erected stick system curtain walls, these gaps can be made up over the installation process by slightly shortening or lengthening the elements. In unit facade construction, connections must accommodate slight dimensional variances but sealants and gaskets have to make up the dimensional difference.[22]

To avoid intersecting or overlapping sealing sections of the units, continuous sealants are installed onsite instead of in the factory for horizontal sealing continuity. This is usually through push-fit seals that connect units laterally. Joining of the prefabricated units results in two profiles abutted against one another. This full frame is necessary for shipping, but can be structurally redundant once erected. Therefore, a balance must be struck between the economies of having large units that are one story or multiple story heights trucked and erected and the size of the unit's frames, glass, and installation methods.[23]

This is not as much of an issue in new construction where this detailing is part of the package, but can be problematic if not coordinated properly. However, in replacing window systems or retrofitting historic construction where dimensional tolerances are large and a prefabricated unit system with tight tolerances is introduced, dimensional discrepancies can emerge. This requires an integrated approach to detailing between the architect, curtain wall fabricator, subcontractor for the structural frame, and the contractor.

LEVINE HALL, UNIVERSITY OF PENNSYLVANIA

The Levine Hall at Penn Campus, designed by KieranTimberlake, is one of the first large-scale applications of a double wall–united glazing system in existence. The curtain wall system encloses a circulation hall that connects two historic buildings. The custom unit system relies on an exterior insulated glass facade, and a single-pane interior surface that is operable separated by 6 in. of vertical plenum space. The air in the cavity is heated by the sun in the winter and taken by the air return to the HVAC system. The air cavity hosts a series of blinds that can be lowered during summer months. The client, seeing the potential energy benefits, adopted this active pressure-equalized double-skin curtain wall. Developed by Permasteelisa Group, the prefabricated double-wall glazed unit system was installed in seven weeks.

This project presented an entirely new method of delivery and installation than had previously been experienced by the crews who installed it. Therefore, the project became a training ground in a new technology. Permasteelisa worked with local subcontractors who were the onsite installers to detail out the system. The hall abutted an existing building and a new section, both of which were in brick. The brick, a much less precise material and given the historicism of being an existing building, caused the glass units to abut the existing wall in a difficult detail producing varied gaps. Other than the existing abutment, the units were installed quickly, with variety, and perform as designed.[24]

continued

Figure 6.12 Levine Hall uses a unitized glazing system that acts as a double-skin thermally active envelope. Eighteen different types of glazing units developed by KieranTimberlake and fabricated by Permasteelisa were packaged in order of assembly and erected to bear on the top and bottom plates of the floor structure.

6.2.6 Cladding Systems

Cladding systems are non-load-bearing building skins that separate the interior from the exterior. As such, some of the functions of the exterior enclosure include:

• Preventing water infiltration from rain and snow

• Retarding water vapor passage as a result of condensation

• Preventing air infiltration

• Mediating thermal transfer due to radiation, convection, and conduction

• Adapting to movements due to moisture, thermal changes, structural loads, and wind loads

• Attenuating sound[25]

Cladding systems may be a single layer of building skin, such as in precast cladding elements, but most often are part of a set of layers that provide building enclosure, as in the case of metal cladding. Each layer performs different functions or multiple functions, as outlined above. Generally, cladding describes the outer layer facing the exterior as the first line of defense against external forces. Providing a barrier to moisture due to wind, rain, and snow is the fundamental job of building skins and therefore cladding. As such, many methods have been devised to ensure proper detailing. For water to move through the skin, there must be both an opening and a force present. In order to keep water out, there are conceptually three strategies:[26]

• Provide a sufficient overhang so that water does not reach the exterior skin. This is the simplest way to reduce water penetration, but is limited to smaller buildings that do not have a large exterior wall surface.

• Barrier walls eliminate openings from the wall by sealing all joints tightly. This is accomplished with waterproofing membranes and sealants. This is nearly impossible to accomplish as buildings have many joints that can be overlooked, and fail in the event of movements due to various loads.

• Rainscreen walls use cladding on the exterior as a first line of defense. A backup waterproofing membrane is provided behind the cladding system. The redundancy in the system allows for water to migrate past the cladding and the wall is designed to remove the water. This does away with sealants in the cladding and allows panels to move under various loads. The system also allows for easy replacement due to mechanical damage or change out due to weathering.

Water moves from exterior to interior by forces of gravity, wind-driven rain, capillary action, surface tension, and differential pressure. Rainscreens provide a pressure equalization chamber that mitigates differential pressure. Detailing cladding in such a way as to introduce labyrinths alleviates the other forces, drip grooves, lapping returns, and reveals in order to resist water infiltration. These types of details, outlined in *Architectural Metal Surfaces* by L. William Zahner, provide more detailed and illustrative examples.[27] More on detailing strategies will be discussed in Chapter 7.

Prefabricated cladding systems rely on factory production of panels that can be mounted on the exterior of the building to a substrate or to the actual structural frame itself. Standard brick veneers and stone claddings are not necessarily prefabricated. Less common, but possible, are brick and terra cotta veneers placed into a frame that acts as a panel to be hung as a facade system on the ex-

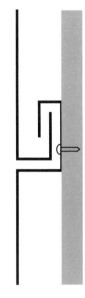

Figure 6.13 This open-joint metal rainscreen cladding is detailed to allow for movement due to thermal stresses but also to mitigate water infiltration from forces due to gravity, wind, surface tension, and differential pressure common with cladding systems.

terior of buildings. Stone and GFRC may have an armature attached to the material so it can be hung on the building as well. This is often done in contemporary retrofits of historic structures. The most common rainscreen cladding systems are in metal and metal composite.

Metal cladding is lightweight sheet that has been cold-formed to act as a rainscreen through folding and stamping. Steel, aluminum, copper, and zinc are common materials. These panels are preformed and prefinished in the factory, prepared for the jobsite installation. Generally, panels are not assembled to subframes in the factory due to the possibility of damage during shipping. Instead, panels are nested until brought to the jobsite. Metal panels experience a high degree of conduction, and, as such, undergo thermal expansion and contraction at high rates. The panels need to be able to move and therefore rainscreen systems are best for these types of conditions. As such, elongated or enlarged

holds are provided for fixing the facade panels and adjusting or detailing the lapping panels allows for movement.

Composite metal panels are also preformed, but then composed with a foam core. The core provides surface durability, keeping the panel from oil canning, dimpling, and denting. The foam composite can be placed with adhesives to polystyrene but, more effectively, is filled with polyurethane injection. Ferrous metals may be used as cladding, but they must be plated so that they are protected from corrosion. Nonferrous metals are also often plated with anodizing in aluminum or tooled to provide a particular aesthetic. When attaching to a wood frame, metal panels may be screwed, but when attaching to a steel frame or concrete frame substructure, a substructure or subframe is needed for attachment.

When dealing with metal cladding, or any metal structure and skin application, issues of galvanic corrosion must be mitigated. Galvanic corrosion is an electrochemical process in which two or more different types of metals, say, steel and copper, come into contact in the presence of acid, salt, or some other electrolyte. The chemicals in the air we breathe can act as a catalyst in this process as well. In galvanic corrosion, the less noble of the two metals will corrode preferentially. There are several ways of reducing and preventing this form of corrosion, including plating the two metals before they are introduced to each other. This will work for a time, but may eventually have to be maintained. The most common method is to insulate the two metals from one another with a polymer insulator such as neoprene, elastomer, or the like ensuring that the insulator is not water absorbent, which will encourage galvanic corrosion rather than resist it. Using metals that are similar so that

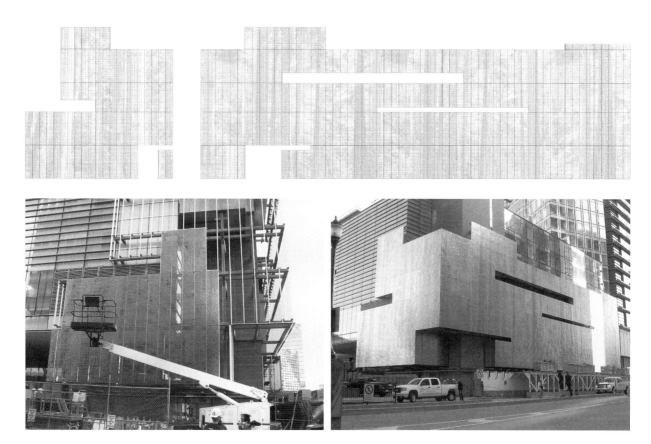

Figure 6.14 Perforated metal rainscreen cladding for the Fairmont Hotel facade in Vancouver, BC, developed by A. Zahner Architectural Metals.

current is minimized is another way to deal with galvanic corrosion. This is especially a problem when sheet metal cladding is not coordinated with either the fastener or the substrate.[28]

Wood cladding may be affixed directly to the substrate or attached to nailers (furring strip), purlins, or battens in a rainscreen condition. The nailers are then attached to the waterproofed structure or sheathing. Cladding may be directly applied to the substrate in smaller single-story and two-story buildings, but should be applied as a rainscreen in projects with greater height due to the exposure of the cladding to the elements. Again, with rainscreens a waterproofing membrane is required behind the wood cladding. Ventilating the wood cladding facade allows the moisture in the system that condenses or is driven in through forces to be released or dry out. Placing nailers vertically with horizontal wood cladding provides a natural ventilation cavity. When applying cladding vertically on horizontal nailers, gaps will have to be introduced in the sequence of the nailers to allow for vertical airflow. This is not of particular concern in dry areas, but in the cold, wet areas of North America this is an important detail. Nailers also make up the differences or variation in the surface of the substrate, especially in all-wood construction when surfaces are not flat.

Wood cladding can be detailed to have open joints or reveals; butt joints with a vertical batten, sometimes called board and batten; lap joints, where one wood element overlaps the other like a shingle; or placed as board siding. Siding configurations may be beveled, shiplap, or tongue and groove. Plywood siding may be applied in larger sheets but require detailing the horizontal end joints between sheets to be capped with aluminum sections. Patterning larger sheet cladding material should be carefully considered as with board siding so that dimensions make logical terminations to maximize the material. Aesthetically, this helps to organize the facade of buildings. Fiber cement board is used as an exterior cladding material much in the way that wood cladding is used and affixed to substrates and nailers. The thin sheet material may come in plank strips of standard wood siding dimensions, but only ¼ or ½ in. thick. The material is more dense than wood, but is more durable to weathering.

Figure 6.15 Wood tongue and groove siding is a cladding system employed on this modular house designed by Michelle Kaufmann and Paul Warner and fabricated and installed by Irontown Homebuilding Company.

The long-term durability of wood is often a concern. Naturally rot-resistant woods such as cedar and American redwood offer natural protection. These woods will continue to deteriorate, but not as quickly as others left to their own devices. In addition, they do not need as much treatment to protect. Some methods of protecting wood exposed to the exterior include natural sealants, such as wax and linseed oils that protect but must be equally maintained, and chemical treatments including varnish, stain, impregnation, and paint. Plywood cladding systems use exterior glues in laminations for durability of the panel and should be finished similarly as siding applications.

Stone, precast, and glass fiber reinforced concrete (GFRC) cladding panels comprise ceramic-based cladding systems that are similar to materials and methods of fabrication and onsite attachment. Ceramic claddings cut precisely with CNC machinery are affixed to a subframe in the factory by using expansion anchors or epoxy set anchors, trucked to the site and installed on the building frame. These systems are designed for wind loading and self-weight primarily. The substructures are generally made of vertical and horizontal steel or aluminum sections. In larger panels of stone or concrete, large steel truss frameworks can be used, or the stone cladding may be post-tensioned to reduce its thickness. Ceramic-based claddings usually are detailed as a barrier wall with grout joints and sealant at expansion joints. Often a light-gauge nonstructural backup wall is used behind the cladding to provide air barrier, insulation, a cavity for service distribution, and a frame to apply interior finishes. These systems are extremely heavy and not the best option for prefabricated wall panel or modular systems. However, thin stone facings may be used with stiffened structural backing or placed on the face of a precast panel.

GFRC panels, similar to precast and stone, use a substructure backing but require much less material for the function. The composite uses glass fiber reinforcing, making the panels a fraction of the weight of precast or stone. The panels therefore can also be placed on lighter gauge metal stud backup walls in the factory. GFRC can also be formed to different colors and textures, unavailable with stone and precast.

Brick veneers are usually formed onsite, one masonry unit at a time. This is both labor-intensive and expensive. Prefabricated panel construction allows brick veneers to be placed either as a brick facing in a precast panel and erected as a precast element, or to be secured in a steel or aluminum frame creating a cladding panel for installation. Brick is a brittle material and extra care must be taken when installing it as a veneer system on a panel or module that will be shipped and set. Masonry grids sometimes have their own logic that determines the overall dimensions of buildings. There have emerged relationships between the width, height, and length of masonry. The most common of these dimensional relationships are:

• Two brick widths plus one mortar joint equal one brick length

• Three brick heights plus two mortar joints equal one brick length

Because of greater ease in design and construction, the vast majority of contemporary brickwork uses modular-sized brick and modular grids. The most common modular dimension system for brickwork uses a 4-in. grid coordinating between brick and concrete masonry units and fits the modular dimensions of other construction materials. Modular di-

Figure 6.16 1" thick GFRC panel with substructure attached in the precast factory at Hanson Eagle Precast. This panel has been developed as a cornice detail for a prominent public building.

mensions in masonry are sometimes called nominal dimensions, because they represent round numbers without accounting for the fractions of an inch represented by mortar joint thicknesses. For masonry elements, the relationship between modular dimensions and the actual dimensions constructed in the field can depend upon the overall length. For longer masonry wall lengths made of modular-sized brick and about four or more brick lengths long, the actual constructed letngth of the element often will be the modular dimension. This is possible because during construction, the mason typically will adjust the horizontal layout of the brick to allow slightly larger or smaller head joints so that the brickwork meets the required dimension.

For shorter masonry wall lengths made of modular-sized brick and less than four brick lengths long, the designer may want to consider the specified dimension of the brick and joint thickness when dimensioning the wall. This is because the amount of adjustment necessary to the thickness of head joints between brick will be larger. Additionally, the mason will adjust the number of courses and the bed joint thicknesses in order to meet fixed vertical dimensions. When the completed elevation is viewed, any slight deviation in mortar joint width or the number of courses generally is not obvious in the brickwork.

The choice of whether nominal or specified dimensions are to be used on drawings is often determined by the type of information that the drawing provides. For drawings that cover large areas, such as elevations and floor plans, use of nominal dimensions is recommended. The overall intent and appearance of the project can be presented without the precision of specified dimensions. When nominal dimensions are used on plans, the drawings must be clearly noted to advise the mason of the intended actual size of the completed masonry elements. For drawings that provide specific information to other trades, those that coordinate the installation of materials, and for shop drawings, the use of specified dimensions is recommended. An easy way to remember this is to use nominal dimensions for drawings in which the scale is smaller than 1/4 in. per foot. Use specified dimensions for drawings shown in 1/4 in. per foot and larger. BIM programs often have the specified dimensions of the brick and mortar joint as input options. Thus, at the designer's discretion, specified dimensions that use fractions can be used throughout the drawings to indicate the desired constructed dimensions of the brickwork. However, doing so may complicate the dimensioning process.[29]

Nonmodular brick, by definition, does not conform to a 4-in. module. However, all nonmodular brick of a certain size creates a module equal to the sum of one brick length and one mortar joint width. This module can be used to establish modular dimensioning for the brickwork in a fashion similar to that used for modular brick. Nonmodular brick that are approximately three times as long as they are wide are usually laid in one-third running bond. When laid

in one-half running bond, brick near wall ends and openings must usually be cut to maintain the bond.

The vertical coursing of both modular and nonmodular-sized brick is similar. A certain number of courses will correspond to 4, 8, 12, or 16 in. in height. This dimension establishes the vertical modular grid used on the brickwork. For example, for a nonmodular standard brick, a vertical grid of 16 in. is used since five courses of brick equal 16 in. total. For a wall constructed of modular brick, a vertical grid is established by three courses (three brick and three mortar joints) equaling 8 in. total.

Most masonry as a unit system is not a prefabricated unit in today's terms; prefabricated wall panel and modules built in a factory may employ a brick veneer that determines the finish size of the module, however. This is the case in the Pierson Student Housing Project at Yale University, designed by KieranTimberlake. This project employed detailed brick veneer on structural steel frame modules. In addition, Blazer Industries in Oregon produces a load-bearing, reinforced block, freestanding bathroom module shipped in two halves with wood framed roofs that are stitched together onsite. SHoP Architects used a brick facing on a precast cladding system for the Mulberry Project in New York City. For prefabricated panels, walls, and modules that use brick and/or block construction, care should be taken to ensure that the factory has experience in working with masonry. Many prefabricators are inexperienced since most masonry is performed onsite. It is recommended that actual dimensions be used for inexperienced factories to ensure that dimensions are exact and detailed before production begins.

Curtain wall and cladding systems are difficult to design by the architect alone. Most systems selected

MASONRY DIMENSIONS

BRICK

- "Modular" brick is the most common type
  - width 3-⅝ in. × height 2-¼ in. × length 7-⅝ in. actual
  - width 4 in. × height 2-⅔ in. × length 8 in. nominal
  - Therefore with mortar, the nominal dimension of a wall is in increments of 4 in. in length. Width of 2-⅔ in. nominal every third course is 8 in. nominal.

BLOCK

- "Modular" CMU is the most common type
  - width 7-⅝ in. × height 7-⅝ in. × length 15-⅝ in. actual
  - width 8 in. × height 8 in. × length 16 in. nominal
  - Therefore with mortar, the nominal dimension of a wall is in increments of 8 in. in length. The height of a wall is in 8-in. increments.
  - Note: Width comes in modules of 4, 6, 8, 10, and 12 in. with 8 in. being the most common.

for use are proprietary. Rarely are enclosure systems developed uniquely for a project. Whether they are proprietary, customized, or both, manufacturers of these systems must be intimately involved to ensure the design and installation is performed according to their expertise. The manufacturer knows the most about exterior prefabricated cladding systems. If the project requires, a cladding specialist may be brought on as a design consultant. This ensures a higher-quality product in the end. The consultant understands the possibilities and can aid in designing a system that is both beautiful and functional.

Placing cladding on a building onsite is labor-intensive. As these systems hang off of the building with fasteners, laborers must put themselves in vulnerable positions and it requires a high degree of focus and balance. Scaffoldings, ladders, and machines onsite must be coordinated. In a factory, panels and modules developed may be skinned with cladding by laying down enclosure panels flat on the ground or placing them at reachable levels from the ground to be manipulated. This allows for quality control in the cladding, ensuring that fasteners are placed correctly and aligned for aesthetics and proper fit. Should cladding need to be further manipulated, these changes are more easily made in the factory. KieranTimberlake used a prefab cedar rainscreen in both the Sidwell Friends School and at the Loblolly House. This allowed for a highly precise attachment and quality that was then craned into place on the building.

Finally, there are an increasing number of panel products and cladding materials available on the market. In terms of relevance to prefabricated panels and modules, these systems fall into two general categories: progressive systems and open systems. For open systems, the installation of panels can occur in any order. A common type of open system is a cas-

sette panel. These are typically sheet metal or wood cladding products, which have an inward-folded edge around the panel. These types of systems do not require any modification or special consideration for offsite construction. These systems facilitate placing some cladding panels on the building in the factory and then placing infill-stitching panels onsite. For progressive systems, the installation must occur in sequence, typically from the base of the building moving upward. A number of clip systems fall into this category. If these systems are to be applied in the factory and onsite, special provisions must be made to provide construction access to the mateline. Project teams must provide a reveal to allow a cladding panel to be placed onsite.[30] Wood, fiber cement, GFRC, and brick veneer cladding panel systems placed on buildings in the factory must also leave areas open for straps, and pick points for loading panels to the truck, securing the panels to the truck, and unloading for setting onsite. Where panels and modules meet, seams must be left clear so that once the joining occurs onsite, the finishes may be stitched together.

6.2.7 Interior Panels

Interior space is the most temporary of all building systems but it also can be the most expensive over the lifecycle of a facility, considering the rate at which change occurs. Interiors can be changed out every time a new tenant or owner moves in. Modular panel partitions systems are not entirely new. Manufacturers

◀Figure 6.17 DIRTT interior partition system includes from left to right and top to bottom: materials come to the factory packed in bundles; they are fabricated into interior partition panels; the panels are loaded into a truck horizontally; plug-and-play electrical system allows for easy change out and adaptation over time; panels are erected in the office space; adjustable height allows for the differentiation of the ceiling height to be mitigated with flexible panels.

have been developing these for years; however, DIRTT uses some unique features that make it attractive to future thinking about prefabrication and interior space. The company has developed ICE, a BIM interface that allows users to create environments in a customized manner. ICE creates a parts and pricing list, and generates code for the factory to order. This allows DIRTT to anticipate materials inventory and eventually be able to run CNC machines. The panels are manufactured from this data and erected in an office or residential flat onsite. The system uses a unique spider plug-and-play to allow for easy electrical and panel material change out. The floor-to-ceiling panels are set on feet that are height-adjustable and can be rearranged easily. Users may change out their entire workspace and panels may be customized with new materials. Instead of gutting the entire office space for a new client, a developer can offer the system for their tenants to reconfigure as needed. This reduces cost and material waste.[31] More will be discussed on the environmental implications of DIRTT and reuse of prefabricated systems in Chapter 8.

6.3 Modules

Modular architecture is often associated with utopian ideals of the 1960s in which architects developed proposals that were temporary, mobile, and used new materials and techniques of erection and disassembly. Today, modular construction is employed for not only utopian ideals, but for standard construction as well, to reduce project durations and increase quality. From high-end residences by Marmol Radziner Prefab, to temporary construction trailers, from green prefabricated houses by Michelle Kaufmann, to wood-framed production housing, modular has become a standard method of building in the United States and it will see much growth as a preferred prefabricated method in architecture.

In the spectrum of degree to which prefabrication is finished, modular is the greatest, offering the possibility of constituting upward of 95 percent complete before setting of the structure onsite. Modules also constitute one of the largest definable industries in prefab architecture. The Modular Building Institute (MBI) was founded in 1983 as a nonprofit trade association serving 300 companies engaged in commercial modular construction. Regular members are manufacturers, general contractors, and dealers of commercial modular buildings. The MBI defines modular construction as:

"An off-site project delivery method used to construct code-compliant buildings in a quality-controlled setting in less time and with less materials waste."[32]

This definition does not distinguish modular from other elements of prefabrication. Mark and Peter Anderson state,

"it is unfortunate that the terms 'modular' and 'prefabricated' have become interchangeable in many people's vocabularies as it greatly confuses the viability and applicability of different available prefabrication systems."[33]

A modular is a standardized unit of construction that is designed for ease of assembly, tends to be more finished than other methods of prefabrication, but it is not restricted in scale. Modules that are larger may be able to have greater levels of finish, but restrict the flexibility of the overall building when compared to smaller modules which, when arranged, can produce customization of an overall composition.

The modular building industry can be categorized by residential and commercial. In residential, there are the classifications of temporary and permanent. Temporary modules are portable and are typically built with chassis. The defining feature, built to the HUD code established in 1976 that certified mobile housing, can be constructed from light gauge metal stud or wood frame. In either case, they are built to lesser standard using shallow profile framing members, thin sheet metal skin, plastic interior paneling, and little insulation. Today mobile homes are otherwise known as "manufactured housing," and can be found throughout the United States as an affordable housing option.

Modular building is also found in the residential sector. Modules are defined by the method of delivery and not the type of construction. Modular residential is primarily Type V construction, built up to a maximum height of three stories. Modules are built to the standard IRC code for smaller dwellings, and the IBC for multifamily housing. The operations of construction are simply relocated to the confines of the factory. Residential modular can be built with steel or concrete; however, it is primarily manufactured in standard wood materials including 2X framing, wood I-joists, glulam beams, and OSB sheathing. Standard methods of siding, housewrap, insulation, and interior gypsum board sheathing are just as common in IBC-built modular as in onsite construction. Although the great majority of residential modular building comes from factories dedicated to this industry, some have crossed over into commercial. Many commercial modular companies also manufacture for residential applications, especially in multifamily housing designed under the IBC.

The commercial modular industry manufactures steel and concrete modular units as well as entire buildings for onsite delivery. Commercial modular are all built to IBC code. This industry can be broken into temporary and permanent structures as well. Temporary commercial modular include construction site trailers, portable classrooms, communication pods, and show rooms. Permanent modular buildings include multistory, multifamily housing, health-care facilities, hotels, government buildings, schools, and any other building type developed in traditional onsite construction. The limitation to the size of commercial modular is only in engineering.

The tallest modular project to date in the United States is the 1968 Hilton on the Riverwalk, in San Antonio, built from precast modules. The hotel is four lower stories of site-cast reinforced concrete. Floors 5 through 21 are constructed from precast modules. The modules were entirely fit out on the interior, each with an exterior window preinstalled in the module. Seventeen units a day were set, with a total of 496 units. Each module had a code number that determined its location. The building was conceived as being able to be changed out over time. Similar projects of the era include Habitat by Moshie Safdie. The reality is that concrete modules are heavy—35 tons each—and the logistic of module change out is not possible when the units depend on one another for structural stability. The Hilton on the Riverwalk project was constructed in 200 days by Zachary Construction Corporation and still stands as a testament to a great feat for 1968.[34]

Since the Hilton in San Antonio, modular achievements in the United States have made very small inroads. Although modular is beginning to make a stronger presence and will see larger projects in the future, the industry is relatively small in comparison to the construction industry at large. The United Kingdom has been working in modular for a couple

Figure 6.18 O'Connell East Architects (OEA) designed a 24-story modular student dormitory for Wolverhampton Development in the United Kingdom. This building contains 805 embedded steel structural modules and was built in 27 weeks.

of decades. In 2010, a 24-story modular student dormitory was built designed by O'Connell East Architects of Manchester. This building contains 805 embedded steel structural modules and was built in 27 weeks. Compared to 500 units in 28 weeks in the Hilton Hotel, this is a more aggressive schedule but one would hope that advances in technology have been made in the 30+ years between the projects. The main argument behind using an offsite modular solution for the Wolverhampton development in the United Kingdom was to increase the speed of construction. By using modular, the project team was able to deliver the building one academic year ahead of a traditional onsite construction, allowing the client to generate revenues ahead of their anticipated schedule.[35]

Jason Brown with MSC Constructors in Ogden, Utah, runs a family construction company established in 1982 by his father, one of the first pioneers in wood modular construction. He states that dealers and manufacturers define the commercial modular industry in the United States contractually. Dealers sell modules to contractors and use outsourced manufacturers to produce the product. Dealers act as either contractor, delivering the project in a turn-key contract, or as a subcontractor to a larger general on a project. Manufacturers sell to dealers but may also be dealers themselves, offering wholesale products to the construction market. Dealers may perform their own sets of modules onsite or have the manufacturer fold this into their subcontract. In addition, third-party installers may perform setting for dealers.

COMMERCIAL MODULAR INDUSTRY

According to the Modular Building Institute, 2007 Commercial Modular Construction Report, dealers and manufacturers deliver the following allocations of building types in their respective sub-industries:[36]

- Dealers:
  - General office (including construction site trailers): 35 percent
  - Education portables: 24 percent
  - Commercial, retail, restaurant, and convenience stores: 23 percent
  - Military, emergency, and government: 8 percent
  - Kiosks, guardhouses, and communication shelters: 4 percent
  - Health care: 4 percent
  - Industrial or workforce housing: 3 percent

- Manufacturers:
  - General office (including construction trailers): 46 percent
  - Education portables: 24 percent
  - Commercial, retail, restaurant, and convenience stores: 10 percent
  - Military, emergency, and government: 10 percent
  - Health care: 5 percent
  - Kiosks, guardhouses, and communication shelters: 4 percent
  - Industrial: 2 percent

6.3.1 Wood Modular

Although precast modular was envisioned as being the answer to fast construction in the 1960s, today it is not used much beyond industrial and prison buildings. Modules of comparable size to wood or steel, maximizing the truck bed, can weigh between 20 and 70 tons depending on the length of the module. Heavy-duty craning equipment is necessary for assembly in precast, often making this option cost prohibitive for residential and light commercial construction. Instead, wood and steel frame modules are common today. Wood modules may be used in construction up to three stories standard. Over three floors becomes uneconomical, requiring robust structure within the module and affecting its price point. This would suggest steel modular or onsite framing methods. Modular wood construction progresses in the following sequence:

1. Floor constructed on factory floor, sheathed, and placed on skids

2. Panel walls constructed and sheathed on factory floor and tilted onto floor

3. Roof built and sheathed on factory floor and craned onto walls (floor, walls, and roof may be simultaneously fabricated on the factory floor)

4. Modules are wrapped

5. Windows are placed

6. Exterior and interior finishes are installed including siding, gypsum board, and roofing

7. Modules are shrinkwrapped and loaded on trailer

8. Semi-trailer transports to site

9. Crane hoists module and sets

10. Modules are stitched onsite

Wood modular construction does not always progress seamlessly in this fashion and variations are made. Often the units cannot be transported due to the oversized height, width, or length of the module. In addition, sloped roofs may present problems and need to be shipped as a separate element. Knockdown methods refer to roofs or panels built in the factory, flat packed and tilted, or propped up and erected onsite. This is not unlike panelization (already discussed); however, the modular company as part of a modular strategy performs the fabrication and erection process. Therefore, the panels are loaded to the trailer in the sequence in which they will be constructed onsite with other elements that may or may not be modular. Roofs may be structured as part of the modular package or met with delivered roof trusses from a truss plant, depending on the project-wide prefabrication strategy.

Irontown Homebuilding Company, located in Spanish Fork, Utah, began as an onsite builder. Over time, they realized that during the long snow season they could factory-produce houses and work year round, constructing indoors and setting in one or two days. Irontown, like many modular residential builders of its kind, uses the same contract structure as traditional onsite construction; however, it brings its subcontractors into the factory including electricians, plumbers, and mechanical trades. This model has brought them business with architects, which they did not anticipate. They have produced wood modular houses for Michelle Kaufmann, Paul Warner, and Alchemy Architects. Their business model in the last year has expanded beyond wood modular into steel modular, as they recently produced a two-story dwelling for Steve Glenn at Living Homes designed by Ray Kappe.[37]

Irontown can set up to six modules in a single day for even highly complex projects. They perform full turn-key delivery offering fabrication, shipping, setting, and stitching. A house at Lake Tahoe designed by Michelle Kaufmann and Paul Warner is priced at $200 per S.F. set and stitched. On the Wee Houses designed by Alchemy Architects, Irontown reports $125 per S.F. for a two-bedroom house. This cost difference is not due to less quality in finishes but because the Tahoe House had structural requirements and the factory has found efficiencies within the Wee House production process that they have now fabricated four times over. These houses by Irontown are being delivered at the same price point of other architect-designed houses in the location they are designed for at half the time to construct them. Additional benefits include reduced waste, increased quality, and added value to the client.

Kam Valgardsen at Irontown has worked with various architects on housing projects. He sees the greatest advantage to prefabricated modules to be predictability. Schedules and budgets are kept to the anticipated program. The greatest disadvantage is the lack of flexibility in the size of the rooms. Even when a larger family room is desirable, the room is limited to how many modules one can stitch together. If posts are not desirable, a method for spanning across modules must be devised and often oversized to meet transportation load requirements. Similarly, Kam sees height as a restriction with modular. Not only does the height of the shop and garage doors leading out of the factory dictate dimensions, but the size of the trailer and highway requirements also limit proportions. Transportation restrictions will be discussed in Chapter 7. Paul Warner relates that a challenge with residential modular is "scope creep." This refers to things that the fabricator puts off to be done onsite. If not carefully planned, many of the tasks inevitably get postponed to be completed in the field. Warner suggests working diligently toward more tasks being completed offsite as a value

LAKE TAHOE HOUSE

In the recent project finished for Michelle Kaufmann and Paul Warner, Irontown delivered the 3,500 S.F. custom house in 22 weeks, including 14 weeks in factory and 8 weeks onsite finishing. The modules were fabricated, shipped to Lake Tahoe, and set in two days during a blizzard. Once Irontown set the modules and ice/water shield was placed on the seams, work inside commenced. The house under construction next door broke ground the same day and had not finished framing when the Lake Tahoe House was already dried in. Paul Warner relates that the project had special requirements in that it used a sloped roof, which is different from most of the flat-roofed houses Michelle Kaufmann Designs has developed in the past, and had to be designed to an astounding 240 lbs/S.F. of snow load. This made the house cost more due to large amounts of structure required for the snow load. Usually transportation loads determine the sizing of structure rather than the loads that the house will experience once set. In this case, due to the high snow load, the opposite was true.

▶Figure 6.19 Sequence of construction for a two-story wood modular house manufactured in Utah and shipped and assembled near Lake Tahoe. 1st row: walls and floor built on the shop floor, which is level within fractions of an inch over entire surface, and then hoisted into place to create modules; 2nd row Left: onsite foundation construction occurring during the factory production of the modules; 2nd row Middle: modules being mocked-up and wrapped; 2nd row Right: radiant floor system carefully being installed in factory; 3rd row: modules being shrinkwrapped prior to transport, modules on lowboy trailers in factory loading dock, modules arrive onsite; 4th row: unwrapped module with belt strap to be hoisted into location onsite, modules being assembled during a blizzard in two days, house during stitching.

in a project. If not committed to pushing the process toward the factory, the scope will naturally, gradually move away from the factory toward the jobsite, where efficiencies decay exponentially.[38]

Blazer Industries, located in Aumsville, Oregon, is also a manufacturer for Michelle Kaufmann, having produced six houses in 2009. In addition, they are currently working with Anderson and Anderson Architects in San Francisco on using temporary chassis-bound portable classrooms employing production methods for customized design. Blazer Industries is a wholesale manufacturer or provider, selling to general contractors or architect/contractors but never directly to clients, owners, or end users. Outside of residential wood modular, Blazer fabricates everything modular, including portable jobsite trailers; doublewide HUD-code dwellings; portable classrooms; and commercial wood, steel, and concrete block modular buildings. Building types range from medical units, equipment shelters, coffee shacks, day care centers, and permanent office buildings.

Blazer Industries produces a concrete block restroom modular. Developed at a rate of one restroom mod per week, the shelters are built in reinforced CMU with an integral framed roof. The modules are in two sections, one for each bathroom in a gendered set. Double-wide manufactured houses are also being produced in the plant at a rate of one per workweek, or five days. This is in comparison to custom houses with architects, which average 8 weeks in the factory for small dwellings, and 12 weeks for larger houses. These numbers illustrate the room that architect-designed modular housing and commercial structures have to go to become more efficient and reduce cost in comparison to structures that Blazer Industries builds every day. Despite the advances in CNC machining, setup time requires a greater investment than standardized modular construction.[39]

6.3.2 Steel Modular

Steel modular is primarily used in commercial buildings that require more robust structural systems such as taller, higher-performing, or seismic-designed buildings. Steel modules have therefore become popular in earthquake-ridden Japan, and with West Coast architects such as Jennifer Siegal with the Office of Mobile Design (OMD), and Marmol Radziner Prefab. The steel frame is strong and rigid and infill panels offer variation to the system. The structure can be less stout because steel is stronger than wood and does not have to be over-structured for transport unnecessarily. The modules are finished out in the factory with insulation, infill framing, wiring, ducting, and so forth in order to complete as near possible up to seams with all the finishes in the building. The level of prefabrication with steel modules is very high due to the strength and precision of the frame.

Figure 6.20 Blazer Industries develops: Left: in and out oil change stations in modular, and Right: prefabricated concrete block bathroom modules for outdoor recreation parks in two halves that are pieced together onsite.

LEAN AND MODULAR

Joe Tanney, Principal at Resolution: 4 Architecture, a prefab housing company in New York City, explained the modular industry in two types of manufacturers: (1) companies that are simply taking construction indoors, relocating the act of construction to a sheltered condition, and (2) companies that are treating prefabrication as a manufacturing process, relying on all the efficiencies of lean production. It is not that stationary modular construction is bad; in fact, great efficiencies are found within that process by virtue of increasing work days, controlling quality, and decreasing overall project schedules, but single-piece flow aids in increasing production productivity, allowing the process of manufacture to play an equal place at the table as questions of construction.[40]

Kullman Buildings Corporation located in Lebanon, New Jersey, is a dedicated commercial modular manufacturer. Kullman only builds in steel and concrete modular permanent structures. It uses a unique method of single-piece workflow with stations for assembly and lean principles to reduce waste in the manufacturing process. Generally speaking, this is rare in the construction industry. This allows value to be added to the project team. The company is separated into three primary types of work:

• Tactical shelters and embassies

• Communication enclosures and data centers

• Education, health care, multifamily, and kitchen/bathroom service pods

Kullman uses an embedded steel frame that allows modules to be stacked up to six stories standard. They are currently developing a system that can be stacked up to 20 stories high. The steel technology Kullman employs is a vierendell truss that allows entire modules to act as a box beam, or large three-dimensional space frame. Although this technology is not new, Amy Marks at Kullman believes this is the time for modular to expand its impact on the building industry. She states that the technology, by way of BIM, has matured to the level that Kullman is able to perform scheduling and cost estimation during project devel-

opment. With BIM as a tool, fabricators of modular are able to truly industrialize the process of construction that could only be talked about in previous years.

Kullman sees themselves not as a construction company, as most modular fabricators do, but rather as a manufacturer in the traditional sense, delivering consumer products. It just so happens that they are deliverables to the construction industry. The benefit to architects, contractors, and project team members is that no longer is "field install" written on the drawings, but the drawings—the 3D, 4D, and 5D analyses—are used for manufacturing the entire delivery of the product through install. In an integrated practice model, Kullman prefers to hold the model, using it for maximizing efficiencies without sacrificing design or production quality.

Amy Marks states,

"The building industry needs to step out of the way things have been done for 100 years. This is a broken process. It is broken because every time a building project begins it is an entire Hollywood production. With industrialized construction leveraging digital technology, lower costs and higher quality are achievable because of the procuring of material happens just in time, because the manufacturer understands the unit characteristics and can anticipate cost and schedule with a high degree of certainty."[41]

Kullman Buildings Corp. notes that architects often ask them the question: "does modular have to be square?" Instead, the fabricator suggests that architects ask: "what are the design and production constraints architects have to work within as the industry moves toward productivity gains in prefabrication architecture?" KieranTimberlake in their thesis *Refabricating Architecture* ask: "why can't architecture and industrialized processes be more congruent realizing increases in productivity and design quality?" Kullman has built two projects with KieranTimberlake: Pierson Modular, a student dormitory at Yale, and the Cellophane House for the Museum of Modern Art "Home Delivery" exhibit in 2008. According to Kullman, the prospect of working with architects more closely is a fruitful partnership to reach a larger and greater critical mass of prefabrication in the building industry. Each step advances offsite fabrication and makes prefab architecture more accessible to the design and construction industries.

These projects designed by KieranTimberlake identify offsite modular manufacturers that are looking forward as Kullman, seeing only roses at the end of the road. Although the economy has suffered in the past couple of years, Kullman is looking at their best year in 2010. All the conventions for other companies seem to be going out the window, as Kullman situates itself to be an innovator in alternative construction for the twenty-first century, delivering complete building packages with complete fit-out including bathrooms and kitchens. Rarely do construction companies have the capacity to perform research and development. At Kullman, this is part of the process of developing and investing in their business model. KieranTimberlake have capitalized on this fact and many other architects are trying to do the same.

6.3.3 Bathroom Modular

Offsite-fabricated bathroom and service modules have been an idea since Buckminster Fuller developed the bathroom pod for the Diaxiom House. The concept of a service core is central to design and construction because it is conceptually efficient. By consolidating piping and high-grade interior finishes into a manufactured module, the quality and control as well as speed can be increased. The module can then be placed inside of a structural frame and be hooked up to services quickly. Traditional finishing of bathrooms and kitchen areas constitute a large amount of onsite construction time and involve various trades including plumbing, electrical, drywall, tiling, and so forth. All of this can be flattened in a factory environment. The critical element is loading, transport, and off-loading. Measures must be taken to ensure that the module does not undergo extreme deflections and cause cracking of finishes.

Bathroom modules in particular make sense when they will be repeated in an office building, hotel, dormitory, or housing complex. One-off bathrooms are not as affordable to accomplish in offsite fabrication, although for experimental purposes were developed by KieranTimberlake in the Loblolly House and the Cellophane House. Tedd Benson developed the modular fabrication method for the Loblolly, while Kullman Buildings Corp. developed the project for Cellophane and Pierson Modular. Today, Kullman is one of only a few companies that actually deliver prefab bathrooms in the United States. This technology has been worked on in Europe quite extensively and is now a market that both architects and builders use in their projects to deliver fast, affordable, high-quality modules on a regular basis.

MODULAR DIMENSIONS

Generally, dimensional requirements for modular construction are determined by transportation restrictions. These will be outlined in detail in Chapter 7, however, from the modular builders contributing to this book, rules of thumb have been assembled below:

- Module Width:
  - 13 ft Common Maximum
  - 16 ft Oversized Maximum

- Module Length:
  - 52 ft Common Maximum
  - 60 ft Oversized Maximum

- Module Height:
  - 12 ft Maximum

- Building Height:
  - 1 to 3 Stories Wood Modular
  - 5 to 12 Stories Steel Modular
  - 12 to 20+ Stories Steel and Precast Specialized Modular

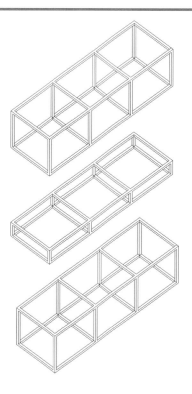

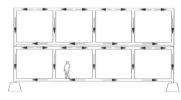

▶ Figure 6.21 Kullman Framing System (KFS) includes: Top: modules with an interstitial module accommodating space for utility distribution; and Bottom: verindeel truss box beam that distributes load to outer vertical module posts and to spot foundation locations mitigating the need for continuous bearing and a stem wall.

▶ Figure 6.22 One-piece workflow at Kullman allows laborers to focus on a set of tasks at one station before the module is moved on to another finish process. The casters and tracks at the base of the modules keep work flowing.

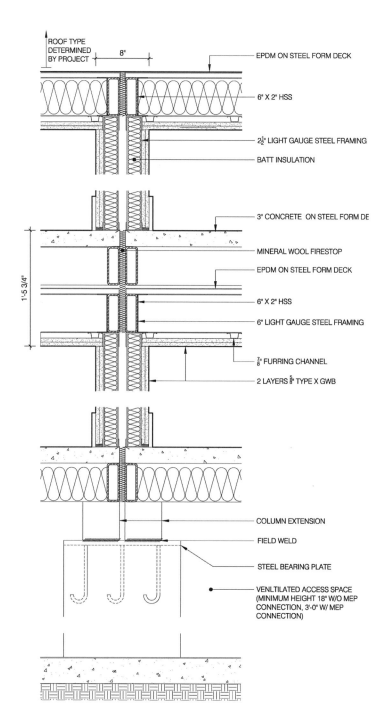

ROOF TYPE
DETERMINED
BY PROJECT

8"

EPDM ON STEEL FORM DECK

6" X 2" HSS

2½" LIGHT GAUGE STEEL FRAMING

BATT INSULATION

3" CONCRETE ON STEEL FORM DE

MINERAL WOOL FIRESTOP

EPDM ON STEEL FORM DECK

6" X 2" HSS

6" LIGHT GAUGE STEEL FRAMING

⅞" FURRING CHANNEL

2 LAYERS ⅝" TYPE X GWB

1'-5 3/4"

COLUMN EXTENSION

FIELD WELD

STEEL BEARING PLATE

VENLTILATED ACCESS SPACE
(MINIMUM HEIGHT 18" W/O MEP
CONNECTION, 3'-0" W/ MEP
CONNECTION)

Figure 6.23 Section of a typical
module-to-module connection for
a two-story stack at roof, floor, and
foundation condition. These are
typical details, with each project
dictating adaptations.

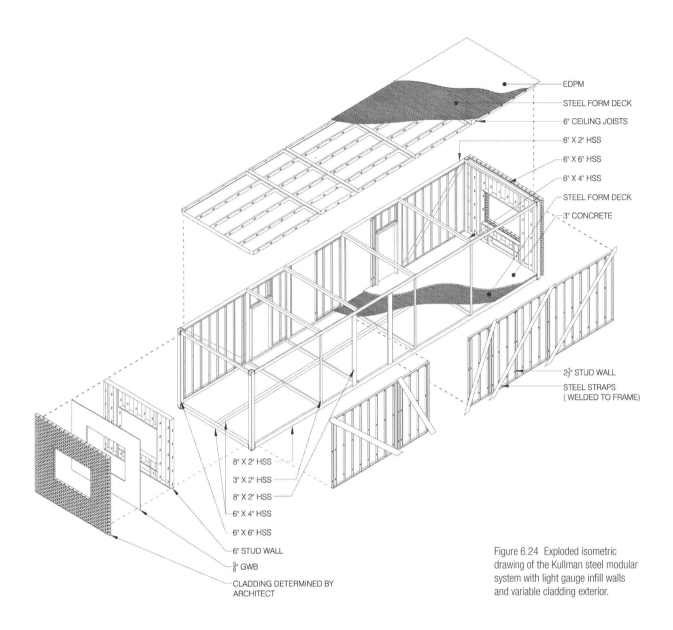

EDPM
STEEL FORM DECK
6" CEILING JOISTS
6" X 2" HSS
6" X 6" HSS
6" X 4" HSS
STEEL FORM DECK
3" CONCRETE
2$\frac{1}{2}$" STUD WALL
STEEL STRAPS (WELDED TO FRAME)

8" X 2" HSS
3" X 2" HSS
8" X 2" HSS
6" X 4" HSS
6" X 6" HSS
6" STUD WALL
$\frac{5}{8}$" GWB
CLADDING DETERMINED BY ARCHITECT

Figure 6.24 Exploded isometric drawing of the Kullman steel modular system with light gauge infill walls and variable cladding exterior.

At Rice University, Duncan and McMurtry College building in 2008, Kullman delivered 178 residential dormitory bathroom pods for two six-story 120,000 S.F. structures. The bathrooms included an outer shell constructed of glass fiber reinforced plastic (GFRP) and were connected to an outer steel frame. The modules are 6 ft × 8 ft including integral wall-hung plumbing fixtures, wall fixtures, and finishes. The modules were delivered onsite, hoisted, and set into place. The final plumbing and electrical connection were then made. Pods may be hoisted into an opening in the side of the building before enclosure is put on, which is the preferred method, or through the top as floors are being erected. The downside to the latter is that coordination is necessary to have modules onsite at different times within the intervals of placing floors. The pods can be rolled into place with a roller, similar to those used in mechanic shops to raise cars or for warehouse applications. Simpler methods are to use air casters on each corner of the module once it is craned into the building. Air casters are quickly replacing rollers as the preferred method of transporting heavy equipment short distances by hand. Using hover technology, air casters can hold from 500 to 10,000 lbs making maneuvering of service pods relatively easy.[42]

Linbeck Construction, the contractor on the Rice University project, commissioned Kullman to fabricate the pods in an effort to reduce onsite construction cost and overall construction time. The bathroom pod approach, according to Kullman, saved the project 50 percent over conventional construction on the bathroom scope. Because construction took place offsite, the pods eliminated construction waste as well as traffic to and from the site by subcontractors, both of which are common with detailed work of vari-

ous trades involved in bathroom finishing. Avi Telyas, CEO at Kullman states,

"Typically, conventionally constructed bathrooms are one of the most inefficient components of a project during the construction phase of a new multifamily-type building… This is usually the result of up to 10 different trades required to work consecutively in such a confined area."[43]

Modular is a growing industry making larger dents each year into the building market. Tom Hardiman of the Modular Building Institute indicates that the largest area of growth during 2009 for the modular industry was in the government projects sector, including the Army Corps. of Engineers, military housing, and administration buildings. The education market is also progressing with schools that have used portable classrooms looking to leverage modular to build entire schools permanently. The advantage to modular for schools is that projects need not require traditional bonding. Therefore, school administrators can sanction build-outs from discretionary funds just as they would a portable classroom. University and community college campuses are also looking at modular prefabrication as an option for temporary or fast construction projects on their campuses. The author has been in numerous meetings where temporary research and office space has been the point of discussion by upper administration trying to determine how to house students and faculty affordably and quickly. Health-care markets are also benefiting from modular, but in small percentage. The advantages

▶ Figure 6.25 Bathroom service units from Kullman are offered in two types. Above: framed modules with integrated mechanical plenum and finished with traditional bathroom finishes such as tile and standard fixtures; and Below: GFRP pods that are smaller but integrate all of the finishes and fixtures as a unit reflecting similar characteristics but slightly larger than airplane restroom units.

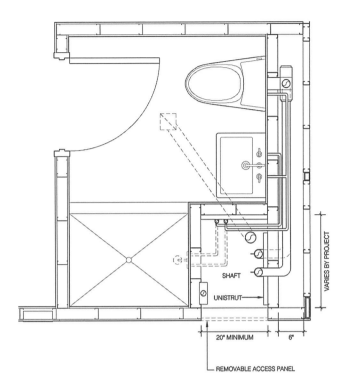

VARIES BY PROJECT

SHAFT

UNISTRUT

20" MINIMUM   6"

REMOVABLE ACCESS PANEL

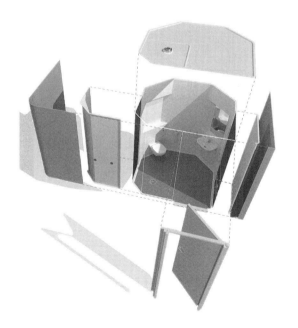

are that facilities may be erected in rural regions to meet the needs of those who cannot access health care. Modules may be fitted out with equipment and furnishings prepared to open upon setting. Other building types include restaurants and quick-service oil change stations. Modular makes sense for corporations that build small commercial buildings because their mission is branding and all buildings need to look the same across each community.[44]

6.4 ISBU Shipping Container

In the early 1930s, regional businessmen and trucking companies in the South began to develop innovative solutions to make shipping more efficient through compartments that were standardized. In 1955, Malcolm McLean, a trucking entrepreneur, studied these earlier efforts at containerization and began planning his own fleet of container ships to increase productivity in his family owned McLean Trucking Company. By 1956, McLean sold his trucking company to form the Pan-Atlantic Steamship Corporation, later renamed SeaLand, a company dedicated to containerized shipping. By 1970, the International Standards for Organization (ISO) container design was introduced.

The ISO intermodal shipping container revolutionized the international shipping trade nearly 50 years ago. Today, 90 percent of all nonbulk cargo is transported by ship, rail, or truck via the intermodal container. With the proliferation of shipping containers around the globe, an excess of containers in some regions is inevitable. This international trade deficit has made unused shipping containers potentially useable in architectural applications. As many as 125,000 abandoned containers currently clog British Ports and nearly 700,000 in the United States exist due to our enormous import industry. Throughout the world, shipping containers are used and are envisioned to fulfill the role of shelter.[45]

Also known as ISBU, or International Standard Building Units, shipping containers are ideal for prefabrication architecture because they are able to be loaded on to different modes of transport with their unique stackable chassis. Because the containers are constructed to transport a wide variety of goods safely in bulk quantity, their engineering makes them suitable to almost any built environment condition. Able to be stacked between 5 and 15 stories easily without additional reinforcement, container architecture will meet most building codes with little modification.

Containers are fabricated with the following specifications:

- Corner fittings for connections
- Corner posts for structural support of individual units
- Bottom side rails
- Top side rails
- Bottom end rail and door sill
- Front top end rail and door header
- Plywood or plank floor
- Front end wall
- Bottom cross members
- Roof panel (corrugated)
- Side panels (corrugated)
- Doors

Containers are constructed of 14-guage (.075 in.) corrugated COR-TEN sheet steel. COR-TEN is used for its natural corrosion-resistance, taking weathering well. The number of corrugations in the sheet metal varies widely on similarly sized containers. These panels are welded to the main structure, which is a 7-guage (.18 in.) tubular steel frame also fabricated in COR-TEN. The top, bottom, side, and end rails are fitted with ISO standardized cast steel corner fittings at all eight corners of the module and are able to withstand a 1,530,000-lb vertical load. Each unit and its floor structure are built to hold 65,000 lbs of weight when stacked up to seven units tall without seismic bracing. Roof panels may be supported by roof bows depending on the use of the container and support for stacking from frame and corner fittings. The tolerances on ISBUs is a remarkable ±3 millimeters. In addition, progressive collapse is mitigated because each unit is structurally sound.

Containers can be obtained at the cost of $1,500 used and $4,000 new. The actual price is contingent upon regional location, current international trade agreements, cost of oil, cost of raw materials to make the containers, and supply and demand economy for containers. Standard sizes of containers are 8 feet wide with variations in height at 8 ft, 8 ft-6 in., and 9 ft-6 in. Containers come in standard 20- and 40-ft lengths. General purpose containers can include some options in addition to dimensional adaptations, including double-end doors, coiling doors, side wall doors, and open sides. Before obtaining containers for architecture, an inspection is required to ensure cracks, breaks, tears, cuts, punctures, or corrosion in corner fittings and sidewall joints are not structurally unsafe.

	40 Foot Typical	40 Foot High Cube	20 Foot Typical	20 Foot High Cube
Ext. Length	40' – 0"	40' – 0"	19' – 10 ½"	19' – 10 ½"
Ext. Width	8' – 0"	8' – 0"	8' – 0"	8' – 0"
Ext. Height	8' – 6"	9' – 6"	8' – 6"	9' – 6"
Int. Length	39' – 4 13/64"	39' – 4 13/64"	19' – 4 13/64"	19' – 4 13/64"
Int. Width	7' – 8 33/64"	7' – 8 33/64"	7' – 8 33/64"	7' – 8 33/64"
Int. Height	7' – 10 3/32"	8' – 10 3/32"	7' – 10 3/32"	8' – 10 3/32"
Doorway Width	7' – 8 3/64"	7' – 8 3/64"	7' – 8 3/64"	7' – 8 3/64"
Doorway Height	7'– 5 49/64"	8' – 549/64"	7' – 5 49/64"	8' – 549/64"
Int. Cubic Capacity	2,390 cu. ft.	2,698 cu. ft.	1,170 cu. ft.	1,320 cu. ft.
Empty Weight	8,070 lbs.	8,470 lbs.	4,755 lbs.	5,070 lbs.
Maximum Payload	59,130 lbs.	58,730 lbs.	62,445 lbs.	62,130 lbs.

Figure 6.26 This chart identifies the ISO standards for intermodal transit of shipping containers.

With all of its benefits of transit-friendly, structural robustness and reuse disassembly capacities there are some disadvantages. ISBU requiring a manipulation of the standard module is going to be breached, reducing its structural capacity. The most effective use of the container from a cost, labor, and structural perspective is to keep the unit intact. This is not useful, however, in most building applications. The 8-ft module also limits the flexibility of the system. The COR-TEN steel must be insulated to avoid thermal transfer in both summer and winter. Methods such as furring out on the interior, adding an exterior insulation skin, or treating the COR-TEN with a ceramic-based insulating coating developed by the aerospace industry are methods that have been employed.

In addition to thermal resistance, soundproofing must also be considered. Because the units do not touch directly, but at points, offering a physical separation by which sound is more easily dampened, this is less of an issue. However, steel is an ideal conductive medium for sound and further attenuation is often necessary between adjacent units. Space for service distribution is limited. Especially regarding wastewater piping, there is not space between stacked units to run large-volume plumbing. A solution is to provide "service" containers that when stacked act as vertical and horizontal distribution modules and utility rooms. Fireproofing is somewhat of an issue, but can be mitigated through careful planning and suppressant measures.

Containers are loaded and unloaded with a forklift, boom/craft, or roll-off truck bed. A compact truck-mounted crane or a boom truck is the preferred delivery method unloading and stacking small-scale building projects. Trucks can deliver a 40-ft or two 20-ft-long containers at one time. Delivery fees increase for 40-ft containers. Site work, including foundation preparation, must be completed, and any additional structural supports must be in place before unloading and placing the containers. For a 20-ft container, 50 ft of straight clearance is required; and for a 40-ft container, 100 ft of clearance. Vertical clearance requirements include 14 ft overhead for roads, and 20 ft over the delivery site (for a one-story structure). The speed of erection is attractive as it limits the amount of labor onsite and the chance for injury.

Interest in shipping containers for architecture has grown in recent years. Architect Wes Jones of Jones Partners Architecture has been proposing the conversion of shipping containers to housing since 1995. His pioneering work pointed to many of the problems and potentials of using this standard unit including issues of site leveling, nesting, capability for compact transport, primary and secondary structural systems, marketing, cultural identity, and so forth. Since this time, many prototype experiments have been developed such as the pioneering work in London called Container City at Trinity Byou Warf in the Docklands in 2000. Container City is now a trademark owned by Urban Space Management Ltd., and has built nearly 20 projects in the United Kingdom. Today, shipping containers are not an entirely experimental building unit, but a viable option to make architecture. Two examples show the possibilities of such application on a large scale, including the "Keetwonen" temporary dormitory in Amsterdam, Netherlands, designed by Nicholas Lacey and Partners, and the UK "Travelodge" Hotel projects using a unique Verbus Systems, an ISBU dealer, engineered by Buro Happold Engineers. Less common in the United States, an example of ISBU by Hybrid Architects in Seattle will be presented in Chapter 9.

Keetwonen is a temporary housing student dormitory in Amsterdam. Commissioned by developer Woonstichting De Key in 2005, the project was intended to serve as housing for five years while land was being banked for a future use. Designed by Architectenburo JMW and built by Tempohousing, its popularity and success have postponed its relocation until 2016. The block consists of 1,000 units, five stories tall. Each unit has a private balcony, bathroom, and kitchen. The complex also includes a cafe, supermarket, office space, and a sport area with inner courtyard for bicycles and circulation for the residents. Keetwonen has integrated a roof topping that connects all the units to accommodate efficient rainwater drainage and provide insulation for the containers beneath. Tempohousing purchased a unique shipping container frame from a manufacturer in China who then transported it to another Chinese factory and fitted it to Temphousing standards. The completed modules were then shipped to Rotterdam and assembled. The cost of fabrication was much less than using onsite labor and using local labor to fit out the containers.[46]

The units used at Keetwonen were completely designed and engineered beforehand for connection, structure, and fit out. The units were designed to be relocate-able to another temporary site as a solution to housing in the Netherlands. But in order for this to be a reality, durability was crucial. Therefore, the design/build team sent advisors to the factory in China to ensure the quality of the ISBU. A complete mockup of the unit was evaluated and approved. In addition to quality, the project benefited from the speed of fabrication: 50 units a week, and speed of erection: averaged six minutes apiece from lifting from a truck with a crane and setting on the foundation or on another unit. Beginning in spring of 2005, 100 units were commissioned and ready for occupancy by late 2005. The entire project of 1,000 units was completed by summer 2006. ISBU was the only solution for fast, durable temporary housing at an affordable cost.

The *Travelodge* is a series of hotels in the United Kingdom that use container-like modules in their construction. Verbus Systems, a conglomerate of

ISBU SUPPLIERS

Tempohousing's Quinten de Gooijer comments that since the Tempohousing project completion:

"We have received a lot of emails from all around the world from people and companies who want to set up local production along the lines of what Tempo has developed and manufactured. Most people underestimate completely how much time and effort it takes to set up a production line that produces the product that you want to have: it is no use trying to set this up for a smaller production quantity than say 500 homes per year…. What we also see that existing shipping container depots around the world (you will find several near each port in the world) also try to get in to this business but they also underestimate what level of detail is required to move from simple site offices on a construction site to professionally manufactured prefab homes that meet all the building requirements that apply to normal residential developments, in particular in relation to in house climate, humidity issues, ventilation and all that but also in relation of high rise, where high standards for stability of the whole building apply, especially in areas with high wind forces or seismic movements."[47]

Buro Happold Engineers and George and Harding Construction, designed the modules specifically for hotel applications. Buro Happold Engineers is an innovative full-service building engineering firm that developed the technology for the Container City. The modules are similar to ISO containers but slightly larger. In order to accommodate the dimensions of a hotel room, a 12 ft × 42.65 ft module was used. The containers used standard ISO fittings so they could be stacked 16 stories without additional structural support. The projects were designed to save an estimated 10 percent on construction costs and as much as 25 percent in construction time, compared to typical onsite construction methods. Apart from time and cost, Adrian Robinson from Buro Happold states that the quality of construction was intended to be just as good as standard construction and that acoustics were envisioned as being superior. During construction, tolerances were not as critical as some other prefab methods.

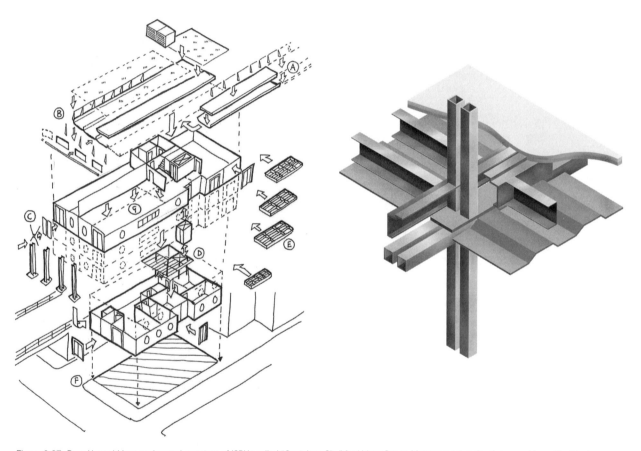

Figure 6.27 Buro Happold has engineered a system of ISBUs called "Container City" for Urban Space Management, a developer working with shipping container architecture since 2000. To date nearly 20 projects have been completed including housing, retail, office space, and day care facilities. Projects by the team are currently being planned for the United States. Left: early diagrams by Buro Happold Engineers identify the elements of the system, and Right: a detail of the connection of the ISBU modules to one another.

Figure 6.28 An exterior image of the 2005 Riverside Project designed by A.B.K Architects and Buro Happold Engineers for Urban Space Management in London's Docklands.

Although the interiors were finished out in China, the major obstacle of using custom containers was the fact that the cladding and structure were made independently and at different times. Cost and time reductions were not as great because of the amount of onsite work that was necessary to structure and skin the building.[48]

Shipping containers make the most sense when a modular, large-scale or rapid build project is desirable. In addition, for sites that are confined or meant to be temporary it is an ideal solution. Given its drawbacks of poor thermal performance and strict limitation on geometry, it may not fit every solution but can provide an effective and affordable

TRAVELODGE UXBRIDGE HOTEL

Recently, the Uxbridge hotel, eight stories tall with 120 rooms, and the Heathrow, a similar 310-room hotel, are being completed. Unfortunately, Travelodge did not use containers because of their plentiful supply. The ISBUs were made specific for the job at hand. However, the benefits of transportation and erection efficiencies weighed out in the end. The savings for a hotel chain is large and Travelodge plans on building 670 new hotels by 2020 using this method. Verbus Systems claims that they have saved 40 to 60 percent on construction schedule and reduced construction waste by 70 percent in comparison to onsite methods. Not wanting to disrupt urban neighborhoods with ongoing construction, the units were set in 20 days. Stitching and finishing included, Verbus Systems saved Uxbridge a documented 10 weeks in total construction schedule duration. In an already rapid construction schedule of 40 weeks with onsite methods, 30-week duration can save Travelodge by increasing operational capital through an early start.

Figure 6.29 The Verbus Systems is an ISBU technology developed by Buro Happold Engineers and George and Harding Construction for the Travelodge Hotel chain. The building is eight stories tall, 120 rooms, and was completed with a reported 10 percent reduction in cost, and 25 percent reduction in schedule. Erected in 20 weeks, the project saved Travelodge 10 weeks, allowing them to recapture capital with an early open date.

method of construction. In the future, used shipping containers should be implemented into construction to reduce embodied energy and increase the benefits to local labor for a given project. This requires architects working closely with the design team, client, and container fabricator or outfitter in order to deliver a quality and affordable product. In the future, port cities may have ISBU fabricators that outfit shipping containers for architectural applications, however, currently the only manufacturers are in China. Buro Happold envisions that this could be a method to offer disassembly and reuse of units for future developments although no projects to date have done such a thing with ISBU construction.

6.5 Conclusion

Moving toward greater degrees of prefabrication from components to panels to modules, flexibility in the systems progressively diminishes. From size limitations due to transport to restrictions in utility distribution, a balance must be struck between design intent and production method. In the end, a hybrid mix of systems may be appropriate taking elements that offer the capacity to increase productivity, but leaving those that sacrifice design freedom behind. In order for this to occur, design and building teams must work together—architects, engineers, contractors, and subcontractors working to find an appropriate project-wide strategy to prefabrication.

chapter 7 ASSEMBLY

Until the late 1700s, manufacturing was a craft-based activity in which one person was responsible for all aspects of manufacturing, including procurement of materials. This method of manufacture had disadvantages: Products were supply- rather than demand-driven, making the capacity to meet an increase in demand impossible. New products or new technologies were inefficient because there was no common building block; and manufacturing methods were inefficient due to a lack of repetitions involved in the work. The Industrial Revolution allowed for more effective sources of power and advances in manipulation. From drilling and milling to lathing and deforming presses, the primary manufacturing technologies have not changed in the history of industrialized manufacturing, only the tools and materials have been improved. These improvements consist of the following:

- Interchangeability: realization of the concept of interchangeability of parts for a given product was developed. This allowed random pieces to be selected and assembled to form a single product.

- Increase in production rate: separation between primary manufacturing and assembly. Fitting is the process of improvement to allow for product functionality while assembly is a secondary process whereby one manipulates the finished parts into a meaningful spatial relationship.[1]

Fitting is the making of parts that when assembled can be a meaningful whole. For manufacturing of automobiles, an assembly may be parts that make up a single door, or the door may be a fitted part that when assembled with the rest of the parts constitute an assembly—the automobile. During the early Industrial Revolution, the act of fitting constituted a great deal of time and energy. Today, fitting is relatively negligible in the manufacturing industry. In the building industry, however, it is quite the opposite. Fitting parts together onsite is standard practice. Much in the way early Fords were run on a production line adding one part at a time to an overall assembly, onsite construction relies on the craft of individuals to piece together buildings into an assemblage. Prefabrication works to implement the concepts of interchangeability and increased production rate discovered in manufacturing and apply them toward construction.

For the sake of this chapter, the manufacturing terms of *parts*, *subassemblies,* and *assembly* will be used and appropriated to prefab construction. They refer to three levels of manufacture and fabrication from material to final building:

- Parts: Parts are fitted products that may be standalone materials or may be components for construction. In offsite construction, parts are not erected onsite, rather joined together in a subassembly in the factory. These are MTS elements.

- Subassemblies: This refers to components, panels, or modules that are pieced together with parts to

create elements to be assembled onsite. These are MTO products.

- Assembly: This is the act of setting subassemblies together onsite in their final location and stitching.

Some of the difficulties of comparing construction to manufacturing can be found in the peculiarity of the construction industry. According to Hook, the peculiarities of onsite construction include the following:[2]

- One-of-a-kind production: Manufacturing uses repetition or similarity between each product in the factory. Product fitting on the jobsite is unique every time.

- Site production: By virtue of the location being on the jobsite exposed to the elements and vulnerable to forces outside of factory control, construction is inefficient in its fitting.

- Temporary organization: Each project is one-off, requiring a temporary site organization of labor, location of materials and tools, and temporary support facilities such as office, computer, restrooms, and break areas. The location of the parts and assemblies are not carried over into the next project.

- Regulatory agency: An organization that carries out the inspection process from the municipality with jurisdiction over the location of the building.

Prefab architecture works to resolve the issues of peculiarities of construction. Both waste reduction and value generation must be taken into consideration to make a prefabrication solution work.[3] Offsite fabrication in buildings suggests that parts come together in the factory to a level in which assembly can occur with ease onsite. The drawback is that buildings are not standardized; therefore establishing fitting parts and subassemblies for building is still an expensive portion of labor and time. For building construction to progress and take advantage of the benefit of factory production, fitting must be expedited leaving final assembly to craft of construction as much as possible in the factory and as little as possible onsite. A movement toward more interchangeable parts and the increase in production rate by favoring direct assembly onsite versus fitting parts onsite will increase productivity.

7.1 Mass Customization

In the 1990s the concepts of lean manufacturing and mass customization were seen as the business strategies of the future, offering a streamlined approach to delivering infinite variability while reducing cost.[4] Although the concepts of lean manufacturing and mass customization are beginning to have an impact on architecture, there is still relatively little connection between design software environments and manufacturing output. Therefore, most products today are still designed with a standardized mentality—shop drawings are submitted, and design and manufacture are rarely integrated. Schodek and colleagues call manufacturers that have CNC tools "islands of automation" that present potentials for mass customization, but require architects to engage in a meaningful collaboration with manufacturing in order to realize these benefits.[5] The prime example of mass customization having reached increased variety with reduced cost is window manufacturers. No windows are made the same, and to do so would not offer any reduced cost that was significant enough to warrant standardization over tightly fitting custom windows.

Mass customization is a result of digital technology and manufacturing tool development. However, the objective can only be realized in its full potential if an end-to-end delivery process is implemented, eliminating potential inefficiencies. This may be accomplished through prefab companies that deliver products such as Project Frog and Blu Homes. These companies, however, are also constantly looking to diversify. Architects may become product developers, as in the case of Michelle Kaufmann, who flattens the entire design-to-delivery process. Or, architects may engage with product developers such as KieranTimberlake with Living Homes, or Resolution 4: Architecture offering designs that are a mass-customized system to be adapted to user needs.

Mass customization is much more common in industrial design, where variation is not an entirely unique building that in no way resembles the one before it, but rather a product that has many similar products with slight adaptations. In short, the differences between architecture and industrial design are in volume and repeatability. Although a fully integrated mass customization model is not entirely possible under the current methods of project development and delivery, a few models exist in industrial design that can be transferred to architecture. As adapted from Schodek and colleagues:[6]

- Component-sharing modularity: same fundamental components with appearance variability within each discrete product (changing cladding options initially from project to project)

- Component-swapping modularity: same configuration of appearance with ability to swap out component function (changing cladding options post-occupancy)

- Cut-to-fit modularity: varying length, width, or height of a product by cutting to size based on a fixed module (standardized cladding that can be increased or reduced in size in production)

- Mix modularity: variation is achieved by mixing products (cladding in which multiple layers can be added or taken away in fabrication)

- Bus modularity: a base structure that supports a number of attachments, sometimes called "platform design" (base frame to which numerous cladding materials and systems can be attached)

- Sectional modularity: parts are all different but share a common connection method (cladding panels may vary, but the connection to frame is always the same)

7.2 Assembly Strategies

The two most important strategies in designing for assembly include:[7]

- Reduce the number of operations in assembly on-site to benefit:

  ○ Reducing assembly time and cost depending on methods and processes

  ○ Potential for less failures resulting in less expensive production rates

  ○ Higher product reliability

  ○ Lower manufacturing cost

  ○ Faster implementation

  ○ Ability to assemble logistically

- Reduce the number of parts in a subassembly and the number of subassemblies in an assembly. The reason that too many products are present for an assembly can be attributed to:

  ○ Cost of fewer parts and subassemblies is higher than more parts in an assembly. This is not the rule, however, as manufacturing has shown that the continual reduction of parts in an assembly overall will yield a project at lower cost.

  ○ Designers and construction professionals rely on conventions in construction, which may be consistent from design to design but are not congruent with developments in manufacturing and production.

When a part or subassembly is not functional or does not clearly benefit the integrated whole, it can potentially be integrated into another part or be removed altogether. Boothroyd and Dewhurst suggest the following questions be asked when determining the need for a part or the possibility of its integration with another: [8]

- Does the specific part or subassembly have to move relative to other parts in order to accomplish its intended function?

- Does it have to be made from a different type of material than others in the assembly?

- Does the part or subassembly enable a capability in the assembly that would not be possible without it?

- Does the part or subassembly need to be replaced or maintained more than others in the assembly?

If the part is not needed it should be removed or integrated into another assembly. This process may include revisiting the other parts and assembly to determine if it needs to be further simplified or reworked to meet the assimilated part functions.[9] KieranTimberlake and Tedd Benson on the Loblolly

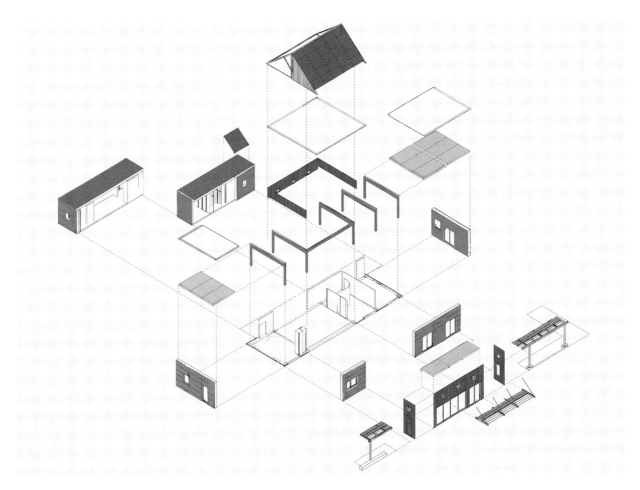

Figure 7.1 Bensonwood, builders of the Unity House at Unity College in Maine, was able to reduce the number of components in the building from 5,000 in traditional onsite construction to 50. Bensonwood developed a panelized and modular system to deliver this net zero house for the president of the college.

House worked to reduce the number of assembly operations onsite to a minimum, this includes finding ways in which to reduce or remove unnecessary parts or to assimilate more parts into a specific subassembly. In the Unity House, built by Bensonwood, this process reduced the number of parts from 5,000 parts to 50 subassemblies.

The act of design necessarily requires a consideration of the act of assembly. KieranTimberlake have developed a system for how they think about assembly and disassembly in the construction sequence. This has fed the methods by which their buildings are produced and erected in the field. A disjuncture between design intent and execution can occur if project teams are not well integrated as assembly decisions are being made during early design stages. This also ensures that disassembly is more possible. Ordering the assembly process during design can greatly impact the aesthetics of

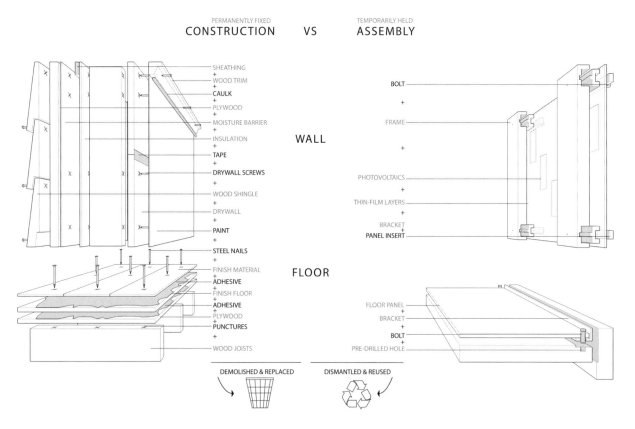

PERMANENTLY FIXED   TEMPORARILY HELD
CONSTRUCTION   VS   **ASSEMBLY**

WALL

FLOOR

Figure 7.2 Assembly diagram that has become a staple of the work of KieranTimberlake outlines the goals of the Cellophane House, designed and built for the MOMA exhibit "Home Delivery." While onsite methods employ many materials and processes of construction that eventually are demolished and replaced, prefab solutions offer the potential for disassembly and reuse.

projects. Designing without this information leads to cost overruns but also settling for something less at the end of the day. Negotiations are part of any design process, however, if the information for design comes from an ordering of assembly sequence the concept is much more closely linked to the actual product.

A useful way of thinking about assembly order is to first evaluate the designed assembly and then begin to systematically disassemble it. Reversing this process can suggest a more effective assem-

bly order. This will require an integration of design, engineering, and detailing. Prefabricated modules, panels, and components made in larger subassemblies allow a shift of the work to the factory where the coordination of MTO products may be better assimilated and integrated. This requires a structuring of the supply chain for flow increasing the probably of timely delivery of subassembly components by reducing the number of intersecting flows.

Buildings that are difficult to build, difficult to disassemble and assemble, will cost more whether in initial bids or in change orders. Prefabricated elements present an opportunity to develop details that are easy to assemble onsite. As every crew has a different set of materials and installation methods, prefab mitigates trade clashes and unforeseen assembly problems that are then handled in the factory. A quality assembly, although usually described by architects as being expressive aesthetically, is not exclusively effective from an assembly and construction perspective. The goal of any effective design process is to find solutions that meet both criteria. For logistical prefabrication, however, assembly principles that are important to consider include the following, list adapted from Allen and Rand:[10]

- Uncut units: Dimensional and modular coordination between subassemblies that will be assembled onsite so that little or no cutting or manipulation is required.

- Minimize elements: This idea is to limit the number of elements to be shipped and erected. This reduces not only labor but also the possibility for failure at joints. The fewer the joints, the better.

- Easy to handle: While designing prefabricated elements, care should be taken to not design elements that are either too large for fabrication, shipping, or erection (hoisting) from a size or weight perspective. There should be clarity in how the element is installed—either it is directionless or is clearly unsymmetrical for easy install. Keying elements with codes is also a coordination method.

- Repetition: When it is unimportant to have special or unique conditions, using repetition in the construction sequence leads to higher-quality and faster erection. This becomes more important on larger projects where standardization cost reductions can be captured.

- Simulation and prototyping: When possible simulations of construction sequencing should be performed to anticipate potential conflicts. BIM has allowed much of this to occur through 4D and 5D analysis. In addition, prototyping and mockups allow for early prefabrication errors to be worked out. Not only mockup of a system in the factory, but a test onsite for assembly ease.

- Accessible mockups: Teams can place prototypes onsite for observation by crews erecting the project. This can especially be important if multiple individuals are installing. Education is critical to the construction process, but it is more important in prefab when efficient design methods are being capitalized.

- Accessible connections: It is vital to design assemblies so that onsite installers can reach work simply. Placing elements at an accessible height to standing and assemblies to occur once the superstructure is erected from the decks themselves allows for ease of installation. Sequences that do not allow workers to access parts in order to bolt, screw, seal, or nail must be reworked onsite. This includes connections that are behind columns, spandrel beams, corners, and so forth. This is also true as connections may need to be accessed for maintenance or disassembly.

- Clearances: Even though a structure might be designed and manufactured to fit snugly, onsite variances as a result of erection dimensional intolerance, and simply maneuvering an element into its final space requires that all details have a little extra space in addition to their own dimension. A common example is a window unit fitting into a rough opening. But this example can be applied to all prefabricated elements in a building construction.

• Clash detections: A classic overrun of cost is due to change orders as a result of conflicting systems in a building. This is common between structure, enclosures, and space systems. Services often conflict with one another and the structural system. In offsite assembly, this can happen between prefabricated elements but more especially between a prefabricated element and a site-built element. Taking an element back to be reworked is cost prohibitive. If not coordinated properly, prefab can cost more than ever imagined in onsite. Clash detection can be mitigated through careful coordination during design via BIM tools.

7.3 Assembly Detailing

Assembly details can be improved upon to decrease onsite setting time. Standard practice or details that are stock solutions may be the simplest way conceptually to achieve a given scenario; however, when addressing new circumstances details should be tried through making. This recognizes that even a well-conceived prefab system of assembly is not fully understood in all of its parameters until it is made in physical. Since this is the area where architects and makers have a shared interest in expression and performance, detailing assembly requires an intimate knowledge of the construction process. The design team must be fully engaged in the act of assembly, visiting manufacturers' and builders' work often to establish the context for design. Detailing for assembly requires that subassemblies and assembly be rehearsed again and again. The improvement of detailing is not only to listen, but also to push. A carefully considered detail in the office may not work in the field, but a detail in the field often cannot get better unless pushed upon by designers.

Building teams must consider weather and climate in detailing for prefabrication and onsite assembly operations. The time of year has a great affect because it determines the temperature, humidity levels, and difficulty of onsite install. Operations such as roofing, painting, laying masonry, and the like cannot be done in certain weather conditions. Although prefabrication offers this to be taken care of in a factory, stitching onsite still presents problems. Precast elements or laminated wood structures that are established in the factory in climate-controlled conditions and then shipped to site where the temperature and humidity levels vary from that of the factory can experience thermal stresses that literally pull panels or modules apart. It is suggested that teams design MTO elements for projects with an understanding of the time of year and the temperature and precipitation expected when built. Its assembly onsite is the most susceptible time in a prefab element's lifecycle. Anticipating potential problems with weather-sensitive operations and mitigating these problems by selecting systems can add to the value of a project. Water affected the assembly of the Pierson College student dormitory, designed by KieranTimberlake, while setting the modules, causing a schedule delay to dry out the units before finishing. The fluctuations in temperature and humidity in Manhattan caused the Alice Tully Hall team to extend their schedule, making interior systems installation spread over an entire year.

7.4 Sequence

Assembly refers to all site installation activities. Therefore, it includes not only a plan for managing parts, subassemblies, and onsite assembly detailing, but also includes operations design, labor supply, crew management, shared resource management,

Figure 7.3   Pierson College modular set in 2004 designed by KieranTimberlake and fabricated by Kullman Buildings Corp.

PARAMETERS OF DETAILING

The following are principles that should be considered by design and construction professionals when devising details for either onsite or offsite construction adapted from Allen and Rand's *Architectural Detailing*[11] and Linda Brock's *Designing the Exterior Wall*.[12]

1. Water:
   - Eliminate openings in building assemblies (barrier wall)
   - Keep water away from openings and building assemblies (overhang)
   - Neutralize forces that move water through openings and assemblies (rainscreen)
2. Air infiltration:
   - Tight tolerances
   - Air barrier surface
   - Seal or gasket joints

continued

3. Energy:
    - Control conduction (insulation, break, air gaps)
    - Control radiation (reflective surfaces, and air gap)

4. Condensation:
    - Keep interior surfaces at temperature above dew point of the air (insulation, breaks)
    - Warm side vapor retarder
    - Ventilate cold side of vapor retarder to release moisture
    - Catch and remove condensation through gravity

5. Sound:
    - Airtight, heavy, limp mediating surface (layered walls, sealant)
    - Quiet attachments (separations of assemblies, pads, and flexible joints)
    - Sound attenuating surface

6. Movement:
    - Temperature movements (control and movement joints)
    - Moisture/phase change movements (removal of moisture, drying)
    - Dead and live loading (abutment joints for dissimilar structures)
    - Settlement and creep (separation joint)

7. Attachment:
    - Protrusions from exterior surface
    - Water removal gutters and downspout attachments
    - Eave, sash, sill attachment
    - Canopies
    - Shading element
    - Parapets
    - Fixity of enclosure
    - Rainscreen to wall attachment
    - Backup wall secured
    - Glass bite
    - Metal spandrel and cladding

site materials management, and commissioning.[13] The following is an offsite fabrication and assembly product sequence checklist, adapted from Gibb, that should be considered when developing a project-wide prefabrication strategy.[14]

- Basic design concept:
    - overall dimensions for transport
    - height, width, and length and weight restrictions
    - crane capacity and access onsite

- Unit construction:
  - lifting points detail
  - jacking point detail
  - transport securing details
- Transportation:
  - route to site
  - access to site
  - permits and clearances
  - details for transport securing
  - road closure
  - delivery times
- Hoisting:
  - access onsite
  - crane location
  - crane selection
  - crane reach and loads
  - permits and clearances
  - road closures for crane
- Insurances:
  - transportation insurance
  - crane insurance
  - lifting insurance
- Method statement:
  - produce detailed method statement
  - delivery cycle
  - night working provisions

  - crane specifications
  - lighting gear details and assembly
  - access routes
  - limitations on other trades
  - structural loadings
- Certifications:
  - Inspections
  - road closures
  - permits
  - crane inspection
  - lifting gear inspections
  - unions
  - insurance documents
  - warranties

Designing for assembly requires that architects and engineering and construction professionals rehearse sequences before construction. This may include developing initial schematic sketches with construction as a design exercise. In addition, during development architects and engineers can use digital tools to map the construction sequence. This process does not stop at the level of jobsite workflows, but can be managed back to source material and to detailing of connections and assemblies to ensure that sequence is well executed. Rand and Allen suggest detailing in the order in which subassembly elements are assembled, thinking simultaneously of the actual construction operations that are represented by each new element of the drawing and trying to see the detail not as an object, but as a process.

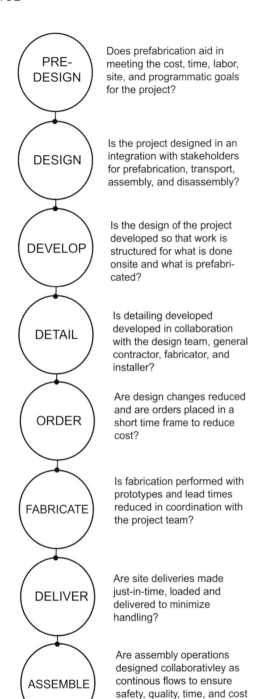

PRE-DESIGN — Does prefabrication aid in meeting the cost, time, labor, site, and programmatic goals for the project?

DESIGN — Is the project designed in an integration with stakeholders for prefabrication, transport, assembly, and disassembly?

DEVELOP — Is the design of the project developed so that work is structured for what is done onsite and what is prefabricated?

DETAIL — Is detailing developed developed in collaboration with the design team, general contractor, fabricator, and installer?

ORDER — Are design changes reduced and are orders placed in a short time frame to reduce cost?

FABRICATE — Is fabrication performed with prototypes and lead times reduced in coordination with the project team?

DELIVER — Are site deliveries made just-in-time, loaded and delivered to minimize handling?

ASSEMBLE — Are assembly operations designed collaborativley as continous flows to ensure safety, quality, time, and cost parameters are met?

The critical path is the engagement of labor. Inefficiencies in schedule as a result of too many trades can slow a project down. For assembly purposes, projects that flatten the manufacture-to-assembly sequence capitalize on using fewer manufacturers. More trades mean more mistakes of intellectual mis-alignments and material and products miss fittings. Striving for assemblies that require a minimum number of trades and visits per trades, needing little or no temporary support, requiring no special tools, and a minimal need for ladders or scaffolding will increase onsite assembly.[15] For componentized and panel-ized elements, truck-to-truck the sequence of onsite erection must be carefully ordered. Within each load on a truck the components must be reverse-sequen-

◀Figure 7.4 Employing prefabrication demands that offsite be considered at each step of a project lifecycle. This outlines the process of offsite construction and the considerations that should be made at each level of project delivery. Note that the project stages do not place responsibility, as to suggest that stakeholders work collaboratively to realize prefab architecture.

▼ Figure 7.5 A truck being flat-packed at Bensonwood before shipment. The panel elements are all placed on the truck in reverse order of how they will be placed onsite. Maximizing the shipping envelope reduced the cost of transport.

tially located in order to accommodate erection process. Items shipped in transit have the potential to be damaged. The contract should carefully spell out who is responsible for items damaged in transit and how recompense will be made.

The specifications for prefabrication should outline how the module, panel, or component is going to be picked up. These are generally called pick points. For lighter elements built all in wood for residential construction, this is relatively simple using a wraparound strap or belt; however, for larger objects this can be costly due to crane sizes and/or labor involved in developing a method for install. Although each element in offsite fabrication may be designed uniquely and any given project may have a myriad of ways in which it "could" be erected, a universal system of picking and setting is desirable as it mitigates differences in hoisting and placing equipment. If not properly handled, elements can be damaged in the hoisting stage not only due to hitting objects, but also due to loads. A wood module, for example, can crack at the back because it was not designed to withstand loads due to hoisting. Often this alone is the reason to go with a chassis or a steel frame base.

7.5 Transportation

Transportation presents a major consideration in the design of the elements and how they come together in the overall structure. Breaking down elements so that they must be shipped limits size of the individual panels, modules, or components but also the final building form aesthetic by determining joints, reveals, and element dimensions. In addition, building subassemblies must be protected during transit so that damage is mitigated.

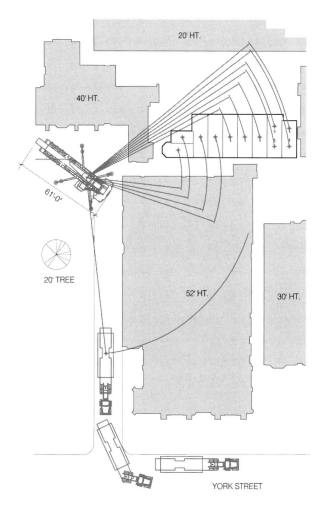

Figure 7.6 Pierson College modular set crane path rehearsed in detail before actuation. The delivery, pick, hoist, and sets were all planned in an integrated manner during the design and fabrication process.

In addition to transport and assembly, sequencing that influences design staging also should be considered. Although ideally offsite-manufactured elements are not standing still, staging does occur on every jobsite. How the materials will be protected is critically important especially if they are finished out and ready to install. Care should be taken to ensure subassemblies are installed as soon as possible.

There are two primary methods of transporting building products from manufacture and fabrication to site for assembly:

- The first method is container shipping. Containers are standardized in size, pick points (method of lifting and locating), attachment between adjacent units and shipping chassis and decks by the International Standards of Organization (ISO), an international organization that develops standards in different industries so they are consistent across international borders. A discussion of the details of size and weight restrictions is presented in Chapter 6 and will not be covered in any detail in this section.

- The second method is called "dimensional" or "cargo" shipping, which refers to abnormal shipping sizes or unique custom dimensions outside of the ISO unit standards. These terms apply to all methods of shipment including rail, truck, ship, air, and on rare occasion, helicopter. Dimensional shipping is applicable to panels, modules, or components that are too wide, high, or long to fit in ISO containers.

ISO containers are brought to an intermodal hub to be shipped out. They are priced and dealt with differently than dimensional shipping at every method of transit. ISO containers are, in general, the most affordable and accessible way to transport without permits and special clearances from transportation organizations.[16] Mark and Peter Anderson experienced that when shipping building elements to Japan—dimensional shipping has been upward of 10 times the cost of shipping elements in ISO containers. Therefore, in international projects in which elements are produced in one country and shipped to another, transportation can account for the majority of the cost of construction. Prefab must com-

pensate for the added cost of shipping to make this option viable.

Although rail transit is efficient, today the United States relies on road transportation through trucking. In 1938, during the Great Depression and in conjunction with the Works Progress Administration, President Franklin D. Roosevelt delineated the first eight-superhighway corridors across the United States. By 1956, President Eisenhower authorized the National Interstate and Defense Highways Act to create a system modeled after the European Autobahn. The 1960s brought about the single-modal use of semitrailer trucks, which are both economical and feasible. This convenient form of transport was faster than rail and became the standardized method by which the majority of all cargo is now delivered.

Although some transport of building products may occur by rail today, prefabricated elements in almost all circumstances arrive onsite by truck. The rare exceptions are sites located directly adjacent to rail lines or seaports in which building components may be loaded and unloaded directly to a train car or boat and then unloaded directly to the location of assembly. Airplane or helicopters, the third option of travel, are most often cost prohibitive. Helicopters should only be considered in the rare instance that the site is too remote or inaccessible.

7.5.1 Truck[17]

Regulations for commercial trucking are set by two agencies, one at the national level—Federal Size Regulations for Commercial Motor Vehicles, U.S. Department of Transportation, Federal Highway Administration (FHWA)—and the other at the state level. Federal guidelines are given for the general national network of interstates. Often they default to the state. Many states have grandfathered guidelines that are respected by the FHWA. The goal of the FHWA is to keep the population safe. Often the difficulty can be in negotiating the trucking regulations as a shipment traverses state lines. In these cases, transportation must follow the more restrictive of the states that are crossed as well as the FHWA. For example, Irontown Homes, while shipping a Michelle Kaufmann and Paul Warner–designed house, had to pass from Utah through California and into Nevada. California was the most restrictive state of the three and therefore required a truck escort the entire trip.

Federal Regulations

- Federal guidelines for commercial truck widths is 8 ft-6 in. Hawaii is the only exception with a 9-ft-0-in. width allowance. These federal limits do not apply to special mobile equipment including military, farm, maintenance, and emergency vehicles such as fire trucks. If states want to allow vehicles more than 8 ft-6 in. wide to operate on interstates in their borders, then the state is federally required to issue a special over-width permit.

- The minimum allowable length limit for a semitrailer linked to a truck tractor is 48 ft, or the grandfathered limit for a particular state. A state may not impose an overall vehicle length limit on a truck tractor–semitrailer combination operating on the national network of interstates or a reasonable access route, even if the trailer is longer than the minimum length required by federal law. A state may not impose an overall length limit on a truck tractor pulling a single semitrailer or a limit on the distance between the axles of such a truck tractor.

- A truck tractor is a non-cargo-carrying powerunit used in combination with a semitrailer. A truck that carries cargo on the same chassis as the power unit and cab, commonly known as a straight truck, is not subject to federal regulations, but is subject to state provisions only. Likewise, a straight truck towing a trailer or semitrailer is subject only to state vehicle length regulations, expect that the total length of its two cargo-carrying units may not exceed a federally established limit of 65 ft.

- The standard configuration for shipping prefabricated elements by road is a truck tractor and semitrailer, or lowboy, to allow for greater height in the prefabricated element shipping. Although trailer regulations are given by states, widely accepted standards have produced set trailer types and sizes for cargo transport.

- Lengths for truck tractors with two trailing units can be 95 ft. This goes up to 111 ft for Colorado. The weight is from 129,000 lbs up to 137,800 lbs in Montana. With three trailing units, the length is 95 ft and 129,999 lbs again. These vary slightly from the previous restrictions. Regulations for states tend to be more space-generous in the West and less so in the East due to infrastructure being more open in the former.[18]

State Regulations

Regulations for shipping by truck mandated by the state vary as discussed. Below is an example of the state of Utah in order to get a perspective on the parameters that one must consider in prefab shipping. The Utah Department of Transportation's Motor Carrier Division has summarized these state regulations in the *Utah Trucking Guide 2009*.[19]

The legal dimensions for shipping products:

- Height: 14 ft

- Width: 8 ft-6 in.

- Length: Semitrailer is 48 ft from front of trailer to the back

  ○ Double trailer combo: 61 ft measured from front of the first trailer to the rear of the second trailer

  ○ An integral truck/trailer or "straight truck" has a limit of 65 ft measured from bumper to bumper

  ○ Overhangs for all conditions may be 3 ft in the front and 6 ft in the back

If dimensions are over these regulations, permits are required. *Oversized permitted vehicles must comply with the following restrictions:*

- Height: 14 ft

- Width: 14 ft-6 in.

- Length: 105 ft

Permit fees for shipping oversized loads should be considered. These fees are marginal, compared to overall shipping costs and the cost of a building project and can usually be absorbed by the company in the bid for shipping generally. *Permit fees for oversized loads include:*

- Single trip: $30

- Semi-annual: $75

- Annual: $90

It should be noted that states may make exceptions for oversized permits of vehicles that are more than 14 ft-6 in. wide, 14 ft high, or 105 ft long if it determines as such. Outside of oversized permitted loads, additional dimensioned loads are allowed in Utah. Loads exceeding 17 ft in width on two-lane routes, 20 ft in width on interstates, or 17 ft-6 in. in height on all public highways may be allowed when accompanied by a Utah Department of Transportation employee and an escort vehicle. These costs are paid by the shipping company, including overtime. Should utility lines, traffic control devices, or other obstacles need to be moved, the associated costs are absorbed by the shipping company as well. In addition, any damage that is incurred during transport is taken care of by the shipping company. Careful planning should be made in these cases to ensure the route, from point of departure to point of arrival, is clear and can anticipate obstructions to make accommodation, obtain proper utility authorizations, clearances, and organize certified pilot escorts. Warning lights, flags, "OVERSIZED LOAD" signs, and other guidelines need to be accommodated by mandate of the state.

Convoys are the movement of more than one permitted vehicle. This is done when trucks in two or more are carrying elements for the building project. The restrictions also vary per state. *Utah convoy shipping restrictions include:*

- Number of permitted vehicles in the convoy shall not exceed two.

- Loads may not exceed 12 ft wide or 150 ft overall length.

- Distance between vehicles shall not be less than 500 ft or more than 700 ft.

- Distance between convoys shall be a minimum of one mile.

- All convoys shall have a certified pilot/escort in the front and rear with proper signs.

- Police escorts or UDOT personnel may be required

Pilot escort for oversized permitted loads are required for the following dimensional conditions:

- 12 ft in width on secondary highways (noninterstate)

- 14 ft in width on divided highways (interstates)

- 105 ft in length on secondary highways and 120 ft in length on divided highways

- Overhangs in excess of 20 ft shall have pilot/escort vehicle positioned to the front for front overhangs, and to the rear for rear overhangs

Two pilot/escort vehicles are required for vehicles/loads which exceed the following dimensional conditions:

- 14 ft in width on secondary highways, and 16 ft in width on divided highways, except for mobile and manufactured homes with eaves 12 in. or less on either roadside or curbside shall be measured for box width only and assigned escort vehicles

- Mobile and manufactured homes with eaves greater than 12 in. shall be measured for overall width including eaves and pilot/escort vehicles assigned

Police escorts are required for vehicles with loads that exceed:

- 17 ft wide and 17 ft-6 in. high on secondary highways; OR

- 20 ft wide and 17 ft-6 in. high on interstate highways; OR

- When required by the department

The maximum gross and axle weight limitations are as follows:

- Single wheel: 10,500 lbs

- Single axle: 20,000 lbs

- Tandem axle: 34,000 lbs

- Tridem axles are dictated by bridge restrictions

- Gross vehicle weight is 80,000 lbs

If in excess of these weights, a permit must be obtained to authorize exceptions to maximum weight.

Limitations are also with regard to times of day in which transfer may be made for certain stretches of road. These include areas with bridges or specific dimensional restrictions not on primary or secondary highways and interstates. Also, restrictions are made for loads that exceed the legal limitations. For example, in Utah, ***oversized loads that are permitted are encouraged at night under the following conditions:***

- Loads may not exceed 12 ft wide on secondary highways, 14 ft wide on interstates, and 14 ft high on all roadways.

- Loads exceeding 10 ft wide, 105 ft overall length, or 10 ft front and rear overhang are required to have one certified pilot/escort on interstate highways and two on all secondary highways.

- Loads exceeding 92 ft overall length are required to have proper lighting every 25 ft, with amber lights to the front and sides of the load marking extreme width, and red to the rear.

Limitations are also made on the acceptable weather conditions in which to travel. ***Loads will not be permitted to travel when the following conditions exist:***

- Wind in excess of 45 mph

- Any accumulation of snow or ice on the roadway

- Visibility less than 1,000 ft

In all cases, vehicles and loads should be reduced to the minimum practical dimensions. This makes sense regarding transport safety as well as cost.

7.5.2 Trailers

There are generally two categories of trailers used for transporting prefabricated elements:

- Box trailer: This is a standard box integrated trailer, sometimes referred to as a dryvan, for transporting components and panels on the interior. It is normally loaded from the rear with a forklift. The benefit of this type is that elements can be kept dry and free from being damaged during transport. Dimension of the box structure should be taken into consideration for shipping dimensions. Trailers come in the following standard exterior dimensions:

  ○ Width: 8 ft or 8 ft-6 in.

  ○ Length: 28, 32, 34, 36, 40, 45, 48, and 53 ft with the final two lengths being the most common

  ○ Height: 8 ft-4 in. above deck

  ○ Weight: 44,000 lbs maximum load

- Flatbed trailer: This is a flatbed chasse that is either one-, two-, or three-axle, depending on the dimensions and weight of the products being transported. There are three types of flatbed trailers commonly used for construction material transport:

- Standard flatbed: This is a standard flat trailer that mechanically hooks to a tractor. It is used when weight and height are not an issue. This is usually a two-axle trailer. The bed is 8ft-6 in. wide and 48 ft long. Because the bed is so high off the ground, the load is limited to 8 ft-6 in., assuming the maximum height is Utah standard 14 ft without permitting. The length of the cargo may be the full flatbed length plus the state-accepted overhang. For Utah, a 48-ft flatbed trailer can hold up to 54 ft cargo length. The maximum weight is 48,000 lbs.

  ○ Single-drop deck: This trailer has a single-drop deck that can be two or three axles. They are used

to haul many of the same types of freight as a flatbed. The advantage is that this trailer can haul a higher load without having to obtain permits for the load. Most trailers are 48 or 53 ft long. The upper deck is either 10 ft long, leaving 38 ft of length for the load on a standard 48-ft trailer. The typical step-deck trailer is a standard 40 in. high at the rear giving the cargo an additional height capacity of 10 ft-6 in. in Utah. The length of the cargo on a triaxle single-drop deck trailer is 50 ft including an overhang at the rear. The construction of the step-deck makes it a heavier trailer than a flatbed, transporting 44,000 to 45000 lbs maximum.

  ○ Double-drop deck: Referred to as a "lowboy," this trailer is able to haul excessively high loads without

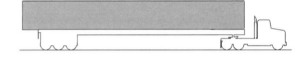

Figure 7.7 Although truck regulations vary according to state, trailers do not necessarily vary. The three standard types of trailers used to transport components, panels, and modules include: Top: flatbed trailer for longer elements; Middle: single-drop deck; and Bottom: double-drop deck for tall elements. Generally, these trailers are progressively more costly to procure from top to bottom.

permitting. The trailer has a "well" in the center of the deck making it able to transport taller but not as long cargo when compared to the single-drop deck. The disadvantage is that it can be difficult to load. Double-drop decks are generally 48 ft long with a lower deck height of 20 in., allowing the height of the cargo to maximize at 15 ft-6 in. without a permit in Utah. The maximum cargo length on a double-drop deck trailer is 40 ft in the well. A variation of this trailer has a removable gooseneck at the trailer-to-tractor connection offering more flexibility in loading and unloading. The payload will vary depending on the trailer.

7.5.3 Modular Transport

Modular, mobile, and manufactured units have the same directives as the shipping guidelines above but have a few added restrictions. Mobile and manufactured units exceeding 14 ft-6 in. and up to 16 ft in wall-to-wall width, transported on their own running gear, may be issued a single trip permit but must comply with tire sidewall guidelines, axle/suspension must not exceed manufacturer's capacity, and all trailers must have operational brakes. Mobile homes in excess of 16 ft wall-to-wall width may be permitted on a case-by-case basis. Mobile/manufactured homes can be moved on all types of trailers.[20]

Often, dynamic structural loads due to transportation are the largest loads placed on a fabricated element that it will experience in its lifecycle. This may be mitigated by flat-packing panels and components, but in the case of modules, this requires carefully determined pick points for loading and offloading as well as the critical dynamic loads that the module will experience in transit. This is often cited as the greatest deterrent to using modular construction, as elements must be over-structured for shipping con-

Figure 7.8 An integrated chasse is used in portable modular classroom and construction site trailers. Jennifer Siegal for the Country School developed this model.

Figure 7.9 If modules are small enough, more than one may be placed on a single trailer. Here ecoMOD has placed two wood modules on a single-drop deck trailer.

ditions. Design teams must carefully consider loads in shipment during the development of elements for building. Prefabricated elements will have to be lifted in the factory to the trailer, transported to site, lifted onsite, transported around the site, and then finally set and placed, leveled and connected to the context, whether other units, superstructure frames, or foundations. Any one of these steps could determine the ultimate structure and aesthetics of the modular system.[21]

Elements must be secured in a specific manner to trailers. This may affect the design of the mobile/ manufactured home. A minimum of four 3/4-in. diameter bolts will be used to directly connect the main support members of the modular to the support frame of the moving equipment. Each of the four bolts shall be at least 4 ft apart. Two bolts each are located not less than 12 ft from the

State	Width	Height	Length	State	Width	Height	Length
Alabama	12' (16')	* (16')	76' (150')	Montana	12'-6" (18')	* (17')	* (120')
Alaska	10' (22')	*	100' (*)	Nebraska	12' (*)	14'-6" (*)	85' (*)
Arizona	11' (14')	* (16')	* (120')	Nevada	8'-6" (17')	* (16')	105' (*)
Arkansas	12' (20')	15' (17')	90' (*)	New Hampshire	12' (16')	13'-6" (16')	80' (100')
California	12' (16')	* (17')	85' (135')	New Jersey	14' (18')	14' (16')	100' (120')
Colorado	11' (17')	13' (16')	85' (130')	New Mexico	* (20')	* (18')	* (190')
Connecticut	12' (16')	14' (*)	80' (120')	New York	12' (14')	14' (*)	80' (*)
Delaware	12' (15')	15' (17'-6")	85' (120')	North Carolina	12' (15')	14'-5" (*)	100' (*)
District of Columbia	12' (*)	13'-6" (*)	80' (*)	North Dakota	14'-6" (18')	* (18')	75' (120')
Flordia	12' (18')	14'-6" (18')	95' (*)	Ohio	14' (*)	14'-10" (*)	90' (*)
Georgia	12' (16')	15'-6" (*)	75' (*)	Oklahoma	12' (16')	* (17')	80' (*)
Idaho	12' (16')	14'-6" (16')	100' (120')	Oregon	9' (16')	*	95' (*)
Illinois	* (18')	* (18')	* (175')	Pennsylvania	13' (16')	14'-6" (*)	90' (160')
Indiana	12'-4" (16')	14'-6" (17')	90' (180')	Rhode Island	12' (*)	14' (*)	80' (*)
Iowa	8' (16'-6")	14'-4" (20')	85' (120')	South Carolina	12' (*)	13'-6" (16')	(125')
Kansas	* (16'-6")	* (17')	* (126')	South Dakota	10' (*)	14'-6" (*)	*
Kentucky	10'-6" (16')	14' (*)	75' (125')	Tennessee	10' (16')	15' (*)	75' (120')
Louisana	10' (18')	* (16'-5")	75' (125')	Texas	14' (20')	17' (18'-11")	110' (125')
Maine	8'-6" (18')	8'-6" (*)	80' (125')	Utah	10' (17')	16' (17'-6")	105' (120')
Maryland	13' (16')	14'-6" (16')	85' (120')	Vermont	15' (*)	14' (*)	100' (*)
Massachuetts	12' (14')	13'-9" (15')	80' (130')	Virginia	10' (*)	15' (*)	75' (150')
Michigan	12' (16')	14'-6" (15')	90' (150')	Washington	12' (16')	14' (16')	*
Minnesota	12'-6" (16')	*	95' (*)	West Virgina	10'-6" (16')	15' (*)	75' (*)
Mississippi	12' (16'-6")	* (17')	53' (*)	Wisconsin	14' (16')	*	80' (110')
Missouri	12'-4" (16')	15'-6" (17'-6")	90' (150')	Wyoming	* (18')	* (17')	* (110')

* Determined entirely by route travelled
( ) Indicates maximum possible dimension which requires permits and/or escorts

Figure 7.10 Regulations for truck transport of elements of prefabrication vary according to the state. This is a list developed by Kullman Buildings Corp. that identifies the dimensional requirements and indicates possible special permits or escorts for over-dimensioned loads. It should be noted that state regulations might change from year to year. The number shown for Utah in this table, for example, is not current with recently published 2010 regulations.

forward and rear ends of the modular. Equivalent methods of fastening may be accepted, provided fastening is not accomplished with clamps that rely on friction contact between the modular home and the moving equipment. In addition to bolting and clamping, two safety chains are used, one each on the right and left sides of (but separate from) the coupling mechanism connecting the tow vehicle and the modular home while in transit. Chains are 3/8 in.-diameter steel capable passing a minimum brake test load of 16,200 lbs; and are securely fastened at each end to connect the tow vehicle and manufactured home and assure that, in the event of a coupling failure, the manufactured home will track behind the tow vehicle. When the mobile/manufactured home is transported on a semitrailer lowboy coupled to the tow vehicles with a fifth wheel and kingpin assembly, the two safety chains are not required.[22]

When transporting modular construction for mobile and manufactured housing, a rigid material of .5 millimeter plastic sheeting based by a rigid grillwork not exceeding squares of 4 ft is required to prevent billowing. This must fully enclose the open sides of the units in transit. For open areas in modular that will connect to other modules, holes in flat roof planes or cavities in floors for stairs and the like must accommodate this, so that air does not pressurize the interiors of modules and cause damage or blow the module off of the trailer.[23]

7.5.4 Rail Transportation

The Federal Rail Administration regulates rail transport. This agency is part of the U.S. Department of Transportation that oversees safety of rail shipping. Rail transport of offsite-fabricated elements is rare but sometimes is used in lieu of truck transport. Some of the advantages and disadvantages of rail include:[24]

Advantages:

- Fuel efficiency

- Heavier loads are possible (3 trucks to 1 railcar conversion)

- Loading and unloading flexibility

- Mitigates driver and equipment shortages in truck industry

- Larger elements possible requiring less disassembly

- No requirement for road permitting, escorts, nighttime, and weather restrictions

- Capacities often allow multiple pieces per railcar reducing per-piece transport costs

Disadvantages:

- Generally more costly in comparison to trucking

- Charge based on minimums; 50,000 lbs or less is same cost generally

- Light-weight construction material such as wood panel and modules are difficult to recoup cost and justify rail

- For heavy elements, load and unload locations must be identified

- If not near the rail where load can be craned from rail-to-rail location, then difficult to truck. If it can be trucked, then most likely the easiest option

- Economies come in density, so flat-pack makes the most sense in rail

The rail industry is separated functionally between East of Mississippi and West of Mississippi regions.

Although many providers exist today in the rail industry, in the East, Northfolk Southern and CSX are the two major providers. Likewise, in the West, Union Pacific and Burlington Northern Santa Fe (BNSF) lead the pack. Although the FRA regulates rail transit, this is primarily a function of ensuring no hazardous chemicals are involved. The rail companies ensure dimensional shipping standards. The West has more liberal dimensional clearances, while the East is restricted by a more dated infrastructure that was established before accommodation of rail. Dimensional clearances of loads must be considered uniquely every time something is shipped. In rail, the entire route is investigated before shipment of large or oversized loads to ensure clearance. This is because the cost associated with this mistake can be significantly higher than that for trucking.

Width:

- West standards:

  ◦ 11 ft or less without a clearance

  ◦ 11–14 ft with a clearance

  ◦ 14 ft or more requires a clearance from the railroad company and a special train that will run on its own without a convoy

- East standards:

  ◦ 10 ft-6 in. or less (Northfolk) and 11 ft or less (CSX) without a clearance

  ◦ 11–14 ft or more requires a clearance from the railroad company

  ◦ 14 ft or more requires a clearance from the railroad company and a special train that will run on its own without the convoy

Height:

Outside of dimensional shipping that uses specialized cars, rail transit also ships containers as outlined in Chapter 6; in this case they are often stacked two components high, or "double stacked" to 21 ft total in height. This sets the height limitation for most trains whether in the West or the East and whether for container, bulk, or dimensional shipping. Height is calculated from top of rail. Elements for buildings are loaded on the deck that is generally 3.5 to 4 ft above top of rail. The height of dimensionally shipped cargo is restricted to 17 ft from the top of rail. Beyond this dimension, clearance is needed from the railroad company in which corridors need to be evaluated for clearance along the entire route. With a 3.5- to 4-ft deck height, modules, panels, and elements cannot be stacked or manufactured higher than 20 to 21 ft.

Of the greatest determinants for shipments that require clearances for width or height are bridges and tunnels. Many of these are historic structures that were built to historic dimensions and no anticipated increase in dimensional shipping. In the event that bridges or tunnels are obstructing a route, circuitous routing is potentially implemented in order to make the route feasible. This adds cost for the increase in mileage and time due to an indirect approach.

Length:

Trains use a flat car for dimensional shipping. Two standard lengths for railcars are 60 and 89 ft, respectively. This is measured from end to end, therefore, elements that are shipped are generally limited to 59 and 88 ft, respectively, to allow for 6 in. of car support on either end.

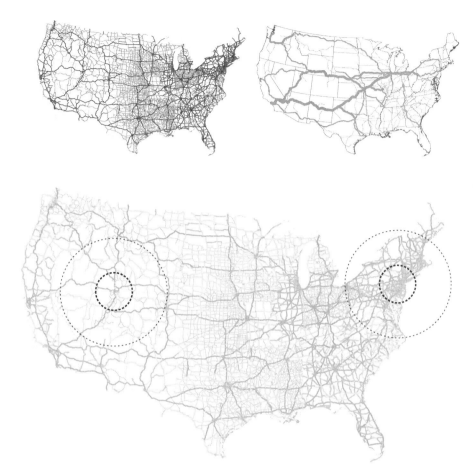

Figure 7.11 Transportation of prefab elements in the United States is restricted to the national network of highways and rail systems. Top Left: This is a graphic of the major highways in the United States. Top Right: This illustrates the rail lines in the country. Comparing the two explains why truck transport is the method employed more than 90 percent of the time due to its accessibility and consequent affordability. Bottom: A rule of thumb for transportation of prefab elements is 125 miles. The inner circle is placed strategically over Spanish Fork, Utah, locating Irontown Home Building Company and Lebanon, New Jersey, the location of Kullman Buildings Corp., represents this. The outer ring is a 500-mile radius, the distance directed by USGBC LEED program that many manufacturers are using as their maximum distance for travel.

7.5.5 Other Modes

A freighter or cargo plane is another means of transport which allows for virtually any size of dimensional shipping. Cargo may also be sent on a passenger plane. Private planes may be chartered for shipping, if project budgets for specialized products allow such. Much of the limitation in shipping by air is the locations of takeoff and landing. If shipping to remote areas where planes cannot land, shipping by boat is necessary. ISO containers are not shipped by plane but by boat. Transporting building elements by boat is more affordable; however, transit time on the ocean should be accounted for. Again, just as with planes,

there are dedicated cargo ships for dimensional shipments outside of ISO container boats.[25]

A Sikorsky S-64E Skycrane helicopter can lift 20,000 lbs above its own weight (10 tons) or move 18,000 lbs with a point-to-point road closure motorcade and a refueling stop every half-hour. The contemporary house weighs per code 60 lbs/S.F. At 1,500 S.F., the house would weigh 90,000 lbs in dead load, or a minimum of six helicopter lifts or "pick" routes. This makes helicopter delivery nearly impossible logistically for both physical and financial reasons for most assembly, unless elements are smaller in dimension and weight.[26]

7.5.6 Cost of Transportation

The size, weight, transportation method, and distance of travel determine transportation cost. Often a radius is determined by manufacturers, calculating the maximum distance to another similar manufacturer, or simply the limits of their capacity to deliver. Of course, there are exceptions to the rule and each situation warrants a cost benefit analysis of distance to site. It is most desirable that elements arrive at the jobsite ready to be installed with a crane. This is due to the difficulty of barricading streets during daytime traffic hours, and in rural settings, leaving elements on the jobsite susceptible to potential damage from construction site mistakes or vandalism. Cost, in many respects, depends on the point of origin and the final destination. There are no set prices for shipments. Shipping companies bid on shipment projects uniquely based on the elements to be shipped and the route.

In making decisions with regard to prefabrication, transportation costs need to be calculated as part of the cost estimate. In smaller buildings that are being transported great distances, the schedule savings may not be significant enough to justify offsite fabrication over onsite methods. Some companies via the Internet offer publicly available pricing, but these estimates should be used as rules of thumb in making larger decisions regarding transportation methods and not considered as overall cost estimates that are accurate for a building project. Fuel prices, increased restriction on regulations, weather, labor shortages, and the like can affect the ultimate cost of shipping regardless of the method.

Seaker and Lee argue in a report in 2006 titled "Assessing Alternative Prefabrication Methods: Logistical Influences"[27] that among the cost of logis-

tical concerns such as material carrying costs from acquisition to install, transportation is the operation attributed to the highest cost increase over onsite operations.[28] This can be attributed to a combination of an increase in total number of shipments, distance and direction of shipments, and shipment configurations requiring higher-cost transportation capabilities. Less fixed overhead and less transportation activity is incurred with onsite methods than with offsite.

The researchers discovered that building elements that are more prefabricated experience higher levels of shipping cost. This is primarily due to the density of the shipping elements. A module, for example, has a lot of empty space and is less dense. In the study, prefab panels had a 70 percent density loss, which increased its cost from $0.53 to $0.93/S.F. Standard modules experienced $1.33/S.F. transportation cost increase above onsite material. Wide loads at 8.5 to 12 ft experienced a $3.27/S.F. increase in transportation costs, while greater than 12 ft were upward of $5.00/S.F. premium. Even with fewer trips, large oversized loads exhibit the highest total costs. It seems that in all categories of shipping construction materials, distance from the manufacturing facility is the greatest factor in transportation cost. Although beneficial for assembly, the addition of fewer subassemblies is not always the answer for the bottom line. Shipping in low-budget projects may require smaller elements in fabrication in the factory or changing to onsite methods altogether.

Notable in the report is the distance at which offsite panels and modules become cost prohibitive—around 150 to 200 miles from the factory. It is at this distance that the cost of transport increases linearly and, in the case of offsite modules at 12 ft or greater, increases exponentially. This study is important because it points to the reality that although production processes by using lean strategies are important, manufacturing and assembly efficiencies have been focused on while transport in general has been neglected. As movements toward larger subassemblies are providing schedule savings, transportation may be just as important in determining the feasibility of fabrication for onsite construction by virtue of project cost. A hybrid approach to using not only modules but also panels and components when needed can be a wise solution for achieving a cost-to-benefit strategy for a given project.

The cost-effective distance of transport found by Seaker and Lee are consistent with numbers established from both ISBU engineer Buro Happold and research performed by the American housing company Pulte. Adrian Robinson from Buro Happold states that, for most projects, a 200 kilometer, or 124 miles, is the limit of cost-efficient transport. This distance was found in research in preparation for the Travelodge projects. The use of ISO containers expedited this benchmark by being able to send the modules through shipping. Had the modules been fabricated near the site, the labor costs would have been cost prohibitive. In developed countries like the United States, prefabrication makes sense when travel distance is closer. Likewise, Mark Hodges from Pulte Homes, who has invested in prefabrication and supply chain integration, and who ships modules for rapid assembly on market rate housing, states that their system is limited to 125 miles from the plant.[29] This number continues to emerge as a standard in the building industry from factory to site. Logistically, it is not cost beneficial to ship from farther distances unless a large margin is made up in labor, time, or material costs.

Although prefabricators will often advertise capacity to deliver upward of 500 miles from factory location, this is more a marketing effort to secure additional work. Tom Hardiman at the Modular Building Institute states that 125 miles, as a rule of thumb, has much to do with the locations of the various modular builders. If a manufacturer or supplier is within a 300 to 400 mile distance, the industry will naturally parse itself into 100 to 150 mile radius sections for shipping. In the modular industry a network of dealers or general contractors who do business, share information and work together to cover territories. For specialized fabricators on projects which demand their services and have accompanying budgets, shipments of great distances can be justified. However, on normative construction projects distance plays an increasing importance into overall project costs. Michelle Kaufmann and modular builder Kullman Buildings Corp., have documented in their operations that although prefabrication distance is decreased by 5 percent, the cost of transportation increases 5 percent for offsite construction. This number considers capital cost only and does not take into account the travel time of crews to and from the jobsite or factory. It is safe to suggest that the number of trips to and from the jobsite is more than to and from a factory location. However, these costs are absorbed by overall project budgets, rarely broken out as a separate line item. Therefore, it is difficult to make an accurate comparison.

7.6 Setting

Prefabricated building elements arrive to the site ready to be placed. Setting and assembling elements is the final step in the process of construction including hoisting, positioning, adjusting, connecting, and stitching. Elements designed for prefabrication and onsite assembly will need to be designed to accommodate lifting points, sometimes called "pick points." Pick points are designed by an engineer to ensure that the lifting points coincide with the distribution of weight of the element. This is critical so the element will stay stable during craning and will be able to be placed square, or on a level plane. Lifting points may be anywhere on the element, but careful consideration should be given to the final aesthetic of the pick point. Questions such as whether the pick points will be covered by finishes or hidden within an assembly makes this decision less critical. Pick points may also be part of the architectural aesthetic or coincide with ultimate attachment points of the element to another element or foundation, floor, or existing building once installed, as was employed in the St. Ignacius

Church by Steven Holl. This can be difficult because forces for hoisting and placing are different than the ultimate loads being distributed in an element once installed. Pick points should be carefully determined if the panel or module is finished to a high degree so that straps, cables, and buckles do not damage the elements while in hoisting. A pick point on a module is calculated at thirds, but always considering uneven weight distributions in a particular unit.

For wooden modules, often a wraparound belt strap is used. This requires the modules to be over-structured so when lifted they do not break at the mid-span. Precast uses lift points, lift lugs, or anchors for transport and assembly. These are embedded into the panel during the precast process in the factory. In order to simplify the positioning of the panels, the ele-

Figure 7.12 This module, for a Marmol Radziner Prefab House in California, is being hoisted with three belt straps and one spreader bar to distribute load to the hydraulic crane.

Figure 7.13 In order to maneuver this on-hook module, the setting crew uses guide ropes to locate the exact placement of the modules.

Figure 7.14 Locating a corner or two during the set is key to getting the exact placement of the module. This may need to be performed a few times in order to get its placement within a tolerable dimension.

ments have reference and fitting surfaces. Often these are scrupulously numbered so there is no confusion about how they are installed. Bar codes, numbering, lettering, and other methods of identification are used to organize the assembly sequence onsite. These can be placed directly on the elements themselves.

Various types of rigs or spreader bars can be used to lift elements. Although direct lifting is an option for smaller elements, spreader bars are used for most projects in order to keep forces perpendicular to the subassemblies, and reduce the possibility of introducing unwanted bending forces within the element. This is especially true for modules. Spreader bars are essentially beams or structures that distribute the loads of lifting over the spreader instead of onto the prefabricated element itself. This is especially critical in modular construction where point loads in conspicuous places may induce eccentric or blunt forces that can permanently damage the module or cause the module to fail structurally. Spreader bars are supplied by the entity performing the setting. However, the design of the interaction of the spreader with the

pick points and the crane should be carefully considered with the design and construction team during early project planning. This may affect the design of the elements for assembly from their size and configuration.

7.6.1 Craning

For most assembly, elements will be lifted directly from the flatbed trailer to their final location. Cranes lift the element and carefully locate its place onsite. Onsite crew guide elements into place and make connections. Ideally, the onsite work process does not impede the maximum workflow of the crane. Rental of large cranes is expensive, and therefore, the machines should be used as much as possible when procured. Once the riggings are in place, the maneuvering of elements "on-hook" is typically performed by one or two guide ropes. Weather conditions will prevent the setting of prefabricated elements when wind speeds exceed 10 mph. Any joints or openings, which remain exposed at the end of the day, are covered with a tarp to protect against possible rain damage.

CRANE TYPES

There are two main types of cranes: mobile cranes and fixed cranes. *Mobile cranes* can be truck-mounted, which have the crane integral to the truck such as in rough-terrain and all-terrain combinations; or they can be crawler cranes, which have a base similar to a front-loader with rotating tracks. The following is a description of the most common crane types used in setting prefabricated elements.

- Truck mounted hydraulic cranes
  - Rough terrain for unimproved worksites in which access is difficult
  - Simple truck-mounted crane can run at highway speeds, but cannot do rough terrain
  - All-terrain truck-mounted crane is combination of the two previous examples
  - Pick and carry capability
  - 40- to 75-ton capacity
- Crawler cranes
  - Greater flexibility onsite
  - Transported on trailer to site
  - 40- to 3,500-ton capacity
  - Ships on eight trucks
  - Self-assembly

The contractor on the job designs cranes. In a project in which the fabrication company is acting as general contractor as well, a decision regarding crane type must be made in tandem with the design of the prefabricated system. General principles of cranes are that their capacity is inverse to the reach or radius. The greater the radius, the lower the weight the crane can hold. However, in order to accommodate greater loads and increase reach, larger capacity cranes must be used. The selection of the type of crane is based on weight and reach. The craning of modules requires a crane of greater capacity than those commonly kept onsite during in situ construction projects. Site cranes often have a capacity of less than 5 tons, whereas the cranes used for lifting modules often have a capacity in the range of 40 to 75 tons.

Selecting a crane depends on the load to be lifted, the height clearance needed, the mobility of the crane to perform multiple jobs, or the reach of the crane, the number of lifts, and the availability of the crane. Tower cranes are much more expensive and are only warranted when multiple levels of installation of prefab are going to be accomplished. For single sets of modules or a few modules, truck-mounted hydraulic telescoping cranes are desirable. This is conflicting, however, because tower cranes have a much larger capacity than truck-mounted cranes, but at the level of building prefab components this is rarely an issue.[30]

Boom size also determines load capacity. For example, a standard truck-mounted hydraulic crane with a smaller 25- to 70-ft boom can handle 22 tons. A 100-ft boom crane can handle 33 tons—larger and

Fixed cranes are not mobile, but can carry greater loads and reach greater heights and distances. Although fixed cranes ultimately are moved, while onsite they move very little for economic reasons. The most common type of fixed crane is a tower crane.

• Tower cranes
  ○ Used when space is a premium
  ○ Up and over reach
  ○ Usually fixed to foundations
  ○ Strategically located for maximum reach

▼ Figure 7.15 Left and Middle: Mobile lifting cranes are versatile, able to move throughout the site and reach distances manageable by small to medium-sized projects. These cranes have a 40- to 75-ton capacity, generally adequate for lifting prefab elements for building construction, and a reach of 180 ft high and 160 ft wide. Right: Tower cranes are stationary and costly but have great lifting capacity and reach.

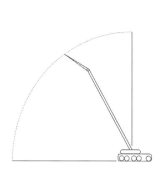  

stronger cranes are readily available, but access of the larger truck will quickly become an issue on residential streets and alleys. Maximum weight allowed for truck transit is 80,000 lbs in gross weight. To put this in perspective, this 40-ton gross weight maximum on highways has a 60 percent weight buffer over that needed for a typical timber-framed house which, at 2,000 S.F. weighs 120,000 lbs or 60 tons, with a code-prescribed dead load weight of 60 lbs/S.F. This means that even if the house were flat-packed as densely as possible, it would generally still weigh less than the maximum weight for truck transit and be able to be lifted by a 25-ft boom in three lifts, or a 100-ft boom in two lifts. In general, it is more economical to go with a small, accessible crane to lift in multiples than with a large crane that will lift once or twice.

7.6.2 Foundations

For modular construction, foundations can either be piers, linear footings, or continuous footings. Wood modules generally place distributed loads on foundations as they distribute loads similar to a bearing wall condition. Depending on how they are developed, steel framed modules, such as those that Kullman Buildings Corp. produces, a point load rather than a distributed load is placed on a foundation. Therefore, slab-on-grade is not a typical solution for this type of modular construction. Rather, perimeter and pier foundation systems are the best solution. Site-cast foundations are never entirely plum; certainly they are much less precise than elements that have been factory produced. Therefore, setting of elements on foundations often includes shims to achieve level.

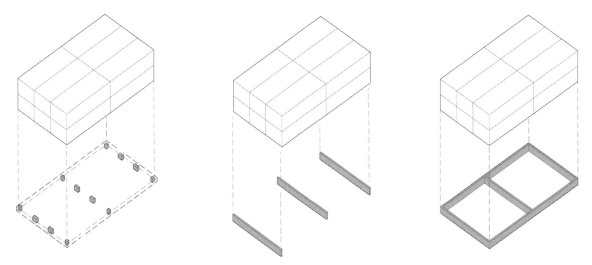

Figure 7.16 Three types of foundations that can be used for modular construction include: Left: piers; Middle: linear stem wall; and Right: full stem wall. Modular construction can be designed to distribute load to vertical structure at corners alleviating the need for full-engaged stem wall bearing at the perimeter of the module.

7.7 Tolerances

Tolerances exist to accommodate the normal manufacturing and installation inaccuracies that occur in construction as a result of moisture, thermal differential movements, material discrepancies, and human error during assembly. During detailing, designers need to work with fabricators and contractors to determine the tolerances for a given project. Each detail has its own accommodation for forgiveness in dimension discrepancy and if two materials are coming together each must respect the other in its accuracies. Larger elements require greater tolerances, especially if they cannot be altered. Calling for increased tolerances does increase the cost of a project. This requires an integrated effort in order to coordinate elements on the jobsite for assembly.

Because factory methods improve the craft of construction, tighter tolerance can typically be achieved in offsite construction relative to onsite construction. Today's equipment and machinery allow for

tolerances up to 20 millionths, given the right temperature requirements. This is used for highly precise work in medical and mechanical applications, but in building, these kinds of tolerances are not necessary. Given the inaccuracies of uneven sites, site-poured foundations without tight tolerance, the precisions of prefab may be high, but the tolerance between the elements must allow for dimensional discrepancy. Therefore, tolerance refers to the desired allowance of dimensional inaccuracy. For prefabricated construction this is between elements themselves, and the elements in relation to onsite-constructed portions of the building.

In prefabrication, tolerances fall into two categories: part or subassembly tolerances and assembly tolerances. *Part tolerance* refers to the tolerance of the parts that make up the component, panel, or module including the making of elements from MTS parts. *Assembly tolerance* refers to the tolerance of the element or subassembly itself and the process of placing the subassemblies onsite.

The ultimate determination for tolerance is dependent on where and how it will be assembled onsite. Tolerances are therefore calculated accumulatively in sets of assemblies, such as a series of modules or panels. For example, in a set of six cladding panels set within a structural bay each having a tolerance of ±1/16 in., the overall dimensional tolerance of the assembly is as follows:

$$= \pm\sqrt{6(1/16)^2}$$

= ±0.153" or an overall dimensional tolerance of 3/16–1/4 in.

Tolerances reflect the dimensional error as a result of onsite construction inaccuracies of human assembly. For example, Office dA designed the Arco gas station to have ±1/64 in. accuracies in the stainless CNC panels. The dimensional discrepancies due to human error during assembly varied upward of ¼ in. Connections are therefore designed with tolerance within them to accommodate this error. Joints that are unforgiving inevitably must be manipulated again in order to fit. Often methods such as slotted holes, neoprene washers, elastic joints, loose fitting joints, and reveals are used to make up this dimensional difference.

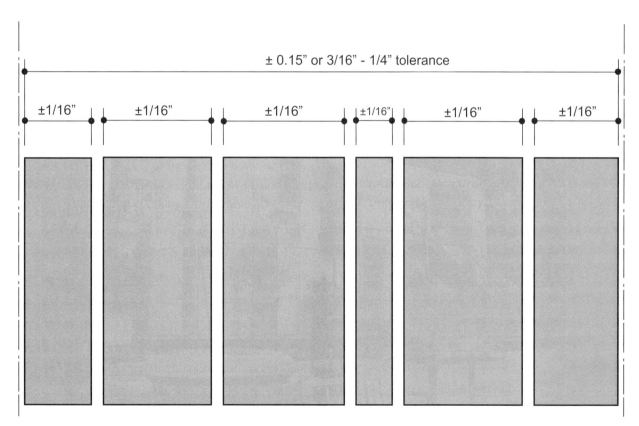

Figure 7.17 This image illustrates the principles of accumulated tolerances in a six-panel column bay. Each panel has a dimensional tolerance of ±1/16 in. The overall dimensional tolerance for this assembly is 3/16 to 1/4 in.

DIMENSIONAL TOLERANCES FOR U.S. CONSTRUCTION

Concrete	
Dimension of footing	−1/2 inch, +2 inches
Squareness of residential footing	1/2 inch in 20 feet
Plumbness of wall	±1/4 inch in 10 feet
Variation of wall from buidling line	±1 inch
Variation in wall thickness	−1/4 inch, +1/2 inch
Plumbness of column	1/4 inch in 10 feet, no more than 1 inch overall
Variation in level of beam	±1/4 inch in 10 feet; ±3/8 inch in any bay; ±3/4 inch for entire length
Variation in level of slab soffit	same as for beam
Structural Steel	
Plumbness of column	1 inch toward or 2 inches away from building line in first 20 stories; 2 inches toward and 3 inches away for above 20 stories
Beam length	±3/8 inch for depth of 24 inches and less; ±1/2 inch for greater depths
Wood	
Floor evenness	±1/4 inch in 32 inches
Wall plumbness	±1/4 inch in 32 inches
Exterior Cladding	
Aluminum and glass curtainwall	varies depending on manufacturer
Structural glass curtainwall	varies depending on manufacturer
Metal cladding (CNC)	±1/64 inch in 15 feet
Interior Finishes	
Plumbness of metal framing	±1/2 inch in 10 feet
Flatness of suspended ceiling	±1/8 inch in 10 feet
Modules	
Wood modules	±1/4 inch in 32 inches
Steel modules	±1/8 inch in any one direction of the individual modules

Figure 7.18 Dimensional tolerances for U.S. construction: These are general rules of thumb and not meant to be standards. Each project may also require a specific dimensional tolerance that deviates from this list for the intended purpose.

MATE-LINE STITCHING

Seams can be concealed or revealed as part of the tectonic of the building. In modular construction walls and ceilings, finishing or "stitching" is accomplished in the field using standard GWB finishing techniques. Flooring can be applied onsite, in the factory, or in a combination of the two. For floors finished entirely in the factory, standard flooring transitions can simply be applied on-site. A combination of factory and site finishing is the most common. Below are a few examples of stitching finishes in modular construction from Kullman Buildings Corp.:

- Carpet: Typically the tack board is installed in the factory and the carpet is sent as ship-loose.

- Ceramic tile: Tile can be set in the factory, allowing one tile to be set onsite over the mate line. It is generally best to perform grouting as a single process onsite.

- VCT is set in the factory such that the tile, which will cover the seam, will be cut about ¼ in. narrower, allowing a precise fit to be made onsite.

- Concrete: Grout or self-leveling compounds can be placed in the seam joint onsite.

- GWB: One full sheet of GWB is left off of the factory finish and applied onsite.

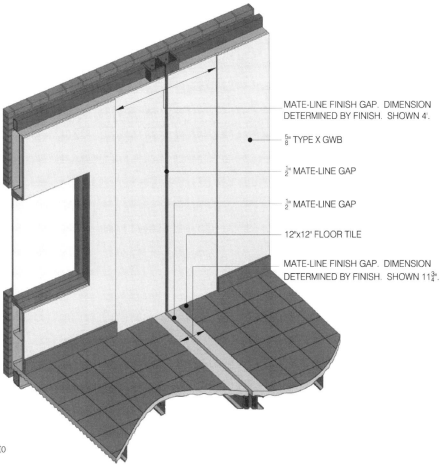

MATE-LINE FINISH GAP. DIMENSION DETERMINED BY FINISH. SHOWN 4'.

$\frac{5}{8}$" TYPE X GWB

$\frac{1}{2}$" MATE-LINE GAP

$\frac{1}{2}$" MATE-LINE GAP

12"x12" FLOOR TILE

MATE-LINE FINISH GAP. DIMENSION DETERMINED BY FINISH. SHOWN 11$\frac{3}{4}$".

Figure 7.19 The interiors of modular and panelized projects have "mate lines" that need to be stitched together onsite in order to seamlessly connect finishes.

continued

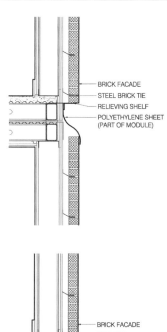

▲ Figure 7.20 This panelized house by Bensonwood has a seam from one floor to the next at the exterior wall. This area has been left clear in order to make a structural connection between the two floors. The exterior siding will be stitched together once the connection is made.

▶ Figure 7.21 This is an example of a brick veneer stitch that occurs between a mate line between two stacked steel frame modules. The mate line, or seam, is left open in order to make a structural connection and then it is: Top: stitched with a flashing detail to cover the seam; and Bottom: in-filled with brick veneer performed onsite.

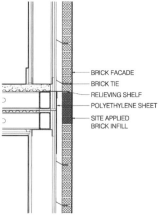

Tolerances are established by individual industry associations such as American Institute for Steel Construction for structural steel frames and Precast Concrete Institute for the precast industry. These standards determine the dimensional accuracy of the manufacturing process to ensure that construction assembly is more easily accomplished. Dimensional discrepancies, when unintended, can present problems and are therefore considered undesirable. However, tolerance is needed in every material part and subassembly so that onsite assembly is smooth and without

labor and schedule increase. Tolerances also increase the quality of the building by providing a means of movement and system change out over time. It is recommended that each project establish its tolerances based on goals and expected outcomes as well as schedule, budget, and availability of labor skill.

Prefabricated elements, when combined with onsite work, often determine the tolerance of construction. On the other hand, if the prefabricated element is small and insignificant to the overall cost of the project, it will be custom fabricated to meet the dimensional needs and tolerances established onsite. Prefabricated wall cladding panels will closely govern the story heights and the length of the building, or part of a building, where they are used. The structural frame is usually erected by site-work methods using site-cast reinforced concrete, and the prefabricated units, whether mass-produced to standard sizes or specially made for the particular building project, are fitted to it. An accurate tie-up between the respective dimensions of structure and cladding units is essential, and only a certain degree of tolerance may subsequently be allowed for either.

Grids for building construction therefore must be established so that onsite and offsite work might be coordinated. This is usually performed with prefabrication based on modular grids, not axial. Modular grids allow for dimensional coordination across elements onsite and offsite. It is necessary, when intending to use extensive prefabrication of components, to design the building from the start on a reference grid related to the intended module.

7.7.1 Joints

Where building subassemblies meet there is a joint. The appearance and performance of joints is important. Joint appearance and location is determined by the system being employed and the grid used. The joints are fixed by production, design, and transport. Joints make up the dimensional discrepancy by virtue of the actual dimension of the joint. Joints must be protected from the weather by virtue of constructional attachment such as lap joints, drip grooves, and other strategies for cladding detailing or are simply joined by sealant. Although sealant may be required or desired for moisture control, details should at all trials work toward quality detailing through geometry and attach-

ment and, as a last resort, chemical sealants. Bolted connections or connections which allow for disassembly have an easier time being recycled. Joints perform moisture and thermal control and acoustical protection. Prefabrication allows for fewer joints in the construction system providing fewer places for a building to fail, less labor to attach or seal, and less labor onsite. Fewer products and subassemblies means less cost, therefore, fewer joints likewise require less onsite assembly time thus reducing overall project cost.[31]

To deal with tolerances in construction at joints, a number of fitting mechanisms can be employed. The following have been taken from Allen and Rand's *Architectural Detailing:*[32]

- Sliding fit: One element overlaps another and is positioned by sliding. If there is a dimensional discrepancy, the gap is covered by one of the elements sliding over the other. If two adjacent elements are fitted against one another, sliding is simple; however, when a third or fourth plane is introduced fitting is more difficult. These sliding planes can be mitigated with three or more dimensions by allowing for generous openings and lapping to occur and adjustable fit joints to allow for the tolerance to occur.

- Adjustable fit: Building elements must be positioned accurately and therefore are designed so alignment can be adjusted during or after assembly onsite. Oversized holes and horizontally or vertically slotted anchors allow dissimilar systems such as an enclosure panel and a structural floor to connect to one another. Once proper alignment is made, a method for securing this detail is needed. It may be a weld or simply friction created at the bolted connection. Disassembly favors bolted friction or slip critical connections over welded or glued connections.

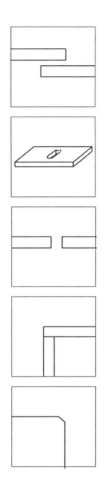

Figure 7.22 The following are fitting mechanisms for negotiating dimensional tolerances from Top to Bottom: sliding, adjustable, reveal, butt joint, and edge.

- Reveal: Offsetting materials so they do not slide past one another but let the tolerance be taken up in the separation dimension is a good way to align elements in relation to one another. The reveal often creates a shadow line that conceals the lack of precision of the detail. Transition of one system or material to another or change in direction from one element to the other element makes a reveal which adds visual interest and tolerance accommodation.

- Butt joint: This detail is an alternative for joining elements at a miter joint. The joint is a lapping of (A) element past (B) element placing the pieces perpendicular to one another in order to hide imperfection in the detail. The real benefit is removing knife joints common with miters. This can be used in connection with reveals and adjustable fit connections. A quirk miter is a corner detail in which elements are joined using a built-in reveal, no knife edges, and is forgiving to retain symmetry of a miter joint.

- Edge: The edge of elements, when exposed, should be carefully considered. A sharp edge is susceptible to nicking, breaking, denting, or the like. On the other hand, chamfered edges allow for easy wearing and will not impale people. In prefabrication this is important to consider and may make end elements different in manufacture than others. Corners may need to be shaped and reinforced differently than other elements in the assembly.

7.8 Conclusion

Architects dealing with offsite fabrication must think more like product designers. In speaking with a product designer about the connection between design and production, he stated that he would not think of designing a product without working to develop the method for production as an integral process. This is because the cost of a project and the time that it takes to manufacture it determines its viability in the marketplace. Product development therefore is the process of including all the activities that take place from market interpretation to finished product designs. Included in this equation are prototype production and test activities. Designers of products and prefab architecture must see their ideas from concept through to end use.

chapter 8   SUSTAINABILITY

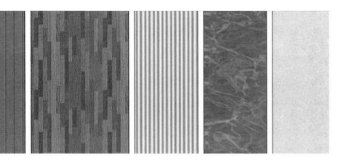

"A thoughtfully integrated ecology of construction can logically lead toward significant reductions in energy and transportation costs; reductions in materials waste and redundant warehousing; the reusability and recyclability of building components; and massive savings of time, frustration, injury, and redundancy on the job site."[1]

—Mark and Peter Anderson

Building is an energy-intensive proposition. The social, economic, and environmental impact of construction, management of the facility during its lifecycle, and end-of-life demolition is anything but ecologically sensitive. Energy data from the U.S. Energy Council 2007 Report[2] illustrates the severity of the situation and the immediate demand for architectural design to aid in solving the challenges of building construction. Considering that we use 26 percent more energy than 20 years ago, buildings account for 39 percent of the energy consumption and 39 percent of carbon dioxide emissions in the United States.

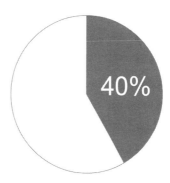

Figure 8.1 Buildings constitute 40 percent of total energy consumption in the United States.

It is projected that the existing building stock in the United States will double by 2030.[3] These numbers suggest an enormous potential for energy savings (and therefore CO_2 reduction) in the U.S. construction market. With more than 100 million households throughout the United States, the housing sector contributed about 17 percent of the U.S. greenhouse gases in 2003, and offers possible energy savings in the range of 25 to 30 percent in gross energy conservation. It would appear that the most sustainable action regarding architecture and construction is to simply not build at all. However, the reality is that the United States, and the world, continues to grow in population, demanding buildings to be constructed or existing buildings to be renovated. This construction growth must be accomplished as sustainably as possible.

Sustainability, as a concept and cultural definition, has become synonymous with reducing environmental encroachment and degradation. However, the U.S. Environmental Protection Agency uses the explanation given by the Brundtland Report in 1987 which defines *sustainability* as "meeting the needs of the present without compromising the ability of future generations to meet their own needs."[4] This broadens the definition of sustainability considerably. A key factor in sustainable practices in construction includes not only environmental impact of buildings during their lifecycle, but economic, social, and cultural considerations as well. The AEC industry must assess sustainability from the perspective of both natural and human capital. A truly resilient system relies on both in order to succeed.[5]

In the book *Prefab Green*[6] Michelle Kaufmann places two seemingly unrelated concepts in one title. Prefabrication does not necessarily mean sustainable building, nor does sustainable building imply the use of prefab. Like with any technology, prefabrication may be harnessed to create sustainable ends. Some of the greatest potentials of prefab and sustainability are with regard to the economic benefits of productivity gains. Prefabrication can remove material and labor waste, thus meeting financial goals of owners, architects, and builders. This is not only true on a specific project increasing efficiencies in the method of design and delivery of construction, but as Eastman and Sacks report, prefabrication is an economic sector growing faster than onsite construction sectors, making it advantageous for project teams to consider offsite production as a longer-term investment.

"The off-site sectors, such as curtainwall, structural steel, and precast concrete fabrication, consistently show higher productivity growth than on-site sectors. Furthermore, the value-added content of the off-site sectors is increasing faster than that of the on-site sectors, indicating faster productivity growth."[7]

The long-term financial sustainability of prefabrication far surpasses that of traditional onsite methods. However, its ability to meet social and environmen-

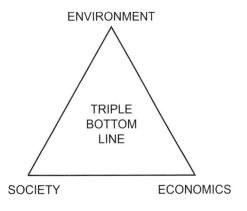

Figure 8.2 The triple bottom line of sustainability includes environment, society, and economics.

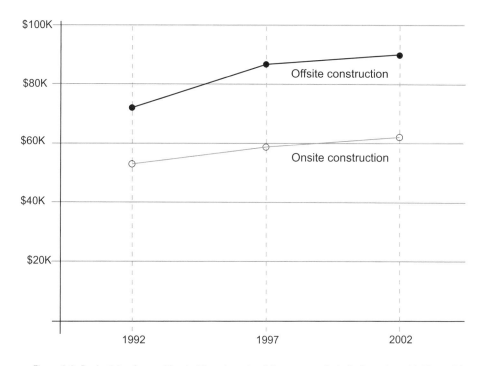

Figure 8.3 Productivity of assembling building elements offsite versus onsite indicating value-added for prefab.

tal goals is difficult to quantify. The greatest of social benefits is regarding labor. In Chapter 4, the principle of safety and reduced labor risk was discussed as an added benefit of offsite manufacture. In addition, pre-fab allows for varied skill workers, and a more consistent daily schedule for a healthier lifestyle. These added benefits, however, are not well researched or documented.[8] Environmental benefits are more easily quantifiable as an objective parameter.

Environmental impact of building requires a quantifiable measurement of impact in total lifecycle from design through facilities management. It stands to reason, therefore, that by controlling the means and methods by which buildings are produced through prefab, architects and construction professionals are able to ensure more sustainable materi-

als and practices for construction as well as have a greater opportunity to predict future energy performance. Horman and colleagues in "Delivering Green Buildings: Process Improvements for Sustainable Construction," evaluate the economic, environmental, and social aspects of prefabrication versus onsite construction in building production. They state that prefabrication is selected based on a broad set of regionally specific economic issues mostly linked to local labor capacity and cost. Although this is the most common consideration for the use of prefabrication, social and environmental considerations make the choice for prefab even more complex.[9]

Prefabrication may be used as a method to revamp the sustainability of construction from the perspective of the total lifecycle of a facility, especially regarding demolition or reuse, as the case may be. The capacity of prefab to deliver buildings that respond to time, change, and reuse/recycle may be its greatest benefit toward total lifecycle sustainability in the future.

8.1 Time

Many cities across the United States during the twentieth century have removed older historic neighborhoods in order to build convention centers and new housing in the name of "urban renewal." Compare this to the urban core of many European cities, whose buildings have stood for centuries and served many generations of owners and clients who have worked to maintain them for future generations. But the U.S. consumption pattern, which we consider as inherent to the order of capitalism and prosperity, has a detrimental effect on the quality and longevity of buildings. The consumptive practices in the U.S. real estate market stem from the concept of product obsolescence.[10] In the United States products become outdated and must be renewed in order to improve their technology and usefulness to society. This can be most often seen in automobiles and electronic products whose design encourages early failure and replacement. This planned obsolescence of products extends to our understanding of the built environment and is how society generally understands the consumptive construction practice in the United States as well.

Stewart Brand in *How Buildings Learn* argues for an architecture that is durable enough to allow change to occur. A diagram of what he calls "shearing layers" reveals that building systems change at different rates historically. The shearing layers include the following, from most durable to least:[11]

- Site: Eternal

- Structure (including foundation and load-bearing elements that last as long as the building does): approximately 50 years

- Skin (including roof and wall enclosures): Due to technology changes in enclosure systems and the end of cheap fossil fuels for heating, it lasts 15 to 20 years.

- Services (such as the HVAC and circulation systems): are updated every 7 to 15 years unless integral to building structure, which often causes a premature demolition of buildings.

- Space (includes the interior partitions, doors, ceilings, and finishes): These are very volatile, being changed out in some degree or another at each new tenant or resident at three-year intervals, on average.

- Stuff (wall paper, paint, and furniture): These change nearly every day at the whim of the inhabitant.

Brand's "six Ss" are taken from Francis Duffy's studies of evaluating building performance over the lifecycle. Duffy illustrates that although the initial costs of a structural system accounts for the majority of capital costs in a building project, structure over the lifecycle of constructing and operating a facility is relatively negligible. In addition to structure, cost related to other initial building systems in the lifecycle of a building are not significant, considering the maintenance and operational costs of energy, water, and so forth. Buildings that were designed and constructed in the 1920s and 1930s were covered up in the 1950s and 1960s with stucco panels and other "modernizations." Many of these buildings have been brought back to the exact state they were in when they were built, with much effort and expenditure. Duffy states,

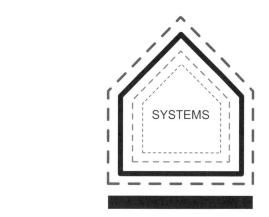

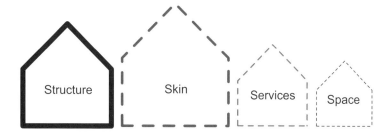

Figure 8.4 The concept of shearing layers illustrates the temporality of construction in the United States. Duffy and Brand's numbers indicate that buildings experience a change out of systems depending on their durability, with the average age of structures being 50 years.

"Add up what happens when capital is invested over a fifty-year period: the structure expenditure is overwhelmed by the cumulative financial consequences of three generation of services and ten generations of space plan changes. That's the map of money in the life of a building. It proves that architecture is actually of very little significance—it's nugatory."[12]

The model of consumptive development that has become standard practice in the United States is obviously detrimental to the environment, requiring buildings to be demolished every 50 years and new buildings to replace them. The sheer amount of material required to do this continues to remove raw materials from the earth, and pollutes our streams, rivers, and air. In addition, treating buildings as consumptive products is not viably economical. The re-cession in 2008 and beyond has created a realization that continual development for the sake of growth will not bring lasting sustainability. On the positive side, the economic crisis has brought a new understanding to the way in which business could be practiced, investing in long-term goals as opposed to short-term profits. This suggests an investment in building methods that are more durable and higher quality for the life of the facility. In addition, consumption practices in the built environment—demolishing buildings a generation after they are built—do not allow cities to establish a social identity. Lasting architecture as harbinger of social and cultural memory is an important part of any city.

More durable, long-lasting materials and methods of construction that make our most beloved historic structures are commonly site built, and assembled from materials of stone and brick. Using these traditional methods to produce infinitely durable buildings is not always feasible or financially possible. Instead, contemporary durability design and production can be understood in the rigorous detailing of lighter yet stronger materials of steel, concrete, and masonry cladding. Prefabrication is only as durable as the design team and fabricators deliver for the given budget. Just as easily, prefab is a tool to produce demounted, reused, or even reassembled architecture. Prefabrication does not solve the issue of time in construction, but it does offer a closer balance between initial and lifecycle costs of a facility.

Obsolescence is not entirely a diabolical plan by the capitalistic demons of society looking out for first costs only; rather buildings do become old regardless of their construction type and need updating. This includes replacing service and enclosure systems that perform more effectively for energy operation, and even augmentation of structure and egress systems to meet current life safety regulations. In addition, materials deteriorate and need to be replaced. On a larger scale, entire buildings need refurbishing, remodeling, and even replacing. But, as Fernandez points out, many of these replacements are made from nonrenewable materials, and therefore are not able to enter the construction stream again easily. Buildings therefore need to be designed for a long life, for a short life, or anywhere in between, with materials that can be recycled or reused in future buildings.

The reality is that the lifetime of buildings is very much out of the control of architects and construction professionals. We cannot anticipate all of the forces that will shape the longevity of buildings. Ironically, although housing is built from some of the most in-

expensive and obsolete materials, their low cost and accessible maintenance makes them relatively durable. However, architects and design professionals may be able to affect how buildings are designed in relation to how they are accepted and how they may accommodate change over their life. Fernandez states,

"Architects are the primary actors in determining the material composition of our buildings and therefore assume the role of primary driver in the extraction, recycling and processing of specific materials, the manufacture and assembly of components and the construction of our buildings."

Architects and construction professionals must therefore assume a larger responsibility to help building owners understand the implications of making such decisions and design to accommodate variable life buildings. Buildings designed with specific lifetimes include strategies that are synonymous with prefabrication:

• Designed for disassembly

• Designed for reuse

• Designed for temporality

• Design for change

8.1.1 Designing for Disassembly

In *Cradle to Cradle,*[13] McDonough and Braungart argue for a revolution in the way we make things. The principles can be summarized by the phrase "waste equals food," that all the refuse of our production and construction processes could one day be completely absorbed into the use stream of new construction. Designing for assembly and disassembly is a strategy for the ultimate cradle-to-cradle cycle. Elements may be assembled in a factory and then reassembled as larger components onsite. At the end of their useful life, these same components may be disassembled for rebuilding elsewhere—reuse and recycle. In this vision, buildings would become organisms of growth, change, decay, and re-growth much the way nature deals with the seasons, years, and centuries that generate its sustainability. Buildings as "industrial nutrients" is certainly far off from where we are today, but as Jane Benyus argues in her book *Biomimicry,*[14] in the sciences and engineering, these ideas may not be as far off as we think.

The steps to realizing a fully integrated lifecycle of material and components in buildings must come from a more structured and organized system. The theories of cradle to cradle, waste equals food, and biomimicry are arguably much more likely to be achieved in a controlled setting off the jobsite in a factory. Perhaps these ideas are even further from the jobsite, couched in research centers that explore the capacity of buildings to be living organisms. Replacing the factory, then the process engineer, biologist, in collaboration with architecture and building professionals, become the new innovators and opportunists of the future sustainable construction industry.

In a lecture in 2001 at the University of Arizona, Glenn Murcutt stated that many of his buildings are designed to use highly recycled materials.[15] The standardized components allow for either reuse on a different building, or to be put back into the manufacturing and supply chain. Many of his buildings therefore take on an assembly aesthetic, bolted instead of welded steel, and fastened instead of glued finishes. This kind of design and building is not easy; in fact, it requires going against construction conventions, but as builders and architects work together to realize a better way of building that uses principles of reduce, reuse, repair, and recycle, moving toward cradle-to-cradle and biomimetic principles in construction, we are forging a better way. Prefabrication is a tool to get us to the 4 Rs and beyond.

Written over four decades ago, *Supports*, by N.J. Habraken, discusses alternatives to mass housing, with prefabrication playing a key role in its achievement.[16] Habraken's words seem more applicable today than in the early 1970s when he wrote the book. He outlines the problem: People need a place to dwell, but the means by which society has developed a solution for housing does not take into consideration the user input nor the ability for change and adaptability by its inhabitants over time. As for prefabrication, Habraken argues that it does not necessarily mean faster, better, cheaper but that in order to be successful a "combination of local, economic, and labo[u]r factors"[17] must be considered. Habraken does recognize that mass housing is interconnected with machine production, but warns that prefab does not mean mass housing, nor does mass housing only reference prefab methods.

Habraken's proposal for building strategy is relatively straightforward: Provide a support structure in which dwelling units may be inserted and removed over time in order to accommodate growth, decay, change, and adaptation of the housing condition as well as the city that supports it. The support structure is not just the skeleton of a building, but "all the dwellings together for the skeleton of the town; a framework for all living and complex organism."[18] On the one hand, images of Archigram's living city come to mind while reading this manifesto, and on the other, a very grounded structuralist ideology is brought to mind.

The theories Habraken purports in his book have been developed further by researchers Stephen Kendall, Jonathan Teicher, and others. In *Residential Open Building for Housing,* Kendall and Teicher write,

---

"…buildings are built and maintained through the concerted efforts of many parties operating at many different levels. It therefore makes sense to structure the interfaces of parts and of decision-makers in ways that improve the responsiveness to end users, while at the same time increasing efficiency, sustainability and capacity for change, and dramatically extending the useful lives of residential buildings."[19]

Open building relies on a theory that:

1. The user is center in the process of design and construction; and

2. Design and construction are open, adaptable, changeable, and flexible.

In order to accommodate the user-informed process and allow construction to be "open" there are:

• Support-level elements, which are common to all users including structure, enclosure, and services. Supports must be site-bound, neighborhood-bound, and context-driven decisions. This will rely on the local labor force to develop and maintain buildings from architectural style, climate, and building codes to local financing and technical restrictions. Supports are related perhaps more to vernacular or to the community that will maintain them throughout their existence.

• Infill is the concept of detachable units from supports so users may specify their dwelling during design and future occupants may replace it upon changeover. The old unit is recycled or taken to another location where the previous user can re-inhabit it in a different supports location. This idea has been tried numerous times in the projects of the metabolists, and more recently in the ISBU constructions of Travelodge Hotels in the United Kingdom. Infill in this regard can be described as an "integrated set of products, carefully prepackaged, custom prefabricated offsite for a given dwelling and installed as a whole.[20]

While supports are more stagnate, infill elements are changed out every 10 to 20 years, on average. They include space partitioning, kitchen and bathroom equipment, outlets, and finishes that are installed as separate systems to be independently replaced by occupants during the lifecycle. This calls for disentangling the systems of buildings; much in the way Tedd Benson envisions the future of building (see Chapter 9). This effort of detangling allows for open building to move in the direction of disassembly as plug-and-play systems. This will allow for an increased level of recycle and reuse, making open building a more sustainable concept by virtue of prefabrication technology.

8.1.2 Designing for Reuse

Buildings are demolished every day whether they need to be or not. Reusing buildings is not always possible because the infrastructure does not necessarily exist for replacement. On a jobsite, when a building is demolished, the separation of materials is twofold: material that can be recycled back into the processing stream and material that will be taken to the landfill because it is too costly to save or its properties have been breached to the level that reuse is not feasible. Phillip Crowther, in his paper "Designing for Disassembly," conceptually outlines four possible strategies of end-of-life scenarios for buildings: building reuse or relocation, compo-

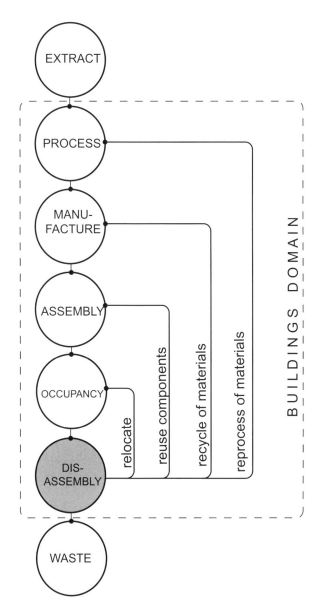

Figure 8.5 Systems of buildings are built to be permanent, and not disassembled. However, with buildings only lasting 50 years on average in the United States, systems need to be disentangled and able to be easily replaced, updated, and disassembled.

nent reuse or relocation in a new building, material reuse in the manufacture of new components, and material recycling into new materials.[21] Design for reuse suggests a range of possible end-of-life scenarios, some more environmentally responsible than others. As disassembly occurs in a project, moving back up the lifecycle of use, the material is increasingly consuming more energy and water, and has a manufacturing impact on the environment. Therefore, as a strategy, reusing as much of the building in its existing form as possible is desirable. This is rarely within existing paradigms of building construction practice, however. Disassembly is not warranted as a strategy because, in some cases, it would be more costly and more detrimental to the environment than to not, such as is the case of low-impact, high-return materials.

Prefabrication offers opportunities to expedite the design for the reuse paradigm. By building in a factory, materials are more easily reduced, reused, and recycled, thus foregoing the waste stream. Prefabrication is a more controlled process and therefore allows for more opportunities for disassembly and reuse, whether in part or in whole. Building disassembly, however, is not a simple feat. There are examples from history, but to date reuse of building components is not a standard practice and therefore an infrastructure for such is rather underutilized. Recycling, on the other hand, is a bit more common, as builders see financial sense in recapturing the cost of buying new materials. Designing for reuse is different than designing for onsite traditional construction. Referring again to Crowther, Figure 8.6 is a list of methods by which designers may plan for future building reuse. Disassembly will require some energy in the reprocessing, but by working by these principles the likelihood of reuse, recycle, and repair is much greater.[22]

DO	DO NOT
Use recycled materials	Use all new material
Use recyclable materials	Use single-life materials
Use a few materials and components	Use many different types of materials and components
Use natural and non-toxic materials	Use toxic and hazardous materials
Use easily separable materials	Use composites that are inseparable
Use mechanical or natural finishes	Use composites that are inseparable
Use mechanical or natural finishes	Use applied coatings and finishes
Provide permanent identification of material type	Use materials that end of life reuse is unknown
Use mechanical connections	Use chemical connections and adhesives
Use a changeable adaptable system	Use fixed unchangeable systems
Use modules, panels, or components	Use non-standard sizes or configuration systems
Use standard construction methods	Use highly proprietary systems
Separate building systems	Compress systems requiring one and all to be changed
Make materials able toe be handled	Make systems that require difficult labor sequencing
Provide a means for handling	Neglect construction sequence process during design
Provide realistic tolerances	Make building too tight
Use fewer connections	Use infinite fasteners and connectors
Design durable joints and connectors	Design one time assembly connections
Provide parallel sequencing disassembly	Detail construction process to accommodate linear path
Use a structural/assembly grid	Make every component and joint entirely unique
Use lightweight materials and components	Use heavy and cumbersome materials and components
Permanently identify points of disassembly	Make assembly and disassembly obscure
Provide spare parts and onsite storage	Make a proprietary system where there is just enough

Figure 8.6 In order for buildings to have a lower embodied energy in their reprocessing, recycle, and reuse, as well as be able to be disassembled more easily, architects and contractors should consider these strategies.

Factory-based production allows for a more controlled setting in which to regulate the use of recycled material into new product. The materials not recycled from other sources can be carefully selected to ensure that they are recyclable, making their end of life a new life. Using less materials and components, easily separable noncomposites, and nonapplied coatings and finishes allows the sorting and reprocessing of materials into the supply stream much more possible.[23] Studies indicate that a difficult sorting process is one of the greatest adversities to recycle and reuse in building construction.[24] Another advantage of factory work is control over toxic and harmful materials used in construction. Adhesives and other chemical-based materials used in connections can be changed out in favor of mechanically fastened finishes and joints. In addition to avoiding VOCs, mechanically fastened connections provide the opportunity to change out components when out of date or in need of repair.[25]

One of the greatest opportunities provided by off-site fabrication is the ability to permanently identify materials for their capacity to be recycled. ISO standards that were established for the plastics industry imprint products for recyclability.[26] Construction materials could similarly identify the material stream for

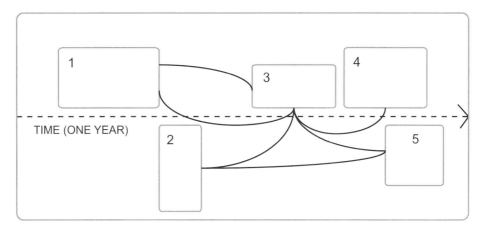

TIME (ONE YEAR)

Figure 8.7 The difficulty with realizing building reuse is the organizational complexity of sharing materials and prefab elements across buildings within a city. This diagram illustrates this paradox where each building is being disassembled or assembled in any one given time, demanding a robust retrieval and supply chain management to be implemented. It is unclear who would serve in this role—a private contracting company or the government—but without regulation, the motivation to do so is very low.

recycle. In addition to recyclables, marking materials and components in a building will allow information concerning the building system, assembly, and disassembly to be forever engrained. In order for these materials to be recycled and reused, however, standard materials and methods must be accommodated. A complex construction sequence or process of procurement will be a deterrent in the reuse of buildings and ease of update and changeability. Conversely, the following are strategies to consider for ease of prefab disassembly:

• Fewer connections

• Deliberate handling connections, such as lifting points[27]

• Easily handled components that are lightweight

• Parallel sequencing of assembly and disassembly[28]

• Identifying points of disassembly

• Providing additional parts onsite in storage

• Designing a system of assembly and disassembly during early parts of schematic design to ensure the client, contractor, key fabricators, and subcontractors are all on board with the strategy

Recycling is an idyllic notion. The reality is that any amount of recycling still consumes energy. Recycling is certainly better than not, but the primary deterrent of such is that materials, in their processing for recycle, are often downgraded in their properties, unable to perform a task in which they were originally created for. For example, plastics, when recycled, cannot be constituted again unless more material, energy, and processing occur. This is called down-cycling. In addition, recycling and reusing have to simultaneously deal with transportation and processing logistics within a city, from a city to a region, region to nation, and nation to world transfers. This process requires transportation energy and becomes a functionally difficult proposition that will most likely not be mitigated unless control and regulations are put in place to encourage reuse of building systems.

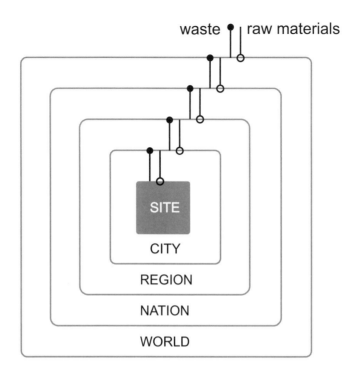

Figure 8.7 Maneuvering building reuse within a municipal space is difficult but easier to imagine than a robust system of material recycle and reuse between the city, region, nation, and world markets. Even in the most direct reuse of prefab modules, for example, at each level of transfer additional construction and transportation energy are required.

Fernandez illustrates that materials flow from the building site out to global space of material trade and back to the site as logistically impossible. From one building to another within a city it is difficult, but for all buildings to be on a time-and-material flow in which they share, trade, reuse, and recycle components, it is just not doable.[29] In order for real progress to be made, these cycles must be connected. Prefabrication offers a first step to evaluating how this might be accomplished, using the control of the offsite location in order to organize the procurement of materials between and through space and time.

8.1.3 Designing for Temporality

Manufactured home construction built on a chassis and construction trailers are built to a lesser stan-dard and fulfill a niche in the market for moveable, temporary constructions. Many architects including Jennifer Siegal, at the Office of Mobile Design, in her work and provocative books on mobile architecture have explored this idea as a permanent housing ideology.[30] To the introduction of Siegal's book *Mobile: The Art of Portable Architecture* poet Andrei Codrescu writes,

---

"Nearly every American house I've lived in has long ago been demolished to make room for some other building. There is a delicious (though painful) paradox here: Americans long for stability, but all they get is station-ary impermanence. No wonder then many of us long to become permanent nomads, snails with houses on our backs, Touareg tribesmen, and Gypsies."[31]

Disaster relief shelters have been designed to meet the needs of natural and man-made calamities. Many of these proposals have made it to market. The systems are fabricated in a factory and deployed quickly. They represent a desire to provide a temporary, durable housing solution to a needy society struck by devastation. A catalog of such solutions is beyond the scope of this book, but can be found in resources such as Architecture for Humanity and Public Architecture publications and websites.[32] An ongoing research project of the author is to identify temporary disaster relief systems in design and on the market across the globe. A key tenant in disaster relief theory is, at first step, to help the community rebuild themselves, thus architectural solutions for stricken societies can be summed up in the statement "the more temporary the better."

8.1.4 Designing for Change

In Schneider and Till's book *Flexible Housing,* the authors state that architects and builders should be developing and designing for "housing that can respond to the volatility of dwelling."[33] Volatility in housing may include changes in lifestyle over a life from young without children, with children, and finally to retired, allowing individuals to "age with grace." Other changes may occur because of philosophical shifts, changes due to life circumstance, financial or otherwise. Changes in life can impact architecture from the rearrangement of furniture to major spatial and enclosure renovation. Design for adaptability, flexibility, changeability can be classified into two primary approaches:

1. *Soft flexibility* refers to designers taking a backseat to users determining the adaptations. An example of a soft change is an open floor plan that allows for change and adaptation over time not predetermining the spatial definition within the structure.

2. *Hard flexibility* refers to architects making decisions regarding the way in which adaptation will occur. An example of this is the Rietveld Schroder House, which employs moveable interior walls that have been located and imposed by the architect.

Hard flexibility is the preferred method used by architects. However, hard flexibility only gives a nod to flexible and lifespan-specific design, and in many cases does more to create obsolescence than it does to eradicate it. "Controlling flexibility" is an oxymoron, the reality being that flexibility in the user creates more ownership and ultimately more reuse potential.

Accommodating the future needs of society is uncertain, but for a truly sustainable theory, this must be considered. Flexible housing allows future generations to choose their destination, that unforeseen technologies, and future systems may be introduced, accommodating social and economic aspects of sustainability. Prefabrication must be exploited to meet these needs not only for systems that are the most flexible such as infill, but for systems that are supports as well. Some ways to design for flexibility include the following suggestions, again by Crowther:

• Design for indeterminacy: designing spaces to accommodate diverse functions

• Raw space: design a specific frame and general space allowing for no over-designed architecture

• Excess or slack space: spaces that are not predetermined but allow the user to employ at a later time, or unfinished space that the user may use as needed

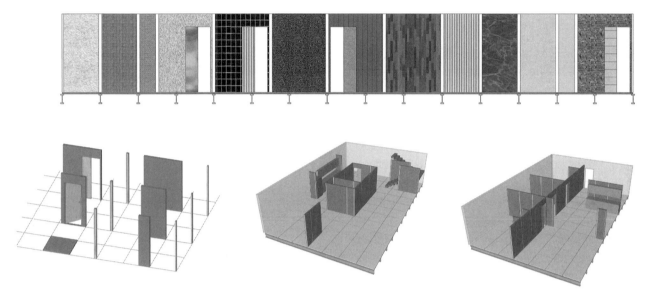

Figure 8.9 This is a proposal for a prefabricated interior partition system for residential architecture. Cleverly called "slips," the panels are connected with a vertical post connector on a grid allowing for easy manipulation of interior spaces. In an age with homeowners updating their interior spaces once every five years on average, a temporary solution such as this would mitigate material waste and make space more flexible on a day-to-day basis.

- Additions: offer the potential of adding on over time, give natural addition spots with regard to site orientation and placement as well as technical connections with structural supports in the correct location

- Expanding within: space that can be joined with another room to make a larger space suggesting walls that are moveable or demountable to be re-configured

- Systems determinants: which systems structure, skin, services, and space should be changed out and how

- Location of circulation: centralized but generic location for vertical circulation

- Moveable parts: design sliding, rotating, or collapsing

Walls, roofs, and floors in contemporary construction today do not accommodate change easily. Although something is prefabricated, if it does not allow for changes later, then a great potential in the system has been missed. Designing for assembly is not always the same as designing for disassembly. Although a building may have a logical sequential order for onsite erection, this may or may not be consistent with a deconstruction sequence. Accommodating disassembly into the prefabrication design process includes more effort, but if subsumed by the process as one of the many parameters including design for manufacture, transport, setting, and assembly, it can be accomplished within the existing project fee structure and workflow. Inflexibility within building systems leads to costly changes later. But a prefabricated system can anticipate this and accommodate change in its method of construction. Examples of realized successes include raised floors and dropped ceilings. Also, easily located and frequent power access panels allow office spaces to go through changes rapidly and inexpensively. These types of strategies can be implemented more easily with prefabrication planning in other building types as well, especially in open built and flexible housing solutions.

8.2 Lifecycle Assessment

The energy consumption of a building generally has two components of consideration:

1. Construction: the energy, embodied in the materials and process of constructing a new facility or renovating an existing one; and

2. Operation: all the energy and maintenance required to operate the building throughout its lifecycle.

The National Institute of Building Science (NIBS) reports that buildings consume 90 to 95 percent of the total lifecycle energy during the operation phase of the building life.[34] Therefore, the consideration of initial energy may seem unimportant by some, thinking that project teams should focus only on operational energy which creates a higher-performing building at the expense of embodied energy. However, as buildings become more and more efficient toward net zero, the concern over the initial energy will increasingly become an important point of research and practice. Prefabrication holds great promise for both initial and operational energy impacts as it allows for reduced material use in initial construction, additional control over materials and their embodied energy, and is more controlled in construction, allowing the building to perform better during its operational life. Between the two, however, prefab has more obvious direct pertinence to construction energy reductions.

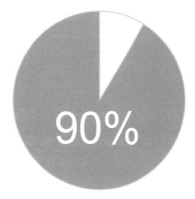

Figure 8.10 Operational energy, or the energy used in post-occupancy, contributes over 90 percent of the total lifecycle energy of a building.

Sometimes referred to as whole building assessment, Lifecycle Assessment (LCA) is an International Organization for Standardization (ISO) 14000 environmental standard. An advantage of using the LCA procedures is that they can potentially cover a wide variety of impacts not accounted for in other types of studies, such as more detailed data concerning the lifecycle energy of specific materials, sometimes called "embodied energy." ISO sections 14040 and 14044 identify four phases of LCA:

1. Goal and scope

2. Lifecycle Inventory

3. Lifecycle Impact Assessment

4. Interpretation

The goal and scope in performing an LCA for offsite construction is to assess the relative debit or savings in construction energy as a result of using prefabrication versus onsite delivery. In order to perform an LCA, a Lifecycle Inventory (LCI) must be compiled. The results of the inventory quantify resources used for construction, including raw and recycled material resource use and its accompanying embodied energy and water use. LCI also considers carbon emissions potential including pollution and sequestration. The process is explained by Jones, Tucker, and Tharumarajah:[35]

• Evaluate the operations involved in the study's scope and system boundary.

• Map the raw material extraction, materials processing, and accompanying energy/water/waste used and generated throughout. This is called a materials flow analysis.

• Quantify the amount of raw material, process material, and energy throughout.

• Calculate the quantity of emissions released into the air, water, and land throughout.

• Track the fate of all emissions released to the air, water, and land throughout.

• Determine how much of each emission is released into the air, water, and land.

• Compare all outputs against inputs to check that mass and energy flow is balanced.

Once an LCI is performed, the next step in an LCA is a Lifecycle Impact Assessment (LCIA). An LCIA quantifies the level of impact on the following factors during the lifecycle process:

• Human health infringement

• Climate change impact

• Ecosystem degradation

• Natural resource depletion

In addition to quantifying construction energy and construction impact, LCA also includes an economic and cultural cost benefit evaluation. Although not many tools have been developed to determine these measures, one called Lifecycle Cost Analysis (LCCA)[36] uses the same method but adapts it toward economic assessment. In addition, software calculators provide the ability to assess impacts real time and allow for consistent and regular updates. Tools such as BEES and Athena Eco-calculator claim to be useful as a design tool in weighing decisions concerning material use in a building project. The major drawback to automated LCA tools is location or context specificity. Each country and company has different mining, forestry, transportation, and production processes. In addition, some software platforms do not allow for the function of prefab factory location or site location to be a parameter in the model, using baseline embodied energy calculations from a database instead. Location of factory and site has a major influence on determining the comparative impact of transportation on construction energy.

As initial investment is always of concern, it is important that prefab elements are assessed for their cost benefit. Prefab architecture, with its increased potential for quality while keeping costs relatively under control, is an ideal method of construction for greener materials per unit of cost. The total energy consumption over the life of a facility can be reduced by employing methods that control the embodied energy of materials in the building, and use a high level of quality in construction that can lead to better performance during the facility operational life. These savings can be reached in traditional onsite construction perhaps with just as much ability, depending on the quality of design proposal for sustainable strategies, but recent materials and methods for residential construction allow for a higher energy performance for the amount of material used. An example is superinsulated systems panels such as SIPs and Kama Wall. Prefabrication potentially can be disassembled and recycled or

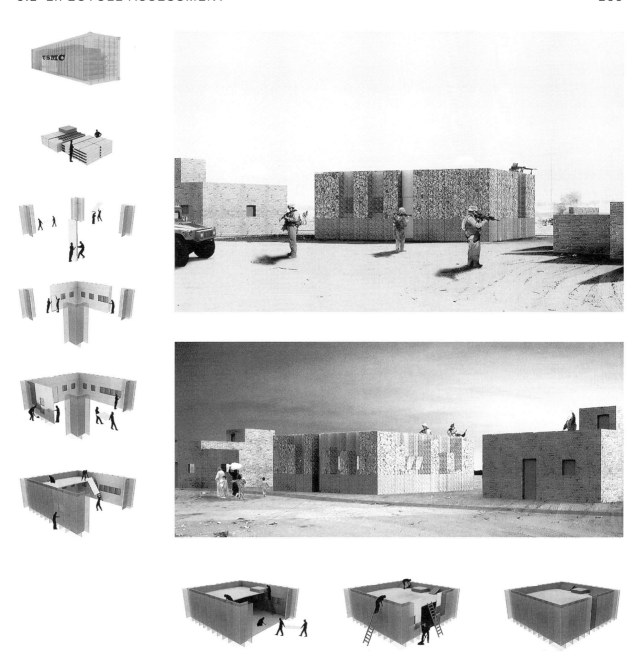

Figure 8.11 This is a proposal for a deployable wall and roof panel system for the U.S. military operations in Iraq. The system contains integral gabion mesh to be filled with local stone for ballistics and relate to the vernacular housing. Once vacated, the building is a dwelling for local residents.

reused, saving the energy for the demolition cycle. Construction energy onsite using power tools that either are pulling power from the grid or using fuel-powered generators in remote sites can be mitigated by using factory power systems. In the future, these can potentially be run by alternative energies, reducing the environmental impact and cost of operations.

Studies comparing the lifecycle costs of facilities built with traditional onsite methods versus nontraditional construction illustrate the value added for prefabrication. Proponents of offsite construction contend that the controlled environment of the factory allows for a higher level of quality and less material exposure to weather. A report from the AIA titled "External Issues and Trends Affecting Architects, Architectural Firms, and the AIA" in February of 2008 identified offsite fabrication as a topic stating:

"The lifecycle expectancy of modular construction is the same as conventional, and in a world where sustainability is gaining momentum each day, there are also several basic principles intrinsic to modular construction process that make it more eco-friendly than conventional construction. They spend significantly less on-site time, a result of a shortened construction cycle (the outcome of the simultaneous activities of on-site development of off-site building construction), notably minimizes the overall impact on the site. And finally, modular construction methods and materials allow a building to be more readily 'deconstructed' and moved to another location should the need arise, so complete building reuse or recycling is an integral part of the design technology."[37]

Lifecycle analysis that focuses on economics alone cannot fulfill the responsibility of our building actions to society and the environment. Offsite construction must also be concerned with environmental considerations due to the combination of less materials waste on the initial site and the capacity for deconstruction at the end of their useful life, reducing landfill waste. By virtue of being more ecological, prefab's cost benefit for lifecycle is greater.

Perhaps the most difficult part of LCA is interpreting the data in order to make design decisions. As with any design decision, construction impact must be weighed against numerous other factors including economics and societal impacts to determine its potential for sustainable results. In some cases verification may be necessary.

8.3 Verification

Verification relies upon post-occupancy data being gathered concerning the building in question. Prefabrication aids in verification in two ways:

1. Prototyping verification

2. Preinstalled performance monitoring equipment

Prefabrication may allow for a prototypical unit to be built before construction commences. The prototype will serve as a study to ensure a system will perform as intended. Verification in prototype or early construction can illustrate quickly whether cost savings are being realized in the production cycle. Site-to-prefabrication relationships are often the point of labor difficulties. If major change orders are required to ensure that connections are not only secure but weather-tight, this becomes an added expense. In addition, verification methods allow short runs in the factory on a large project to ensure that the shop operations have been optimized. This is difficult, however, because manufacturers who have been producing for decades are continually developing more efficient methods for production of goods and may be reticent to change their approach to manufacture. As prefabrication becomes a more common practice, the practice of lean manufacturing will increase, and waste and potential for error will decrease. Verification through early and frequent failure will provide the information necessary to overcome the challenges of oversight in the planning stages.

In addition to verification prototypes, prefab offers potentials to embed energy, air quality, and water usage real time monitoring equipment in offsite-fabricated elements to evaluate their performance over their lifecycle. In a recent research project by the author, two SIP houses were wired with thermocouple wires and hooked to a data logger to determine the performance of the houses for alternative energy and efficiency technologies. The installation of monitoring equipment can be completed relatively easily in the factory, during wiring for electrical in a prefab panel or module. In prefab architecture, these evaluation tools and feedback technologies could be embedded within the system of the building, allowing building teams and building occupants to receive real-time information on the systems performance.

8.4 Challenges

The major obstacle in performing an LCA to determine the contribution of savings as a result of prefab is in the time and resources required to perform such a study. Tracking the path of material flow is a full-time job, one that is difficult to justify in smaller projects, or even in budget-sensitive, larger projects. The reality is that LCA may not always be the best option for any given situation. In prefabrication, however, much of the up-front research for LCA can be performed as a project is developing. Project

teams can hold suppliers and product manufacturers accountable to provide accurate data on the environmental impacts of the materials used in their MTS and MTO products.

8.4.1 Certifications

Green product certification systems are working to move the building industry supply chain to be more responsible for its impact on the plant and its people throughout the lifecycle. Prefab allows for the procurement process to identify which MTS materials and products are certified and meet stringent environmental goals. In addition, in developing new products, the regulations can be mandated to manufacturers. Master specification systems such as MASTERSPEC and Building Systems Design (BSD) are also helping with this effort by providing green specification data. They both offer GreenSpec, a specification listing that uses inhouse research to verify material manufacturer claims and testing data in order to include products in their line, having continually been updated since 1997. It is unclear how these systems will evolve in the future and how they will be managed to certify the level of "greenness" of materials.

Relying on certifications and specification systems is important because most designers and builders do not have the time or resources to become experts in lifecycle assessment of each material being used in factory-assembled elements. Although offsite fabricators should have more of a knowledge and control of the products used in their assemblies, most also do not have resources to spend on full lifecycle research either. Unfortunately, internationally recognized certification entities such as the International Organization for Standardization (ISO), American National Standards Institute (ANSI), and the American

Standards of Testing Materials (ASTM) do not have an active verification process for determining the environmental impact of materials. Therefore, most of the green product standards currently available are developed outside of the formal consensus process that is recognized by industry and governments alike.

The sustainable certification of MTS can be organized into certification levels, referring to the degree of separation from the certifying organization and the company that develops the product. The first level is a statement by the company that produces the MTS material or product. This should be taken essentially as a word-of-mouth claim, and should be considered with little validity. The second level can be described as verifications from trade organizations or a consulting firm that the production company has hired. The most reliable is a third-level verification that is from a testing laboratory that gives a certificate of compliance with standards understood by the science industry as meaningful for determining the ecological impact of construction materials. Third-party verifiers may also receive approval from ANSI, recognizing the validity of the certifier as an objective party.

The ISO defines different types of labels that can be used for products, depending on what is being claimed. Type I labels provide a seal of approval for meeting a multiple-attribute set of predetermined requirements. Type II labels are verifiable single-attribute environmental claims for such things as energy consumption, emissions, or recycled content. According to ISO, Type II labels can be first-party self-declared claims of the manufacturer, but manufacturers are increasingly seeking third-party verification of those claims. Type III labels display comprehensive and detailed product information. Certifications available in the United States today lead mostly to Type I and Type II labels, although not all meet ISO's requirements.[38]

Some examples of third-level certifiers include:

- Multiple type certification
  - Green Seal
  - Eco Logo—Environmental Choice
  - Sustainable Choice—EPP, Environmentally Preferred Products
  - Cradle to Cradle—C2C
  - SMaRT—Sustainable Materials Rating Technology
- Forestry certifications that certify sustainable forestry practices to ensure longevity of the forests for use in building construction
  - FSC—Forestry Stewardship Council
  - SFI—Sustainable Forestry Initiative
  - AFTS—American Tree Farmer System
  - CSA—Canadian Standards Association
- Indoor air quality standards that primarily regulate emissions from volatile organic compounds, or VOCs, that are toxic to human health
  - Greenguard
  - Green Label Plus (for carpets)
  - California Section 01350
  - FloorScore
  - Indoor Advantage
- Energy Performance
  - Energy Star (for products)
  - CEE/ARI Verified Directory
- Water
  - WaterSense (verified by U.S. EPA)

8.4.2 Reliability of Data

Although quantification is valuable, it also points to the problem of computation in general—Is the data reliable? In the event of bad data, the problems are obvious. However, often data-driven design also does not give space for the designer to look at a problem qualitatively and intuitively in order to manipulate spatial environments and natural materials to emerge as a context-responsive solution. In addition, data in tools are only as good as the algorithms that drive them. These methods are built upon smaller-scale studies and verification needs for simulation. Therefore, current buildings are being designed using quantification performance software that is based upon best practices known. As additional data is discovered through verification the algorithms may change.

This is especially true in qualitative measuring methods such as LEED. Armpriest and Haglund report that although the Seattle City Hall was designed to a LEED standard in 2004, it is a poor energy performer.[39] The *Seattle Post-Intelligencer* wrote, "Seattle's new City hall is an energy hog" on July 5, 2005.[40] Based on data from the local utility, operating costs due to energy for the new City Hall ranged from 15 to 50 percent higher than for the building it replaced. Granted, the new building has a higher occupant-to-space ratio; however, the new building is smaller than its predecessor and other design elements such as extensive glazing and double height spaces have made anticipating the performance difficult. Though commissioning has mitigated many inefficiencies in the environmental controls, in 2005, the energy company report showed that in the summer months, the building performs very well, but suffers in the cold winter and spring. This building is a victim of the sustainability hype that surrounds many cases of new "green" architecture.

Without quantification, relying on qualitative measures for sustainability assessment during and after design may lead to more conscientious owners and designers but not necessarily better-performing buildings. Perhaps the best outcome of the Seattle City Hall is the lessons to be learned that can drive revision and development of future LEED and other qualitative rating systems. This is an example of operational energy; however, the point is made about qualitative methods of assessment as it relates to construction impacts.

Qualitative systems also have difficulties with heavy-laden bureaucracies. In order to gain credits or evaluate for green building quality, they rely upon a top-down imposed system of order. This inherently places bias regarding the special interests of the organization administering the evaluation system. For example, in LEED a point system is used, giving equal weight to parameters that may or may not have as much environment impact with regard to the building at hand. The previous example of the Seattle City Hall illustrates that a building may gain a LEED rating but not be truly sustainable from either an environmental, social, or economic perspective. In this case, because it is difficult to measure the success of the building socially, it is failing from the perspective of both environment and economics. Larry Scarpa of Pugh + Scarpa stated in a recent lecture on green building, "an energy hog community loved building is more sustainable than a green community loathed building."[41]

8.5 USGBC LEED

LEED is undisputedly the leading qualitative rating system on green building in the United States today. The industry uses it to design buildings by architects and to evaluate their performance of meeting goals.

As the industry standard, the role of prefabrication in the LEED rating system will be evaluated. In 2009, LEED updated its new construction and major renovation categories. The emphasis on performance seems to be a common theme that will increase over time—requiring quantification either in calculation or in simulation as well as more documentation that credits are being met. Most points awarded in the LEED system have no respect to whether or not prefabrication is considered. As such, manufacturers, suppliers, designers, and owners must evaluate what is beneficial and what is not with regard to modular, panelized, and componentized systems for building structure, skin, service, and finishes. Offsite fabrication in some instances, however, may make LEED more attainable.

The Modular Building Institute recently commissioned a report from Robert Kobet, AIA, LEED-AP that aligned the modular building industry with Prerequisite and Credit requirements imbedded in the USGBC's LEED rating system. The report, "Modular Building and the USGBC's LEED Version 3.0 2009 Building Rating System" evaluates LEED New Construction, Major Renovations, and LEED for Schools. For the purpose of the study by Kobet, modular building was defined broadly as prefabricated building components, parts, pieces, and subassemblies assembled under controlled conditions and shipped to become part of a larger, primary building project.

It is important to note that if prefabricated elements are used in the context of a larger building they must meet the LEED criteria that apply to them but also are subject to the LEED rating system as it relates to the finished building type under consideration. The individual components or subassemblies do not, in themselves, receive LEED certification. In the case of modular building units, the completed unit may be the subject of the LEED rating application and certification effort and may ultimately be the finished project that receives LEED certification. The following is a summary of this report in the categories of Sustainable Sites, Water Efficiency, Energy and Atmosphere, Materials and Resources, IEQ, Innovation and Design Process, and Regional Priority.

8.5.1 Sustainable Sites

This category rewards construction techniques that limit site disturbance and keep affected areas to within the space adjacent to the building footprint. Offsite methods meet these goals as the process of construction erection can be carefully planned to mitigate site disturbances.

SS Credit 6.1: Site Development—Protect and Restore Habitat may be met more easily through offsite methods. Option One in this credit applies to construction done on green fields or sites not previously disturbed or developed. The intent of the credit is to stay within 40 ft of the building perimeter; within 10 ft of sidewalks; and utility trenches serving connection of 10 in. in diameter or less, within 15 ft of trenches with larger utility connections, and within 25 ft of areas intended to remain permeable. Because offsite components and complete modular building units are fabricated elsewhere and delivered by a variety of transport, it is possible to achieve tighter site control and less disturbed area in the project perimeter. Industry representatives need to coordinate delivery of modular components with contractors to ensure the site tolerances for SS Credit 6.1 can be maintained.

8.5.2 Water Efficiency

Water conservation and reuse is becoming an increasingly important consideration in green building. However, there is not significant advantage to using offsite construction for achieving benefits of water efficiency over traditional construction in the LEED credits. The nature of predictability of offsite building warrants that this topic should be part of the process, and perhaps team members can strategize to meet water reduction and catchments goals.

8.5.3 Energy and Atmosphere

Offsite construction has many benefits to energy and atmosphere. The control of the factory allows for infusing high R-value enclosure and ensuring the quality of such in controlled conditions. High performance envelopes may be carefully crafted as panels, modules, or components with joining methods carefully planned in sequence and execution in steel, aluminum, and energy-efficient fenestration of windows and doors. This does not inherently have a benefit over onsite construction; however, in commissioning, offsite methods may find great benefits.

EA Prerequisite 1: Fundamental Commissioning of the Building Energy Systems Commissioning is the art and science of using diagnostic tools, experience, and building forensic knowledge to guarantee, to the greatest extent possible, that a building will perform and be operated and maintained as it was intended. LEED requires fundamental commissioning of the HVAC and controls, lighting and controls, domestic hot water systems, and renewable energy systems if they are included. Commissioning differs from traditional testing and balancing of the startup primary space conditioning equipment by manufacturer suppliers or subcontractors in that

commissioning must ensure that all systems are working collectively as intended. In the case of prefab building, commissioning will be applied to a finished project. If a prefab module is fully assembled prior to delivery and the systems that must be commissioned are installed and operational, most fundamental commissioning activities can take place in the factory. However, offsite methods are subject to additional commissioning activities onsite if connecting to the civil infrastructure, site-mounted renewable energy systems, site water supply pressure testing, and so forth. These activities can only happen in the field and are required for a complete commissioning report. One of the most important roles a commissioning authority has when a project involves prefabrication is to act as the liaison between the manufacturing plant and the construction site. The commissioning plan should address how commissioning activities that vary in scope and location will be coordinated and reported.

8.5.4 Materials and Resources

Offsite construction is by definition a resource-efficient method of delivery. Prefab reduced materials and resources as its major impact on the LEED rating system in all forms for new construction, existing buildings as well as LEED for homes. The economies in resource management of manufacturing panels, modules, and components in controlled factory conditions are found in the ability to produce repetitive units and remove material waste associated with onsite construction. In modular and panel construction, whole assemblies including interior finishes can significantly reduce onsite-generated waste. These materials can be reused in the factory or put more easily into the recycling stream for use in making other materials and products.

Specifically, LEED rewards projects for recognizing where materials come from, how they are used onsite, whether or not they are salvaged during renovations, and how the residual waste stream is managed. Special recognition is given to using existing buildings, materials with recycled content, and those that are mined, harvested, extracted, and assembled within 500 miles of the construction site. Finally, LEED rewards projects that use products grown using good stewardship practices, and are lightly processed or have low embodied energy. In order to accurately evaluate the role of materials and resources in prefabrication and LEED projects the following must be understood:

• There are no LEED certified products

• A product cannot give a LEED project points

• A product can contribute toward or comply with LEED credit requirements

In LEED products fall into two categories of credits: Contribution Credits and Compliance Credits. Contribution Credits require a calculation to determine what percentage of the project's materials meet the requirement set forth by the LEED rating system that the project team is applying for certification. Compliance Credits require all related materials to meet a certain requirement set forth by the standard. All products related to the credit must all pass the standard. These credits are pass or fail. In order to facilitate the LEED application, prefab suppliers must be intimately familiar with the nature, source, and manufacturing processes associated with the MTS assembled in the MTO for site assembly. The Prerequisite and LEED Credit opportunities in the Materials and Resources section are:

MR Prerequisite 1: Storage and Collection of Recyclables is a prerequisite common to all LEED

projects and not specific to offsite building. The project team must illustrate how glass, aluminum, paper, corrugated cardboard, and plastic are collected, stored, and then removed from the project site whether or not a municipal waste collection program is in place. This is typically the responsibility of the design team.

MR Credit 1.1: Building Reuse, Maintain 75 percent of Existing Walls, Floors, and Roof

MR Credit 1.2: Building Reuse, Maintain 95 percent of Existing Walls, Floors, and Roof

MR Credit 1.3: Building Reuse, Maintain 50 percent of Interior Nonstructural Elements

These credits only apply to LEED projects that involve existing buildings. In LEED 2009, MR Credit 1.1 is awarded two points. It is possible that the existing building in question is a panelized or modular building. It is also possible that the project involves adding modular or panelized building elements or new construction that contains modular, panelized, or highly specialized components to an existing building. In each case an inventory of the building is conducted to calculate the percentage of each involved. These credits stay in play unless the new construction being added to the existing building (if any) exceeds the size of the existing building by 200 percent, at which point these credits drop out and the existing building materials segue into MR Credits 2.1 and 2.2, Construction Waste Management.

MR Credit 2.1: Construction Waste Management, Divert 50 percent from Disposal

MR Credit 2.2: Construction Waste Management, Divert 75 percent from Disposal

One of the significant economies associated with offsite construction is the ability to manage construction waste. LEED rewards construction waste management at the construction site by being able to account for the materials, by weight or by volume, that are diverted from landfills. This includes all nonhazardous materials excluding cut and fill and organic material removed from the site. One direct benefit of reducing the overall waste stream is the simplification of construction waste management at the site and the resultant reduction in dumpster costs and hauling fees. In addition, there may be "Innovation Points" available to LEED project teams that can illustrate similar waste management practices are implemented at the prefab manufacturing facility. In order to apply for an Innovation Point the project team must be able to do a similar "upstream" evaluation to determine the amount of construction waste material generated in the fabrication of MTO products at the plant and the amount also diverted from landfills.

In order to calculate MR Credits 3.1 through 5.2, LEED requires project teams to calculate the cost of building materials in MasterFormat Divisions Two through Ten, less labor and transportation costs. This number then forms the denominator in the calculations used to determine compliance with the MR Credit requirements in each. Achieving these credits requires a working knowledge of the source of the materials, their composition and the point of purchase. Prefab dealers and suppliers should familiarize themselves with the full range of credit requirements detailed in the LEED Reference Guides. Only materials that are permanently installed qualify for inclusion in MR Credits 3 through 7.

MR Credit 3.1: Material Reuse, 5 percent

MR Credit 3.1: Material Reuse, 10 percent

LEED rewards reuse of building materials in new construction and major renovation. To date this practice is very limited in the manufacture of new prefab com-

ponents. However, it is quite possible that extensive prefabrication could be used in LEED projects where other aspects of the overall construction could feature these materials. The percentages listed refer to the percentage of Divisions Two through Ten material costs that are represented by reused materials.

MR Credit 4.1: Recycled Content, 10 percent (postconsumer + half preconsumer)

MR Credit 4.2: Recycled Content, 20 percent (postconsumer + half preconsumer)

LEED recognizes the contribution of material manufacturers that use both postconsumer and preconsumer recycled content. Postconsumer recycled content is that which is manufactured from such items as plastic bottles and cans which, once used, find their way back into the manufacturing process. Preconsumer recycled content is that which transfers from one industry to another without interfacing with consumers. Fly ash in concrete or wheat straw substrate are two examples of preconsumer recycled content. In order to participate in obtaining these credits the product manufacturer must be able to identify and quantify the nature and percentage by weight of recycled content in the materials used in offsite construction. These include but are not limited to materials commonly found in the modular construction industry: oriented strand board (OSB) and insulation polymers found in structural insulated panels (SIPs); agriculturally based substrates, linoleum, aluminum, metal, and glass window assemblies; medium and light gauge steel framing; carpet systems; floor tile; acoustic ceiling tile; cabinetry; interior drywall partitions; surface treatments and fabrics; doors; metal roofing; and so forth. Each must be evaluated for recycled content and cost relative to the overall cost of the modular component or unit, less labor and transportation. Because transportation costs associated with transporting MTO products is documented separately from the MTS products, this information simply needs to be recorded and provided to the appropriate LEED submission contact person.

MR Credit 5.1: Regional Materials, 10 percent Extracted, Processed, and Manufactured Regionally

MR Credit 5.2: Regional Materials, 20 percent Extracted, Processed, and Manufactured Regionally

These credits recognize the economic and environmental benefits of building with materials that are found in proximity to the construction site. The percentages listed refer to the portion of the total material cost less labor and transportation of materials in Divisions Two through Ten. In order to qualify for these points the location of the MTS and MTO products must be within a 500-mile radius of the project site. The fabricator must then be able to identify what building products used in the construction of the MTO product were extracted, processed, manufactured, and purchased within that same 500-mile radius. For homogenous materials this can be a relatively easy assessment. For materials that are complex or which derive a portion of their materials outside the 500-mile radius, this can be an involved calculation. The 1,000-mile diameter that results from the 500-mile radius is a significantly large area and many LEED projects get one or both of the points associated with these credits. It should be noted that the 10 and 20 percent of the value of the materials on the project are calculated against the total cost of materials including site development.

MR Credit 6: Rapidly Renewable Materials are those that are derived from raw materials that come

to market in a 10-year cycle or less. These include materials such as bamboo, Agrifiber, linoleum, cork, wool, and cotton. LEED awards a point for projects that have at least 2.5 percent of the cost of the materials in Division Two through Ten in the entire project represented by materials that have these attributes. In order to qualify for this credit and the available point, the MTO supplier must be able to identify and quantify which materials comply. These are then evaluated against the total project cost of materials in those divisions and a determination is made.

MR Credit 7: Certified Wood is that which comes from sources certified by the Forest Stewardship Council's Principles and Criteria. These include but are not limited to structural framing, subflooring, wood doors, and finishes. In order to qualify for this credit and the available point, 50 percent of the value of the wood-based products in the completed project that are permanently affixed must come from FSC-certified sources. The MTO supplier should be able to identify and quantify what those products are and have proof of the chain of custody that accompanies FSC certification. If the FSC-certified source is within 500 miles of the construction site, credit can be taken for MR Credit 5.1-Regional Materials.

8.5.5 Environmental Quality

Architects such as Michelle Kaufmann, Anderson Anderson Architecture, and Jennifer Siegal, as well as prefabrication dealers such as Project Frog, have exploited modular construction for its capacity to meet indoor environmental goals. "Indoor environmental quality" includes air quality, fresh air, and removal of contaminants as well as sound quality. Offsite manufacture is not fundamentally any better than onsite from an indoor air quality perspective; however, the control over what material is placed in the building during construction is easier to manage by way of trades. Modular construction by nature of separation of building units has a better acoustical performance than onsite methods.

EQ Prerequisite 3: Minimal Acoustical Performance (LEED for Schools only) contains this prerequisite which is intended to provide minimum acoustic performance in core learning spaces in academic buildings. Attaining the credit is based on designing classrooms and other learning spaces to meet the Reverberation Time (RT) requirements of ANSI Standard S12.60-2002, Acoustical Performance Criteria, Design Requirements, and Guidelines for Schools. Also, classrooms and other core learning spaces must meet Sound Transmission Class (STC) requirements except for windows, which must meet an STC rating of at least 35. In addition, a background noise level of 45 dBA must be met using the methodologies described in annexes B through D of ANSI Standard S12.60-2002. Or, classrooms and other core learning spaces must achieve an RC (N) Mark II level of 37 with HVAC equipment and installations as defined in the 2003 *HVAC Applications ASHRAE Handbook,* Chapter 47. Panel and modular units can be optimized to meet these criteria as they are seldom fabricated of heavy masonry construction or massive materials that reflect sound. SIP construction, metal studs with multiple layers of drywall mounted on resilient clips, acoustic ceiling tiles, and other acoustic design techniques can all be applied. The strategy for meeting this prerequisite and the associated EQ Credit 9: Enhanced Acoustical Performance can be formed around materials and construction techniques commonly used in prefab construction. The overall approach must be considered against the site context, whether or not the finished project is multistory and ambient noise conditions.

EQ Credit 3.1: Construction IAQ Management Plan during Construction. The criteria for maintaining acceptable IAQ during construction are based on the Sheet Metal and Air Conditioning Contractors National Association (SMACNA) *IAQ Guidelines for Occupied Buildings Under Construction,* 1995, Chapter 3. When applied to conventional construction projects, the intent is to ensure that work in place is protected, the project site is generally clean and free of excessive water, materials are effectively stored and kept dry, and ductwork is kept clean, especially if the HVAC system is used during construction. In MTO manufacturing plants, the conditions are often ambient, reducing the need for supplemental space conditioning during construction. The assembly areas are not subject to excessive moisture or extremes in temperature and are generally controlled to provide acceptable working conditions. It is assumed that factory-finished MTO products are shipped and installed in ways that also maintain the intent of the credit that assumes the precautions are observed until the project is completed.

EQ Credit 3.2: Construction IAQ Management Plan before Occupancy. LEED rewards project teams that build with allergen-free nontoxic material and building practices as defined in EQ Credits 4.1 through 4.6, described below. As an extra precaution, EQ Credit 3.2: Construction IAQ Management Plan Before Occupancy is available to ensure that any residual indoor air pollutants are removed. This is done by either flushing out the completed building or measuring the same using IAQ testing procedures focused on the following:

- Formaldehyde (HCHO) not to exceed 50 parts per billion
- Particulates not to exceed 50 microns per cubic meter

- Total Volatile Organic Compounds (TVOC) not to exceed 500 micrograms per cubic meter
- Carbon Monoxide (CO) at 9 parts per billion and no greater than 2 parts per million above outdoor levels
- 4-phenylcyclohexane (4-PCH) not to exceed 6.5 micrograms per cubic meter

In order to ensure superior air quality in any completed structure it is important to build with allergen-free nontoxic materials and maintain the same with ecologically acceptable cleaning products. Prefab is no exception and factory control should be leveraged to meet these IAQ goals.

EQ Credit 4: Low Emitting Materials. MTO suppliers are scrutinized more than those of site-build construction for their ability to provide usable habitats with acceptable indoor air quality. The combination of growing awareness of the consequences of poor indoor air quality coupled with LEED and the growing high-performance green building movement has made compliance with this collection of credits very desirable. In LEED 2009, the following four Low Emitting Materials Credits are contained in this credit grouping in LEED for New Construction and Major Renovations:

EQ Credit 4.1: Low Emitting Materials—Adhesives and Sealants

EQ Credit 4.2: Low Emitting Materials—Paints and Coatings

EQ Credit 4.3: Low Emitting Materials—Flooring Systems

EQ Credit 4.4: Low Emitting Materials—Composite Wood and Agrifiber Products

Each of the above material categories are governed by organizations that set maximum allowable limits for volatile organic compounds in the products eligible for credit consideration. They are listed in the respective reference guides along with the submission requirements and allowable alternative compliance paths for calculating VOC budgets if a product does not comply. In essence, project teams are challenged to use only benign products with low or zero VOC content. These materials are now readily available and largely cost neutral, especially if purchased in bulk. Prefab has two unique situations that impact achieving LEED points for these credits. By assembling building components and units in controlled environments it is possible to critically meter and effectively apply only the amount of material necessary. Material off-gassing and airborne overspray can be controlled. Controlled temperatures and humidity provide for optimum product storage, application, and curing conditions. This is not true if building products and units are manufactured and/or assembled in whole or in part outdoors. The second situation is when, technically, these credits only consider materials applied onsite. As in all credit categories, only the finished LEED project is considered. If none of the materials evaluated in EQ Credits 4.1 through 4.4: Low Emitting Materials are applied onsite, then the credits and associated points are not available. Conversely, if even small amounts of the subject materials are applied in the field, perhaps in touching up or final installation, then the entire application of the material in question must be evaluated.

8.5.6 Innovation and Design Process

Offsite construction, because it is not traditional, is innovative by nature. Therefore, this area is where offsite can shine, but it requires project teams to qualify and quantify the benefits of offsite methods for environmental sustainability in order for reviewers to justify their validity. Pursuing previous area credits and pushing further reaches these credits. A few ways in which offsite construction may foster innovation and design point arguments in the LEED system are discussed herein:

Exemplary performance: This means the team has moved beyond the last increment of the credit in the category and would like to achieve more points for a certain sustainability effort in water, reduction of waste management, and so forth. For offsite construction, Materials and Resources may be the most appropriate area to consider as it reduces onsite waste and can regulate the quality of the materials used and recycled in the waste stream.

Original innovation: In this case, the LEED team needs to document the intent, requirements, and the means by which the idea was achieved. Original ID credits are most successful if they quantify the results the project is trying to achieve. The ability to quantify savings and/or the environmental benefits to the project is central to achieving the LEED points. Offsite construction capitalizes on the ability to move production indoors, and maintain tight inventory control and project schedules. It is inherently waste conscious and can have minimum site impact if delivered carefully and strategically with respect to site constraints. Prefab elements purchased within 500 miles of the construction site offer other LEED ID point opportunities, as does the installation of low VOC materials offsite.

Among production methods, offsite fabrication offers some of the best strategies for construction waste management, material efficiencies, and indoor air quality. Sustainability is a balance of social, economic, and environmental considerations. Each of these principles must be weighted more or less de-

pending on the values of the project as they come from the owner, design team, contractor team, and community stakeholders. As previously stated, a LEED certification does not necessarily guarantee a higher-performing building from either a construction or an operational perspective. This listing of credits in relation to prefabrication is meant to be an overview of the potentials of prefab, but also how it might be leveraged to achieve the industry standard in green building certification.

8.6 Market

In 2008, Michelle Kaufmann's firm wrote a white paper titled "Nutritional Labels for Homes: A way for homebuyers to make more ecological, economical decisions"[42] in which her firm performed an environmental performance study of conventional onsite code standard construction to her factory-based green housing. The study illustrated that her homes in post-occupancy are performing at over half the energy consumption and over half of CO_2 emissions than the code standard house. She then proposes a labeling system that would place "sustainability facts" on buildings much in the way that "nutritional facts" are placed on food products. Just as we are careful about what we put into our bodies, so we should be careful about what our buildings are made of and how they perform. This rating system would allow for owners to make more informed decisions regarding buying and selling, and place green building as commodity in the real estate markets. Kaufmann uses the following determinants:

• Annual energy consumption in kbtu

• Annual CO_2 emissions in lbs

• Average annual H_2O use in gallons per day

• Insulation values in resistance for walls, roof, and floors

• Window U-value

Percentages in the rating system are based on national averages to help consumers understand the performance in comparison to market standards. This type of rating is not unlike the German Energy Pass that was implemented to provide comprehensive information about energy consumption and the energy status of respective buildings to increase market transparency for tenants and buyers. The energy passes merely serve for information purposes and do not constitute any legal grounds. Renovation recommendations are also included in each energy pass. These are intended to act as an incentive for upgrades and energy-saving measures. In Germany, legislation has approved two variants of the energy pass: the so-called demand-oriented and the consumption-oriented iterations. For the demand-oriented energy pass, building envelopes, construction materials, and heating systems are analyzed. Afterward the total heat loss of the building is determined based on this data. The result is an objective picture of a building's energy quality, independent of the behavior of individual consumers. The consumption-oriented energy pass, on the other hand, states the actual energy consumption per square meter. For this type of energy pass, the corresponding data is determined on the basis of the heating costs for the last three years. For nonresidential buildings, additional details about the power consumption are required.[43]

The idea of a sustainability facts or energy pass program for total lifecycle energy in the United States would offer an opportunity for issues of sustainability to become a tradable commodity along with other aspects of real estate including location, aesthetics, and quality making it a player in resale and equity markets.[44] Sometimes referred to as market-based incentives, offsite construction within the factory for housing, schools, and commercial could make provisions for performance inspection in the factory before shipping and assembly onsite. The examples above are primarily for operational performance; however, a similar system could be set up to account for construction-related environmental impacts. This would allow sustainability to be bought and sold embodied within building products produced in the factory. Just as trade organizations certify fabricators for quality assurances so design teams and owners can have confidence in their products, a certification process of prefabrication companies to deliver energy pass buildings would streamline what is essentially the goal of LEED and other rating systems to control the quality and performance of sustainable architecture.

8.7 Conclusion

Although we do need more precise methods of evaluation for green building and sustainability in general, these methods also need to be accessible so that users may implement such. For a whole building assessment, LCA is the most thorough and in-depth, but data does not always exist or may not be available to carry out this type of evaluation. Whether or not buildings are more sustainable and if prefabrication is used to accomplish this, is determinant upon people being able to integrate in order to deliver on these promises.

The National Renewable Energy Laboratory (NREL) performed an in-depth case study of six high-performing buildings.[45] The research has spawned numerous additional studies and metrics that have taken cues from this precedent. The evaluation focused on understanding the culture of practice of architecture and planning that aided the process of sustainable design, construction, and more specifically, high-performing energy buildings. It found that the greatest contributors to realizing high-performing architecture were communication among partners with owner-driven goals and an integrated approach to project delivery. Integration in the process of design and construction delivery is the key to reaching green building and prefabrication objectives and goals whether they are high-performing architecture or some other aspect of green building.

Although changes will continue to refine the tools and methods for environmental analysis, ratings systems, and the certification methods for MTS products, real success is not uncovered in technique, but will be found when a balance is struck in environment, society, and economics for a sustainable system. Integrated teams of architects, engineers, owners, subcontractors, facility managers, and the like can use a process of designing for disassembly, lifecycle assessment, verification and rating systems, in part or whole, to determine the appropriate prefabrication methods to employ to meet sustainability goals.

PART III

CASE STUDIES

chapter **9** Housing

"Isn't prefabrication a method of building, not a stylistic outcome? What is the correlation? ...Who knows? What I do know is that although there is sometimes a symbiotic basis for the relationship between modern design and prefab, the marriage is more an outgrowth of intention than style. The manufacturing process doesn't care."[1]

— Tedd Benson

This quote, from an offsite builder, explains a common perspective on the current prefabrication hype that has emerged in the United States. Prefab has become synonymous with modernist detached dwellings set in idyllic landscapes. Certainly this is a part of prefabrication in architecture that has just as much or more to do with pop culture than with architecture. But reading the magazines and websites and attending the exhibits in which architects' prefab work is being discussed, there seems to be little difference between the two. The reality is that buildings are more industrialized than ever before, especially housing. Housing will always be a need for the populations that are growing, and architects will seemingly always find joy in designing the object.

There are some defining moments in the last decade, however, that have led us to this modern prefab fetish. In 2000, *Dwell Magazine* emerged as a pop culture modern chic magazine for architects, designers, and mid-century consumers. At the time, Senior Editor Allison Arieff, also a writer, had an obvious fascination with design which showed forth in her books on airstream and other topics. Arieff and Bryan Burkhart wrote a case study book titled "PREFAB," published in 2002, that featured a history of prefab dwellings by architects and others from the industrial revolution forward. Perhaps and Dwell's greatest contribution to contemporary prefab housing, with Arieff at the helm, was in the 2004 competition call for a 2,000-S.F. dwelling under $200,000. Sixteen designs were submitted and one firm won—Resolution: 4 Architecture—with its "Modern Modular." Among those who fared well were emerging talents that, in addition to Joe Tanney of Resolution: 4, took their designs and developed companies out of them. They included architects Charlie Lazor with his "Flat Pack" panelized house, Michelle Kaufmann with her modular wedge "Glidehouse," Jennifer Siegal with her prefab prototype, and Marmol Radziner with their steel frame and infill system.

Others who have made headway in prefab housing the past decade include Rocio Romero and the LV House; Steve Glenn and Living Homes, who have collaborated with Ray Kappe and now KieranTimberlake to produce modern kit and modular systems, Hive Modular, Alchemy Architects, Hybrid Architects, Bluhomes, Project Frog, and even Daniel Liebenskind announced a prefab prototype dwelling. The intrigue does not stop at industry; schools of architecture are looking to prefab as a possible solution for design/build programs with the John Quale EcoMod program at University of Virginia, and Dan Rockhill's Studio 804 at University of Kansas. Today there is a flurry of websites, blogs, and case study books dedicated to the popular modern detached dwelling and the movement sees no signs of slowing except for economic challenges.

The opening of "Some Assembly Required: Contemporary Prefabricated Houses," organized by Andrew Blauvelt of the Walker Art Center in Minneapolis in 2006 and 2007, and "Home Delivery: Fabricating the Modern Dwelling" that showed in 2008 at the Museum of Modern Art (MOMA) in New York City, have further solidified the modern prefab movement. The premise of both exhibits was that the current resurgence of interest in prefab is owed to recent developments in digital technology. The idea is that industrialization with customization could potentially make the prefabricated dwelling commonplace in the United States, offering both variability and predictability.

The MOMA show was arguably one of the most thorough collections of history, theory, and practical thought on prefabrication and housing ever to be presented in one setting. We should applaud Bergdoll and Christiansen, curators of the show, and all those who participated. The exhibit also took modern prefab to a higher level of art and a wider audience of designers and design consumers. But design culture needs to move beyond stylistic discussions of prefabrication in architecture as it is portrayed in the magazines, blogs, and coffee table books, toward a more meaningful discussion about what are the opportunities and challenges of offsite fabrication in architecture and construction in a myriad of building types and conditions, especially with regard to realizing affordable housing. This is why Witold Rybczynski stated recently that the current prefab fad is more about industrial chic than about construction efficiency and affordability.[2]

While MOMA was showing some of the most recent thoughts on prefabrication in housing including the installation of five prefab modern dwellings just outside the museum on its 54th Street lot in Manhattan, 2008 brought unexpected challenges to the United States and the rest of the economic world. The conventions under which we understood the building

HOUSING PRODUCTION STATISTICS

Prefabricated housing can be categorized into modular, mobile (HUD code), production builder, and panelized. Below is the market share and descriptions:[3]

- 63 percent of all new housing is being built by builder/dealers

- 56 percent is panelized

- 33 percent production is onsite building

- 7 percent is modular

- 4 percent is HUD-code mobile

Modular: 225 modular home manufacturers in the United States make assembled sections of housing inside factories. Modules are made in complete boxlike sections, multisection units, and stack-on units. Up to 95 percent complete when they leave the factory, modules are sold directly or through local builders or builder/dealers. In 2008, 127,000 modular homes and apartments were sold.

Mobile home: Since the 1976 passage of U.S. Department of HUD Manufactured Home Construction and Safety Standards (HUD code), exterior frame construction of mobile units has been a popular solution to affordable housing. Eighty companies operating in about 250 factories use this technique that is similar to modular but with generally lighter construction and with metal chassis as part of the floor system. These homes are sold through dealers on display lots or from model homes in subdivisions. In 2008, about 82,000 HUD-code homes were sold, and about half of those were double- or multisection units.

Production builders: These builders produce single-family homes and low-rise multifamilies. More than 95 percent of the nation's 7,000 large production builders use factory-fabricated roof trusses. Other components of prefab such as floor trusses and wall panels are growing rapidly because of site labor and construction loan costs. Production builders, however, sell their homes directly to end buyers rather than in builder/dealer networks which distinguishes them from panelized home manufacturers. In 2008, production builders sold 622,000 units.

Panelized: This is the largest and most diverse section of the U.S. housing arena. These types include hundreds of conventional panelizers who sell their packaged homes through builders and builder/dealers; over 200 log-home kit builders, who sell direct or through dealers; mass merchandiser chains and local lumber yards and home centers, who perform all functions of a package home producer; producers of dome homes and other alternative systems including light-gauge steel, lightweight concrete, SIPs, ICF, and firms who cross over into package homes. In 2008, the estimated 3,500 panelizers collectively built just over a million units, slightly exceeding production builders.

Component manufacturers: These are independent companies that operate facilities and make components mostly for sale to production builders. Ninety-six percent of these manufacturers make roof trusses, 90 percent make floor trusses, 60 percent produce wall panels, and 6 percent machine and prehung doors. Other components include gable ends, tees, stairs, cupolas, agricultural out buildings, prefab garages, and metal-plate-connected rough openings for windows and doors. Output is not measured in units because component manufacturers sell mostly to production builders counted in the production builders' number. There were 2,100 component manufacturers in the United States in early 2009.

continued

Special unit manufacturers: These factory builders produce commercial structures of all types. There exist about 170 of these companies that build 777 structures per year. They sell direct or through dealers. They also have a model of leasing units. Their output is built to a commercial building code and includes classrooms, offices, banks, hospitals, construction offices, equipment shelters, restaurants, kiosks, jails, airport terminals, strip shopping centers, and dozens of other commercial buildings. This industry is one of the fastest growing. Owners are discovering the speed, cost, and quality advantages of specifying modular commercial buildings. The housing producers mentioned above can also build commercial buildings. The total prefabricated output of commercial builders and housing producers that also manufacture for commercial was estimated at 382,000 units in 2007.

industry have changed in many regards. The gratuity of the 1990s with its curving metal facades and smooth transparent glass curtain walls are appearing less and less attractive. Even modest modern prefab dwellings can be seen as exorbitant. Given the fact that Michelle Kaufmann, Empyrean Homes, and Marmol Radziner all either closed their doors or downsized as a result of the current economic climate in 2009, and many modular dealers and providers closed shop in 2009, even modest prefab designers and fabricators are having to rethink things. In the current economic state architects, engineers, and builders are left wondering: What is the future of housing and prefabrication?

Production builders today are more prefabricated than ever. Leveraging automation, production home companies, such as Pulte Homes, have developed an integrated CNC prefabrication and supply chain. Pulte has developed a packed modular system regulated by their Pulte Home Sciences which ships modules for rapid assembly. One of the reasons for this expansion is the consolidation of the building industry into larger and larger companies that are doing more of the market share. Whereas a decade ago the top 10 homebuilders nationally were doing 8 percent of the work, today, the same 10 companies are doing 25 percent of the work.[4]

A myriad of design software packages are used to develop truss and framing systems in a parametric model. Pulte uses precise 3D software to model the entirety of houses before production to work out any clashes and eliminate seams and joints. Accurate engineering and assembly reduces settling, cracks, and poor window operation. In addition to CNC equipment, companies are working to refine the schedule improvements and strive for supply chain integration using just-in-time approaches for house-by-house assembly. Today, some production builders are reporting that they can assemble panelized and packed houses from foundation to dried-in in a week or less. By going to a componentized system of prefabrication for housing, whether panels or modules, manufacturers can save substantial cost in schedule, material, and labor. Just in material, Dietzen, from Keymark, states that conservatively prefab is cutting costs by 6 to 8 percent on exterior shell and 10 percent on framing time.[5]

These advances in design software improvements and linkages to manufacturing and scheduling are not limited to mass-production builders. George Petrides designs, builds, writes, and presents on automation in construction. His company, Petrides Homes LLC, builds three or four custom homes a year in New England. Unlike the production build-ers, Petrides uses outsourcing regularly to Conner Homes of Vermont for production and erection of shell components. Petrides Homes' strategy is to dry-in the structure within three days so that work can continue onsite in shelter. Although not building 30,000 units a year like Pulte did in 2005, Petrides uses the same principles to build more efficiently and with quality on three to five homes a year.[6] These are the same principles being capitalized by modern prefab architects.

If we learn anything for the past couple of years in the housing depression, it is that "American consum-ers desperately want and need affordable housing, and would flock toward better-built, lower-cost alter-natives to what the market currently offers."[7] While visiting dozens of housing developments, factories, and developers in the past few years, two determina-tions can be stated: (1) the current system of housing delivery is broken, fraught with waste, litigation, and inequity, needing fixing in order to continue to provide housing in the future; and (2) the technology exists for prefabrication to make inroads into providing afford-able quality housing and that the benefits for finan-cial institutions, design professions, owners, and the building industry would be incalculable. For the sake of society's need for affordable, durable housing and for the sake of the construction industry we must do better.

Comparing the situation in the United States to Scandinavia and Japan we can learn much about style versus production. These societies have built prefabricated housing for decades. Modern or not, prefabrication is simply a better, more efficient way to build. In fact, today in Scandinavia a site-built house is, bottom line, a more expensive house. But prefab-rication has a rocky past in the United States, as dis-cussed in previous chapters. During the post–WWII period, prefabrication proposals were many but, un-like Scandinavia and Japan, the U.S. market adopted onsite framing as its construction method for mass housing. Sandy Hirshen, former director of the UBC School of Architecture, has been working in the pre-fab area since 1965 and has focused on rural, poor housing. He states,

---

"Prefab never took off in the States mostly because unions and banks traditionally didn't want to link them-selves to housing not attached to the ground. Developers don't make much money from building the structures— they make it by densifying the land and getting low interest rates."[8]

The reality is that modern prefab dwelling as it is deliv-ered today is not a solution for the masses—far from it. Prefab architecture in the United States is costing two to three times more than onsite traditionally built houses and, therefore, four times the cost of existing manufactured housing. Although these houses may be built better, without VOC materials, and have ef-ficient HVAC systems, they are still detached, only able to serve one family, and are often the family's second home. This is not a solution to the housing crisis, but these are experiments in prefabrication, whose lessons can hopefully be leveraged to help solve the social, environmental, and economic ills of today.

Modernist prefab architects have learned much about what does and does not work, when to harness standardization assembly line production, and when to use CNC technology to customize accordingly. The following case studies document interviews with principals of architecture firms and fabricators who are currently working in prefab housing. The lessons learned from these architects and construction professionals are informative and help to glean process and product answers, or lack thereof, to the issues of quality affordable housing.

• Rocio Romero Prefab

• Resolution: 4 Architecture

• ecoMOD Project

• Michelle Kaufmann

• Marmol Radziner Prefab

• Jennifer Siegal Office of Mobile Design

• Hybrid Architects

• Project Frog

• Anderson Anderson Architecture

• Bensonwood

9.1 Rocio Romero Prefab

Rocio Romero is an architect located in Perryville, Missouri, using a kit home concept to deliver modern streamlined dwellings. The LV Series, named after Romero's home Laguna Verde, Chile, is designed on the principles of simplicity, spatial quality, and sustainability. Kit houses have been in existence since the first portable cottage sent out to colonies of the British Empire in Australia and South Africa. Aladdin and Sears made kits popular and many early houses in the United States were built under the kit house concept. Romero's LV Series is a kit that comes with plans, instructions, and parts for the exterior construction of the shell of the house. The plans are detailed enough to be permitted by the local jurisdiction in which the house is built. Instructions include a con-

struction manual, materials list, schedule, specifications, and an informative DVD illustrating the system and construction method to be employed. This is to provide "how to" information for an owner to build the kit house by themselves or for a general contractor to build.

The LV Series comes in the following options:

• LV Home: Living room, dining room, kitchen, two bedroom, two bathroom, and closets starting at $36,870. 1,150 S.F. (25 ft-1 in. × 49 ft-1 in.)

• LVL (LV large): Living room, dining room, kitchen, three bedroom, two bathroom, and closets starting at $42,950. 1,453 S.F. (25 ft-1 in. × 59 ft-6 in.)

• LVM (LV mini): One bedroom, one bathroom, kitchen, living/dining area starting at $24,950. 625-S.F. studio (25 ft-1 in. × 25 ft-1 in.)

• LVG (LV garage): starting at $20,570. 625-S.F. garage (25 ft-1 in. × 25 ft-1 in.)

Other options include an LVT (tower), an LVC (courtyard), and upgrades for seismic and high wind areas.

Including onsite construction that must be completed on the kits, on average, the LV Home costs $120 to $195 per S.F. to build by employing traditional construction materials and techniques for residential building. All of the units have a standard width of 25 ft-1 in., but vary in length. The LV units are designed to be freestanding or combined to create a larger home or campus.

The kit-of-parts, manufactured and shipped by Branstrator Corp. out of Indiana, consist of wall panels, post and beam, roof structure, and exterior siding.

• Wall panels are delivered in either 2 × 6 or 2 × 4 framed exterior wall with ½ in. OSB affixed to the stud framing. Studs are predrilled for onsite electrical wiring to be performed by the owner's electrician. The panelized walls also do not include interior finishes, sill, and top plates. LV uses a faux wall panel as well. This is a non-load-bearing exterior wall that is placed on the exterior of the load-bearing panels to create a cavity for added insulation. This system allows walls to be R-38 with batt insulation, and R-50 with rigid foam insulation. The faux wall also conceals the low-slope roof as a parapet. Between the two walls, a downspout is concealed. The thickness between the two walls also offers a natural overhang to shade windows.

• Post and beam consists of 4 in. × 4 in. steel posts and glue lam beams that create large openings in the fenestration. The 4 in. × 4 in. steel posts are prefabricated with welded top and bottom plates. These plates have predrilled holes for connections to the foundation and to the roof beam. The glue lam beams are 5-1/2 in. × 11-7/8 in. and come in large 24-ft sections that can either be hoisted into place with a boom truck or cut to size as indicated in the plans and hoisted into place manually.

• The roof structure consists of I-joists at 24 in. O.C., I-joist hangers, and 4 ft × 8 ft- 5/8 in. CDX PLYWOOD. Installation of the roof structure is similar to normal stick construction. The roof package does not include nails or the 2 in. × 4 in. strapping that goes beneath the I-joists.

• The LV comes standard as Kynar 500 coated galvanized steel. All of the Kynar is included in the kit: the flashing, the flat panels, and the corrugated metal. However, no door and window pans, nails, bolts, rivets, screws, and silicone are included. All

Figure 9.1 LV House by Rocio Romero uses a panelized wall system and components that are shipped as a kit of parts to owners who must hire their own contractor.

the Kynar flat panels have hems on the back, which hook into cleats allowing the system to conceal fasteners and appear cleaner.

Romero capitalizes on the kit home concept well understood by consumers. The house is marketed as a product, so owners know what they will get as part of the package. The system can be deployed as outbuilding or a second home, but has also recently been used to deliver larger high-end homes. The hidden amount of construction that must occur in addition to the structure and siding kit is the large majority of the budget in a project and can be deceiving to first homebuyers. It is remarkable that despite the uncertainty of how the house will be completed it has been famously successful. This can be attributed to its strong image and the marketing strategy by the company including many published articles and a well-designed website. Romero built the first LV House for herself and opens it to potential clients.[9]

9.2 Resolution: 4 Architecture

Joe Tanney started Resolution: 4 Architecture (Res4) in 1990 to create urban domestic spaces. Working with spatial modules in creating linear lofts is something Tanney had been researching and developing long before his interest in modular housing. The company's traction in prefabrication began in 2002 when Tanney developed a series of typologies of unitized housing evaluating the possibility of variability within a standardized system. During this research he notes three tiers of residential fabrication: kits, panels, and modules. Going to the most finished of all the systems, Tanney has developed mass customized architecture, exploiting the robust wood modular industry found throughout the United States to deliver high-quality modern modular architecture. In 2003, the firm won the *Dwell Magazine* prefab housing competition and built its first modular dwelling the following year. The firm has since designed dwellings that have been installed across the United States from Maine to Hawaii.

Res4 has developed a comprehensive knowledge of the modular industry and the efficiencies and deficiencies of such. The firm works with a myriad of providers trying to find ways to design and deliver more productive architecture without sacrificing quality. A factory they are currently working with can produce up to five modules per day, but with this output, quality is bound to recede. Res4 has also noted that prefab for wood modular is geographically sensitive. The Northeast United States is home to many more modular manufacturers than the West. This is because modular has existed in the East longer, but also can be attributed to the high labor costs and fewer immigrant workers found in this part of the country. Tanney sees a great difference between western and eastern

modular providers. He has noted that, in general, factories in the East use more lean manufacturing principles building on assembly line and single piece workflow concepts. As a result, higher-output modular manufacturers are building 200 to 400 homes a year and 2.5 modules a day. These modular manufacturers for housing are beginning to move more aggressively to multifamily housing.

Res4 has developed what they call the "modern modular series." This is a design process by which modular typologies have been developed not as purchasable kits or packages, but as concepts of what can be done within the designed system. The concept is a two-type modular design including communal and private modules. In addition to the two modular types, Resolution 4 has developed with manufacturers standard methods for detailing, lighting, mechanical systems integration, finishes, and so forth. Much in the way that architectural firms develop a language and method for detailing, Tanney's firm has taken office standards to the level of modular fit-out concepts and factory floor operations.

To date Resolution 4 has designed and built dozens of houses across the United States. The houses average $250 per S.F., including site improvements. Architectural fees are 15 percent due to the level of coordination needed with the factory and value added to the customer. The designed system is usually bid out to three to five modular providers. Projects usually have a general contractor who prepares the site, foundation, and utilities. The GC purchases the modules from the factory as part of the project bid. Joe Tanney sees an average 5 percent markup by the GC for the modules above the wholesale cost from the modular provider.

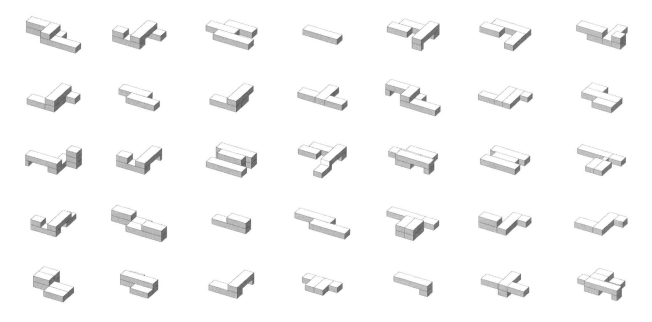

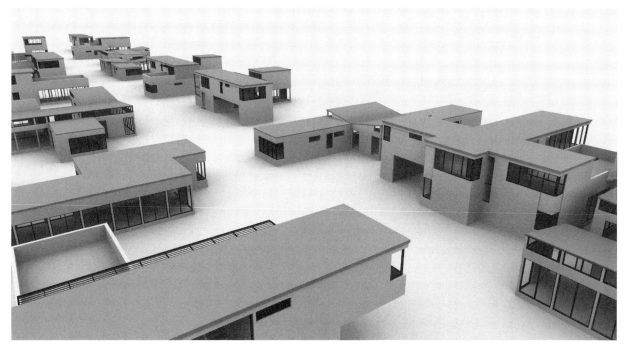

Figure 9.2 Top: Resolution: 4 Architecture's designed modular system uses predetermined blocks that can be customized to assemble into any configuration for housing. These are 35 of numerous other options by the architectural firm. Bottom: The modern modular program by Resolution: 4 Architecture envisioned as a community of models using the same base modules configured in different ways.

MODULES OF COMMUNIAL USE

MODULES OF PRIVATE USE

ACCESSORY MODULES

Figure 9.3 Resolution: 4 Architecture has developed a system of customizable modules based on three functions of community, privacy, and accessory.

Figure 9.4 This sequence is of The House on Sunset Ridge including design, fabrication, set, and finish. Resolution: 4 Architecture is able to achieve a highly customizable solution for owners within a set of standard modules.

RESOLUTION: 4 ARCHITECTURE HAS DEVELOPED A FOUR-PHASE AND FOUR-MONTH PROCESS:

- Phase 1: Design and documentation with client including programming, module design adaptation, customization

- Phase II: Engineering coordination, factory, and general contractor (GC) coordination and regulatory agency approvals

- Phase III: Shop drawing development, review, and approval. This requires a deposit from client to begin the fabrication process. As the factory is procuring materials and products for the project, the contractor is prepping the site. Procurement of materials to the factory for the project often takes longer than actual fabrication. Modules are online at the factory for one to two weeks.

- Phase IV: Setting and finishing of the house can take up to 16 weeks depending on the capacity of the GC and complexity and location of the site.

Although Res4 sees great potential in their current model and it has proven successful on numerous projects, they still see the "modern modular" as an ongoing research project to increase productivity while not sacrificing quality. Tanney states that architects spend the majority of their time on developing the design of buildings, without any thought to how those buildings will be produced. But there are many prefabrication systems and methods in existence being used for everyday buildings that architects can leverage to design a higher quality product for a better value. The greatest barrier Joe Tanney has seen in working with clients is the culture of consumption that does not place value on quality, rather on speed. The fear is that architecture will become faster, and cheaper, but not necessarily better, from either a product or design perspective by virtue of prefab.

In conclusion, Joe Tanney's goals are, in the short term, to continue to build better each day from house to house, in the mid-term, to continue to collaborate with manufacturers to find more affordable ways to deliver quality housing, and in the long term, to build communities of homes in higher density as well as other building types including infill housing in urban cores. Currently, Tanney is working on a three-story structure mixed-use infill system with commercial on the bottom floor and two levels of housing on the top, all in modular construction. This is the promise of prefabrication for affordable housing and one that is active among visionaries and research-based practices such as Resolution: 4 Architecture.[10]

9.3 EcoMOD, University of Virginia

In 2000, the University of Virginia, School of Architecture led a group of students and faculty in the U.S. Department of Energy's Solar Decathlon. The decathlon asks universities to design and build a prefabricated solar dwelling and place it on the mall in Washington, D.C. for a week of judging. The experience was positive for student learning and faculty research, but little was transferable to affordable housing, as the competition is just as much about the quantity of photovoltaic arrays (PVs) as it is about design. The entry from UVA topped out at $400,000 for 750 S.F. of space. However, the lessons learned about sustainability and prefabrication led to envision architecture and engineering educational experience that has become known as ecoMOD.

John Quale, ecoMOD director, and his collaborators in engineering, landscape, and information technology have evolved the Solar Decathlon experience into an affordable prefab housing research, education, and service program. EcoMOD moves building projects beyond design and construction to include more sophisticated control systems, energy modeling, and post-occupancy monitoring. UVA engineering is constantly working on evaluation processes, bringing their own objectives and talents to bear. The project runs on the mission of DESIGN – BUILD – EVALUATE. EcoMOD works with affordable housing providers to deliver modular-built projects to needy neighborhoods. The program is scheduled on the university calendar, designing the dwelling in one year, a summer session of construction in a warehouse on campus,

followed by one academic year of evaluation. This allows the project to extend beyond public service to provide real research on affordability and prefabrication in housing. EcoMOD has built four projects in the past eight years.

ecoMOD 1: Two-story modular in the region

ecoMOD 2: Steel channel and foam panelized system for post–Hurricane Katrina neighborhoods

ecoMOD 3: Historic renovation and modular addition in the region

ecoMOD 4: Two-story modular in region

EcoMOD architecture and engineering students manufacture the panels and modules in an airport hangar on campus during the summer months. The

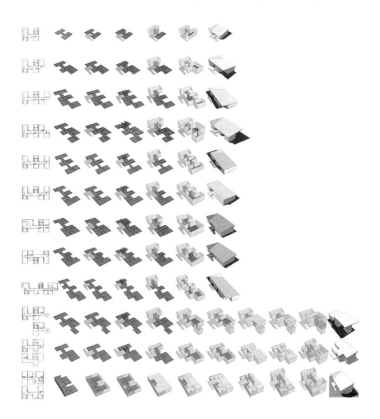

Figure 9.5 EcoMOD variations and sequencing options for the student-designed and fabricated modular projects at the University of Virginia.

Figure 9.5 EcoMOD process images. Top: students design and build a modular, students factory fitting a light gauge steel channel and foam panel system before flat packing it and shipping it to site; Middle: modules being set on site, interior photo of a modular project; Bottom: L—note the mate-line that is covered with a built-in millwork ribbon that wraps the ceiling of the room, and R—stairwell photo lit from side and top.

program works consistently with the same transportation, craning, and setting companies to ensure communication and a smooth installation process. Quale states that modular construction is an evolutionary delivery with each project gradually becoming simpler. It requires more planning for anticipating where straps and pick points will occur, sometimes causing decisions about design to be made based on the method of install.

As the name indicates, ecoMOD is a prefabrication program that is researching the possibilities of affordable net zero ecological design for housing. Quale and his collaborators purport the following research claims:

- CO_2: Carbon emissions included in transportation of workers are the largest contribution in construction. Prefabrication finds a savings environment by bringing workers inside rather than to and from a jobsite. Prefabrication requires a smaller labor force, reducing the amount of carbon as well.

- Waste: Prefabrication requires less material in comparison to onsite construction. In a well-managed onsite delivery, this can be mitigated and the argument is reversed, as transport requires greater amounts of material in the structure of the modules.

- Control: Time can be saved as prefabrication forces thinking through the procurement process from material acquisition to final stitching of modules. Prefabrication allows for increased control of the quality of fabrication and installation.

The long-term goal of ecoMOD is to continue to integrate with not-for-profits to deliver a greater quantity of modular housing. This requires a great deal of energy for fundraising to study aspects of the projects beyond the base construction costs provided

by the nonprofit developers. In order to increase the quantity of affordable housing output, ecoMOD is performing much less fabrication and working on design efficiencies with fabricators. Modular builders throughout the East Coast could become partners with ecoMOD design and nonprofit developers in a new model for housing production. Currently, ecoMOD is working with Habitat for Humanity in Charlottesville to develop a mixed-use, mixed-income housing that consists of 22 units in 11 duplexes in an old trailer park under redevelopment.[11]

9.4 Michelle Kaufmann

"It wasn't that we set out to create a company that focuses on prefab. Rather, it turned out to be a means to an end. Prefabrication allows us to prepackage the green solutions. It allows us to combine the different sustainable materials and systems."[12]

Michelle Kaufmann set up her company, mkDesigns, in the early 2000s with a mission to find a better, more sustainable and healthier way to build housing. Her first experiment was a house for herself, which led to requests for houses just like it. Intrigued by this idea, Kaufmann looked into using factory fabrication to produce her design called the mkGlidehouse®. Initially built for her husband and herself onsite in 14 months, the same house would later take only four months at 20 percent less in cost to produce in a factory.

Adding to her series of prefabricated homes is the mkBreezehouse™, which opens up the center of the home to cross ventilation; the mkSolaire®, designed for narrow lots; mkLotus®, a vacation house; and mkHearth®, a modern farmhouse. At its height, mkDesigns employed 30 individuals and held a fac-

PREFAB STATISTICS FROM MICHELLE KAUFMANN

During the extent of working in the prefabrication arena, Kaufmann has consistently collected data about the process to be able to quantify how well they are doing as a company, but also to be able to sell prefabrication as a viable benefit to clients and future owners. Some of the company's findings on prefab building include:

• Modules can be completed up to 95 percent coming from the factory

• 50 to 75 percent less waste than onsite construction

• 30 to 50 percent faster than onsite construction

• 20 percent less cost, on average, for factory production

• 20 to 30 percent increase in structure due to transportation loading

• 5 percent increase in transportation cost

• Less actual miles traveled

tory in Lakewood, Washington, called mkConstructs. Just as Kaufmann began with indoor air quality as her major concern, prefabrication is more of a tool to accomplish the goals of green architecture than the end.

In Kaufmann's experience, the cost of prefab architecture varies significantly from traditional costs. There are soft costs related to nonphysical design, financing, and planning fees, and hard costs related to bricks and mortar costs. Soft costs in prefabrication are higher than in traditional delivery. This seems counterintuitive. If design is already established, then why must the price of design be higher? Kaufmann explains that the collaboration and coordination that must occur between the factory and the designer require increased design fees. This investment saves on the hard costs in the lifecycle, however. Often owners have difficulty investing in what may initially seem to be a more expensive process. Kaufmann averages 15 percent of total construction costs for design services includ-

ing engineering and construction administration for a typical project.

Prefabrication hard costs include factory manufacture, shipping, setting, and stitching. In addition to the factory production, site preparation and foundation work constitute 50 to 60 percent of the overall construction budget. Transportation costs for a Michelle Kaufmann design varies depending on the distance from the factory to the site. Generally, the transportation of a standard module (14 ft-0 in. wide by 48 ft-0 in. long) from Blazer Industries to San Francisco, some 600 miles, costs approximately $10,000. The cost of setting and securing to foundations is $4,100 per module for any location within California, $3,500 for Oregon, and $3,000 within Washington. For example, the two-bedroom mkGlidehouse® consists of two 14 ft-0 in. wide by 48 ft-0 in. long modules. The transportation and setting costs for this model to a location in northern California is approximately $28,000. Kaufmann's houses range in total cost from $250 to $300 per

Figure 9.7 Michelle Kaufmann has designed a 16-module development for the Sisters of St. Francis Marycrest Convent in Denver, Colorado, her first modular co-housing development to date.

S.F. for flat sites. Factory production costs average $200 per S.F.

Since its beginnings in 2004, mkDesigns has built over 51 green modular homes. As the houses became more and more popular, Kaufmann partnered with others who had experience in industrial manufacturing. Paul Warner became a partner in 2007 to lead factory transitions, along with Lisa Gansky, with an IT background, Scott Landry, and Joseph Remick.[13] The vision by Kaufmann was to assemble a team that could develop a unique software tool to allow for mass customization or configuration by the client of basic standard designs. The system was envisioned to allow for user preferences not only in materials and finishes, but also in water-saving devices, upgrades on windows, and so forth. Warner oversaw the transition of site-built methods to factory-built, saving 20 percent on average in comparison to site-built homes of similar scope. But in May of 2009, amidst the housing crisis and lending freeze, two of the firm's major modular providers went under, leaving mkDesigns in a vulnerable position. In 2009, Kaufmann sold the assets of mkDesigns to Massachusetts-based Blu Homes.

Currently, Michelle Kaufmann is doing essentially what she did before, but focusing on larger-community developments that can benefit from economies of scale, making quality, sustainable prefabrication more affordable to the general public. Her most recent project is Casa Chiara, a co-housing development within a new community called Aria Denver, in Denver, Colorado, built for Sisters of St. Francis Marycrest Convent. This project is a 16-module development set in two rounds, one in July of 2009 and another in the following month. The added benefit of modular is that units often must travel at night, reserving daylight hours for setting. From start to finish Michelle Kaufmann's blog illustrates a rigorous two-month setting and stitching schedule.[14] The modules were shipped less than 500 miles from the site and materials used in the modules were also acquired within 500 miles, reducing the overall footprint of the project. Kaufmann will continue to work at Aria Denver and other multifamily and co-housing projects in the future, seeing greater potential in these markets for the principles of modular prefabrication.[15]

9.5 Marmol Radziner Prefab

Marmol Radziner, a full-service architectural firm in Los Angeles, entered the *Dwell Magazine* competition in 2003. In 2005, it produced the competition design as a prototype in the Desert House in Desert Hot Springs, California, built for partner Leo Marmol. Marmol Radizer then opened up a new section of its company dedicated to highly customized modernist prefabricated steel frame dwellings. In 2006, a second house was developed and delivered in 2007 to Utah. Since this time 10 to 11 additional homes have been completed. The benefit of prefabrication from the architect's perspective is complete end-to-end delivery. The architectural firm handles everything from foundations to button-up onsite. Todd Jerry at Marmol Radziner believes this is the part of prefabrication that clients are attracted to, the complete turn-key approach that leaves fewer questions unanswered.

Marmol Radziner Prefab, until the summer of 2009, held its own factory in Los Angeles, developing and fabricating steel frame modules. Since volume has slowed and lending has been frozen by the economic recession, the company is looking to outsource its designs for fabrication. Manufacturing is concerned

Figure 9.8 Marmol Radizer process images: structural tube steel frame is fabricated outside near the factory; frame floors are installed inside the factory; infill metal stud construction infill between the modular fram; interior finishes and millwork are completed in the factory; modules are brought outside in preparation for wrapping and shipping; modules are shrink wrapped and shipped; modules are hoisted and set; and modules are stitched together onsite.

with finding cost efficiencies within the fabrication process of the factory, but the architecture firm has found that when building custom, the efficiencies are offset by transport and install. They learned that it is difficult to build custom houses one at a time and drive price points down. The overhead by keeping a factory open could not be justified with the volume of production. Todd Jerry, who now runs the prefab-

rication arm of the firm, believes that in order to run a factory as a prefabrication architect, volume is the most essential element.

For Marmol Radizner Prefab, 2009 was a slow year, designing just three houses. In order to outsource fabrication, the firm is searching the country to find other factories that can build the steel frame system

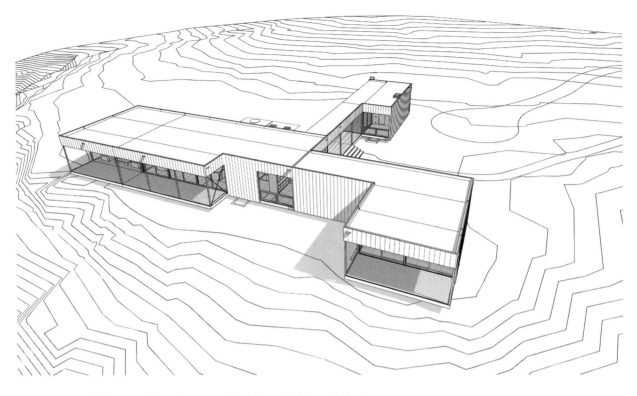

Figure 9.9 An architectural rendering of the Desert House in Desert Hot Springs, California.

and execute the quality desired. They have found prospects in the commercial modular industry with companies able to perform steel fabrication at a larger scale. As part of this new business model, Marmol Radziner Prefab is working with *Dwell Magazine* on the 12 homes collection with Lindel Cedar Homes, a kit provider, which is the second of *Dwell Magazine's* prefabrication efforts. In addition to this work with Lindel Cedar, Marmol Radziner recently announced an agreement with Haven Custom Homes, a factory in Pennsylvania, to deliver the new home designs. This collaboration will allow the company to bring down their original $400 per S.F. costs 25 percent to $300 per S.F. and still be able to serve the high-end market.[16]

9.6 Jennifer Siegal, OMD

The Office of Mobile Design (OMD) has been producing portable and prefabricated projects since its inception in the 1990s. Jennifer Siegal's innovative mobile structures include customized, prefab, green modernist homes and education facilities. OMD began its practice by looking at the possibility of taking portable classroom fabrication into a project called the Mobile EcoLab, funded by a grant to rethink the portable classroom. This lab was used to teach students about the environment. After a process of researching local fabricators and manufacturers of modular construction, Siegal determined to use the same portable chassis and steel moment frame, common in seismic-active California portable

Figure 9.10 Country School by Siegal process images: site plan of the school campus; modules fabricated with a steel moment frame for seismic and transportation loads with an integral chasse as well as longer spans for open classrooms; modules are placed in a tight site with a small forklift; and finished images of the school.

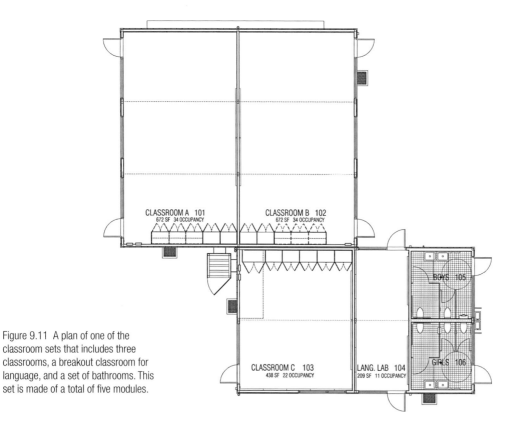

CLASSROOM A 101
672 SF 34 OCCUPANCY

CLASSROOM B 102
672 SF 34 OCCUPANCY

BOYS 105

GIRLS 106

CLASSROOM C 103
438 SF 22 OCCUPANCY

LANG. LAB 104
209 SF 11 OCCUPANCY

Figure 9.11 A plan of one of the classroom sets that includes three classrooms, a breakout classroom for language, and a set of bathrooms. This set is made of a total of five modules.

classrooms. Brandal Modular in southern California was selected as the fabricator of the Mobile EcoLab, having 20 to 30 years of experience in portable construction. Since this time, Siegal has worked closely with Brandal Modular to develop numerous modular dwellings and schools using the same steel system. Over the past decade, the maturation of the system has grown and efficiencies are now found more easily.

OMD uses a turn-key contract, giving the fabricator the responsibility for site and fabrication. This works well in both the houses and schools. A recent project that was delivered under this model is the private Country School, located in Valley Village, California. Having seen Siegal's work in publications, the school contacted OMD to consider a master plan strategy.

The project evolved into an existing elementary and nursery school remodel and middle school modular addition. Although the master plan was initially to upgrade the elementary, later the school found that by using portable modular, it was able to integrate a new landscape and create a new middle school.

The middle school comprises grades six through eight, including art, science, and administration, as well as boys and girls restrooms. Eleven modules make up this portion, each slightly varied in size. Each classroom in the middle school is 20 ft × 40 ft consisting of two 10 ft × 40 ft modules. Butterfly sloped roofs allow for water to be collected and directed to the garden, situated between the elementary, nursery, and middle school. Using a steel frame allows the prefabrication

SIEGAL ON PREFAB

Siegal reports that her houses generally range from $240 to $280 per S.F. for turn-key, including site improvements and site utilities. The school was much more affordable at $150 per S.F. This price point was possible because there were no kitchens in the design, and bathrooms were standard grade. In addition to cost savings, prefabrication allows OMD to cut time from the construction schedule. To achieve these savings, however, does not come just by virtue of using prefabrication. Siegal states that if architects want to engage in prefabrication for its cost, schedule, and other benefits, they must have an incredible amount of passion, focus, and humility to be willing to collaborate with the fabrication industry.

"This is a much more holistic process that takes a certain way of practice than conventional design practice. However, this process is rewarding because it is changing the system of delivery, it is avante garde, it is intuitively better. However it is still difficult and requires a great deal of effort. This is because the process is not conventional, requiring a commitment and thick skin from opposition from clients to regulatory agencies, from engineering consultants to contractors and even fabricators on occasion."[17]

portables to span longer distances. This is especially important in schools where clear spans of space are necessary for open-plan classrooms. Siegal has since taken the steel frame modular and added SIP infill walls for lateral stability and thermal enclosure.

9.7 Hybrid Architects

Robert Humble and Joel Egan founded Hybrid Architects in 2003 with a specific mission in envisioning solutions to urban dwelling. The partners believe that architects and builders can have an impact on the disparate economic gap between the rich and poor that currently does not offer housing options to lower-income members of society. In addition, buildings are demolished and enter the landfill, with new ones replacing them. Flexible building systems and modular assemblies facilitate building deconstruction, the relocation/adaptation of buildings to new sites, and temporary occupation of urban lots that would otherwise remain vacant. Hybrid capitalizes on existing industrial infrastructure and economies

of scale. Rather than reinventing the wheel on every project, the firm adapts established materials and technologies to new uses. As such, Hybrid focuses on prefabricated multiunit urban dwellings rather than single-family residences so as to maximize the efficiencies of an assembly-line-based approach to construction and increase urban densities.

9.7.1 99K House

In 2007, Hybrid Architects with Owen Richards Architects, both operating in Seattle, Washington, submitted a winning entry to the 99K competition in Houston put on by the Houston AIA. The competition called for a 1,400 S.F. three-bedroom, two-bath prototype house situated on a 50 ft × 100 ft lot in Houston's Fifth Ward. The design was to be built for $99,000. As part of the competition, the house was prototyped through onsite framing using MTS components. A similar version has since been created for Habitat for Humanity in the Seattle area but envisioned as a panelized system. Similarly, in connection with GreenFab.com, Hybrid has further adapted

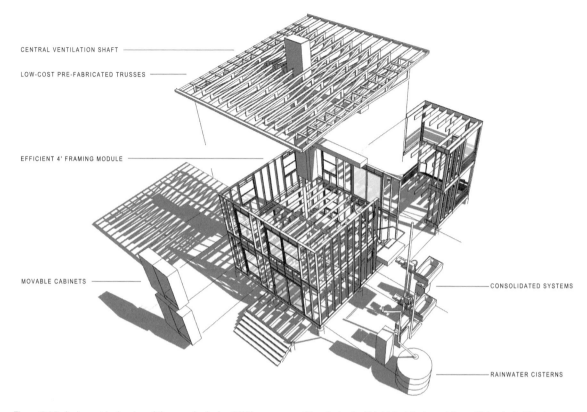

CENTRAL VENTILATION SHAFT

LOW-COST PRE-FABRICATED TRUSSES

EFFICIENT 4' FRAMING MODULE

MOVABLE CABINETS

CONSOLIDATED SYSTEMS

RAINWATER CISTERNS

Figure 9.12 An isometric drawing of the award-winning 99K house competition design by Hybrid Architects and Owen Richards Architects.

the design in modular construction. The house is set up on a standard 4-ft grid amenable to onsite framing, panelization, or modular.

9.7.2 Urban Modular

While the 99K house was being envisioned, Hybrid Architects with Mithun Architects collaborated on a two-year feasibility project to develop a standardized modular system for Unico Properties LLC, a Seattle-based real estate development company. The partnership developed a new model of stacked urban dwelling units to meet the needs of singles which comprise two-thirds of the housing market in downtown Seattle. The study compared using

stick framing, ISBU, and wood modular units. The options priced at only $1,000 in variation. Shipping containers would require a factory to be established. Modular could be erected three to six months faster than onsite stick framing. As speed of construction played a major factor in the study, wood modules were determined to be an appropriate solution. In the end, the design team located a company 65 miles from downtown that had the capacity with CNC tools to produce the desired quantities of 2,500 units across five apartment buildings for the first development. Two units, called "Inhabit," were fabricated, the smaller 15 ft × 32 ft stacked on the larger 15 ft × 45 ft and set in Seattle, was host to over a 1,000 visitors.

1 Computer-Generated 3-D Model: The factory creates a three-dimensional model of each module from the architectural drawings, which guides the automated machinery to precisely cut and assemble building components.

2 Optimizing Saw: The auto-saw reads CAD files and optimizes standard-length lumber stock, cutting it into precise lengths for each wall, floor or ceiling, minimizing waste with each cut.

3 Wall Framing: The framing station creates interior and exterior walls in 34-foot lengths. It utilizes automated nail guns, nail plate presses, multistage drills and an integrated routing mechanism.

4 Floor/Ceiling Build: Parts kits for each floor are preassembled in semi-automated shops and staged while waiting for installation into the appropriate floor or ceiling.

5 Interior Sheathing: The multi-function bridge combines tools that nail, rout and staple sheathing materials onto a wall. After fastening all materials securely, it routs all openings, within 1mm of accuracy.

6 Wall Installation: The walls, now 90 percent complete, are lifted by crane and installed on the completed floor system.

7 Interior Wall Finishing: The final coats of mud and tape are applied in an enclosed environment that helps capture dust from the sanding process and contain fumes and dust during the installation of texture and paint.

8 Interior Finishes: Upon its exit from the enclosed sanding and painting stations, the module travels into the finishing stages where cabinets, fixtures, flooring, appliances and hard surfaces are installed.

Figure 9.13 Wood modular system developed for urban sites in Seattle and beyond. Hybrid Architects designed this project in collaboration with Mithun Architects for Unico Properties, LLC.

9.7.3 Cargotecture

Hybrid also works in shipping containers. Waterfront real estate is expensive. During an economic time in which large investment is a risk, landowners may sit stagnant on their property or land bank to wait for real estate to bounce back from the recession. Land that is currently used for parking lots now and for the next 10 to 15 years could be inhabited with a temporary development that would generate revenue in the interim. As part of a competition entry, Hybrid developed what they term "Cargotecture," or the use of ISBU to develop multistory, mixed-use projects that occupy land-banked sites temporarily. With access to shipping containers on the port city of Seattle, Hybrid developed a system that could be deployed rapidly and save material waste through recycling of the containers.

Developers are unwilling to invest heavily in a five- to ten-year building, making temporary projects low budget. Hybrid has worked to develop wood, steel, and ISBU modular projects that are pricing out at just over $100 a S.F. The benefit of using shipping containers is that units could be fitted out quickly so that site work literally progresses from slab to all-enclosure in one week. Located in the Georgetown neighborhood in Seattle, Hybrid has designed two separate two-story buildings comprising 7,200 S.F. Onsite stick framing for the development would have taken 14 months to build. With Cargotecture, Hybrid delivered the project in six months, saving the client five months to recoup cost in early operation. This cost savings has been estimated at 5 percent by Hybrid.

Cargotecture did not reduce design and construction costs. However, the project was brought within the desired budget by design innovations by care-ful subthreshold code, which removed the need for an elevator, sprinkler, and more than one stair, and eliminated exterior fireproofing. Also, measures were taken to remove the need for structured parking and underground water detention systems. From the experiences of Inhabit, wood modular construction has been proven by Hybrid to be just as fast and to save at least 1 percent when compared with the capital investment of ISBU architecture. This finding suggests that ISBU for two- to three-story modular dwelling is used solely for aesthetic and waste reduction functions. Its greatest benefits are in higher than five-story structures and large quantities of units. Buro Happold in the Travelodge ISBU projects, and Tempohousing in the Keetwonen project in Amsterdam, have seen greater benefits, but the sheer volume of the projects warrants the use of ISBU manufactured in China. Until the United States sees a factory that produces and retrofits containers for building application, it is rare that they will be used for small-scale application beyond one-off prototypes.[18]

9.8 Project Frog

Project Frog stands for Flexible, Responsive to Ongoing Growth. The company grew out of research by the founder's architecture firm. Mark Miller from MKThink was researching ways in which to increase the quality, energy performance, and sustainability of education facilities and had the idea to begin a product company that sold prefabricated green classrooms. Miller spun off the company in 2007. Project Frog (PF) offers componentized and panelized customizable systems for schools. Portable trailers are an obvious problem: thin walls, poor insulation, flimsy metal skins, and permanent. Portable schools are poorly designed and produced: poor light, poor ventilation, and high-VOC-content materials. In response

Figure 9.14 An ISBU project by Hybrid Architects sited in the Georgetown neighborhood of Seattle employs twelve shipping containers spanned by framed floors.

to these concerns, the USGBC has developed LEED for Schools in 2007 which makes accountancies for indoor air quality, acoustics, daylighting, views, and mold protection. PF has developed a prefabricated panel system that, while being able to be erected quickly, meets the LEED for Schools requirements and beyond. *Forbes* magazine rated PF one of its top 10 "Ideas Worth Millions" in 2009.[19]

PF offers a full range of services working with general contractors or providing turn-key solutions. Consisting of 25 employees, and located in San Francisco, the company does not focus on design alone, rather on the product development and marketing. PF is a dealer, partnering with providers to manufacture semi-customizable kits for onsite erection. PF is constantly operating through efficiencies, working to flatten the complete process of workflow and supply chain.

According to Ash Notaney, in charge of supply chain and strategy operations, PF, like any product developer, offers customization where customers are willing to invest. This increases the value to the customer and decreases the cost and efficiencies of the dealer. Larger, more invasive options such as ceiling height changes require too much customization to be cost beneficial. The structure and infill system of PF makes sense for a mass-customized model because the base frame and modules are established; however, clients may customize the module relationships to one another and the materials within the infill panels. This variation of multiple relationships within the set systems allows for a great deal of flexibility without added cost for PF. The greatest advantages of prefab for PF beyond the sustainability aspects are speed of construction and cost.

PF has a 30-day average design and approval process due to an established kit-of-parts that are pre-cisely budgeted. PF is constantly reworking their process to ensure efficiencies. For example, the system has received California DSA precertification allowing for over-the-counter permits based on site planning. The system has been tested for speed of manufacture, delivery, and onsite assembly to as little as six weeks total onsite installation time. Inspections by the local jurisdiction occur primarily in the factory to expedite site inspection requirements. PF claims a 25 to 40 percent lower project cost than for similarly specified buildings using traditional construction methods. The speed of installation reduces site overhead and the potential to reduce lifecycle costs through net gain in operational energy costs that has been monitored and documented at 30 percent.

PF is not a true panelized or modular system; instead, it is a componentized system of structural framing and infill panels. The advantage is that the company has streamlined the design, delivery, and installation to take advantage of prefabrication concepts without having to ship large modules or panels. Componentized design also allows for a greater degree of customization by the customer. PF uses a finished structural steel frame powder-coated in the factory. Infill panels are prefinished as well with gypsum wallboard that is taped and sanded in the factory and painted in the field. Restrooms are not preplumbed, but electrical is installed in the panels before installation onsite.

The design, however, is modular-like, with set elements that can conceptually be added or removed. The modules consist of a central high volume, which is called the spine, and wings that are placed on either or both sides of the spine. Plans may be circular, linear, or clustered in form. Projects are developed in Solidworks, a software package common among product designers and engineers, but not among

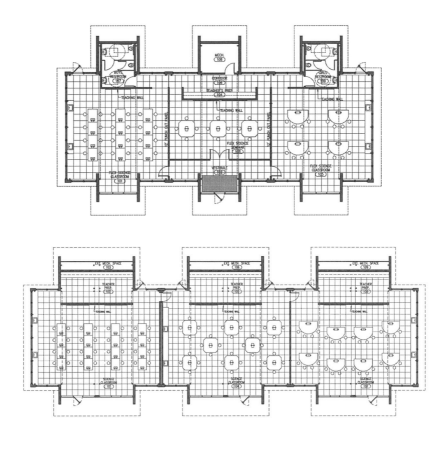

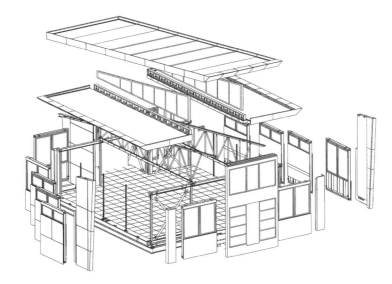

Figure 9.15 Project Frog's panelized system is designed as a series of predetermined modules that can be combined to increase or reduce space. PF uses prefabrication in order to control the quality and sustainability of materials used in the construction of their projects. Cost and schedule reductions have been documented by PF in comparison to similar specified projects of its size.

LACK OF INNOVATION IN CONSTRUCTION

Mr. Notaney at Project Frog explains that a constructed wall that is 10 ft × 30 ft and a thickness of 8 in. might cost $10,000. This is the cost of a modest car. A wall is a 2D object that cannot do anything on its own, especially not be able to be driven for a decade or more with dynamic loading. Further, if a Boeing 737 can be built in 11 days, supply chain management theory says that buildings should be able to be as well. Notaney also relates PF's model to fashion design, the industry he came from. Zara, a clothing company, revolutionized the fashion industry by flattening the delivery of clothing from one year, design to market, to six weeks. As styles change or new technology emerges, Zara is able to quickly adapt, meeting the needs of their consumers and saving money in the process. This delivery, otherwise known as end-to-end, is the model that PF has adopted.

architects, requiring engineers and contractors to include information concerning materials, welds, fasteners, and the like during development. This software feeds the CNC manufacturing process to allow for increased streamlining of outputs. PF is always looking for ways to quickly translate design information into information for manufacture.

PF does not manufacture its products, but has factory partners that work in an integrated fashion to better the product progressively. These factory partners may produce various components of the system and PF acts as the dealer, organizing the product, working with the client to deliver the project in quality, on time, and on budget. PF uses a three-tier manufacturer model of raw material, manufacture, and fabrication to manage their commodities. Their model is not unlike the automobile or aerospace industry which uses an outsourcing model to procure elements concurrently from many providers into a whole. This obviously requires a greater degree of integration and coordination than a traditional process between PF dealer and their outsourced partners.

PF uses an extended producer responsibility model, offering extended warranty for their product, the entire building, giving the client an added value while they own the building. Instead of "take it up with the brake supplier" mentality in many building ventures, PF is the supplier for the entirety of their product, making the building more affordable, of higher quality, and faster to fruition, but also exposing the company to greater innovation and risk in the process. This new model of horizontal distribution, when architecture is indistinguishable from manufacturing, can be seen as a future of prefabrication in architecture and one that architects, engineers, and builders may consider as a viable option to project delivery.[20]

9.9 Anderson Anderson Architecture

Mark and Peter Anderson are brothers, builders, and architects. This is how they described themselves at a lecture at the University of Utah in late 2009. Working on the marriage of design and production since 1984, the brothers have researched and developed applications of industrialized building in design. Their recent book, *Prefab Prototypes*,[21] documents prefabrication thoughts, theories, and projects they have produced over two decades of a design-build practice. Among these projects are streams of prefabrication investigations including componentized systems of CNC timber manufacturing, panelized

Figure 9.16 The sequence of PF system: panelized frames are knocked down and laid flat for shipping; panelized frames are quickly erected onsite; enclosure panels are installed with custom cladding options; night view of finished project, and student sitting in a day-lit PF classroom.

Figure 9.17 Exploded perspective drawing of a CNC timber frame house.

systems of factory-framed and SIP wall structures, metal building system investigations, precast concrete, and, most recently, investigations into shipping containers and portable commercial modular construction. The Andersons work collaboratively with fabricators to envision how existing production methodologies might be exploited to create more innovative architecture.

9.9.1 Panelization

Early experiments in prefabrication began with prototype projects that were panelized using 2 × 6 framed and sheathed walls that could be built up to 8.5 ft × 45 ft, or the general size of a semitrailer bed. This research led to the deploying of the system in the Fox Island House to take advantage of the cost-saving efficiencies of factory building without giving up the benefits of adaptation to specific requirements of individual building sites. With a particular focus on working with the hillside terrain common to the Pacific Northwest, the Fox Island House uses prefabricated 2 × 6, 8-ft-wide vertical panels which remain standardized from the main floor and above, but are lengthened or shortened at their lower ends to adapt to varying slopes and lower floor configurations. This system was taken to Japan in the Andersons' Amerikaya and Garden Pacific Prototypes. The Fox Island House and Japanese prototypes did not move beyond one-off experiments, but they presented opportunities of shortened building schedules and improved predictability that the Andersons have taken into other projects and explorations in prefab.

9.9.2 Chameleon House

The Chameleon House in rural Michigan uses 6.5 in. SIP construction for walls, roof, and floors to enclose 1,650 S.F. of space on nine different levels including a roof deck. The idea of prefabrication was part of the design concept, speaking to the sensibilities of the owner who works for Steelcase Manufacturing which develops prefabricated office systems. The house was designed on a 4-ft-wide modular grid to employ the benefits of standardized SIP widths. Walls were also kept within SIP modular standards for height. The building is skinned with translucent acrylic slats that reflect the surrounding and play with light during the day, earning it the name of Chameleon. A large three-story glazed surface faces the major view. This opening was difficult for SIPs to structurally negotiate with large lateral loads from wind. Therefore, the Andersons designed a steel moment frame that provides horizontal shear and is a welcome aesthetic complement to the main living spaces contrasting the finish plywood interiors.

9.9.3 Steel Modular

The Andersons have employed SIPs and steel frame combinations in other projects as well. In the Cantilever House, built before both SIP houses, the Andersons investigated the potential of prefabricating a steel moment frame, craning the entire frame of the house to a remote site and infilling with SIP panel walls, roof, and floor. This allowed for the greatest benefits of SIPs—not structural, but as enclosure and substrate for finishes and exterior skin. In addition, in the earthquake region where the house was built, SIPs as structure requires special engineering, of which the cost was absorbed by using the moment frame. This experiment in moment frame continued in a collaboration with Joss Hudson at Eco Steel, developing a number of proposals for using a metal building system and metal composite foam panels to build two- to three-story condo-style dwellings of

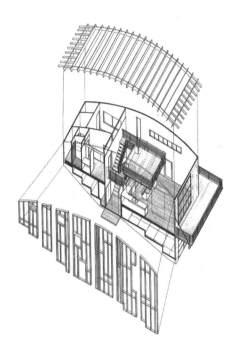

Figure 9.18 Wood panel systems explored by Anderson Anderson Architecture include early experiments with 2X panelized walls at the Fox Island House in Washington State, and Amerikaya and Garden Pacific prototypes in Japan (Top). These prototypes were further refined in the SIP panel Chameleon House in Michigan (Bottom).

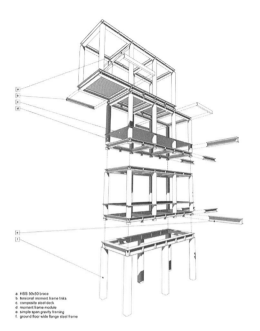

Figure 9.19 Early experimentation with prefabricated steel frames can be found in the Cantilever House, which uses a single moment frame craned into place with non-load-bearing SIP infill panel enclosure walls (Right). Further developments with metal building system manufacturers and suppliers have given way to a proposal for a moment frame stackable modular frame for mid-rise projects in cities across the United States (Left).

proprietary steel modular systems in American cities including San Francisco, Charlottesville, and Tulsa. The system was explored at a much larger mass-housing level for urban sites in the Wuhan housing project which uses a prefinished, prefabricated living unit concept through steel modular construction.

Wuhan Blue Sky Prototype seeks to provide a highly rationalized steel construction system that is cost-effective; appropriate to the current site, program, and project partner production facilities; and readily adaptable to future diverse sites, programs, and environmental conditions. The Andersons collaborated with Bao Steel and SBS Engineering Construction Company to develop a modular moment frame box assembly that can be easily stacked at full building height without temporary bracing or scaffolding, before in-fill beams are placed and floor slabs are cast.

This construction sequence allows for extremely rapid, precise erection, with immediate working floorspace providing safety and efficiency at each step in the building process. Each of these modules is designed to be prefabricated offsite for optimum efficiency and quality assurance, and is sized to match the international standard high-cube shipping container dimensions. A prototype unit was constructed in connection with a separate commission that acts as a portable environmental education pavilion for sporting events. All professional services were pro bono by the Andersons in the interest of advancing environmental education and construction prefabrication technologies.

9.9.4 Portable Modular

Although these projects did not develop beyond design and prototype, the collaboration with fabri-

Figure 9.20 A prototype for portable environmental education at sporting events uses the same dimensions and pick points detailing as shipping containers, making relocation relatively simple.

cators and engineers presents a model of practice that, when integrating solutions that would otherwise not have been imagined, can become more affordable and customized for a given condition. Their most recent exploration has taken the Andersons from one spectrum of prefabrication in proprietary componentized systems to complete portable modular units that are 100 percent completed in the factory. The Harvard Yard Child Care Center is a response to the university not having the funds to build a permanent facility but wanting to invest in a green temporary building that would occupy a site for 18 months during fundraising for a permanent facility. The Andersons worked with the general contractor and Triumph Modular to develop a double-wide portable classroom that employs a number of green elements, including low-VOC and recycled content materials, natural ventilation, views, natural daylight, quiet HVAC systems, and energy performance measures. Unlike traditional portables, the modules are designed to reduce sound transmission. Although built in an assembly line with other portable classrooms, the project exceeds onsite construction code standards and minimizes waste.

Figure 9.21 The Harvard Yard Child Care Center is a green portable modular project designed by Anderson Anderson Architecture in collaboration with Triumph Modular. It is a double-wide portable classroom that employs low VOC materials, natural daylighting, and quiet HVAC systems.

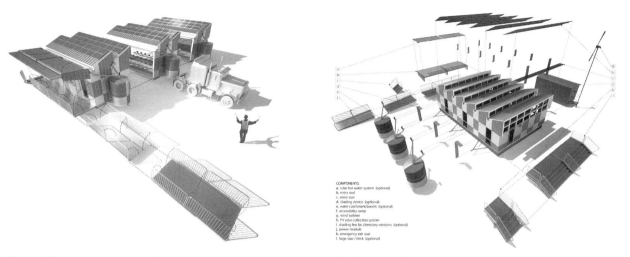

COMPONENTS
a. solar hot water system (optional)
b. entry roof
c. entry stair
d. shading device (optional)
e. water catchment barrels (optional)
f. accessibility ramp
g. wind turbine
h. PV solar collection system
j. shading fins for clerestory windows (optional)
j. power module
k. emergency exit stair
l. large stair / deck (optional)

Figure 9.22 An energy-neutral portable classroom prototype for Hawaii developed with Blazer Industries in Oregon.

After it is used as a child care center, the modular was designed to accommodate interior and exterior finish change-out to perform a different function on campus. The green portable classroom has instigated discussions for other school boards and universities needing space expansion quickly, but not wanting to sacrifice energy performance and interior air quality measures.

The Energy Neutral Portable Classroom developed in collaboration with Blazer Industries in Oregon takes the ideas of the Harvard project further to evaluate the feasibility of creating an affordable, portable, net zero energy classroom for K through 12 education. The classroom maximally conserves as well as collects and generates natural resources, including electrical energy, daylight, wind energy, and rainwater. As well as being strong, efficient, and conserving, natural forces and resources are highlighted and exposed throughout the structure, and all systems and performance criteria are monitored and broadcast to the web. The building acts as a learning tool for occupants, other schools, and the general public. The design optimizes photovoltaic roof surface orientation, naturally shaded north-facing daylight glazing, and modulated natural ventilation. All of these forces are balanced with the additional criteria of manufacturing and transport efficiency, functionality for classroom use, low operating costs, and ease of maintenance.

The building is prefabricated in either two or three easily transportable modules, reducing initial cost and energy, and facilitating ease of transport and reuse in the future, minimizing waste. A steel frame and steel and rigid foam sandwich panel floor and roof systems minimize material use; maximize insulation and heat reflection; and deter pests and mold in the cavity-free structure. A simple, double-wall metal cladding, along with metal roofing shaded by solar panels above a 3-in. ventilated airspace, creates a ventilated double skin, greatly reducing heat gain. All glazing is operable and north-facing and/or shaded to prevent direct sunlight, and to optimize natural ventilation and comfortable airflow. Interior surfaces are low-VOC products. Exposed beams

ANDERSON ANDERSON ARCHITECTURE ON PREFAB

For Mark and Peter Anderson, establishing a practice around offsite architecture has been both challenging and rewarding. The lessons learned over the past two decades have allowed Anderson and Anderson Architecture to establish a network of industrialists who are able to make their projects a reality. They are now looking at how projects can emerge not from discrete elements of prefabrication, but a hybrid of systems that will allow for a balance between standardization and customized options. The brothers state that architects rarely realize the capacity and culpability of manufacturing and fabrication and that the first step is to get designers and builders into the factory to collaborate. The Andersons summarize their experience in prefabrication in advantages and disadvantages:

Advantages: The greatest advantage to offsite fabrication is in predictability. Predictability refers to time and cost expectation. For owners, architects, and builders this is invaluable as all understand the scope, schedule, and cost and are more confident that these project goals can be met through supply chain management. Time is saved at each step, but not necessarily in overall time. In their research of smaller single-family houses versus larger developments in urban settings they claim that modular construction and componentized systems are much more feasible from a cost perspective in commercial multifamily using steel or wood modules than in detached one-off projects.

Disadvantages: Prefabrication is not necessarily the cheapest way to accomplish a project for lowest initial cost. Quality and sustainability may be more easily achieved through control of the product. CNC equipment and automated processes including assembly line production of building elements is expensive to set up; therefore, using existing production systems has been the preference of the Andersons. They see the greatest potential for the future of industrialized building not in CNC fabrication for mass-customized outputs, but in using standardized systems and methods of production and finding ways in which to exploit existing manufacturing infrastructure.

---

are FSC certified paralams, with exposed structural steel tracing primary structural forces. Interior walls are naturally finished, recycled rice straw panels. Daylighting analysis indicates that excellent work light levels are achieved throughout the typical school day in most locations without electric lighting. Thermal comfort analysis indicates the classroom will be comfortable in most high heat climates without air conditioning, although an efficient mechanical air conditioning system is planned as an option for school sites where air quality, or noise conditions, preclude natural ventilation.[22]

9.10 Bensonwood

Tedd Benson, President of Bensonwood Homes, began producing timber frame houses in 1975 and has slowly moved to bringing more of the operations of construction into the factory. Trained as a builder, Benson believes that houses should be well-crafted, beautiful, and affordable. Today, Bensonwood Homes works with architects and alone to create custom prefabricated housing. By moving the construction process indoors, Bensonwood can implement plumbing, electrical, and finish systems within walls and modules. Panelized operations at Bensonwood are producing exterior walls that are superior in structure, thermal performance, and finish quality. This process is accomplished by a flattening of the disciplines placing architects, engineers, timber framers, carpenters, woodworkers, and IT staff in one environment. As a result, this company has become an example of integrated housing delivery.

Bensonwood's work is allocated by 50 percent in high residential, 25 percent in mid-level residential, and 25 percent in commercial. With the economic downturn in 2008, Bensonwood is working to diversify its services and find solutions to mid-level and affordable housing as well as commercial building delivery. Bensonwood houses price out at $120 to $200 per S.F. for low to middle range, and $220+ a S.F. in high-end residential. Although Tedd Benson began by producing timber frames, the acquisition of Hundegger equipment and the operations of the factory have allowed them to become a premier prefabricator for quality homes and architectural projects across the country. Prefabrication at Bensonwood stems from a prem-

ise that Tedd Benson calls "dissing the homebuilding industry," that residential building today in the United States is "disorganized, disintegrated, dysfunctional, disenfranchised, disinterested, and disposable."

This conceptual framework has led Bensonwood to be able to deliver and erect a timber frame in 12 days in 1976, frame and shell in 15 days in 2004, and a frame, shell, and complete enclosure in a finished house in 15 days in 2009. These houses use a panelized frame wall system, floor and roof panels, and modular bathroom and kitchens. The only remaining portions of the houses onsite are final stitching of finishes and mechanical hookups. From mastering the art of building elements in shop through digital modeling, shop cutting, fitting appropriate tolerances, and refining connections, Bensonwood has developed a system of design, fabrication, shipping, onsite workflow, and craning and rigging safety. Their ideology of open-building system borrows conceptually from architects Habraken, Brand, and Kendall. Bensonwood uses eight principles in its operations to better the twenty-first-century homebuilding design and delivery.

Figure 9.23 Bensonwood began in 1975 as a timber frame company and has emerged as a leader in prefabrication thinking. Walls are now prefabricated in their shop in New Hampshire on tracks complete with plumbing, finish, and even base boards.

9.10.1 Disentanglement

The first step is to separate the supports from infill, or shell and infill. *Shell* refers to complete wall structures that are developed as high-performance envelopes. Bensonwood develops these walls as robust structural elements with R-40+ insulation. Working on the wall as a building science element, moisture, vapor and air infiltration are all tested. In Tedd Benson's operations this is accomplished by establishing a differentiation between shell and infill. The shell is therefore the most expensive portion of Bensonwood's process. Tedd Benson argues that instead of investing in home theaters, granite countertops, and other expendable elements, shell elements need initial capital investment to be able to pay off in the lifecycle. Therefore, the shell must be manufactured at a high level of quality and investment so that the nebulous "stuff" of a building may be changed out in future iterations. The company works everyday in a dry factory environment to better their shell support system to last for 100 or more years.

Bensonwood works to not only conceptually separate shell from infill, but literally produces components, panels, and modules that are physically separate systems and separate layers to facilitate adaptations in the future. The relationship between these systems allows Bensonwood to evaluate lifecycle needs for future alteration during design and execute them for disassembly in construction. The systems are organized to optimize assembly sequencing and increase inhabitant control. In order to accomplish this, Bensonwood has reorganized building system layers as distinct elements including: frame system, floor system, mechanical system, and support panel system in a unique take on supports and infill concepts.

9.10.2 Regulating the Grid

By regulating the three-dimensional spatial grid, Bensonwood finds that an empowering of control over space occurs. The grid is predictable, dimensions are stable, and cost is controlled. The design therefore considers materials and component manufacturers' sizes and capacities. This grid includes divisible multiples accordingly:

Timber structure: 2 ft × 2 ft or 2 ft × 4 ft

Infill: 3 in. × 6 in. or 6 in. × 12 in.

Vertical dimension: 7.5 in.

	SHELL	INFILL
IMPACT	Public control, Regulation	Private freedom
INTENT	Long term durability, Sustainability	Easy change and modification
PLAYERS	Architects, Engineers, Agencies	Inhabitants, Interior professionals

Figure 9.24 This table, developed by Tedd Benson, illustrates Bensonwood's purpose regarding disentangling building systems into shell and infill that have impact, intent, and players.

9.10.3 Virtual First

Bensonwood has realized the power of BIM during design to be able to develop the 3D qualities and understand clash detections, but also to simulate the sequence of construction prior to its beginning so that components can be broken down into assemblies. The automated project management information at Bensonwood including costs, supply chain, shipping, and install is virtually simulated before construction. This allows the company to automate cutting and shaping machinery through CNC code. Digital information is fed directly to CNC machines that are able to expedite the in-door labor of prefabrication.

On the Loblolly House, Bensonwood took the design BIM model from KieranTimberlake and continued to develop it during fabrication. As prefabrication is concerned with assembly, Bensonwood uses BIM to develop a project-wide strategy for fabrication, shipping, and install. In this process, everything is modeled including lights, connection, and even bolts and screws. The Autodesk Revit model from KieranTimberlake was developed in CADWorks at Bensonwood to allow for CNC machinery operation. The manufacturing process therefore allows for custom stock components to be milled concurrently and stored for the project based on material efficiencies. For example, window trim may be milled with rough framing. By nesting elements according to size and shape maximizing material, Bensonwood is able to control cost. There are technically no shop drawings in this process. This requires most of the cost to be in processing of information and not in actual labor of assembly as is the case in onsite construction. As Bensonwood updated the CADWorks model, KieranTimberlake continued to update their BIM model based on fabrication information. Sharing the digital model back and forth, architecture and construction were closely integrated.

9.10.4 Design Assemblies

By using proven libraries of families and objects in BIM, buildings are designed as a series of assemblies and systems. Called "design patterning," Bensonwood uses this method to develop parametric objects that can be reused and reworked for different projects. Structure and skin connections, for example, with their details and variability are kept as key elements to assure quality and variety, cost, and fit of the building as a whole. Reminiscent of Palladio's kit-of-parts, Bensonwood uses an open kit of parts to develop "open-built compositions" including interior modules, panelized walls/floors/roofs, and windows, doors, and interior millwork. This allows the company to reduce the number of pieces in a building from the tens of thousands in onsite construction to 50 or so elements.

9.10.5 Modular

While site work is occurring, a parallel process of building components is occurring in the shop. Bensonwood looks to combine systems as much as possible for added assembly value. Examples of this include kitchen and bathroom modules that can be craned into place on the jobsite and finished once in place. The company is always looking for ways to include more of the components in a prefabricated wall, floor, or roof including electrical, plumbing, finishes, and even baseboards.

9.10.6 Site for Assembly

The site is the worst place to attempt to control quality, efficiency, cost, and time. As such, site is used only for assembly of the prefab elements and connecting the systems of the building together. This reduces the potential for error. In order to accomplish this, Bensonwood not only has to develop a method for fabrication, but a sequencing model for packaging, flat packing on truck beds, and unloading so that elements go on the truck in the reverse order of how they will be assembled onsite. Elements are all numbered so that the assembly sequence is fast and predictable.

9.10.7 Play the Whole Team

By integrating the entire team, all the disciplines during the entire process under one company, Bensonwood is able to collaborate with architects, engineers, and building specialists during design. Decisions regarding prefabrication and onsite assembly are therefore present from the very beginning of design. This might seem to be a hindrance for creativity by some architects, but Bensonwood as a fabricator and builder sees it as critical to achieving cost and quality control.

9.10.8 Good Jobs

Finally, Bensonwood believes in a culture of discipline in training and mentorship seeing the building trades as just as valuable to the process of building as the design professions. The current building industry does not allow for real mentoring or apprenticing that teaches higher expectation on skills, efficiency, values, integrity, and ethics. This kind of mentoring allows experience, craft, knowledge, and the disintegration of hierarchy to occur. This is even more important for projects that are looking to prefabrication as the process demands a horizontal structure and flow of information freely.

Outside of working with KieranTimberlake on the Loblolly House, Bensonwood has worked with other architects as well, bringing their conceptual

and physical capacities to bear on a project and delivering well-designed and sustainable projects. In the Unity House, inhouse designers at Bensonwood in collaboration with Kent Larsen, professor at MIT, designed a net zero energy house for the President's House at Unity College. Bensonwood fabricated and assembled an open-built superinsulated enclosure with R-40 walls and R-67 roof. The exterior skin is able to be adaptable and changed over time. The house employs interior walls that are moveable and finishes that are replaceable. The design intent was to express architecture as pedagogy including: visible systems, energy monitoring, and transforming spaces. Distinct, disentangled, and accessible layers were implemented; it was designed for disassembly, and the composition became a library of components that could theoretically be reused on future projects.

For fabrication, Bensonwood set up a series of tracks in their factory, much like a Fordist assembly line, in which exterior wall panels were layered up to achieve performance. This not only allowed the crews to control the quality of the product, but also to assemble walls much faster. Including building wrap, windows, siding, interior finish, and even baseboards, the wall panels were shipped to site to be installed. A service bar on one side of the house was developed as a module in the factory with fixtures and plumbing preinstalled. Shipping was performed in flat pack with walls, roofs, floors, and modules neatly wrapped and secured to minimize damage during transit. Unity House works to reduce the number of components

▶ Figure 9.25 The Unity House fabricated by Bensonwood is a net zero energy house for the President of Unity College. The house design was assimilated into 50 elements of prefabrication. Components and panels were developed as structural and infill elements in the factory and were erected onsite. Bathroom and kitchen modules were finished in the factory preassembly.

in a building site from 50,000 (average) to 50 so that site assembly took five days to complete the install of the enclosure with stitching and finishing to follow.

Although Bensonwood uses bathroom and kitchen modules, they do not subscribe to whole modular construction for building structure and envelope. The reason is that they believe high-quality architecture is one of the key ingredients of the built environment and modular is difficult to achieve the variability needed. Panels and service modules have provided the company with a set of components that, when combined, provides a customized solution. Bensonwood is trying to work toward developing solutions that enhance quality of building and the quality of architecture. Tedd Benson therefore sees modular, panels, and components all as arrows in a quiver of prefabrication methods that must be employed when appropriate to reach project goals of cost, schedule, scope, and quality.[23]

chapter **10** COMMERCIAL
AND INTERIORS

Chapter 9 focused on housing and residential scale prefabrication case studies. These projects primarily consisted of affordable modular and panelized systems that could be produced and set quickly to provide added value to the customer. The large majority of prefab architecture is at this scale. However, perhaps the greatest opportunities to recoup the investment in prefabricated systems are in larger-scale architecture that use sizable elements and have more flexible budgets to invest in research and development. As such, the projects in this chapter focus on commercial and interiors that use prefabrication for its capacity for control to produce innovative architecture. The following architects will be presented:

• KieranTimberlake

• SHoP Architects

• Steven Holl Architects

• Moshie Safdie/VCBO Architects

• MJSA Architects

• Neil M. Denari Architects

• Office dA

• Diller Scofidio + Renfro

10.1 KieranTimberlake

Founded in 1984 by Stephen Kieran and James Timberlake, the Philadelphia full-service architectural firm has become a global leading voice in research-based practice. KieranTimberlake works collaboratively with clients, engineers, manufacturers, and fabricators to lead a process of research and discovery in design problems. This process has led the firm to become an industry innovator in integrated process and building technology, namely, prefabrication. Their book *Refabricating Architecture* is a manifesto on how "manufacturing methodolo-

▼ Figure 10.1 The Loblolly House is an experiment in prefab architecture designed by KieranTimberlake. The house has four major systems that were thoroughly modeled in BIM, fabricated in the factory, and set onsite. From left to right: Using Bosch aluminum sections, the frame of the house was precision-cut and erected with bolted connections onsite. Floor and wall panels were fabricated with utility systems embedded within. Service modules were craned from atop the structure. Rainscreen cedar cladding panels were installed last. This project was fabricated and assembled by Bensonwood.

gies are poised to transform building construction."[1] The book argues that architectural style is dead, that the new "avant-garde" are the actual production methods by which building comes into being. KieranTimberlake also stands behind their philosophy, committing a portion of their gross revenue and a professional staff of researchers toward research, development, and innovation. They have developed new materials, processes, and products of offsite fabrication and apply them into design projects that test these theories in practice.

10.1.1 Loblolly House

The Loblolly House is a prototype for both process and product research in design. Prefab as presented in many of the housing projects discussed in Chapter 9 suggests that prefabrication is about the simplifying of elements, flattening the materials to larger panels and chunks so that construction may be simply a pro-

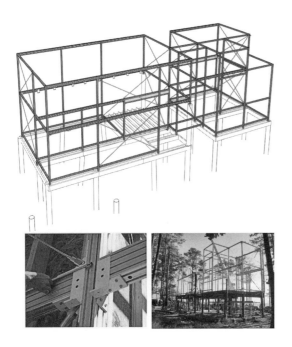

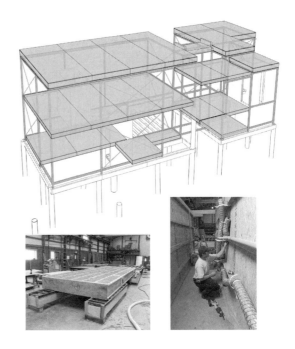

cess of a few assemblies. These systems tend to be proprietary, using complete modules that are difficult to disassemble, recycle, and reuse. Also, proprietary panel and modular systems do not allow for variation. KieranTimberlake determined to create a site-specific industrialized house made of MTS materials in the factory of Bensonwood and assembled onsite. The house is broken into five major building systems: piles, scaffolding, cartridges, blocks, and equipment. Kieran and Timberlake discuss the process thoroughly in their book *Loblolly House: Elements of a New Architecture.*[2]

The house is situated on the Chesapeake Bay, making driven piles the solution for a foundation to raise it above the nontidal marshes. The piles were driven at angles, taking their cue from the forest that surrounds the house. Driving piles is not as precise as the prefabricated elements that would follow; therefore, two layers of collar beams and a gasket make up this difference. The scaffold or structural frame of the house is an aluminum frame built from precision-cut Bosch 90 Series Profiles often used in industrial applications that are bolted with a T-slot connection. These connections allow the frame to conceptually be completely disassembled. Tension rods placed in the scaffold bays provide lateral bracing. Floor, roof, and wall cartridges were developed that could be set complete with integrated structural joists, insulation, and utilities. The floor cartridges have radiant heating, microducts, and electrical conduit throughout providing the primary distribution of services in the house. Wall cartridges came to site with insulation, integrated windows, a waterproofing layer, and cement board. A rainscreen of cedar planks sheathed the exterior of the building relating to the context of the wooded site surroundings. Three blocks, or service modules, include a bathroom, closet, and mechanical room unit, a guest bathroom mechanical unit, and a mechanical room and closet unit.

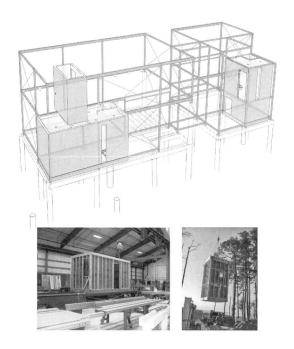

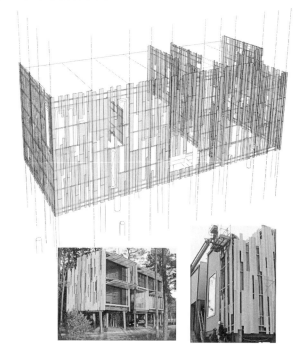

The Loblolly House is innovative not only in its method of prefabrication of components, but in the process of supply chain management employed by KieranTimberlake. A BIM modeling process allowed for the architect and fabricator, Bensonwood, to refine the design to take advantage of the sequencing of construction and the procurement of materials for fabrication and assembly. Kieran and Timberlake explain that working in BIM is simulation, not representation; the intentions of the architects were not interpreted from 2D typical illustrations, rather every connection was modeled. Bensonwood used the BIM model to develop a CADWorks model for fabrication. Although translation between the KieranTimberlake Revit model and the Bensonwood CADWorks model was not seamless, it provided a medium for collaboration. The model was so dimensionally accurate at the end of the design process it served to manage the supply chain, allowing the architect to assign tasks to either the onsite builder (Arena Program Management) or the offsite fabricator and onsite assembler (Bensonwood Homes). Parts were ordered directly from the model, such as the aluminum sections for the structure. Submittals and shop drawings disappeared during this process.[3]

10.1.2 Cellophane House

The Loblolly House led to a further exploration into BIM, supply chain management, and prefabrication in the Cellophane House, developed for The Museum of Modern Art exhibit "Home Delivery: Fabricating the Modern Dwelling" in 2008. Building in "integrated component assemblies,"[4] KieranTimberlake took the ideas of Loblolly House into a four-story structure that appeared to be anything but permanent. The structure employs the same aluminum frame bolted together with hand tools found at Loblolly as well as floor cartridges and service cores

(blocks) but adds interior wall panels, windows, and a PET film skin. This thin-film wrapper is an adaptation of their early work with Dupont on embedded PV systems in a polymer SmartWrap™, displayed at the Cooper Hewitt National Design Museum in 2004. KieranTimberlake detailed out the assembly sequence as an intricate process. Working outside of the realm of stylistic determinism, the house is an expression of the act of construction and the beauty of utility in what appears to be an intense experiment into assembly and disassembly. The commercial building prototype was designed and developed in collaboration with Kullman Buildings Corporation, who acted as the supply manager and fabricator to manufacture the service blocks and ship and erect the elements of the building. The building was assembled in sixteen days from arrival of elements to completion.

Since these house prototypes, Steve Glenn from Living Homes, a developer of modern modular housing products, has hired KieranTimberlake to develop a line of steel modular designs that can be prefabricated and delivered to customers' desires. Living Homes developed its first prototype with architect Ray Kappe.[5] KieranTimberlake is intrigued by this new role of developer of prefabricated sustainable housing, seeing an opportunity for impact into the production housing markets. The real measure of Loblolly House and the Cellophane House, however, is not whether the prototypes are repeated in mass customization. The real success of the projects will be determined in the impact that KieranTimberlake has on the housing supply chain in the United States. The company anticipates a day in which housing providers like Steve Glenn and others will streamline the supply chain management and integrated prefab assemblies process and products to produce affordable, quality architecture.[6]

Figure 10.2 The Cellophane House was developed by KieranTimberlake for The Museum of Modern Art exhibit in 2008 titled "Home Delivery." Using the aluminum frame system, KieranTimberlake devised a modular structure that could be fabricated at Kullman Buildings Corp. and installed in four stories onsite in an empty lot near the museum. The building is wrapped in a PET skin and was erected in one week.

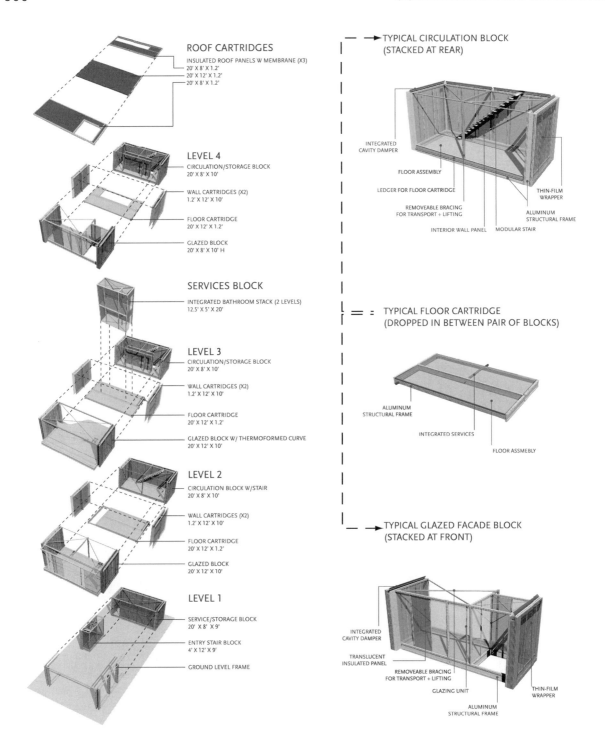

ROOF CARTRIDGES
INSULATED ROOF PANELS W MEMBRANE (X3)
20' X 8' X 1.2'
20' X 12' X 1.2'
20' X 8' X 1.2'

LEVEL 4
CIRCULATION/STORAGE BLOCK
20' X 8' X 10'

WALL CARTRIDGES (X2)
1.2' X 12' X 10'

FLOOR CARTRIDGE
20' X 12' X 1.2'

GLAZED BLOCK
20' X 8' X 10' H

SERVICES BLOCK
INTEGRATED BATHROOM STACK (2 LEVELS)
12.5' X 5' X 20'

LEVEL 3
CIRCULATION/STORAGE BLOCK
20' X 8' X 10'

WALL CARTRIDGES (X2)
1.2' X 12' X 10'

FLOOR CARTRIDGE
20' X 12' X 1.2'

GLAZED BLOCK W/ THERMOFORMED CURVE
20' X 12' X 10'

LEVEL 2
CIRCULATION BLOCK W/STAIR
20' X 8' X 10'

WALL CARTRIDGES (X2)
1.2' X 12' X 10'

FLOOR CARTRIDGE
20' X 12' X 1.2'

GLAZED BLOCK
20' X 12' X 10'

LEVEL 1
SERVICE/STORAGE BLOCK
20' X 8' X 9'

ENTRY STAIR BLOCK
4' X 12' X 9'

GROUND LEVEL FRAME

TYPICAL CIRCULATION BLOCK
(STACKED AT REAR)

INTEGRATED
CAVITY DAMPER

FLOOR ASSEMBLY

LEDGER FOR FLOOR CARTRIDGE

REMOVEABLE BRACING
FOR TRANSPORT + LIFTING

INTERIOR WALL PANEL   MODULAR STAIR

THIN-FILM
WRAPPER

ALUMINUM
STRUCTURAL FRAME

TYPICAL FLOOR CARTRIDGE
(DROPPED IN BETWEEN PAIR OF BLOCKS)

ALUMINUM
STRUCTURAL FRAME

INTEGRATED SERVICES

FLOOR ASSMEBLY

TYPICAL GLAZED FACADE BLOCK
(STACKED AT FRONT)

INTEGRATED
CAVITY DAMPER

TRANSLUCENT
INSULATED PANEL

REMOVEABLE BRACING
FOR TRANSPORT + LIFTING

GLAZING UNIT

ALUMINUM
STRUCTURAL FRAME

THIN-FILM
WRAPPER

10.1.3 Pierson Modular

KieranTimberlake's relationship with Kullman Buildings Corporation did not begin with the Cellophane House, but a decade ago when Yale University hired the firm to renovate Pierson College Upper Court, a 1930s residential college. In addition to bringing the building up to code standards for life safety, replacing bathrooms, and installing modern fire protection systems. KieranTimberlake was asked to restore finishes in the historic portions of the building and extend the building program into basements and attics, for social and recreational spaces. The primary goal of Yale was to maximize the bed count to capture students who were increasingly moving off campus because on-campus housing was not available.

The site for the project is a quadrangle surrounded on two sides by shallow light wells between Pierson College and other buildings. A larger space for sports was located just outside the existing dormitory. It is in this void that KieranTimberlake proposed a 24-bed addition. Due to the land-locked site and short construction schedule, KieranTimberlake suggested steel modular construction that could be craned in from above the existing historic buildings blind, being guided by radio and cameras. The design consisted of three stories, six rooms on each floor, bathrooms, and stairs. Pierson was modularized into 24-plumbed, wired, and finished boxes. The greatest challenge in using offsite construction for Pierson was in meeting the strict university standards for steel-framed windows and veneer plaster and wood floors that were not prefinished. A brick veneer exterior presented problems with stitching onsite.

◀Figure 10.3 The Cellophane House consists of stacked blocks on the front and rear ends of the building with floor cartridges spanning between the blocks.

Chris Macneal, at KieranTimberlake, relates that after design development was completed and before moving to prefabrication definitively, KieranTimberlake, Yale University, and the construction manager all priced the project using conventional construction methods.[7] The proposal for modular required the convincing of the New Haven Building Trades Council, 20 people at the university, the construction manager, the modular assembly company, the fire marshal, and the building inspector. Prefabricated modules were estimated as slightly more affordable. As such, the added benefits of the modular system were not in initial cost savings, but in schedule and control of the product. Including early occupancy revenue, prefab is estimated to have generated 15 percent cost savings when compared with onsite methods.[8] KieranTimberlake finished design development with Kullman in a design-assist mode to produce shop drawings that became the documents for permitting and construction. KieranTimberlake visited Kullman every other week for approval of an accelerated schedule. Working with a subcontracted mason in the factory, KieranTimberlake and Kullman developed a brick veneer method that is still used by Kullman today. Setting of the modules took place on Spring Break, when there was clear access to the site. Hoisting and setting was difficult with the crane operator not being able to see the site directly.

Once set, the modules had to be stitched together. The brick was a full module veneer consisting of a 2.5 in. cavity and 2 in. of insulation on the outside of the substrate and steel frame. Insulation was also placed in the framing cavity. Shelf angles at the bottom of each module limited deflection of the veneer. The brick was detailed as a rainscreen with vents at the top and bottom of each module. KieranTimberlake and Kullman devised a method by which the module joint was revealed with a recessed course and joint sealant. The modularity was therefore expressed on the exterior of the building. This added some brick detailing to what was otherwise a simple running bond veneer. At the base of the modules on the first floor is a cast stone veneer that is consistent with other Yale buildings in the quadrangle.

Atwater Commons at Middlebury College in Vermont, also designed by KieranTimberlake, required 60 workers over 16 months to drive an estimated 2 million miles to and from work. At Pierson, the residence hall was fabricated at Kullman in New Jersey, allowing it to be more quickly assembled over Spring Break by around 15 workers who racked up 30,000 miles. Kieran and Timberlake argue that the emissions reduction by virtue of prefabrication offsets any energy expenditures added by offsite production, especially when other efficiencies are considered.[9]

10.1.4 Sidwell Friends Middle School

KieranTimberlake designed a 39,000 S.F. three-story renovation and addition to the Sidwell Friends Middle School, a private institution in the Washington, D.C., area. The project includes a number of sustainable functions including water catchments, innovative HVAC systems, and a solar chimney consuming 60 percent less energy than conventional code construction, making Sidwell the first ever LEED platinum project for K through 12 schools. The concept for the building skin was to increase energy performance and waste reduction of the green building, and to act as an aesthetic bridge between the upper level of the old building and the new addition.

Richard Hodge at KieranTimberlake states that the goal of the skin was to develop a high-performing envelope. In order to do this, control of the product was needed. The panels would have to respond to all four cardinal coordinates, performing different functions on each elevation. On the north, the panels would have no solar shading, on the south, horizontal aluminum louvers, and on the east and west, vertical fins to block the azimuth angle of the sun in early morning and late evening. This resulted in 20 to 30 variations of the panels, each one being slightly different from the other. The common theme between the panels was a wood cladding taken from old fermentation barrels. The reclaimed western red cedar cladding was oriented vertically in a pattern of 1.25 in. to 5 in. in width, spaced ½ in. apart. The panels were 8 and 12 ft, typical widths at two-stories high. In order to expedite the construction of the panel strategy, a fabricator in Rhode Island was selected to work collaboratively to develop the enclosure system.

The final panel system consisted of 6 in. of staggered metal studs couched in 8-in. top and bottom metal channels. This allowed for no thermal bridges. The cavity was filled with batt insulation. A vapor barrier was placed just inside of the gypsum board. Wood windows with exterior aluminum cladding were placed in the panels in the factory. One of the major problems the team experienced was the air barrier that was applied in the factory as a fluid. This was still wet when panels arrived to the site. In retrospect, a membrane would have been more functional for fabrication. Weld plates were installed on the panels in the factory for a slip fit and to secure to plates onsite. The system was developed in consultation with the DOW and exterior wall specialist Paul Totten of Simpson Gumperz & Heger Inc. in Washington,

▶ Figure 10.4 Pierson College is a student dormitory project at Yale University that consists of 24 modular units stacked three stories high including bedrooms and bathrooms. The system was devised by KieranTimberlake and fabricated by Kullman Buildings Corp. It is estimated that the use of modular construction saved the university 15 percent including the early open date.

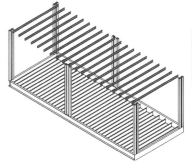

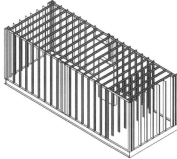

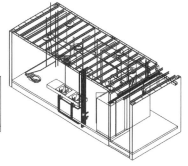

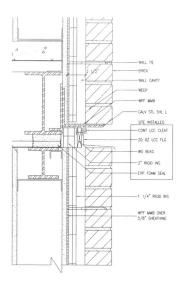

Figure 10.5 At the Sidwell Friends Middle School, KieranTimberlake developed a prefabricated enclosure panel system with Simpson Gumperz & Heger Inc. The 20 to 30 variations of the two-story panels were fabricated on standard light-gauge steel framing and skinned with a reclaimed western red cedar cladding hung vertically.

KIERANTIMBERLAKE ON PREFAB

KieranTimberlake's design emerges from a deep research process that looks first at principles and develops the projects from a series of research queries. As part of their process, the firm tries to use off-the-shelf (MTS, ATS, and MTO) rather than proprietary (ETO) products. KieranTimberlake's prototypes and commercial projects work to manage the supply chain making quality and efficiency more accessible. In the Cellophane House, it is reported by the fabricator Kullman Buildings Corp. that when the pieces arrived from the manufacturer, they did not always come together as easily as anticipated, manifesting gaps in the supply chain and indicating the need for further refinement through collaboration. James Timberlake states, "everyone wants to get from here to here (in a diagonal line as if to climb steadily, quickly) but the only way to really get there is stair stepping."[11]

Some might say that buildings built from a kit-of-parts is just as utopian an idea as some sort of stylistic agenda, but KieranTimberlake's hybrid approach demonstrates a much more viable methodology that can have a lasting impact on the environment, economics, and finally society in a positive way. KieranTimberlake is not a manufacturer, nor intends to be, but their work illustrates a provocative notion that the future of design and construction practice can and should be better. In the words of James Timberlake concerning the Loblolly House,

"We decided to make our private effort, our experiment, public in order to address those fears and dispel the critics who said it could not be done. That we could not improve design and construction. That we could not improve the supply chain. That we could not do better. Nonsense."[12]

D.C. Because the panel system presented risk to the owner, Totten worked with KieranTimberlake and the fabricator during the design to devise the best method for execution.[10]

10.2 SHoP Architects

SHoP summarizes their attitude about architecture and building practice in the quotes that flash on their website homepage:

"Use technology to build practice, see practice as technology"

"How it's built doesn't matter except when it's the only thing that matters"

"Efficiency and great design are not mutually exclusive"

"Building buildings is better than talking about buildings"

SHoP Architects is concerned with matters of construction. Since its inception in 1996, the principals Chris Sharples, Coren Sharples, William Sharples, Kimberley Holden, and Gregg Pasquarelli have grown the firm to include 60 employees and a portfolio of projects that range from master planning and high design to the opening of a branch of the company, SHoP Construction, a fully applied technology, BIM, and project delivery services firm for the design and construction industry. SHoP's interest in the connection between design and production can be traced to

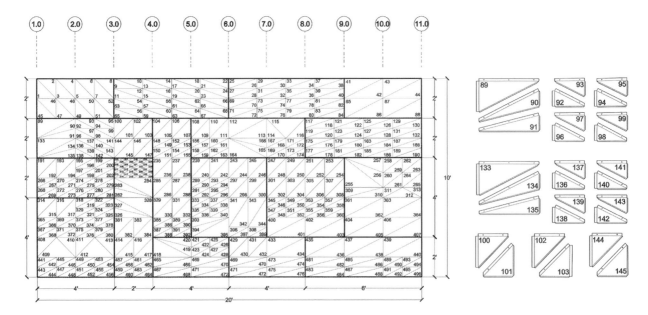

Figure 10.6 A-Wall in 2000 was developed as a trade show booth for *Architecture Magazine*. The wall is 20 ft long and 10 ft high and is fabricated from laser-cut metal and acrylic. This image is the shop drawing development by SHoP in preparation for fabrication.

early experiments in fabrication such as Dunescape in 2000, which exploits CNC truss fabrication methods to produce a 2X cedar lofted landscape that acts as an artificial beach. Another project, A-Wall in 2000, is a trade show booth for *Architecture Magazine* measuring 20 ft long and 10 ft high fabricated from laser-cut metal and acrylic.

10.2.1 Camera Obscura

Following these early projects, SHoP was commissioned to master plan and design pavilions for Greenport, New York's Mitchell Park in 2005. One of the four pavilions, Camera Obscura, is an experiential public dark room through which an optical lens and mirror project live images of the park surroundings onto a flat circular adjustable table at the center of the room which users may manipulate to focus images. SHoP used this opportunity to continue its research and development into CNC fabrication. The first of its

type, the firm constructed the building entirely from digitally fabricated components. The experiment was to evaluate the capacity of digital information to drive multiple CNC processes and then fit them together with tight tolerance onsite. The project was manageable enough that coordination was seamless.

10.2.2 Porter House

The Porter House used the principles of CNC fabrication on the larger scale of a condo development. Located in the Meatpacking District of Manhattan, the Porter House is a renovation and addition of a six-story, 30,000-S.F. warehouse built at the turn of the twentieth century. The addition cantilevers out 8 ft beyond the warehouse building and four stories above it.

▶ Figure 10.7 Camera Obscura is a park pavilion of which every element in the building construction is designed and fabricated entirely from digital information. SHoP Architects.

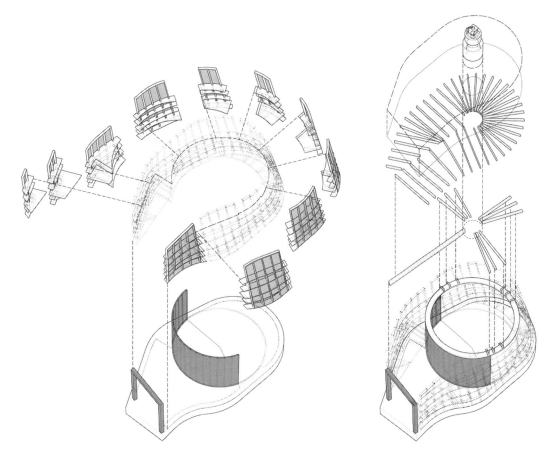

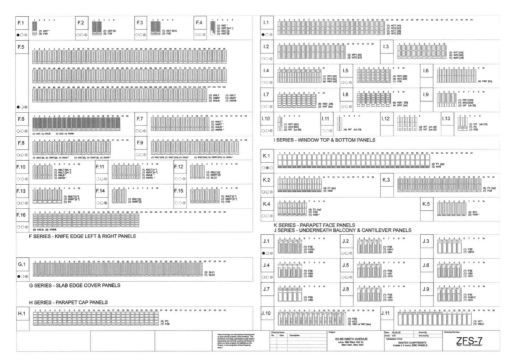

Nested Zinc Panel Components

SHoP worked in a joint venture with Jefferey M. Brown as developer on the housing project and therefore had an invested interest in both initial cost and resale value. As such, the firm employed a custom zinc fabricated panel system for the facade and exterior windows. The project team worked closely with a fabricator, using software standard to the sheet-metal industry to develop an elevation pattern based on the most efficient layout of panels on a standard width of sheet material. Since the panels were cut and bent directly from digital files, an economy of scale was achieved in the manufacturing process while accomplishing a highly custom look with variable sized panels.

10.2.3 290 Mulberry

At 290 Mulberry in 2009, SHoP developed an innovative solution to condominium housing using decorative brick facing embedded in precast concrete cladding panels. Sited in New York City's Nolita District, the context consists of detailed historic brick buildings. The condo is 13 stories high with commercial space located on the ground floor. Each condo averages 2,000 S.F. In order to respond to the context, SHoP devised a rippled brick design that was developed in advanced modeling software. Using parametric-based modeling as a solution for resolution of complex geometries and digitally fabricated components, SHoP undertook this building as a pilot project to initiate the use of Building Information Modeling as part of its operation. The firm employed scripts that were developed inhouse by project teams to control

◀Figure 10.8 The Porter House, constructed in 2003, exploits digital fabrication in an architecture and developer joint venture. Porter House is a four-story addition to an existing six-story warehouse, jetting out to use unoccupied air rights of the adjacent building. The Porter House employs 15 different types of zinc panels that, when nested, create fabrication efficiencies for the manufacturer. The arrangement of the panels makes each seem unique in the composition onsite.

the brick panels' geometry and manufacture. The final model incorporated engineering and cost data, and was used to fabricate the precast molds for the variation in the system.

SHoP worked closely with precasters during design to develop a method for panel fabrication. The fabricator was reluctant to risk time and material on the tests before having a contract in hand, so the project demanded that the owner invest in preconstruction services by providing funding for design-assist subcontractor consultation during the early design stages. The base building, developed as a building information model, allowed live links to various forms of output that facilitated communication with the owner's consultants, contractors, and engineers for systems coordination. This integrated process allowed for predictability and open communication, which led to innovation in the precast brick cladding system.

10.2.4 Barclays Center

Most recently, SHoP is collaborating with corporate firm Ellerbe Beckett on the design of the Barclays Center at Atlantic Yards. Scheduled to be completed in 2011, this is a sports and entertainment venue in Brooklyn. Integrated into one of the busiest urban intersections in the New York metro area, the center is purposed to sustain a dialogue with the surrounding context. It is designed as a performative street engagement. The civic gesture of the arena is heightened by a spectacular 30-ft high canopy, which contains an oculus that frames the view of the arena. The Main Public Entrance plaza links Atlantic and Flatbush avenues and creates a flexible, welcoming yet grand civic space. Views and physical access both into and out of the arena will be plentiful, easy, and accommodating, thus ensuring a strong connection to the surrounding urban environment.

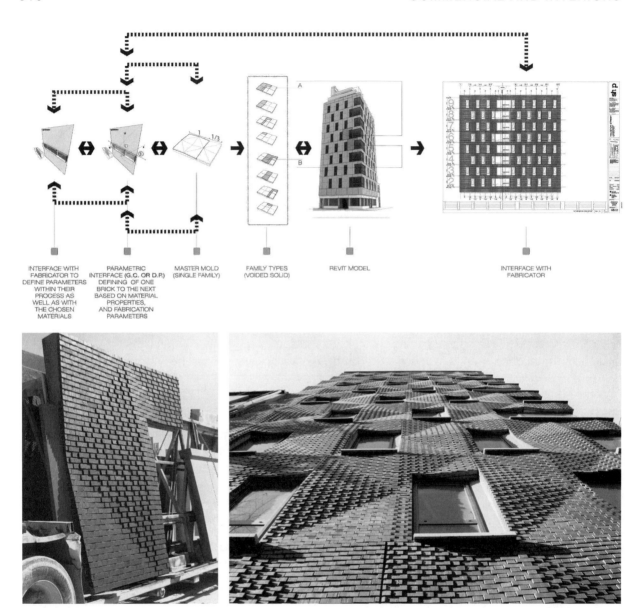

INTERFACE WITH FABRICATOR TO DEFINE PARAMETERS WITHIN THEIR PROCESS AS WELL AS WITH THE CHOSEN MATERIALS

PARAMETRIC INTERFACE (G.C. OR D.P.) DEFINING OF ONE BRICK TO THE NEXT BASED ON MATERIAL PROPERTIES, AND FABRICATION PARAMETERS

MASTER MOLD (SINGLE FAMILY)

FAMILY TYPES (VOIDED SOLID)

REVIT MODEL

INTERFACE WITH FABRICATOR

Figure 10.9 The 209 Mulberry Project is a condo development that uses complex curving precast panel with a brick veneer. The panels were modeled parametrically through script writing and using an immersive BIM process in the office that was used to fabricate from in the factory. Precast panels designed by SHoP Architects arrived onsite and were installed as the cladding on the 13-story structure in Manhattan.

SHOP CONSTRUCTION

SHoP has recently opened a new business called SHoP Construction, led by partner John Malley. The branch of SHoP Architects evaluates projects from a fabrication and constructability perspective early in the process. Using software, costs and implications are evaluated with builders and clients. SHoP Construction is the integrator between design and builder/fabricator on the Barclays Center, where the company will joint venture with a manufacturer to produce a custom weathered steel cladding system based on solar angles and orientation of the curved building. The project has become a performance-based design that quantifies energy, cost, and scheduling data via BIM tools. SHoP Construction is using AutoCAD, Rhino, and Revit in developing technical drawings and performing complex geometrical modeling in CATIA. SHoP Construction now makes BIM, construction simulation, and design-assist part of their operational cannon.

Barclays Center employs a 250,000-S.F. metal facade that wraps the arena. The firm has been given the task of ensuring that the complex skin system on the project is designed and delivered. The skin tapers and forms a 100-ft canopy with a larger oculus. Weathered steel in a locking pattern will morph, creating hundreds of different shapes, louvers, ducts, entrance points, and so forth. This is in comparison to the 15 different types in the Porter House. SHoP has worked with A. Zahner in a design-assist process from the beginning on Barclays to ensure a level of cost control is implemented. Using digital software, SHoP has developed a schedule to determine how cladding panels can fit on a trailer bed and how many picks will be implemented to time the duration of street closure. Often owners are not interested in investing in design-assist or early simulation studies for construction efficiencies, however, this is necessary if a tight bid package is going to be developed and costs are going to be controlled.[13]

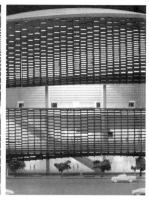

Figure 10.10 The Barclays Center in Brooklyn is scheduled to be completed in 2011. It employs a curving, mutating, and changing metal skin using hundreds of different panels. Working in a design-assist delivery, the system was developed in collaboration with sheet metal manufacturers to gain the greatest variety and cost control as possible. The sequence of construction, including shipping and installation, have been carefully simulated and managed by a project management arm of the company called SHoP Construction.

10.3 Steven Holl Architects

10.3.1 St. Ignatius Chapel

Located on the University of Seattle campus, the St. Ignatius Chapel, by Steven Holl Architects and OSKA Architects, is an example of a low-cost, rudimentary construction system misused in an elegant manner. Tilt-up concrete is usually associated with warehouse and industrial projects. It is affordable and fast in its construction. A simple rectangle in plan, the "box" of the chapel is constructed from 21 tilt-up slabs. Although not technically precast, these slabs were poured horizontally onsite, cured for 18 days, and then raised in only 12 hours.

At the building's four corners, the tilt-up slabs interlock like a Chinese box to expose the load-bearing thickness of the concrete. Window openings are formed when cuts at the slab joints engage when the slabs are tilted into place. Integral-color tilt-up concrete slabs define a tectonic that is more direct and far more economical than stone veneer, the material originally envisioned for the project. While the famous tilt-up slabs of Rudolph M. Schindler's King's Road House were lifted by block and tackle, at the Chapel of St. Ignatius, a sophisticated multiboom crane lifted, turned, and placed pieces weighing as much as 80,000 lbs. Embedded in the walls, pick-pocket points used for lifting and balancing the slabs remains intentionally visible on the building's exterior, being capped with a cast bronze protective cover as a finish.[14]

The panels were cast face up, rather than face down, to expose the pick points on the exterior of the building envelope.[15] During the lifting process special precaution was taken to make sure that each panel was erected in the order described in the construction documents. Once erected, the panels were not

Figure 10.11 St. Ignatius Chapel at University of Seattle campus is designed by Steven Holl Architects. This project employs industrial tilt-up construction methods in an innovative use in a religious building type.

Figure 10.12 Final interior and exterior images of the St. Ignatius Chapel in Seattle.

released from the crane until the tilt-up panels were properly braced. Connections between individual tilt-up walls were then made, which entailed welding splices of steel ledger angles.

Tilt-up construction was a collective decision between Steven Holl Architects, the contractor; architect of record OSKA Architects; and the owner.[16] Holl's decision to use tilt-up construction substantially improved the process by adding to savings in cost, time, labor, and design. The project fell within the desired budget because the contractor, Baugh Construction, was both the general contractor and the tilt-up contractor. The installation of the building envelope was erected in less than 20 days from the original tilt-up pours.[17]

10.3.2 Simmons Hall

In the St. Ignatius Chapel, Steven Holl Architects used an already existing building technology; how-ever, at Simmons Hall, a dormitory at MIT, the design and construction team took advantage of the versatile characteristics of concrete to create a new system of precast. In response to the site and project goals of creating a flexible, open and "porous" building, Steven Holl Architects and engineer Guy Nordenson designed a grid precast structural system dubbed "PerfCon," short for perforated concrete.[18] The system comprises precast concrete units weighing an average of about 10,000 lbs each, which were assembled to form a kind of exoskeleton—in effect, a giant Vierendeel truss—to carry the building's primary structural forces. The steel reinforcing bars in the separate precast units were grouted together onsite so that they would behave as continuous elements.[19] Each panel ranged in size with a maximum dimension of 10 ft tall and 20 ft wide.

There are several ways that the PerfCon panel system resolved the project conditions. First, the prefab sys-

Figure 10.13 Béton Bolduc, a Canadian precaster manufacturing 6,000 unique PerfCon panels in the factory using an automated precast process in preparation for the Simmons Hall dormitory on MIT campus designed by Steven Holl and engineered by Guy Nordenson.

tem maximized the allowable number of floors for the site up to 10 stories. The use of precast elements sped up the erection process. Prefabrication allowed for the PerfCon to be cast at the same time the foundation and excavation was occurring. Once the foundation was done, it only took about two weeks per floor to erect the panels. In the beginning of the project both the contractor, Daniel O'Connell's Sons, and owner thought the idea of using prefabrication was risky and unconventional. Using prefab was the most controversial aspect of the whole project and design process.

Béton Bolduc was chosen to manufacture the PerfCon panels. Béton Bolduc is a Canadian precaster located about seven hours away from MIT. Fortunately, the subcontractor was willing to work within the budget. With the plant a mere 350 miles from the site on MIT campus, a union worker was able to drive directly to the site without stopping or sleeping. Béton Bolduc was selected early in the process, during design development (DD). The pre-

caster provided mockups and test runs during the development phases in order to ensure a quality and timely product during construction.

In addition to the variance in panel shape and size based on the design of the overall building, each individual PerfCon panel was configured according to structural loads and stress factors. To accommodate this variety, the panels were cast on a moveable steel formwork. This formwork allowed for the panels' shape to be manipulated in order to create the design of 6,000 unique PerfCon panels.[20] Béton Bolduc produced two casting beds so that while one mold was being poured the other mold was drying or being removed. Most of the formwork was manufactured concurrently with the excavation and foundation work on the jobsite. This accelerated the construction time of the building and produced precise panels because each piece was cast in a controlled environment. The accuracy of computer analysis, and the ability to use only one formwork system rather than

Figure 10.14 PerfCon panels arriving onsite and being hoisted into location in the building.

multiple site-cast forms increased the consistency in form and finish within the variability of each panel.

10.4 Moshie Safdie/VCBO Architects

10.4.1 Salt Lake City Library

The new Main Library in Salt Lake City embodies the idea that a library is more than a repository of books and computers—it reflects and engages the City's imagination and aspirations. The building, which opened in February 2003, doubles the previous space with 240,000 S.F. to house more than 500,000 books and other materials, and room to grow the collection. The six-story curving wall embraces the public plaza, with shops and services at ground level, reading galleries above, and a 300-seat auditorium. A roof-top garden, accessible by walking the crescent wall or the elevators, offers a 360-degree view of the Salt Lake Valley. The Urban Room between the library and the crescent wall is a space for all seasons, generously endowed with daylight and open to valley views.

The crescent wall of the library is a double-curving wall, radiused in plan and curving in section from perpendicular to the ground to sloped toward the interior and then back to perpendicular as the wall diminishes from five floors to one and travails from exterior to interior to exterior. The wall is an urban icon standing 150 ft tall at the high end and sprawling an eighth of a mile. As a result of the vertical and horizontal curvature, the steel framed wall had to be clad in 1,580 custom precast panels, each one unique geometrically. Many precasters were approached about the project. Once bids were received the project team selected Mexico precast company Pretesca as their bid was $1 million less than any other. Through multiple trips to Mexico and conversations in broken English, the team of local professionals including VCBO Architects and Reaveley Engineers devised a method for fabricating the panels.

Figure 10.15 The Salt Lake City Library, designed by Moshie Safdie and VCBO Architects has a curving precast clad crescent wall that houses study carrels in five floors and forms a space between it and the triangular library volume that houses the majority of the programs and stacks.

The geometry of the wall was developed as a 3D model. This *x,y,z* information was extracted and rationalized to allow for fabrication. The 650-ft-long wall was broken into seven sections, called warps by the project team. Each warp had a close enough geometry to build standard precast formwork. In order to make each panel unique within the warp, Pretesca devised shim inserts so, when cast, each panel would be custom. The fabricator did not use automated casting equipment; all the panels were cast by hand. Rather than adding a color agent, the color was matched to a historic building next door by adding earth to match the tone. This gave the panels a consistent color throughout. As the precast ages over time, the color will weather consistently across the wall surface. Pick points and attachment points were designed by Reaveley Engineers; HHI Corporation, the installer; and Big D Construction, the general contractor to expedite the handling and setting process.

HHI Corporation from North Salt Lake, Utah, had never worked on a project over a couple of stories. The library called for HHI to furnish and install 87,000 S.F. of architecture precast. The difficulty of making panels in Mexico City and shipping to the United States was not foreseen. HHI and the design team visited the plant before the bidding process to ensure they had the capacity and then visited numerous times during manufacture for color match and quality assurance. The panels were well fabricated and were not the issue. The problems surrounded transportation. Union workers from HHI Corp. could not go past the border to acquire the panels, and Pretesca could not get clearance to cross the border and hand them off. The shipping difficulty hit a fever pitch when all 2,120 panels (including curved and straight panels on other areas of the building) had to be x-rayed at the border. Finally, the teams were allowed to bring them across into the United States and up to Utah some 2,330 miles in

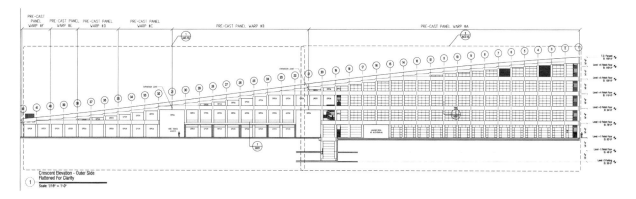

Figure 10.16 The precast panel geometry was developed in 3D model. The 650-ft wall was broken into seven warp sections, each one corresponding to a formwork that was developed by the precaster Pretesca in Mexico City.

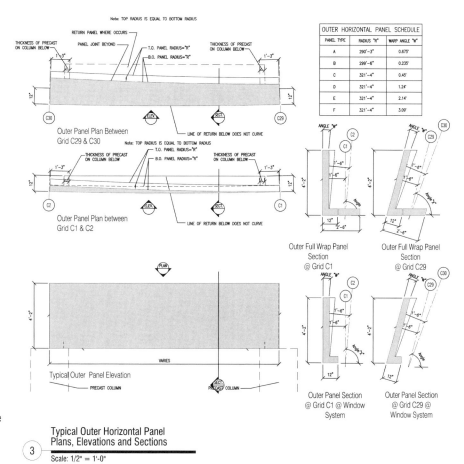

OUTER HORIZONTAL PANEL SCHEDULE		
PANEL TYPE	RADIUS "R"	WARP ANGLE "W"
A	290'-3"	0.675'
B	299'-6"	0.235'
C	321'-4"	0.45'
D	321'-4"	1.24'
E	321'-4"	2.14'
F	321'-4"	3.09'

Figure 10.17 Detail of the precast panel geometry. Shims were placed in the seven formworks to cast 1,580 unique panels.

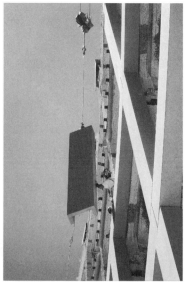

Figure 10.18 Precast panel process: panels are precast in Mexico City at Pretesca; panels being loaded to a flatbed trailer by forklift; cladding being affixed to the structural frame onsite; a column cladding panel being hoisted into place; and precast cladding panels near completion.

140 loads. The panels had a total weight of 4 million lbs for a combined distance of 326,220 miles, or 13.1 times around the world. Although the project did not use local fabrication and had an unfathomable carbon footprint, it is remarkable that the project team—architects, engineers, and HHI Corp.—were able to safely erect the panels on time and with minimal added cost for border crossing.[21]

10.5 MJSA Architects

10.5.1 Marriott Library, University of Utah, Salt Lake City

The Marriott Library on the University of Utah campus was built in the 1960s as a site-cast post-tensioned structure three-stories high with precast concrete cladding on the exterior. During an assessment of the building it was determined that the precast panels would have to be replaced as they posed a safety hazard of falling in the event of an earthquake. In addition, being a Seismic D zone in Salt Lake City, the entire structure as well would have to be braced and upgraded. The precast panels had been secured to the site-cast structural frame for gravity load only, therefore a seismic event would cause a progressive collapse potential. In order to get light into the building, the panels were removed and replaced with glazing.

With this program in mind, Salt Lake architects MJSA Architects (MJSAA) devised a method for the replacement. The edges of the floor slabs had to be repaired, but the PT slab could not be obstructed. Therefore, the PT slab was scabbed over on the edges in order to provide a clean and uniform sur-

Figure 10.19 Precast panels on the Marriott Library on the University of Utah campus being removed in preparation for a new glazed enclosure system as part of a major seismic retrofit and remodel of the 1960s library.

Figure 10.20 Unitized glazing
system arriving onsite in crates.

face by which the glazed units could be attached. The scabs also had embeds and leveling devices cast with them to accept the prefabricated glazing unit panels. The existing structure both vertically and horizontally was not true and varied in overall dimension from 1 to 3 in. The reason for choosing an offsite unit system of glass was because the library was to be occupied during construction, therefore each side of the building would be taken down and the system installed quickly. The process of precast cladding removal and glazed unit installation was repeated on each side systematically. Slotted connection in both vertical and horizontal directions allowed for aligning the panels plumb.

The unit sizes, attachment method, specifications, and sealing system were designed by MJSAA in collaboration with Steel Encounters, the subcontractor of the glazing units, and Jacobsen Construction, the general contractor. The manufacturer of the panels provided engineering. The roof overhang made the installation difficult, so a special method of jacking was developed to allow Steel Encounters to install the glazing units. During the design process the mechanical engineer feared too much heat gain, therefore, a ceramic frit was imposed on the glass to reduce the gain and glare. In addition to the glazing units, metal panels were also devised at spandrel locations provided by Centria and had to be coordinated with the prefabricated glass units. Because the glass units were so large and precise, the tolerance between them and the imprecise existing structure caused gaps to occur. These had to be filled with backer and up to a 3-in. maximum of joint sealant. This cannot be seen standing at ground level but presents problems with maintenance in the long term.

Figure 10.21 Prefabricated glazing units installation sequence: Suction-lifted panels are installed through radio control. Adjustable joint allows for the panels to tolerate dimensional adjustments during installation. Panels being lifted onto the building floor in preparation for being suction-lifted into place.

The installation of the panels was accomplished with laborers inside and a crane operator outside. The panel meditated between the two, making visual connection obstructed. Using a suction lift the panels were placed while the teams communicated by radio. Once the attachment was made, the panel was plumbed and tightened so the suction could be released. According to Derek Losee at Steel Encounters, the size of the glazing units presented problems, but was far superior to any onsite stick-framed method. The Marriott Library project would be the largest panel he would be willing to risk his company on. The entire project team was impressed with the lack of waste that the prefabricated system offered in comparison to stick-framed glazing systems onsite. All of the panels fit and none had to be reconstructed.[22]

10.6 Neil M. Denari Architects,

10.6.1 Highline 23, with Front Inc.

Highline 23 (HL23) is a 14-story condominium project in New York's West Chelsea Arts District developed by Alf Naman and designed by Neil M. Denari Architects (NMDA) out of Los Angeles in collaboration with associate architect Marc I. Rosenbaum. The building was designed to respond to the adjacent High Line at 23rd Street. The spur of the elevated tracks restricts the footprint of the building to 40 ft × 99 ft at the ground level. To maximize the floor area ratio of the zoning envelope, NMDA designed a morphing geometric tower that progressively curves beyond its footprint. The building contains one unit per floor that has three separate facades. In order to accommodate these various facades, NMDA developed a custom nonspandrel curtain wall on the south and north sides and a steel panel facade on the east facing the High Line.

NMDA identified Front Inc., an innovative curtain wall designer, to develop the design during schematics. Having been on the project during the early design-assist process, Front Inc. was the natural choice for developing the enclosure system from detailing to install. Front Inc. was established in 2002 as two partners from Dewhurst Mcfarlane Partners in New York and the United Kingdom split off to form their own specialized practice. Initial projects by Front Inc. include the Seattle Public Library and Beverley Hills Prada Store, both designed by OMA Rem Koolhaus. They were also the curtain wall subcontractor on the Toledo Museum of Art, designed by SANNA and the Walker Art Center, designed by Herzog and de Meuron. These projects have established Front Inc. as a leader in taking complex glass and metal cladding projects from start to finish offering fully integrated design services for large-scale commercial projects using state-of-the-art digital modeling techniques and fabrication methods.

Figure 10.22 Front Inc. employs what they call megapanelization at the Highline 23 project in New York City, designed by Neil Denari Architects. The glazing units were fabricated in China and shipped to New York for install.

HL23 demanded a high level of geometrical complexity. Therefore, 3D modeling became the method of communication between design and production. NMDA provided a Rhino model that defined the face of the skin and joint lines preferred. Front Inc. then developed the Rhino model into a CATIA and SolidWorks iteration to allow engineering analysis in structure, thermal analysis, clash detection, and fabrication output. The CATIA model was built with parametric intelligence to allow fast changes to be made without having to rebuild the entire model. The model was also built to include details such as all of the silicon sealants and nuts and bolts to ensure risk was managed. The model takes into consideration tolerances of parts and pieces, taking advantage of traditional curtain wall elements and details when possible and deviating to accommodate the customization of the project when necessary.

Megapanelization and preassembly were used to minimize site labor—which is costly in New York—and control quality, but this also presented problems. NMDA designed the skin to trace the superstructure. The subtle thermal and wind load deflections that caused the structure to move potentially would have an effect on the less flexible curtain wall. Spans of the floor were over 30 ft, making the floor deflect more than the joints in the seams of the individual glass unit panels. Hanging the large glass panels from the columns and not the floor to accommodate movement mitigated this. The system works completely independent of the floor structure.

Front Inc. prefers to develop curtain wall and metal cladding systems as prefabricated units to control quality and mitigate risk. In effect, the company then only has to worry about the factory quality and joints at installation instead of every joint that emerges in onsite construction relying on the individual installer

FRONT INC. AND DIGITAL MODELING

According to Min Ra, Principal at Front Inc., digital technology has made more things possible than anyone could have imagined a decade ago. He sees using CATIA and other software as not only an innovation tool, but also a method by which risk is managed being able to anticipate and predict the fabrication and installation challenges that will be encountered. However, more than technology, project teams must engage in a method of thinking and collaborating that works toward innovation. No software can make that happen. Not all materials are fabricated from digital information. Front Inc. still relies heavily on traditional 2D-generated drawings so shops in China can cut, weld, and grind elements together to produce the megapanelized glazing units. Some parts can be fabricated from a digital model when necessary. But many things are still done in a very rudimentary way because they don't have to create a new process for production.

of the system for quality assurance. In the case of HL23, the panels were all fabricated in China due to lower cost. In this process, Front Inc. investigated the factory floor–to-site logistics process thoroughly including group transport of panels, local handling, and handling strategies. Front Inc. represents a new generation of suppliers that are able to flatten the process by which innovative projects occur, bridging the gap between design ideology and physical construction.[23]

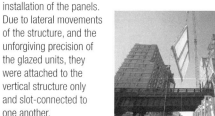

Figure 10.23 Onsite installation of the panels. Due to lateral movements of the structure, and the unforgiving precision of the glazed units, they were attached to the vertical structure only and slot-connected to one another.

10.7 Office dA

Started in 1991 in Boston by Nader Tehrani and Monica Ponce de Leon, Office dA has become recognized for its rigorous yet diverse design process, which engages expertise and interests traditionally considered outside the field of architecture and construction. Through early experiments with digital fabrication, Office dA has developed a working method by which they engage manufacturers and fabricators to produce unexpected geometrical and material solutions to complex problems. Office dA's experiments in production have carried over into larger commercial projects including the Rhode Island School of Design (RISD) Library renovation and Arco, a gas station for British Petroleum in Los Angeles.

10.7.1 RISD Library

The Fleet Library at RISD, completed in 2006, is a 55,000-S.F. restoration and renovation of a historic library located in the main hall of the former Fleet Bank–owned Hospital Trust Bank building in downtown Providence. The banking building is a 50-ft-tall barrel-vaulted space with traditional detailing and materials. The design consisted of three distinct architectural responses: preserve the existing building, engineer accessibility and provide mechanical and fire safety upgrades, and install an architectural intervention of two interior pavilions—all for a modest budget of $167 per S.F.

Given the impossibility of fitting the new program into the existing square footage, two new pavilions housing key programmatic components were positioned within the barrel-vaulted void of the main hall, enabling the addition of new study spaces, a reading room, and a circulation island. The inserted objects not only house these programs, but also make use of every surface and pocket of space to maximize their functionality. The study pavilion houses study carrels within niches set below a stepped reading surface to act as the main reading room. The information pavilion houses reference desks and a range of other functions. The pavilions are conceived as colossal pieces of furniture framing a reading lounge in the center envisioned as a collective "living room" for the student dormitories housed above the library. They enhance the composition, character, and strength of the existing hall, without mimicking its architecture.

Both pavilions were prefabricated and CNC-milled offsite to allow them to be installed and dismantled, if need be in the future, in the most efficient manner and with minimal disturbance to the space. The fabrication was performed in Connecticut at an experienced millwork shop that was tooling up their process from manual to CAD/CAM; therefore, Office dA worked in close collaboration to deliver the design and fabrication of the pavilions. The firm researched the means and methods to develop a design response that was at once spatial and also tectonic, enabling fabrication to occur affordably and quickly. The pavilions at the RISD Library were created through a 2D milling process. Initially conceived in wheat board, an interior finish panel made of byproduct from the agricultural industry, team members had to reconsider as early experiments presented milling problems when being machined. The material was subsequently changed to MDF. Because labor is becoming more and more expensive, eating up a greater percentage of overall cost than materials, investing in finding ways to reduce onsite labor is one of the benefits of using CNC-milled interior panels.

The process of design to fabrication produced a very refined product in panels that were milled to ±.0001 of an inch. Although panel-to-panel tolerances for

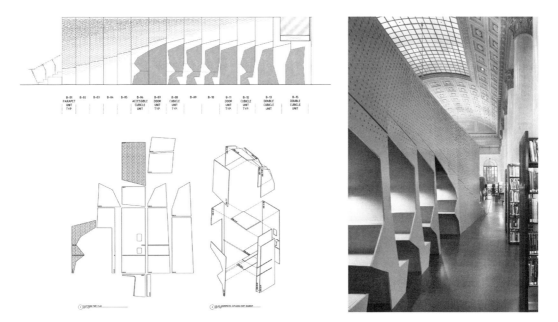

Figure 10.24 Study pavilion at the RISD library: elevation of the living room pavilion fabricated with CNC-milled MDF panels; an assembly diagram by the architect, Office dA; and a flattened cutting diagram; installed image of pavilion.

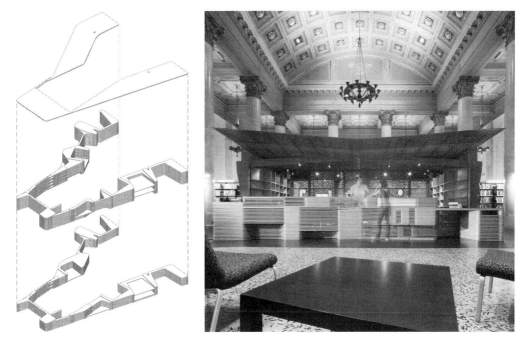

Figure 10.25 Information pavilion at the RISD library: horizontal layering of the MDF-milled panels and installed image of the pavilion.

fitting are tight, the exactness of the pavilions presented discrepancies with the existing uneven floor of the historical library. Upon inspection, the project team found that the floor experiences inches of variation over the surface where the pavilions would be installed. These variations were accommodated by providing an adjustable base condition that is recessed within the pavilion to allow for the MDF panels to hover ¼ to 2 in. above the floor. The pavilions were assembled completely in the factory before disassembling, shipping, and installing them in the library. This coordination with fabrication ensured a lower cost than was expected in a shorter amount of time, but put greater responsibility on all project team members to ensure the MDF furniture elements were fabricated and installed properly.

10.7.2 Arco

Located in Los Angeles at the intersection of Robertson and Olympic boulevards, a conventional gas station was built in the mid-1970s. Arco is a project to upgrade the original station in an environmentally conscious manner by recycling old materials and installing sustainable and recyclable new materials. Office dA conceived of the station as a "learning lab," to stimulate dialogue, promote education, and foster discussion on the topic of environmental stewardship. The water, heat, energy, lighting, and material systems of Arco were all built to maximize sustainability and energy efficiencies. Arco uses architecture and design to reinvent the gas station experience and does so with a refined metal tessellated canopy that morphs from stall to stall and envelops the corner of the street.

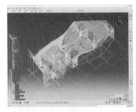

Figure 10.26 The process of fabrication for the Arco canopy: CATIA model to develop the geometry. Fabrication prototyping was used to produce 1,653 stainless steel panels into 52 transportable subassemblies for onsite installation.

Figure 10.27 Final images of the Arco Station in Los Angeles.

OFFICE DA ON PREFAB

Nader Tehrani states that Office dA's work moves between materials and processes of manufacture rather than subscribing to a set of formal fabrication methods. Since their early days in fabrication prototypes, the industry has changed with many architects researching or even becoming manufacturers, challenging the ways in which machinery is used to create space. Initially these types of projects always came in high on budget, but this is now the preferred method by the firm and Office dA sees greater time and cost savings as they become more proficient at engaging fabricators in a process of collaboration. Tehrani encourages architects:

"Specialized disciplines are stratified, making it easy to get immersed in your small practice, doing what you do well. The danger in practice today is that if one does not get acquainted with new technologies and the evolving ways in which practice is being conducted, one can easily be led into irrelevance of obsolescence. But we can find intelligence in shared platforms of practice with other disciplines and specializations to advance our own mission through collaborative practice. This can be accomplished with willingness for early and ongoing experimentation and research. Approach fabricators directly. The capacity to own the procedure is immeasurable."

The design of the canopy is the most emblematic feature of Arco. While conventional gas stations combine functionally distinct elements (canopy, kiosk, and sign), this project develops a unique formal logic to integrate all of those elements into one seamless whole. Using a structural bay as a starting point, the cladding system unifies the relationship between column base, shaft, and capital with the canopy. Furthermore, the surface works parametrically to incorporate various architectural and technical features using the same technique. Thus, the pay kiosk, the structure, the fin panels (as signs), and the canopy are all shaped from the same faceted surface. The triangulated stainless steel panels reconcile complex, and sometimes contradictory, requirements of the site, program, codes, and zoning ordinances, and establish the site identity.

In keeping with the goal of sustainability, the fabrication and design systems were optimized to conserve labor costs and reduce material waste throughout the project. Developed with a design-build fabricator, the canopy incorporates 1,653 stainless steel panels into a prefabricated assembly system. Fastened together offsite, the canopy is comprised of 52 transportable components, which were erected onsite in just four weeks. The back building and screen wall were constructed in a modular fashion, then assembled onsite and hooked up to fueling and infrastructural systems in just two weeks. The efficiency and precision of these techniques tap into the potential of mass customization, using the controlled environment of a shop to calibrate modular components with unique geometric conditions, which facilitate efficient site installation.

Arco was a collaboration between British Petroleum (BP), BIG, a concept and marketing firm, and Office dA with Johnston Marklee. Tehrani and Ponce de Leon worked with Buro Happold Engineers and Carlson & Co., design-build fabricators, to devise the canopy system. Located in Los Angeles, Carlson & Co. had extensive experience in Hollywood set fabrication and therefore had complex capabilities. Using Rhino to design and Gehry Technologies Digital Project, Office dA worked with the engineers and fabricator collaboratively to determine how the geometry could be rationalized and developed into a surface that could be fabricated. Conventional stainless steel was selected as the material because it does not require extensive maintenance and provided the aesthetic qualities desired by the architect. Tolerances became a problem because onsite erection time was very short. The system had millwork-like tolerances and was intended to be erected as a piece of furniture, much like the RISD library; however, a short schedule created a hurried installation crew that reduced the quality of the end product with gaps in seams varying from ¼ to 1 in.[24]

10.8 Diller Scofidio + Renfro

10.8.1 Alice Tully Hall, New York City, with 3Form + Fetzers

Alice Tully Hall is located at the Lincoln Center for the Performing Arts in New York City. Completed in 2009, the hall was redesigned by Diller Scofidio + Renfro (DSRNY) in collaboration with FxFowle Architects. The hall sits under the Julliard School of Music in the shell of the Piertro Belluschi's building. The goal of the project was to transform the multi-purpose hall into a premiere music venue including street identification and upgraded facilities. The interior of the hall was a functional yet blank space and DSRNY wanted to raise it to the level of a vibrant intimate performance experience. The hall design is a skinning of the interior surface in an undulating and flowing orange hue of African moabi that acts as finish, doors, cavities for lighting, and noise attenuation.

The wood panels illuminate, as a metaphor for the raising of the chandelier or the parting of the curtain at the start of a performance. In this hall, the space itself performs for the visitor as an intimate welcoming to the performance.[25]

The blushing walls are a development of a collaboration with DSRNY and fabricators Fetzers Architectural Woodworking, an international finish wood panel manufacturer known for its projects fitting out retail stores, churches, and LDS temples as well as millwork for the Apple Retail stores around the globe; and 3Form, an interior resin panel manufacturing company that has produced a patented system of recycled resin panels that embed materials, including wood veneers, in the matrix. Working closely with the architect, Fetzers and 3Form developed a method by which the interior panels could be manufactured with reverse curvature. The process unfolded through DSRNY providing Rhino model that had been further developed with the help of Gehry Technologies in Digital Project (DP) to create developable surfaces. The DP model was used as a collaboration tool for a three-year process in which critical surface geometry from the architect was developed into mechanical information for manufacture and fabrication.

A challenge in accomplishing the geometry developed by DSRNY was material capacity. Fetzers held the contract with Turner Construction, the general contractor for fabrication of the interior wood surfaces, as most of the hall consisted of nonblushing panels, but subcontracted to 3Form for the wood blushing walls that required wood veneer not to be placed on a composite substrate, but to be sandwiched within polymer. The project team engaged in a research effort to find a wood and resin com-

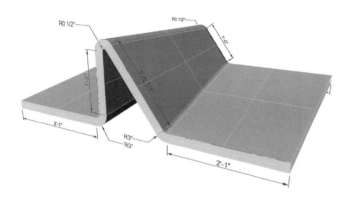

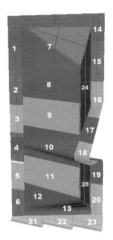

Figure 10.29 Images of the interior space after installation just before a performance begins.

posite that would be able to create the geometries desired. Resin can virtually create any shape, but the wood, because of its grain, had difficulty performing reverse curvature. Most areas were easily manipulated, but one particular zone, called the nose, where the most acute curvature occurred was mocked-up with various woods until a compromise of geometry and material capacity was achieved. Both 3Form and DSRNY had to negotiate to get their desired end. Before installation, two full-scale mockups with lighting, geometry, and wood type studies were performed.

◀Figure 10.28 DSRNY-designed Alice Tully Hall at Lincoln Center in Manhattan. The interior panels were developed and fabricated by 3Form and Fetzers Architectural Woodworking, both located in Salt Lake City. Backlit translucent wood panels were fabricated using complex geometrical CAD/CAM processes and multiple mockup prototypes

The design team, based on acoustical properties, determined the thickness of the panels. Laying up the panels to create the geometry was done by CNC milling forms from MDF and then veneering the MDF substrate and vacuum bagging the panel for 24 hours. Similarly, the 3Form panels took impregnated wood veneer, heated it to a temperature where the polymer became supple, and then were laid on CNC milled forms to be vacuum bagged. The final sizing and tooling of the panels was performed again by precision CNC milling. A strip of the same wood was placed under joints between panels in a splice and groove configuration. Tapped connections on the back of the panels attached to an armature that was then secured to a unistrut system that was affixed to the structure of the shell of the hall. The panels were all built from a 1/16-in. veneer with composite backer or resin impregnation making the entire hall built from one peeled Moabi African Cherry Tree. The fabrication and installation process encountered challenges from the differentiation of moisture from Utah to New York. Not only was the humidity an issue, but also variations of weather and humidity within Manhattan urban corridors made the panels expand and contract. The installation extended in duration from October 2007 to October 2008, as the panels continued to move every day, each impacting the other.

Willie Gatti at 3Form and Ty Jones at Fetzers (now working with 3Form) state that this project would not have occurred logistically without a budget to support it. Fetzers and 3Form in collaboration used a model of "fail early and often" in order to be able to find a path that would yield the most appropriate solution to the problem. Fortunately, Liz Diller refused to take no for an answer, always pushing the fabricators to develop a better, more refined product, making the project a success.[26]

PART IV

CONCLUSION

C-1: The Chameleon House overlooking Lake Michigan is a SIP wall and roof constructed tower house designed by Anderson Anderson Architecture.

▲ C-2: 209 Mulberry is a condominium in Manhattan with brick veneer embedded precast cladding panels designed by SHoP Architects.

▶ C-3: Alice Tully Hall is an interior performing arts renovation project at Lincoln Center in New York. It features translucent wood impregnated resin panels that are backlit during performances designed by Diller Scofidio Renfro.

C-4: The Apple "Cube" on 5th Avenue in Manhattan is one of many glass and metal fitting staircases designed by Bohlin Cywinski Jackson.

C-5: Camera Obcura is a pavilion in Mitchell Park in New York. The pavilion was completely designed and fabricated from digital models, and then assembled onsite in components. Design by SHoP Architects.

C-6: Container City is a series of shipping container architecture projects in the UK designed by various architects and engineered by Burro Happold Engineers.

▶ C-7: The Fairmont Hotel in Vancouver, BC, received a new perforated metal rainscreen developed, fabricated, and installed by A. Zahner Architectural Metals.

▼ C-8: The Arco Station in Los Angeles is a digitally designed and fabricated metal gas station canopy designed by Office dA.

C-9: Salt Lake City Library urban room with unique double curving precast cladding panels designed by Moshe Safdie Associates and VCBO Architects.

C-10: RISD Library renovation added custom CNC milled MDF pavilions designed by Office dA.

C-11: The Loblolly House is located on the Chesapeake Bay. It is entirely offsite fabricated in frame, floor, and wall cartridges, service blocks, and a panel rainscreen. KieranTimberlake designed the house.

C-12: Project Frog: an architectural product designer has developed a kit system that is customizable and features green materials and high-performance specifications.

◀C-13: The Porter House is a condominium project in New York that features custom metal fabrication skin designed by SHoP Architects.

▶C-14: Canopy designed and fabricated with CNC milling by Anderson Anderson Architecture.

C-15: The first of the ecoMOD projects in Charlottesville, a design-build program at University of Virginia School of Architecture led by Professor John Quale.

C-16: The LV House by Rocio Romero is a siteless kit house that can be ordered and built by patrons much in the tradition of pre-cut kit houses in the early 20th century.

C-17: The House on Sunset Ridge is one of many in Resolution: 4 Architects' Modern Modular program led by principal Joe Tanney.

C-18: The twisting tower at the De Young Museum in San Francisco is clad with a perforated, dimpled copper skin designed by Herzog de Meuron and fabricated by A. Zahner.

▲ C-19: The Unity House at Unity College in Maine is a net zero energy house developed in 50 components and assembled onsite by Bensonwood.

▶ C-20: St. Ignatius Chapel in Seattle is an uncommon architectural use of tilt-up concrete construction designed by Steven Holl Architects and OSHA.

chapter 11 CONCLUSION

Technology is capability; embodied knowledge in an artifact, method, or process. Technology transfer then refers to the exchange of capability from one party to another to the mutual benefit of both. The transfer of technology may occur between government, industry, and the university in any direction or combination. It is the fast appropriation of technologies to industries in which they were not originally intended that often is more applicable or better suited to have a sustainable future. For prefabrication to thrive as a building production, an understanding and implementation by architects and construction professionals into this process is necessary.

According to Williams and Gibson, technology transfer occurs in four ways:[1]

1- Appropriation: This points to quality research and development that assumes that when the idea is good enough it will sell itself.

2- Dissemination: This emphasizes the dissemination of knowledge to the user. Once linkages are secured the knowledge will continue to flow.

335

3- Utilization: This emphasizes interpersonal community between technology researchers and clients by identifying facilitators and barriers to the transfer process.

4- Communication: This method sees the transfer process as interactive, an exchange of ideas continuously.

Numbers 1 through 3 are linear modes of transfer. Although all require a giving and receiving end, thus suggesting some form of communication, the last method of understanding technology transfer requires an open, collaborative model of working. Option 4 is a dynamic nonhierarchical network that suggests prefab as an ongoing exchange that involves process and product technology, sharing knowledge for the mutual benefit of all. Technology is not then transferred just from the automobile and aerospace industry to construction, but is also transferred from business and other models of collaboration to architectural practice itself. This view of technology, therefore, is not a transfer of actual theories or tools but in process models for effective integration.

David E. Nye defines three levels of technology and associated professionals. He illustrates that inventors, scientists, and theorists provide a prediction function to technological development offering breakthrough inventions that are not realized until the long term, if ever. Engineers and entrepreneurs forecast innovations by developing the technology for markets some 10 years out. However, it is designers and those who market products, such as subcontractors and builders, who determine new models less than

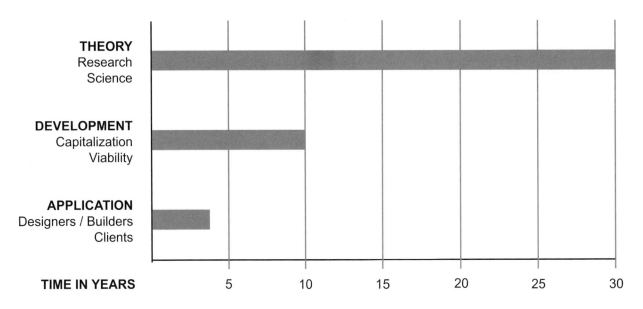

Figure 11.1 The three levels technological development are mapped against duration. Theory includes research and scientific discovery; development includes the financing or capitalization of the idea to evaluate its viability; and application of the technology occurs by virtue of design. This illustrates that whether a technology such as prefabrication takes hold is the responsibility theory, development and application stages, but owners and architects making decisions regarding prefabrication on a daily basis on building projects can have immediate impacts.

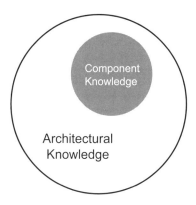

Figure 11.2 Architects need to foster what computer science refers to as component knowledge, knowledge of the core technologies in a building; and architectural knowledge, knowledge of how the components are integrated.

three years out from conception.[2] Although in other fields, designers many not have as much control over projection markets, in architecture the opportunity is increasingly changing. Architects are having a resurgence of interest and participation in all phases of technological development including predicting, forecasting, and projecting materials and digital technologies into the market sector. However, in order to do so knowledge is required.

Computer science has adopted *architecture* as a term to describe the conceptual design and operational structure of a computer system. With regard to knowledge, Henderson and Clark, in "Architectural Innovation," indicate that computer engineers should have both component knowledge (knowledge about each of the core design concepts) and architectural knowledge (knowledge about the ways in which the components are integrated and linked together into a coherent whole).[3] Although critical to being an effective collaborator, architects should have more than just macrolevel knowledge concerning how the different components are linked together in a building.

Architects need to also develop component knowledge, or an understanding of the role that each player contributes to the team, using a joining effort to innovate on a project. The advantages to sharing one's specific knowledge in a building team are obvious. Buntrock states,

"With rapid technological change and the increasing complexity of buildings today, not one field can demonstrate sufficient understanding of all the issues facing the building team. The generalist tendency in the profession serves a very real purpose in drawing together the opposing values of other members of the team…Architects, however, cannot truly be generalists without a deep understanding of construction. Collaboration must, of necessity, occur before and during construction."[4]

Instead of assuming that there is a theory or tool in the pipeline waiting to solve our fragmentation and disjunction in building practice, we should focus on the players and how they integrate into a building collaborative. There is a player in the process of building who holds the key to innovation—the subcontractor, including fabricators and manufacturers. The subcontractor fabricates, manufactures, and does all the buying and selling on a building project. Subcontractors are increasingly becoming more innovative and advanced as tools for manufacture are more accessible. By collaborating with manufacturing, architects have an increased chance to deliver more efficient and innovative products, assemblies, and buildings.

The integration paradigm requires reworking the fundamental missions of schools of architecture, engineering, and construction toward cross-disciplinary learning. On the university campus, this can take the role of integrated environments where architecture, engineering, and CM students come together to learn how to solve complex problems in a collaborative manner. It may also include integrating industry within the classroom much in the way that industrial design education hosts companies to come and share in the activities of envisioning next-generation design. Sponsored studios in architecture schools are nothing new. Although they may appear as a breach of educational ethics, they present students with life-long industry mentors who can help them realize their professional goals in a controlled environment of the classroom. Bringing in industry partners puts fabricators, contractors, and owners in the realm of the thinking academics where the conventions of construction may be challenged in an intellectual manner as to suggest a better way that is often a threatening conversation in the thrushes of a building delivery. In this new

Figure 11.3 EcoMod at the University of Virginia invites students to participate in the process of designing and delivering a modular low-income house. The education of architects therefore is concerned with teaching the collaborative skills necessary so that students will become master facilitators in the integrated process.

paradigm for education, future professionals in the construction industry then feel empowered to make decisions that will affect the innovation of construction in the future. Prefabrication is therefore an integral part of any education that claims to prepare students for the future, whether in a theoretical or applied education model.

Eric von Hipel, a professor at MIT's Sloan School of Management, coined the term "lead users" to describe forward-thinking and innovative individuals who anticipate market forces before competitors. Dana Buntrock calls architects who similarly exploit construction industry materials and processes in order to innovate "lead users." "Lead users do not, and perhaps cannot, work alone in a market as technologically diverse as the construction industry. Manufacturers also benefit from working closely with these designers, as their input can encourage innovation and help industry to project future demand more accurately."[5]

This paradigm shift in architecture toward an integrated collaborative provides the opportunity for architects, engineers, and builders to be lead users, players who can exploit industry resources, working with subcontractors, fabricators, and manufacturers in order to innovate. In order to prepare for an integrated construction industry, stakeholders need to break down the barriers of cultural stifling, work toward the development of updated contractual/legal structures, and assume more risk in the process.

The future of construction as outlined in this book is ambitious: an integrated process that involves all parties, using the full range of capacities in the manufacturing industry and transferring it to the construction industry to increase design and production quality. But if we are going to move forward,

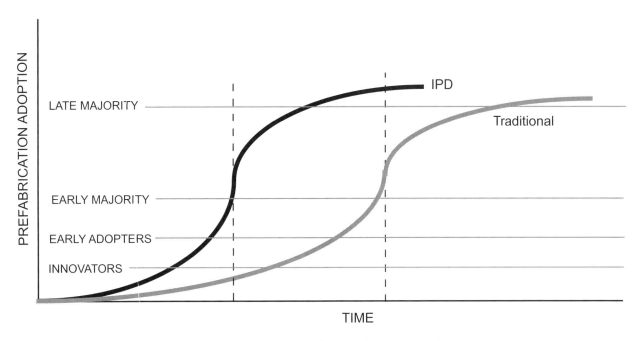

Figure 11.4 The industry needs innovators and early adopters that are willing to implement prefabrication for a more efficient and innovative delivery of construction. Prefabrication adoption will be expedited by the employment of integrated delivery.

a better way must be found. Prefabrication exists. It has been successful in many other industries and is now making its way in the construction sector. Prefab is an improvement as it increases productivity, innovation, and quality. The developments and implementation of prefabrication in architecture are occurring in an evolutionary growth. In order to expedite this technology at a more rapid pace, the industry needs owners, architects, engineers, and contractors who are willing to blaze the trail of offsite construction today for a better construction industry tomorrow.

ENDNOTES

Front Matter

1. Fernandez, John. *Material Architecture: Emergent Materials for Innovative Buildings and Ecological Construction.* Burlington: Architectural Press, 2006, pg. 10.
2. *Merriam-Webster Online Dictionary*: "prefabricate." http://www.merriam-webster.com/dictionary/prefabricate. Accessed 02.09.10.

Chapter 1 - History of Industrialized Building

1. H. Pearman, "Creative Lego: are prefabricated homes architecture or building?" *Gabion: Retained Writing on Architecture.* Commissioned for The Sunday Times. (First Published August 2003. http://www.hughpearman.com/articles4/creativelego.html) Accessed November 19, 2009.
2. B. Bergdoll, "Home Delivery: Viscidities of a Modernist Dream from Taylorized Serial Production to Digital Customization" *Home Delivery: Fabricating the Modern Dwelling.* B. Bergdoll and P. Christensen (Eds.) (New York: Museum of Modern Art, 2008): 12.
3. A. Arieff and B. Burkhart, *Prefab.* (Layton: Gibbs Smith, 2002): 13.
4. G. Herbert, *Pioneers of Prefabrication: The British Contribution in the Nineteenth Century* (Baltimore: Johns Hopkins University Press, 1978): 6.
5. Ibid: 8
6. Louden, John Claudius. *The Encyclopedia of Cottage, Farm, and Villa Architecture and Furniture* (London: Longman, Orme, Brown, Green and Longmans) 1839.
7. G. Herbert, *Pioneers of Prefabrication: The British Contribution in the Nineteenth Century* (Baltimore: Johns Hopkins University Press, 1978): 11–12

8. C. Davies, *The Prefabricated Home* (London: Reaktion Books, 2005): 44–47.
9. Herbert: 30.
10. Ibid: 149–156.
11. *The Illustrated London News* (July 6, 1850): 13.
12. A. Mornement and S. Holloway, *Corrugated Iron: building on the frontier* (Singapore: W.W. Norton & Company, 2007): 10–14.
13. C. Peterson, "Prefabs in the California Gold Rush, 1849." *Journal of the Society of Architecture Historians* (1965): 318–324.
14. D.D. Reiff, *House from Books: treatises, pattern books, and catalogs in American architecture, 1738–1950, a history and guide* (University Park: The Pennsylvania State Press, 2000).
15. R. Schweitzer and M.W.R. Davis, *America's Favorite Homes: mail-order catalogues as a guide to popular early 20th-century houses* (Detroit: Wayne State University Press, 1990).
16. Bergdoll. *Home Delivery*: 48.
17. R. Batchelor, *Henry Ford: mass production, modernism, and design* (Manchester University Press, 1994): 93.
18. C. Sabel and J. Zeitlin, "Historical Alternative to Mass Production; Politics, Markets and Technology in Nineteenth-Century Industrialization," Draft of article for *Past and Present* (London, 1985): 2.
19. Davies: 53–55.
20. A. Bruce and H. Sandbank, *A History of Prefabrication* (New York: Arno Press, 1972): 26–27.
21. Arieff: 16.
22. T.T. Fetters, *The Luston Home: the history of a postwar prefabricated housing experiment* (McFarland & Company, Inc. Publishers, 2002).
23. U. Jurgens, T. Malsch, and K. Dohse. *Breaking from Taylorism: changing forms of work in the automobile industry* (Cambridge University Press, 1993): 2.

24. J. Ditto, L. Stern, M. Wax, and S. B. Woodbridge, *Eichler Homes: Design for Living* (San Francisco: Chronicle Books, 1995).

25. B. Vale, *Prefabs: A History of the UK Temporary Housing Programme* (London: E & FN Spon, 1995): 52–59.

26. Manufactured Housing Institute, "Understanding Today's Manufactured Housing," *US Department of Commerce, Bureau of the Census*: 1.

27. A. D. Wallis, *Wheel Estate: The Rise and Decline of the Mobile House* (Johns Hopkins University Press, 1997).

28. *Automated Builder*. Manufactured Housing Institute. Online Trade Journal. http://www.automatedbuilder. com/industry.htm. Accessed 12/16/09.

29. Davies: 69–87.

30. G. Staib, A. Dorrhofer, and M. Rosenthal, *Components and Systems: Modular Construction, Design, Structure, New Technologies*. (Edition Detail, Birkhauser, 2008): 21–22.

31. J. F. Reintjes, *Numerical Control: Making a New Technology* (New York: Oxford University Press, 1991).

32. L. Mumford, *Technics and Civilization* (New York: Harcourt Brace & Company, 1963): 9–59

33. M. R. Smith, "Army Ordinance and the "American system of Manufacturing" *Military Enterprise and technological Change: Perspective on the American Experience* (Cambridge: MIT Press, 1985): 39–86.

34. Ibid:13–15.

35. D. Schodek, M. Bechthold, J.K. Griggs, K. Kao and M. Steinberg, *Digital Design and Manufacturing: CAD/CAM Applications in Architecture and Design* (Hoboken: John Wiley & Sons, Inc, 2004): 17–25.

36. Ibid: 25.

Chapter 2 - History of Industrialized Architecture

1. U. Pfammatter, *The Making of the Modern Architect and Engineer: The Origins and Development of a Scientific and Industrially Oriented Education* (Basel: Birkhauser, 2000): 8–14.

2. Ibid: 281.

3. M. N. Woods, *From Craft to Profession: The Practice of Architecture in Nineteenth-Century America* (Berkeley: University of California Press, 1999): 30–31.

4. Ibid: 154–158

5. Pfammatter: 280–291.

6. Ibid: 284–290.

7. L. M. Roth, *Understanding Architecture. Its Elements, History, and Meaning* (Boulder: Westview Press, 1993): 464–465.

8. W. Gropius, "Dessau Bauhaus—Principles of Bauhaus Production," *Conrads, Programs and Manifestoes* (March 1926): 95–96.

9. C. Davies, *The Prefabricated Home* (London: Reaktion Books, 2005): 20–21.

10. I. Osayimwese, "Konrad Wachsmann: Prefab Pioneer." *Dwell Magazine The Prefab Issue: Real Homes for Real People* (February 2009): 98,100.

11. G. Herbert, *Dream of the Factory-Made House: Walter Gropius and Konrad Wachsmann* (Cambridge: MIT Press,1984).

12. Roth: 471.

13. Ibid: 471–472.

14. P. Blake, *The Master Builders: Le Corbusier, Mies van der Rohe, Frank Lloyd Wright* (New York: W.W. Norton & Company, 1976): 414.

15. Ibid: 288.

16. "Snapshot of an Infant Industry," *Architectural Forum* (February 1942): 84–88.

17. B. Kelly, *The Prefabrication of Houses* (Cambridge: MIT Press, 1951): 60.

18. A. Bruce and H. Sandbank, *A History of Prefabrication* (New York: Arno Press, 1972): 18–21.

19. Davies: 33–34.

20. B. Huber and J. Steinegger, *Jean Prouve: Prefabrication: Structures and Elements* (Zurich: Praeger Publishers, 1971): 11.

21. Davies: 33–34.

22. Ibid: 35.

23. B. Bergdoll, *Home Delivery: Fabricating the Modern Dwelling*. B. Bergdoll and P. Christensen (Eds.) (New York: Museum of Modern Art, 2008): 94–96.

24. Davies: 36.

25. A. Arieff and B. Burkhart, *Prefab* (Layton: Gibbs Smith, 2002): 33.

26. A.E. Komendant, *18 Years with Architect Louis I. Kahn* (Englewood: Aloray Publisher, 1975): 1–24.

27. N. Silver, *The Making of Beaubourg: A Building Biography of the Centre Pompidou, Paris* (Cambridge: MIT Press, 1994): 19–22.

28. Ibid: 134.

29. Interview with Rick Smith, mechanical engineer credited with bringing CATIA from Boeing to Gehry's office in the 1990's. Smith was the model manager for the Concert Hall project.

30. Davies: 203.

31. K. Frampton, "Seven Points for the Millennium: an untimely manifesto." International Union of Architects Keynote Address. Beijing, 1999.

32. M. Anderson and P. Anderson, *Prefab Prototypes: site specific design for offsite construction* (Princeton Architecture Press, 2007).

33. Davies: 203.

34. T. T. Fetters, *The Luston Home: the history of a postwar prefabricated housing experiment* (McFarland & Company, Inc. Publishers, 2002).

35. "Taking Care of Business." *Dwell The Prefab Issue: Real Homes for Real People* (February 2009): 107.

36. Fetters.

37. Herbert: 247.

38. A. Gibb, *Off-site Fabrication: Prefabrication, Pre-assembly, Modularization* (Scotland: Whittles Publishing distributed by John Wiley and Sons, Inc, New York, 1999): 228–229.

39. Ibid: 226–228.

40. *Dwell:* 105.

Chapter 3 - Environment, Organization, and Technology

1. L. G. Tornatzky and M. Fleischer, *The Process of Technological Innovation* (Lexington Books, 1990): 153.

2. C. Eastman, P. Teicholz, R. Sacks, and K. Liston, *BIM Handbook: A Guide to Building Information Modeling for Owners, Managers, Designers, Engineers and Contractors* (Hoboken: John Wiley and Sons, Inc., 2008): 382.

3. Ibid: 117.

4. M. Konchar and V. Sanvido, "Comparison of U.S. Project Delivery Systems." *Journal of Construction Engineering and Management* (American Society of Civil Engineers, 1998): 124(6): 435–444.

5. Eastman: 118.

6. C. Geertsema, E. Gibson, and D. Ryan-Rose, "Emerging Trends of the Owner-Contractor Relationship for Capital Facility Projects from the Contractor's Perspective" *Center for Construction Industry Studies* (Report No. 32, University of Texas Austin): 50–51.

7. "Integrated Project Delivery: A Guide, Version 1" *IDP Guide*. AIA National/AIA California, 2007. Available gratius download at the AIA's website: www.aia.org.

8. ConsensusDOCS consists of twenty-one member organizations, including the Associated General Contractors of America (AGC), the Construction Owners Association of America (COAA), the Construction Users Roundtable (CURT), Lean Construction Institute (LCI), and a large number of subcontractor organizations. *See* http://www.consensusdocs.org.

9. P.J. O'Conner, *Integrated Project Delivery: Collaboration Through New Contract Forms* (Faegre & Benson, LLP, 2009): 23.

10. S. Stein and R. Wietecha, *Whose Ox Is Being Gored?: A Comparison of ConsensusDOCS and AIA Form Construction Contract Agreements* (Stein, Ray & Harris, LLP, 2008): 8.

11. IDP Guide.

12. AndersonAnderson website http://andersonanderson.com.

13. "So Many Materials, So Little Time." *Architecture Boston* (Volume 8. March – April 2005): 21.

14. M. Dodgson, *The Management of Technological Innovation: An International and Strategic Approach* (Oxford University Press, 2000): 166.

15. S. Thomke, *Experimentation Matters: Unlocking the Potential of New Technologies for Innovation* (Cambridge: Harvard Business School Press, 2003): 10–14.

16. A. Gibb, *Off-site Fabrication: Prefabrication, Pre-assembly, Modularization* (Scotland: Whittles Publishing distributed by John Wiley and Sons, Inc, New York, 1999): 226–228.

17. M. Dodgson, *Technological Collaboration in Industry: Strategy, Policy and Internationalization in Innovation* (London: Routledge, 1993): 152.

18. H. Ford, *Today and Tomorrow* (Productivity Press, 1988).

19. J. Liker, *The Toyota Way* (McGraw Hill, 2003): 15–21.

20. J.P. Womack and D.T. Jones, *Lean Thinking: Banish Waste and Create Wealth in Your Corporation* (London: Simon and Schuster, 2003).

21. Y. Kageyama, "Toyota banking on famed production ways in housing business." The Associated Press, *The Seattle Times*. June 15, 2006. http://seattletimes .nwsource.com/html/busniesstechnology2003062192 toyotahousing15 Accessed August 2009.

22. J. Miller, "Workstream Kaizen for Project Teams." Gemba Pana Rei http://www.gembapantarei.com/ 2005/12/workstream_kaizen_for_project.html Accessed August 2009.

23. Womack: 15–29.

24. "Prefabricated Housing: A Global Strategic Business Report." Global Industry Analysts, Inc., 2008.

25. Kageyama.

26. M. Horman and R. Kenley, "Quantifying Levels of Waste Time in Construction with Meta-Analysis." *Journal of Construction and Engineering Management*. (ASCE, January 2005): 52–61.

27. Eastman: 330–331.

28. D. Sowards, "Manufacturers Need to Look At Lean Construction." *Leadership in Manufacturing*. Industry-Week.com. May 05, 2008.

29. Tornatzky: 9.

30. T. Mayne, "Change or Perish: Remarks on building information modeling." *AIA Report on Integrated Practice*. (Washington D.C.: American Institute of Architects, 2006).

31. U. Jurgens, T. Malsch and K. Dohse, *Breaking from Taylorism: changing forms of work in the automobile industry* (Cambridge Press, 1989): 1–5.

32. Liker.

33. D. Buntrock, *Japanese Architecture as a Collaborative Process: Opportunities in a Flexible Construction Culture* (London & New York: Spon Press, 2002): 105–106.

34. Dodgson, 2000: 19.

35. J. Woudhuysen, *Why is Construction so Backward* (Academy Press, 2004): 50.

36. B.J. Pine, *Mass Customization: The New Frontier in Buisness Competition* (Harvard Buisness Press, 1992).

37. P. Goodrum, D. Zhai, and M. Yasin, "The relationship between changes in material technology and construction productivity. *ASCE Journal of Construction Engineering and Management*. 2008: 135(4): 278–287.

38. D. Schodek, M. Bechthold, J.K. Griggs, K. Kao and M. Steinberg, *Digital Design and Manufacturing: CAD/CAM Applications in Architecture and Design* (Hoboken: John Wiley & Sons, Inc, 2004): 184–185.

39. WP 1202 'Collaboration, Integrated Information and the Project Life Cycle in Building Design, Construction and Operation,' *Construction Users" Roundtable*, 2003.

40. www.gsa.gov

41. T. Sawyer, "Soaring Into the Virtual World: Build It First Digitally," *Engineering News Record*, October 10, 2005.

42. S. Kieran and J. Timberlake. *Refabricating Architecture* (McGraw-Hill, 2003): 79–80.

43. Eastman:180–181.

44. Ibid: 20.

45. J. Gonchar, "Diving Into BIM." *Architectural Record* December 2009 Issue.

46. P.J. Arsenault, "Building Information Modeling (BIM) and Manufactured Complementary Building Products." *Architectural Record* December 2009 Issue.

Chapter 4 – Principles

1 . "The Partnering Process – Its Benefits, Implementation and Measurement Construction Industry Institute (CII)." (Clemson University Research Report 102–11, 1996).

2. *Advancing the Competitiveness and Efficiency of the U.S. Construction Industry*. (National Research Council. 2009): 1.

3. As quoted in C. Eastman, P. Teicholz, R. Sacks, and K. Liston, *BIM Handbook: A Guide to Building Information Modeling for Owners, Managers, Designers, Engineers and Contractors* (Hoboken: John Wiley and Sons, Inc., 2008): 8–10.

4. R. E. Smith, *Outline Specifications*. Salt Lake City: ARCOM Education www.arcomeducation.com. Chapter 1.

5. C. Ludeman, "Prefab Is Not the Answer to Affordable, Modern, and Green Homes." *Jetson Green*, September 16, 2008. http://www.jetsongreen.com/2008/09/prefab-is-not-t.html Accessed January 18, 2010.

6. A. Gibb, *Off-site Fabrication: Prefabrication, Pre-assembly, Modularization* (Scotland: Whittles Publishing distributed by John Wiley and Sons, Inc, New York, 1999): 33.

7. Tedd Benson Lecture, ITAP, Fall 2009 University of Utah, School of Architecture.

8. Gibb: 44.

9. "Prevention: A Global Strategy: Promoting Safety and Health at Work." *International Labor Organization 2005,. Genea.* http:www.ilo.org/public/englisth/protection/safework/worldday/products05/report05_en.pdf

10. "Census of Fatal Occupational Injuries 2008." *U.S. Bureau of Labor Statistics*. http://www.bls.gov/iif/oshwc/cfoi/cftb0240.pdf Accessed November 2009.

11. H. Lingard & V. Francis. *Managing Work-Life Balance in Construction* (Abingdon: Spon Press, 2009).

12. Nutt-Powell, T. E. "The House that Machines Built." *Technology Review* 88 (8), 1985: 31–37.

13. P. Goodrum, D. Zhai, and M. Yasin, "The relationship between changes in material technology and construction productivity. *ASCE Journal of Construction Engineering and Management*. 2008: 135(4): 278–287.

14. Gibb: 45.

15. C. M. Harland, "Supply Chain Management, Purchasing and Supply Management, Logistics, Vertical Integration, Materials Management and Supply Chain Dynamics." *Blackwell Encyclopedic Dictionary of Operations Management*. N. Slack (Ed. (UK: Blackwell Publishing, 1996).

16. M. K. Lavassani, B. Mohavedi, and V. Kumar, "Transition to B2B e-Marketplace enabled Supply Chain: Readiness Assessment and Success Factors." *Information Resources Management (Conf-IRM),* 2008, Niagara, Canada.

17. J. Schwartz, and D. J. Guttuso, "Extended Producer Responsibility: Reexaming its Role in Environmental Progress." *Policy Study Number 293*. (The Reason Foundation, Los Angeles, 2002).

18. J. Broome, "Mass housing cannot be sustained." *Architecture and Participation*. Blundell Jones (Ed.) (London: Spon Press, 2005): 65.

19. M. Hook, "Customer Value in Lean Prefabrication of Housing Considering Both Construction and Manufacturing." *Proceedings IGLC–14* (July 2006, Santiago, Chile): 583–594.

20. N. G. Blismas, "Off-site Manufacture in Australia: Current State and Future Directions." (Brisbane: CRC for Construction Innovation, 2007).

21. Eastman: 8–10.

Chapter 5 - Fundamentals

1. S. Brand, *How Buildings Learn: What Happens After They're Built* (Penguin Publishers, 1995): 13.

2. G. Staib, A. Dorrhofer, and M. Rosenthal, *Components and Systems: Modular Construction, Design, Structure, New Technologies*. (Edition Detail, Birkhauser, 2008): 59.

3. C. Schittich, *In Detail: Building Skins* (Basel: Birkhauser, 2006): 29.

4. Ibid: 40.

5. C. Sauer, "Interior Surfaces and Materials." *In Detail: Interior Surfaces and Materials: aesthetics technology implementation*. C. Schittich (Ed.) (Basel: Birkhauser, 2008): 145–157.

6. J. Fernandez, *Material Architecture: emergent materials for innovative buildings and ecological construction* (Architectural Press, 2006).

7. Ibid: 85–87.

8. T. Herzog, J. Natterer, R. Schweitzer, M. Volz, and W. Winter, *Timber Construction Manual* (Basel: Birkahauser, 2004).

9. Fernandez: 116.

10. Ibid: 138

11. L.W. Zahner, *Architectural Metal Surfaces* (Hoboken: John Wiley and Sons, Inc., 2005).

12. E. Allen, *Fundamentals of Building Construction. 4th edition* (Hoboken: John Wiley and Sons, Inc., 2003): 444.

13. A. Bentur, "Cementitous Materials: nine millennia and a new century: Past, Present and Future." ASCE, *Journal of Materials in Civil Engineering* (Vol. 14, No. 1: 2–22).

14. Fernandez: 216–222.

15. Ibid: 153.

16. Ibid: Section 3.4.

17. Staib: 42–43.

18. Ibid: p.45.

19. T. Herzog, R. Krippner and W. Langet, *Façade Construction Manual* (Basel: Birkhauser, 2004): 48–49.

20. Ibid: 51.

Chapter 6 - Elements

1. Staib, G., A. Dorrhofer, and M. Rosenthal. *Components and Systems: Modular Construction, Design, Structures, New Technologies* (Munich: Reaktion DETAIL, 2008) 41.

2. Interview with Joshua Bellows, Euclid Timber Frames, Heber, Utah - December 2009.

3. P. Paevere and C. MacKenzie, "Emerging Technologies and Timber Products in Construction – analysis and recommendations." *Market Knowledge and Development Project No. PN05.1022* (Forest and Wood Products Research and Development Corporation, March 2007).

4. Interview with Kip Apostel, Euclid Timber Frames, Heber, Utah - November 2009 and Janaury 2010.

5. A. Deplazes, *Bauen + Wohnen, ½*. (Zurich: 2001): 10–17.

6. Ibid.

7. D. Buettner, J. Fisher, and C. Miller, *Metal Building Systems. 2nd Ed.* (Cleveland: Building Systems Institute, Inc., 1990): 1–7.

8. Ibid.

9. Interview with Michael Gard, Fast Fab Erectors, Tucson, Arizona – December 2008.

10. Interview with Joss Hudson, EcoSteel, Park City, Utah – October 2009 and December 2009.

11. Interview with James McGuire, Hanson Eagle Precast, West Valley City, Utah. December 2009.

12. C. Eastman, P. Teicholz, R. Sacks, and K. Liston, *BIM Handbook: A Guide to Building Information Modeling for Owners, Managers, Designers, Engineers and Contractors* (Hoboken: John Wiley and Sons, Inc., 2008): 270–271.

13. E. Allen, *Fundamentals of Building Construction: materials and methods 4th Ed.* (John Wiley and Sons, Inc. 2003): 560–565.

14. Automated Home Builder Magazine website, http://www.automatedbuilder.com/industry.htm Accessed January 3, 2010.

15. M. Crosbie, "Making Connections: Innovative Integration of Utilities in Panelized Housing Design." *Without a Hitch: New Directions in Prefabricated Architecture.* Clouston, P., Mann, R. and Schreiber, S. (Ed.) (Proceedings of the 2008 NE Fall Conference, ACSA, University of Massachusetts, Amherst, September 25–27, 2008): 86–204.

16. Interview with Debbie Israelson & Clint Barratt, Burton Lumber, Salt Lake City, Utah - November 2009.

17. D. Simpson and R.E. Smith, *Features, Benefits and Applications of Structural Insulated Panels: AIA and CSI Continuing Education Course*. AEC Daily Online, 2007.

18. Interview with Tom Riles, Premier Building Systems, Belgrade, MT – September 2009.

19. Interview with Mervyn Pinto, Minean International Corporation, Vancouver, BC – November 2009.

20. *Modular Advantage*, eNEWS from the Modular Building Institute. www.modular.org

21. Interview with Eric Miller, FoamBuilt, Park City, Utah – March 2009 and August 2009.

22. U. Knaack, T. Klein, M. Bilow, and T. Auer, *Facades: Principles of Construction* (Basel: Birkhauser, 2007): 60.

23. Ibid: 46.

24. S. Murray, *Contemporary Curtain Wall Architecture* (Princeton Architectural Press, 2009): 95–97; and S. Kieran and J. Timberlake, *Refabricating Architecture* (McGraw-Hill 2003): 40–143.

25. Interview with Udo Clages and Zbigniew Hojnacki, POHL, Inc. of America, West Valley City, Utah – November 2009.

26. Allen: 720–722.

27. W.L. Zahner, *Architectural Metal Surfaces* (Hoboken: John Wiley and Sons, Inc., 2005).

28. Interview with Gary Macdonald, GMAC Steel, Salt Lake City, Utah - August 2007.

29. "Dimensioning and Estimating Brick Masonry." *Technical Notes and Brick Construction* (The Brick Industry Association, February 2009).

30. *Modular Architecture Manual.* Kullman Buildings Corp. 2008

31. Interview with Lance Henderson, DIRTT Product Representative, Salt Lake City, UT – August 2009.

32. Interviews with Thomas Hardiman, Modular Building Institute (MBI), January 2010; and Kendra Cox, Blazer Industries, January 2010.

33. M. Anderson and P. Anderson, *Prefab Prototypes: Site-Specific Design for Offsite Construction* (Princeton Architectural Press, 2006): 183.

34. "21-Story Modular Hotel Raised the Roof for Texas World Fair in 1968." *Modular Building Institute Website.* http://www.modular.org/htmlPage.aspx?HtmlPageId=400 Accessed 01/27/10.

35. "O'Connell East Architects Design 24-Story Modular." *Modular Building Institute Website.* http://www.modular.org/htmlPage.aspx?name=24_story_modular Accessed 01/27/10.

36. Modular Building Institute 2007, Commercial Modular Construction Report. http://www.modular.org.

37. Interview with Kam Valgardson, Irontown Homebuilding Company, Spanish Fork Utah – November 2009.

38. Interview with Paul Warner, Architect, San Francisco, California. December 2009.

39. Interview with Kendra Cox, Blazer Industries, Aumsville, OR – November 2009.

40. Interview with Joe Tanney, Resolution: 4 Architecture, New York City, NY – November 2009.

41. Interview with Amy Marks, Kullman Buildings Corporation, Lebanon, NJ – January 2010.

42. "Reducing Bathroom Waste: Rice's Prefabricated Pods." July 28, 2008. http://swamplot.com/reducing-bathroom-waste-rices-prefabricated-pods/2008-07-28/ Accessed January 18, 2010.

43. "Bathroom "pods" coming to Rice University student residence halls;. *Building Design & Construction*, 4/1/2008 http://www.bdcnetwork.com/article/382232Bathroom_pods_coming_to_Rice_University_student_residence_halls.php Accessed January 18, 2010.

44. Thomas Hardiman, MBI.

45. J. Kotnik, *Container Architecture* (Barcelona: Links Books, 2008); and P. Sawyers, *Intermodal Shipping Container Small Steel Buildings* (Paul Sawyers Publications, 2008).

46. Interview with Jeroen Wouters, Architectenburo JMW, Tilberg, NL – July 2009.

47. Interview with Quinten de Gooijer, Tempohousing, Amsterdam, NL – July 2009.

48. Interview with Adrian Robinson, Burro Happold, UK. October 2009.

Chapter 7 - Assembly

1. A. Redford and J. Chal, *Design for Assembly: principles and practice* (Berkshire: McGraw-Hill Book, 1994): 3–4.

2. M. Hook, "Customer Value in Lean Prefabrication of Housing Considering both Construction and Manufacturing. *Proceedings IGLC–14* July 2006, Santiago Chile: 583–593.

3. G. Ballard, "Construction: One Type of Project Production System." *Proceedings of IGLC–13*, Sydney, Australia, 2005.

4. J.B. Pine, *Mass Customization: The New Frontier in Business Competition* (Boston: Harvard Business Press, 1993).

5. D. Schodek, M. Bechthold, J. K. Griggs, K. Kao, and M. Steinberg, *Digital Design and Manufacturing: CAD/CAM Applications in Architecture and Design* (Hoboken: John Wiley & Sons, Inc, 2004): 341.

6. Ibid: 156–157.

7. Redford: 140.

8. G. Boothroyd, and P. Dewhurst, *Design for Assembly Handbook*. (University of Massachusetts, Amherst, 1983).

9. Shodek: 317; and G. Boothroyd, *Assembly Automation and Product Design.* (New York: Marcel Deker, Inc. 1992).

10. E. Allen and P. Rand, *Architectural Detailing: Function - Constructability – Aesthetics. 2nd Edition* (John Wiley & Sons Inc., 2006): 163–186.

11. Ibid.

12. L. Brock, *Designing the Exterior Wall: An Architectural Guide to Designing the Vertical Envelope* (Hoboken: John Wiley and Sons, Inc., 2005).

13. G. Ballard, Lean Construction Institute - Prefabrication and Assembly and Open Building Championship Area.

14. A. Gibb, *Off-site Fabrication: Prefabrication, Pre-assembly, Modularization* (Scotland: Whittles Publishing, distributed by John Wiley and Sons, Inc, New York, 1999): 222.

15. Allen & Rand: 187–188.

16. Interview with Kelly L'heureux, Ocean Air, Connecticut – October 2009.

17. *Utah Trucking Guide*. Motor Carrier Division, Utah Department of Transportation, 2009 Edition. http://utahmc.com/trucking_guide/ accessed 12.15.09

18. Code of Federal Regulations (CFR), 23 CFR Part 658. Statutory provisions U.S. Code (USC), 49 USC 31111, 31112, 31113, and 31114.

19. *Utah Trucking Guide*.

20. Ibid.

21. Interview with Jason Brown, MSC Constructors, South Ogden, UT – October 2009.

22. *Utah Trucking Guide.*

23. Interview with Kam Valgardson, Irontown Homebuilding Company, Spanish Fork, Utah – December 2009.

24. Interview with Jermey Young, Over-dimensional Products. Progressive Rail Specialized Logistics, Headquarters in Minnesota – November 2009.

25. Kelly L'heureux.

26. F. Zal and K. Cox, "Pre.Fab: Myth, Hype + Reality." *Without a Hitch: New Directions in Prefabricated Architecture*. Clouston, P., Mann, R., and Schreiber, S. (Eds.) Proceedings of the 2008 NE Fall Conference, ACSA, University of Massachusetts, Amherst. September 25–27, 2008: 128–141.

27. R. Seaker and S. Lee, "Assessing Alternative Prefabrication Methods: Logistical Influences." *Advances in Engineering Structures, Mechanics and Construction*. M. Pandey et al. (Ed.) (Netherlands: Springer, 2006): 607–614.

28. J. R. Stock and D. M. Lambert. *Strategic Logistics Management, 4th ed.* (Boston: McGraw-Hill Irwin, 2001).

29. "Demand Drives Homebuilders to Build Fast and Innovate." *Engineering News Record*. McGraw Hill 2005. http://enr.ecnext.com/comsite5/bin/enr_description_docview_sav.pl Accessed January 4, 2006.

30. American Institute of Steel Construction. *Teaching Tools - Cranes*. www.aisc.org Accessed December 2009.

31. K. Willer, Industrielles Bauen 1. Grundlagen und Entwicklung des Industrielen, (Energie- und Rohstoffsparenden Bauens. Stuttgart/Berlin/Cologne/Mainz 1986): 96.

32. Allen & Rand: 163–183.

Chapter 8 - Sustainability

1. M. Anderson and P. Anderson, *Prefab Prototypes: Site-Specific Design for Offsite Construction* (Princeton Architectural Press, 2006): 16–17.

2. "2007 U.S. Energy Report." U.S. Department of Energy.

3. A.C. Nelson, "The Boom To Come, America Circa 2030." *Architect*, 95, no. 11 (Hanley Wood Business Media, October 2006): 93–97.

4. *1987 Report of the World Commission on Environment and Development: Our Common Future.* United

Nations General Assembly. Transmitted to the General Assembly as an Annex to document A/42/427 – Development and International Co-operation: Environment. Accessed February 2009.

5. P. Hawken, A. Lovins, and L. Hunter Lovins, *Natural Capitalism: creating the next industrial revolution*. (Snowmass: Rocky Mountain Institute, 2010).

6. M. Kaufmann and C. Remick. *Prefab Green* (Layton: Gibbs Smith, 2009).

7. C. Eastman and R. Sacks, "Relative productivity in the AEC industries in the United States for onsite and off-site activities." *Journal of Construction Engineering and Management*, 134 (7): 517–526. 2008.

8. N. Blismas and R. Wakefield, "Engineering Sustainable Solutions Through Off-site Manufacture." *Technology, Design and Process Innovation in the Built Environment*. P. Newton, K. Hampson, & R. Drogemuller (Eds.) (Spon Press, 2009).

9. M. Horman, D. Riley, A. Lapinski, S. Korkmaz, M. Pulaski, C. Magent, Y. Luo, N. Harding, and P. Dahl, "Delivering Green Buildings: Process Improvements for Sustainable Construction." *Journal Green Building*: Volume 1 Number 1 10/5/05.

10. J. Fernandez, *Material Architecture: emergent materials for innovative buildings and ecological construction* (Architectural Press, 2006): Chapter 2.

11. S. Brand, *How Buildings Learn: What Happens After They're Built* (Penguin Publishers, 1995): 12–13.

12. F. Duffy, "Measuring Building Performance." *Facilities.* (May 1990): 17.

13. W. McDonough and M. Braungart, *Cradle to Cradle* (New York: North Point Press, 2002).

14. J. Benyus, *Biomimicry: innovation inspired by nature* (New York: William Morrow and Company Inc., 1997).

15. G. Murcutt, Leccture at the University of Arizona School of Architecture, Fall 2001.

16. N. J. Habraken, *Supports: An Alternative to Mass Housing*. B. Valkenburg Ariba (Trans.) (London: Praeger Publishers, Architectural Press (Trans.), 1972).

17. Ibid: 51.

18. Ibid: 69.

19. S. Kendall and J. Teicher, *Residential Open Building* (Spon Press, 1999): 4.

20. Ibid: 36.

21. P. Crowther, "Designing for Disassembly." *Technology Design and Process Innovation in the Built Environment*, P. Newton, K. Hampson, & R. Drogemuller (Eds.) (Spon Press 2009): 228–230.

22. Ibid: 230–235.

23. M. Pawley, "XX architecten." *World Architecture,* 69. 1998: 96–99.

24. T. Dowie and M. Simon, "Guidelines for Designing for Disassembly and Recycling." Manchester Metropolitan University. http://sun1.mpce.stu.mmu.ac.uk/pages/projects/dfe/pubs/dfe18/report18.htm Accessed 1998.

25. T. Yashiro and N. Yamahata, "Obstructive factors to reuse waste from demolished residential buildings in Japan." *Sustainable Construction, Proceedings of CIB TG 16 Conference*. Tampa, Florida, November 6–9, 1994: 589.

26. T. E. Graedel and B. R. Allenby, *Industrial Ecology* (Englewood, NJ: Prentice Hall, 1995): 263.

27. M. A. Hassanain and E. L. Harkness, *Building Investment Sustainability: Design for Systems Replaceabiilty* (London: Minerva, 1998): 100.

28. G. Miller,"Buildabilty: a design problem." *Exedra*, 2 (2), 1998: 34–38.

29. Fernandez: 58–62.

30. J. Siegal, *Mobile: The Art of Portable Architecture*. (Princeton Architectural Press, 2002).

31. Ibid: Introduction.

32. Architecture for Humanity Website: http://architectureforhumanity.org/ Public Architecture Website: http://www.publicarchitecture.org/

33. T. Schneider and J. Till, *Flexible Housing* (Architectural Press, 2007): 4–7.

34. 'Annual Report to the President of the United States.' National Institute of Building Sciences 2003.

35. D. Jones, S. Tucker, and A. Tharumarajah, "Material Environmental Life Cycle Analysis." *Technology Design and Process Innovation in the Built Environment*. P. Newton et al. (Ed.) (Spon Press, 2009): 55–56.

36. S. Fuller, *Life-Cycle cost Analysis (LCCA)*. National Institute of Standards and Technology (NIST). 2005.

37. "External Issues and Trends Affecting Architects, Architectural Firms, and the AIA." *American Institute of Architects,* February 2008.

38. "Behind the Logos: Understanding Green Product Certifications." *Environmental Building News*. BuildingGreen.com Accessed 02.01.10.

39. D. Armpriest and B. Haglund, "A Tale of Two City Halls: icons for sustainability in London and Seattle." *Eco Architecture: Harmonisation between Architecture and Nature*. Broadbent and Brebbia (Ed.) (WIT Press. Southampton, UK. 2006): 133–142.

40. K. Mulday, "Seattle's new City Hall is an energy hog." *Seattle Post Intelligencer*, July 5, 2005.

41. L. Scarpa, University of Utah, College of Architecture + Planning, Spring 2008 Lecture Series.

42. M. Kaufmann and K. Melia-Teevan, "Nutritional Labels for Homes: A way for homebuyers to make more ecological, economic decisions." Michelle Kaufmann Companies 2008. http://blog.michellekaufmann.com/wp-content/uploads/2008/09/nutrition_labels_for_homes.pdf Accessed 01/31/10

43. Interview with Joerg Rugemer, Assitant Professor University of Utah, School of Architecture – August 2009.

44. K. R. Grosskopf and C. J. Kibert, "Market Based Incentives for Green Building Alternatives." *Journal of Green Building*. Volume 1 Issue 1 Winter 2006: 141–147.

45. P. Torcellini, S. Pless, M. Deru, and B. Griffith, "Lessons Learned from Case Studies of Six High-Performance Buildings." U.S. Department of Energy, National Renewable Energy Laboratory. Report No. NREL/TP–550–37542. June 2006.

Chapter 9 - Housing

1. T. Benson, "What Good Is Prefab?" Posted September 24, 2008 http://teddbenson.com/index.php?/categories/2-Prefab-Homes Accessed 12/31/08

2. W. Rybczynski, "The Prefab Fad." *Slate*. http://www.slate.com/id/2171842/fr/flyout. Posted August 8, 2007. Accessed 11/19/09

3. Manufactured Housing Institute 'Automated Building' trade journal. http://www.automatedbuilder.com/industry.htm. Accessed 12/16/09.

4. Engineering News Record. http://enr.ecnext.com/comsite5/bin/enr_description_docview_save.pl McGraw Hill 2005. Accessed January 4, 2006.

5. Engineering News Record. http://enr.ecnext.com/comsite5/bin/enr_description_docview_save.pl McGraw Hill 2005. Accessed January 4, 2006.

6. Engineering News Record. http://enr.ecnext.com/comsite5/bin/enr_description_docview_save.pl McGraw Hill 2005. Accessed January 4, 2006.

7. S. Goldhagen, *The New Republic*. February 8, 2009.

8. D. Egan, "The Prefab Home is Suddenly Fab." May 31, 2005. *Tyee News*. http://thetye.ca/News/2005/05/31/PrefabHome/ Accessed 12/16/09.

9. This case study was developed by Ryan Hajeb, student at the University of Utah, School of Architecture in the summer of 2009.

10. Interviews with Joe Tanney of Resolution: 4 Architecture, New York City, NY - November and December 2009.

11. Interview with John Quale, ecoMOD Project - November 2009.

12. M. Kaufmann and C. Remick. *Prefab Green* (Layton: Gibbs Smith, 2009): 61.

13. M. Drueding, "Top Firm: Michelle Kaufmann, AIA, LEED AP Leadership Awards 2008." *Residential Architect*. (November – December 2008): 32–36.

14. M. Kaufmann, Michelle Kaufmann's blog. http://blog.michellekaufmann.com Accessed 1/8/10.

15. This case study was developed by Chase Hearn, a student at the University of Utah, School of Architecture. Interview with Michelle Kaufmann December 2009.

16. This case study was developed by Chase Hearn, a student at the University of Utah School of Architecture. Interview with Todd Jerry, Marmol Radziner Prefab, November 2009.

17. This case study was developed by Chase Hearn, a student at the University of Utah School of Architecture. Interview with Jennifer Siegal, Summer 2009 and November 2009.

18. Interview with Joel Egan and Robert Humble, Hybrid Architects - November 2009.

19. Q. Hardy, "Ideas Worth Millions." *Forbes magazine*. 01.29.09 http://www.forbes.com/2009/01/29/innova-

tions-venture-capital-technology_0129_innovations. html Accessed 01/28/10.

20. Interview with Evan Nakamura and Ash Notaney, Project Frog, San Francisco, CA – November 2009.

21. M. Anderson and P. Anderson, *Prefab Prototypes: site specific design for offsite construction* (Princeton Architecture Press, 2007).

22. The author studied under Mark Anderson at UC Berkeley. Subsequent interviews in 2007, 2008, and in September 2009.

23. T. Benson, ITAP Fall 2009 Lecture, University of Utah; and Interview with Tedd Benson of Bensonwood, October 2009 and January 2010.

Chapter 10 - Commercial and Interiors

1. S. Kieran and J. Timberlake, *Refabricating Architecture* (McGraw-Hill, 2003).

2. S. Kieran and J. Timberlake, *Loblolly House: Elements of a New Architecture* (Princeton Architectural Press, 2008).

3. S. Kieran, Keynote Address at *Without a Hitch: New Directions in Prefabricated Architecture Conference*. NE Fall Conference, ACSA, September 25–27, 2008 University of Massachusetts, Amherst.

4. B. Bergdoll and P. Christensen, *Home Delivery: Fabricating the Modern Dwelling*. (New York: Museum of Modern Art, 2008): 224–227.

5. Interview with Steve Glenn, Living Homes, Santa Monica, CA – August 2009.

6. Interview with Billie Faircloth, KieranTimberlake, Philadelphia, CA – October 2009.

7. Interview Chris MacNeal, KieranTimberlake – January 2010.

8. J. Newman, INSIGHT: Mod Mods: Manufacturing Markets for Modulars. ArchNewsNow.com. January 11, 2008. http://www.archnewsnow.com/ features/images/Feature0239_03x Accessed 12/16/09

9. A. Chen, "Teaching Tools." July 25, 2007 MetropolisMag.com. www.metropolismag.com/story/20070725/ teaching-tools. Accessed 12/16/09

10. Interview with Richard Hodge, KieranTimberlake – January 2010.

11. K. Jacobs, "Industrialists Without Factories." July 16, 2008. Metropolismag.com http://www.metropolis-mag.com/story/20080716/industrialists-without-factories. Accessed 12/16/09.

12. Kieran, *Loblolly House*: 158–159.

13. Interview with Chris Sharples and Greg Pasquerelli, SHoP Architects, New York City, NY – December 2009.

14. S. Holl, *The St. Ignatius Chapel* (Princeton Architectural Press, New York, 1999).

15. Interview with Tim Bade, Steven Holl Architects, New York City, NY – July 14, 2009.

16. Interview with Tom Kundig, OSKA Architects, Seattle, WA – July 17, 2009.

17. This case study was developed by Brian Hebdon, University of Utah School of Architecture.

18. J. Cohen and G. Moeller, Jr. (Eds.) *Liquid Stone: New Architecture in Concrete* (New York: Princeton Architectural Press, 2006).

19. Interview with Guy Nordenson, Structural Engineer – August 2009.

20. T. Gannon, *Simmons Building: Steven Holl* (New York: Princeton Architectural Press, 2004); and the casting beds were analyzed by James McGuire from Hansen Eagle Precast during an interview in August 2009.

21. Interview with Steve Crane and Nathan Levitt, VCBO Architecture, Salt Lake City, UT – November 2009.

22. Interview with Christiane Phillips, MJSAA, and Derek Losee, Steel Encounters, Salt Lake City, UT – January 2010.

23. Interview with Min Ra, Front Inc. San Francisco, CA – December 2009.

24. Interview with Nader Tehrani, Office dA, Boston, MA – November 2009.

25. DSRNY website. http://www.dillerscofidio.com/

26. Interview with Jeremey Porter, Ty Young and Willi Gatti, 3Form, Salt Lake City, UT – October 2009.

Chapter 11 - Conclusion

1. F. Willams and D. Gibson, *Technology Transfer: a communication perspective* (California: Sage Publications,1990): 15–16.

2. D. Nye, Technology Matters: Questions to Live With (MIT Press, 2007): 33-35.

3. R. Henderson and K. Clark, "Architectural Innovation: The Reconfiguration of Existing Product Technologies and the Failure of Established Firms." *Administrative Science Quarterly March 1990.* (Cornell University Graduate School of Management 1990): 4.

4. D. Buntrock, Japanese Architecture as a Collaborative Process: Opportunities in a Flexible Construction Culture (Taylor & Francis, 2002): 170–171.

5. Ibid: 40.

ILLUSTRATION CREDITS

Cover Courtesy Michelle Kaufmann

Chapter 1

F1.1   Adapted from A. Gibb, *Off-site Fabrication: Prefabri-cation, Preassembly, and Modularization* (John Wiley & Sons Inc., 1999): 10, Fig. 1.2.

F1.2   Excerpted from *South Australian Record*, November 27, 1837, illustration attributed H. Manning.

F1.3   British patent number 10399: John Spencer, November 23, 1844.

F1.4   Courtesy of the National Archives, Air Force RG 342-FH-3a3929656.

F1.5   Excerpted from Aladdin "Built in a Day" House Cata-log, 1917.

F1.6   Photo by Peter Goss, Courtesy University of Utah, School of Architecture.

F1.7   Credit: Author

F1.8   Credit: Author

F1.9   Courtesy Thomas Edison Archives

F1.10 © 1800s, Source Unknown

Chapter 2

F2.1   Credit: Author

F2.2   Excerpted from *Teknisk Ukeblad*, 1893 Technical Journal in Norway.

F2.3   © 1905, Chicago Architectural Photo Company

F2.4   © 1900, Source Unknown

F2.5   © 1909, Source Unknown

F2.6   Photo by Matthew Metcalf, University of Utah, School of Architecture.

F2.7   © 1920, Source Unknown

F2.8   Source Unknown

F2.9   Source Unknown

F2.10 Photo by Scott Yribar, University of Utah, School of Architecture.

F2.11 © Moshie Safdie Associates

F2.12 Courtesy Paul Rudolph Foundation and Library of Congress Prints and Photographs Division.

F2.13 Photo by Dijana Alickovic, University of Utah, School of Architecture.

F2.14 Photo by William Miller, Courtesy University of Utah, School of Architecture.

F2.15 Source: Dell and Wainwright, EMAP/Architectural Press Archive.

Chapter 3

F3.1   Adapted from L. Tornatzky and M. Fleischer, *The Pro-cess of Technological Innovation* (Lexington Books, 1990): 153.

F3.2   Photo by Xiaoxia Dong, University of Utah, School of Architecture.

F3.3   Credit: Author

F3.4   Excerpted from G. Elvin, *Integrated Practice in Ar-chitecture: Mastering Design-Build, Fast-Track, and Building Information Modeling* (John Wiley & Sons, Inc., 2007): 22, Fig. 2-3.

F3.5   © Anderson Anderson Architects

F3.6   Adapted from MacLeamy Curve: *Construction Users Roundtable's "Collaboration, Integrated Information, and the Project Lifecycle in Building Design and Con-struction and Operation"* WP-1202, August 2004.

F3.7   Adapted from *A Working Definition Version 1—May 2007 Integrated Project Delivery.* AIA California Coun-cil and McGraw-Hill Construction.

F3.8   Credit: Author

F3.9   Photo by Dijana Alickovic, University of Utah, School of Architecture.

F3.10 © 3Form

F3.11   Adapted from A. Gibb, *Off-site Fabrication: Prefabrication, Preassembly, and Modularization* (John Wiley & Sons Inc., 1999): 228, Fig. 6.1.
F3.12   Credit: Author
F3.13   Credit: Author
F3.14   Credit: Author
F3.15   Credit: Author

Chapter 4

F4.1   Source: Engineering News-Record, 254 (1): 12–13.
F4.2   Courtesy Paul Teicholz
F4.3   Credit: Author
F4.4   Adapted from M. Kaufmann and C. Remick, *PreFab Green* (Gibbs and Smith Publishers, 2009): 18–19.
F4.5   Adapted from *Modular Architecture Manual*. Kullman Buildings Corp., 2008.
F4.6   Credit: Author
F4.7   Credit: Author
F4.8   Credit: Author
F4.9   Adapted from "Pre-Assembly Perks: Discover why modularization works," *The Voice*. 2007 Fall Issue (Cincinnati, OH: Construction Users Roundtable, 2007): 28–31.

Chapter 5

F5.1   Adapted from S. Brand, *How Buildings Learn: What Happens After They're Built* (Penguin Publishers, 1995): 13.
F5.2   Credit: Author
F5.3   Credit: Author
F5.4   Credit: Author
F5.5   Photo by David Scheer, Courtesy University of Utah, School of Architecture.
F5.6   Credit: Author
F5.7   Photo by VIA, Courtesy Front, Inc.
F5.8   © Kullman Buildings Corp.
F5.9   Credit: Author
F5.10   Credit: Jonathan Moffitt
F5.11   Credit: Jonathan Moffitt
F5.12   Credit: Jonathan Moffitt
F5.13   Credit: Author
F5.14   Credit: Author
F5.15   Credit: Jonathan Moffitt

F5.16   Credit: Jonathan Moffitt
F5.17   Credit: Jonathan Moffitt
F5.18   Zahner Architectural Metals
F5.19   Credit: Jonathan Moffitt
F5.20   Joshua Michael Weber, University of Utah, School of Architecture.
F5.21   Credit: Author
F5.22   Credit: Author
F5.23   BURST*008 Douglas Gauthier and Jeremy Edmiston
F5.24   © 3Form
F5.25   Credit: Author
F5.26   © 3Form
F5.27   Credit: Author
F5.28   Credit: Author

Chapter 6

F6.1   Adapted from *Modular Architecture Manual*. Kullman Buildings Corp., 2008.
F6.2   Provided by Hundegger USA
F6.3   Provided by Hundegger USA
F6.4   © Eco Steel, Courtesy Joss Hudson.
F6.5   ©Eco Steel, Courtesy Joss Hudson.
F6.6   Credit: Jonathan Moffitt
F6.7   Photo Courtesy of Hanson Structural Precast, Inc.
F6.8   Credit: Jonathan Moffitt
F6.9   Photo by Jennifer Gill, ITAC, University of Utah.
F6.10   Mervyn Pinto, President, Minaean International Corp.
F6.11   Courtesy Eric Miller, Foambuilt.
F6.12   © KieranTimberlake
F6.13   Credit: Author
F6.14   Zahner Architectural Metals
F6.15   Irontown Housing Company, Inc.
F6.16   © Hanson Eagle Precast, Courtesy James McGuire.
F6.17   © DIRTT, Courtesy Lance Henderson.
F6.18   © OEM
F6.19   Irontown Housing Company, Inc., Courtesy Paul Warner, Architect.
F6.20   © Blazer Industries, Courtesy Kendra Cox.
F6.21   © Kullman Buildings Corp.
F6.22   © Kullman Buildings Corp.
F6.23   © Kullman Buildings Corp.
F6.24   © Kullman Buildings Corp.
F6.25   © Kullman Buildings Corp.
F6.26   Credit: Adam Lafortune

F6.27   © Buro Happold (2010), Courtesy Adrian Robinson.
F6.28   © Buro Happold (2010), Courtesy Adrian Robinson.
F6.29   © Travelodge

Chapter 7

F7.1   Bensonwood
F7.2   © KieranTimberlake
F7.3   © KieranTimberlake
F7.4   Adapted from G. Ballard, "Lean Construction Institute Prefabrication and Assembly and Open Building Championship Area."
F7.5   Bensonwood
F7.6   © Kullman Buildings Corp.
F7.7   Credit: Author
F7.8   Office of Mobile Design
F7.9   Courtesy ecoMOD Project, University of Virginia.
F7.10   © Kullman Buildings Corp.
F7.11   Credit: Author
F7.12   Marmol Radizer Prefab, Courtesy Todd Jerry.
F7.13   © Resolution 4: Architecture
F7.14   Courtesy ecoMOD Project, University of Virginia.
F7.15   Credit: Author
F7.16   Adapted from *Modular Architecture Manual*. Kullman Buildings Corp., 2008.
F7.17   Credit: Author
F7.18   Adapted from E. Allen and P. Rand, *Architectural Detailing: Function—Constructability—Aesthetics,* 2d Ed. (John Wiley & Sons Inc., 2006): 165, Table 12-1.
F7.19   © Kullman Buildings Corp.
F7.20   Bensonwood
F7.21   © Kullman Buildings Corp.
F7.22   Credit: Author

Chapter 8

F8.1   Credit: Author
F8.2   Credit: Author
F8.3   Excerpted from C. Eastman and R. Sacks, "Relative Productivity in the AEC Industries in the United States for On-site and Off-site Activities," *Journal of Construction Engineering and Management*, 2008:134 (7): 525.
F8.4   Adapted from S. Brand, *How Buildings Learn: What Happens After They're Built* (Penguin Publishers, 1995): 13.

F8.5   Adapted from P. Crowther, "Designing for Disassembly," *Technology, Design and Process Innovation in the Built Environment*. P. Newton, K. Hampson, and R. Drogenmuller (Eds.) (Spon Press, Taylor and Francis, 2009): 230.
F8.6   Adapted from P. Crowther (2009).
F8.7   Credit: Author
F8.8   Adapted from J. Fernandez, *Material Architecture: emergent materials for Innovative Buildings and Ecological Construction* (Architectural Press, 2005): 61.
F8.9   Prefab Course Project by Aaron Day, University of Utah, School of Architecture.
F8.10   Credit: Author
F8.11   Assembling Architecture Project by Eric Hansen, University of Utah, School of Architecture.

Chapter 9

F9.1   © Rocio Romero
F9.2   Resolution 4: Architecture, Courtesy Joe Tanney.
F9.3   Resolution 4: Architecture, Courtesy Joe Tanney.
F9.4   Resolution 4: Architecture, Courtesy Joe Tanney.
F9.5   Courtesy ecoMOD Project, University of Virginia.
F9.6   Courtesy ecoMOD Project, University of Virginia and Scott F. Smith.
F9.7   Michelle Kaufmann
F9.8   Marmol Radiner Prefab
F9.9   Marmol Radiner Prefab
F9.10   Office of Mobile Design, Dave Lauridsen
F9.11   Office of Mobile Design
F9.12   Hybrid Architects/Owen Richards
F9.13   Robert Nay, Courtesy Hybrid Architects and Mithun.
F9.14   Courtesy Hybrid Architects
F9.15   Project Frog, Inc.
F9.16   Project Frog, Inc.
F9.17   © Anderson Anderson Architects
F9.18   © Anderson Anderson Architects
F9.19   © Anderson Anderson Architects
F9.20   © Anderson Anderson Architects
F9.21   © Anderson Anderson Architects
F9.22   © Anderson Anderson Architects
F9.23   Bensonwood
F9.24   Credit: Author
F9.25   © Naomi Beal Photography, Courtesy Bensonwood.

Chapter 10

F10.1   © KieranTimberlake and Bensonwood
F10.2   © KieranTimberlake
F10.3   © KieranTimberlake
F10.4   © KieranTimberlake
F10.5   © KieranTimberlake
F10.6   © SHoP Architects
F10.7   © SHoP Architects
F10.8   © SHoP Architects
F10.9   © SHoP Architects
F10.10   © SHoP Architects
F10.11   © Steven Holl Architects
F10.12   Photo by William Miller, Courtesy University of Utah, School of Architecture.
F10.13   © Steven Holl Architects
F10.14   © Steven Holl Architects
F10.15   Credit: Author
F10.16   © VCBO Architecture
F10.17   © VCBO Architecture
F10.18   © VCBO Architecture
F10.19   © University of Utah, Courtesy MJSAA.
F10.20   © Steel Encounters, Inc.
F10.21   © Steel Encounters, Inc.
F10.22   Photo by VIA, Courtesy Front, Inc.
F10.23   Photo by VIA, Courtesy Front, Inc.
F10.24   © Office dA and © John Horner Photography
F10.25   © Office dA and © John Horner Photography
F10.26   © Office dA
F10.27   Courtesy Joerg Rugemer
F10.28   © 3Form
F10.29   © Iwan Baan Photography, Courtesy 3Form.

Chapter 11

F11.1   Adapted from D. E. Nye, *Technology Matters: Questions to Live With* (The MIT Press, 2006): 33–35.
F11.2   Credit: Author
F11.3   Courtesy ecoMOD Project, University of Virginia.
F11.4   Credit: Author

Color Credits

C1   © Anderson Anderson Architects
C2   © SHoP Architects
C3   © Iwan Baan Photography
C4   Courtesy Dijana Alickovic
C5   © SHoP Architects
C6   © Buro Happold (2010)
C7   Zahner Architectural Metals
C8   Courtesy Joerg Rugemer
C9   Credit: Author
C10   © John Horner Photography
C11   Bensonwood
C12   © Project Frog
C13   © SHoP Architects
C14   © Anderson Anderson Architects
C15   © Scott Smith Photography
C16   © Rocio Romero
C17   Resolution 4: Architecture
C18   Zahner Architectural Metals
C19   © Naomi Beal Photography, Courtesy Bensonwood
C20   Photo by William Miller, Courtesy University of Utah, School of Architecture.

INDEX